Understanding the Boundary between Disability Studies and Special Education through Consilience, Self-Study, and Radical Love

Critical Issues in Disabilities and Education

Series Editor: Eric Shyman, St. Joseph's College

The social, legal, and political history of persons with disabilities in the United States as well as internationally has been significant, especially in the areas of social justice, civil rights, and cultural inclusion. This series will focus on various critical perspectives on issues involving the social, political, and cultural experiences of people with disabilities. Manuscripts in this series will address topics such as: (1) legal developments (such as issues with the Americans with Disabilities Act, Individuals with Disabilities Education Act, Education for All, and others) at both the national and international level; (2) social and cultural models of disability and its outcome on the inclusion and/or exclusion of individuals with disabilities; (3) the benefits and challenges of the current educational system for children and adolescents with disabilities, including specific methodologies and categories of students (e.g., educational approaches for students with Autism Spectrum Disorder, inclusive education for students with disabilities, etc.); (4) philosophical perspectives of special education/education for students with disabilities; (5) issues regarding transitional support services and approaches to community support for adults with disabilities. This series would be open to scholars representing education, psychology, sociology, philosophy, human relations, business and management, cultural anthropology, speech and language pathology, and medical sciences (among others). Manuscripts published in this series would be appropriate for use in scholarship and coursework at colleges and universities, as well as be written in a way to be accessible and appealing to a general intellectual audience.

Titles in the Series:

Understanding the Boundary between Disability Studies and Special Education through Consilience, Self-Study, and Radical Love
  edited by David I. Hernández-Saca, Holly Pearson, and Catherine Kramarczuk Voulgarides

Disabling the School-to-Prison Pipeline: The Relationship Between Special Education and Arrest
  by Laura Vernikoff

Understanding the Boundary between Disability Studies and Special Education through Consilience, Self-Study, and Radical Love

Edited by
David I. Hernández-Saca, Holly Pearson,
and Catherine Kramarczuk Voulgarides

LEXINGTON BOOKS
Lanham • Boulder • New York • London

Published by Lexington Books
An imprint of The Rowman & Littlefield Publishing Group, Inc.
4501 Forbes Boulevard, Suite 200, Lanham, Maryland 20706
www.rowman.com

86-90 Paul Street, London EC2A 4NE

Copyright © 2023 by The Rowman & Littlefield Publishing Group, Inc.

All rights reserved. No part of this book may be reproduced in any form or by any electronic or mechanical means, including information storage and retrieval systems, without written permission from the publisher, except by a reviewer who may quote passages in a review.

British Library Cataloguing in Publication Information Available

Library of Congress Cataloging-in-Publication Data

Names: Hernández-Saca, David I., editor. | Pearson, Holly, editor. | Voulgarides, Catherine Kramarczuk, editor.
Title: Understanding the boundary between disability studies and special education through consilience, self-study, and radical love / Edited by David I. Hernández-Saca, Holly Pearson, and Catherine Voulgarides.
Description: Lanham, Maryland : Lexington Books, [2023] | Series: Critical issues in disabilities and education | Includes bibliographical references and index. | Summary: "In this book, the authors explore what constitutes boundary work at the intersection of traditional special education and critical disability studies in education. Readers will consider how their personal, professional, and programmatic actions can lead to freedom from the hegemony of traditional special education and White and Ability supremacy"— Provided by publisher.
Identifiers: LCCN 2022040517 (print) | LCCN 2022040518 (ebook) | ISBN 9781793629135 (cloth) | ISBN 9781793629159 (paperback) | ISBN 9781793629142 (ebook)
Subjects: LCSH: Children with disabilities—Education—United States. | Special education—Study and teaching—United States. | Educational equalization—United States. | Educational change—United States.
Classification: LCC LC4015 .U56 2023 (print) | LCC LC4015 (ebook) | DDC 371.90973—dc23/eng/20220825
LC record available at https://lccn.loc.gov/2022040517
LC ebook record available at https://lccn.loc.gov/2022040518

♾️™ The paper used in this publication meets the minimum requirements of American National Standard for Information Sciences—Permanence of Paper for Printed Library Materials, ANSI/NISO Z39.48-1992.

Contents

Acknowledgments   vii

Introduction   1
Holly Pearson, Catherine K. Voulgarides, and David I. Hernández-Saca

1   Practicing Consilience—Thoughts from a Career-long Attempt   11
     David J. Connor

2   At the Nexus of Disability Studies in (Special) Education: Toward Consiliencatory Frameworks for Critical Emotion Praxis Liberation   31
     David I. Hernández-Saca

3   Anti-ableism in Teacher Education: Celebrating Disability Identity Through Self-study and Radical Love   53
     Sarah Arvey Tov

4   Teaching in the In-Between: Opportunities and Factors Informing Inclusive Reform in One School District   75
     Amy J. Petersen, Danielle M. Cowley, Deborah J. Gallagher, and Shehreen Iqtadar

5   On the Margins of the Marginalized: Protecting and Loving on Black Children with Intellectual Disability and Emotional and Behavioral Disturbances   95
     Lydia Ocasio-Stoutenburg

6   Boundaries of Disability Studies and Special Education: Radical Pedagogy and Relatedness   125
     Jane Strauss

7	Critical Coalition with/in the Boundaries: A Radical Love Response to Neoliberal Debilitation in Special Education *M. Nickie Coomer, Ashley Cartell Johnson, Ganiva Reyes, and Brittany Aronson*	147
8	Introspecting the Radical Love Boundaries between Deaf Studies and Special Education in an African Setting *Martin Musengi*	171
9	Ethics of Care/ing Work/ers at the Boundary of Critical Dis/ability Studies and Special Education *Christina A. Bosch*	193
10	Daring to Speak/Teach from Our Hearts: A Self-study of Critical Disability Studies Teacher Education at the Boundaries of Ableism, Racism, and Sexism as Faculty of Color *Shehreen Iqtadar and David I. Hernández-Saca*	215
11	Grappling with the Tensions: Cultivating Justice-Oriented Praxis through Collaborative Autoethnographic Poetry *Amanda L. Miller, Chelsea Stinson, and Maria T. Timberlake*	235
12	Checklists and Merit Badges: On Whiteness, Ability, and the Boundary between Special Education and Radical Love *JPB Gerald*	261
13	Female Inclusive Educators of Color: Challenging White Privilege and the Mechanism of Dis/ablement Through Radical Love *Sarah Schlessinger*	281
14	Blurring Boundaries: Dreaming/s of a Neurodivergent-Teacher-Parent-Student-Researcher *Ananí M. Vasquez*	303
15	I Still Have Joy: Disability Justice as Praxis, Theory, and Research in a Special Education Teacher Preparation Program *Gloshanda Lawyer*	325

Conclusion *Holly Pearson, Catherine K. Voulgarides, and David I. Hernández-Saca*	343
Index	347
About the Contributors	357

Acknowledgments

This book came together during the onset of the COVID-19 pandemic in March of 2020 and the racial trauma associated with the murder of George Floyd in Minneapolis, Minnesota, in May of 2020. The conditions of our coming together forced us to lean into our ethics and values as we collaborated, learned, and grew together as co-lead editors. We want to acknowledge this process as we lifted each other up and also leaned upon each other in times of need.

We also acknowledge each of the authors for their willingness, openness, and take-up and application of the main theoretical and conceptual frameworks of the book to their areas of research at the boundaries between traditional special education and disability studies in education for critical praxis: consilience (unity of knowledge), self-study in teacher education, radical love (care, responsibility, knowledge, and respect), and the Disability Justice Principles.

Introduction

Holly Pearson, Catherine K. Voulgarides, and David I. Hernández-Saca

Dear readers,

Before we dive into this book, we want to ask you to take a moment to check in with yourself. How am I doing? Where am I feeling the tension in my bodymind? What brings me here to this moment? This is not about a moment of judging as we often do this too quickly and too often. This is about taking a moment to recognize and acknowledge what is taking place along with what we may need. Too often, we are on autopilot, switching gears left and right. Consider, when was the last time you were fully present in the moment? Intentionally being in the moment? For some folks, this is a quick recall, while for others, it is an "oh shit . . . I honestly don't remember." Again, this is not about judgment. This is about recognizing and acknowledging.

"Why?"
"Why are you asking me this?"
"Why does this matter?"

We are asking because this is a core component when doing boundary work as this kind of work takes a toll on our bodyminds. Our curriculum/training does not teach us or reward us on self-care and community care. These forms of care have the least built-in accountability compared to teaching a class or attending meetings. Think about it. When was the last time you not only asked yourself but also asked your colleagues about how they are caring for themselves? We are not talking about the classic American interaction of "Hey, long time no see! How are you doing?" "I'm doing good. How about yourself?" "I'm doing good too!" This is AUTOPILOT. What if this was different? What if we recognized that we have a limited number of spoons (Miserandino, 2022) and time available?

If we take this approach, then this is about being intentional about where we invest our time. Yes, there are times when we have no control such as in a work meeting, teaching in class, along with paying the bills but, outside of that, we do have a choice. But if we are on autopilot, we are missing out on not only making choices but being aware of the choices that we ACTUALLY do have. We actually can say NO—to accepting another project, working past 6 p.m., or stepping away from a toxic dynamic, while saying YES to time to decompressing and disconnecting, engaging in work that you are passionate about, or building community spaces of kinship. Shifting away from autopilot means listening and trusting your instincts. Anytime you feel that inkling of "No, this is not cool," "I think I'm burnt out," or "What is happening?!" trust it. This is the damaging reality of autopilot as it actually encourages us to become estranged within our bodyminds—psychic disequilibrium (Rich, 1994).

The reason why we are gently nudging you to intentionally check in with yourself is simply that if we do not know how to do this, we cannot instill the value within the folks we work with. Furthermore, we cannot expect the folks we work with to know how to do so if we do not know how to do so. This creates an intergenerational ripple effect of the normalization of being disconnected from within. Trusting yourself is so vital because it allows us to be open to alternative ways of understanding/engaging while setting boundaries. The irony is in doing boundary work involves setting boundaries at times. To know how to pace yourself. To know when to stop. To know that you have a choice. Remember, you are amazing as you, and you are doing the best you can in this moment. Trust yourself.

This book stems from collective pain, trauma, dehumanization, suffering, and violence we encountered in boundary work. This is how we came to find each other—a strong desire to make sense, seeking affirmation and kindred spirits, dreaming of radical love, community care, and interdependence (Berne et al., 2018), and spaces where we can breathe. As with amazing relationships, our encounters came out of the blue, unexpected. By chance, we happened to encounter each other at various shared spaces, which led to follow-up via emails, texts, and then zoom meetings.

Through these interactions, slowly the pain, trauma, dehumanization, suffering, and violence we experienced floated to the surface—transformed into shared pain and trauma rooted in dehumanization, suffering, and violence in the academy and beyond. We came to realize that we were not alone with our thoughts and feelings. Coming together crushed the illusion that we were alone and what we were feeling/experiencing was not real.

The entwinement of shared pain, trauma, and pedagogical beliefs and values leads to collective movements (yes plural) of co-constructing safe spaces. Safe spaces are not neutral nor singular moments in time. Instead, safe spaces mean we made mistakes as we unlearn years of ingrained toxicity. Toxicity stems from neoliberal capitalistic white supremacist, ableist, heteronormative, Christian, transphobic, and masculine values where bodyminds are stratified and violence toward certain groups is seen as normal and/or justified. Unlearning in these space(s) involved moments of tension and confusion. Why? Because it is one thing to believe in certain pedagogical values, it is another thing to practice those values daily.

There were moments of tension, pausing, stepping back, coming back, and redefining the boundaries of our project and our relationships. We gently nudged each other to not feel the need to be apologetic, to listen and honor how we were feeling, and to drop the bullshit pretentiousness in order to disrupt and dismantle autopilot mode. Therefore, this book is us opening our hearts, souls, minds, and spirits—inviting you to join as you. There is no need to be apologetic, to prove your worth, or to feel you need to be something else. You are you in this time and moment. That is all we ask—is for you to be your authentic self. To trust in yourself and know your damn worth.

INTENTIONS OF THE BOOK

The spirit of this book is about leaning on each other and embracing vulnerability while recognizing that the whole solitude, independence, and pulling yourself up by your bootstraps is bullshit. To disrupt boundaries involves leaning on each other. To create spaces of vulnerability while unlearning years of toxic programming. Without building in community care, we will not survive, and instead, our hearts and spirits become weakened, damaged, and fatigued. Together, munching is vital in processing, healing, and dreaming. Munching is the act of engaging in intentional "chewing" of a particular thought that we are trying to digest. Munching is not about finding the perfect answer, but it is about being present while understanding what the hell is going on while supporting each other in unlearning.

Thus, this book is not about providing answers, especially in the form of merit badges and checklists (Gerald, in press). Instead, this book is about the possibilities of applying *a disability justice radical love meta-critical emotionality consiliencatory boundary* work praxis to the long-standing debate at the boundaries of Disability Studies in Education (DSE) and (Special) Education. We call for a critical emotion revolutionary praxis (Allman, 2007), the coupling of critical thinking, feeling, reflection, and action (Artiles & Kozleski, 2007; Zembylas, 2021) that helps us all transcend the boundaries, both internal and external, at the nexus of DSE (Danforth & Gabel, 2006; Pearson et al., 2016; Ware, 2006) and special education.

By dis/Ability we mean the social, cultural, political, economic, emotional, affective, spatial, and material construction of both ability and disability. We acknowledge that the slash in dis/Ability is a contested and controversial issue in the field. As disabled and dis/Abled scholars and co-conspirators ourselves, we acknowledge arguments from the disability community themselves about the importance of saying the word, "disability," given the legacy of pride and identity that disability in society and education has come to mean, for some. However, the slash and the accompanying capitalization of "A," is an intentional reframing and counter-narrative to the master narratives of disability in society and K-12 and beyond education as reclamation given misdiagnosis and the insidious entanglements at the nexus of race and disability that have caused intersectional disablism to Black, Indigenous, and Youth and People of Color (BIPOC) given the 60 plus old problem of disproportionality in special education. By reclaiming our abilities, in the social and emotional construction of dis/Ability, we firmly humanize ourselves and disrupt deficit thinking and language on our humanity. However, within and across the chapters, please note that each author(s) chose how to write disability according to their own conceptual framework.

Furthermore, DSE scholars struggle with their department's rigid guidelines on what constitutes inclusive theories, philosophical perspectives, pedagogies, and praxis. These departments are oftentimes departments of special education. In addition, it is pertinent to acknowledge the persisting disconnect between the ivory tower and the surrounding communities. Therefore, community scholars' and activists' critical philosophical stances and praxis are often disregarded, wrongly appropriated, excluded, or absent within the neoliberal capitalist university and society (Cheek, 2019). This creates a false ableist illusion that special education "expertise" is solely generated and contained within the ivory tower.

The boundary work between DSE and the system and canon of traditional special education (Akkerman & Bakker, 2011; Danforth & Gabel, 2006; Ware, 2004) is a subject of long-standing debate. Within the current disciplinary formation, traditional special education includes teacher preparation for both general and special education systems (Ashby, 2012; Pearson et al., 2016; Petersen et al., 2018; Waitoller & Kozleski, 2013). Each discipline has a different historical, ontological (i.e., the study of what it means to be a person or being), epistemological (i.e., the study of knowledge and its origins), axiological (i.e., the study of ethics), and most importantly etiological (i.e., the study of the causes of disease, conditions, or impairments) conceptualization, implementation, and relationship to theory, research, practice, and praxis (i.e., critical thinking and feeling before acting). Special education has spurred the discursive, material, and ethical construction of "what counts" as an educational disability on the one hand—high-incidence special education categories such as Specific Learning Disabilities, Emotional Behavioral Disorder, Autism, Intellectual Disabilities, and Speech and Language Impairment, for example—while DSE has advanced an agenda of critical theory, pedagogy, and heuristic to understand and critique special education.

For many scholars in these fields, conflicting theorizations of identity (disabled, non-disabled, self-identified, non-identifying disabled, and disidentification; Munoz, 2008) create tensions within their individual and collective work. Critical and traditional special educators, DSE teacher educators, and educational researchers negotiate these boundaries as a means of engaging in boundary work. The dominance of traditional special education has both afforded critical and special education scholars and constrained DSE scholars at the individual and systemic levels when addressing the rights and access of children and adults with dis/Abilities in educational settings from K-12 and postsecondary institutions.

Furthermore, at the fault lines between these two systems and paradigms lie historically multiply marginalized dis/Abled students (with dis/Abilities) at their intersections of power and identities, along with the professional personnel, across K-20 and beyond, in the U.S. education system. These two parallel systems of support have invested historical interest in the understanding and development of their own paradigmatic views on topics ranging from the meaning of and practice of services for historically multiply marginalized youth and adults with dis/Abilities. However, the dominant ideologies of traditional special education wield considerable influence and power indoctrinating medicalized views of disability, inclusion, access, and equality among these same groups. Furthermore, given that the medical model of disability is institutionalized within the traditional special education model, multiple layers of the system have been framed at the epistemological, axiological, and etiological levels from this traditional lens. This includes national standards not only for students, but teacher education and federal laws such as the Individuals with Disabilities Education Act (IDEA, 2004) to boundary work through publishing (Artiles, 2011; Artiles et al., 2011; Baglieri et al., 2011; Valle et al., 2006).

ENGAGING WITH BOUNDARY WORK

This book is long overdue as it addresses personal, professional, and programmatic identity work (Artiles, 2003; Watson, 2008), politics (hooks, 1994), and affects of both pain and privilege (Maxwell & Aggleton, 2013) at the boundaries that have historically structured educational research (Arzubiaga et al., 2008) of doing educational research and in higher education. The consequences of having a boundary or a wall between traditional special education and DSE are multiple. On an individual level, this boundary potentially creates traumatic silos that have institutional and cultural tensions. These tensions, however, offer opportunities for individual, institutional, and societal transformations, if we reframe the tensions at the boundaries between DSE and special education by centering *a disability justice radical love meta-critical emotionality consiliencatory boundary work praxis that anchors self-study in teacher education* for personal, professional, and programmatic levels of the self.

Boundary work requires vulnerability and transparency that can lead to a consiliencatory framework at this nexus and boundary work (Akkerman & Bakker, 2011) of DSE and SPED. By consilience we mean, *the jumping together for the unity of knowledge* (Wilson, 1998) that centers both practical and theoretical knowledge production that is not only technical but explicitly critical and interdisciplinary. This involves disruption of hegemonic forms of knowing, being, and doing that reproduce the dominance of traditional special education, and allows for a reframing of foundational perspectives for a more liberatory, humanization, and consiliencatory praxis on the ground. In the spirit of disability justice's commitment of collective liberation, liberation, and recognizing and valuing all bodyminds, the book intentionally brings together a diverse group who are committed to disability justice, equity, inclusion, and access for all (Berne et al., 2018). This involves *collective interconnected accountability* during boundary work rather than engaging in identity politics that perpetuates falsified binary hierarchies. Utilizing the consilienc-*ing*, radical love-*ing*, and self-study-*ing* as a conceptual springboard, we move toward our individual and collective boundary-crossing and objects of DSE, (SP)ED, and/or beyond for socio-historical, spatial, cultural, emotional, affective, and discursive development at the axiological, epistemological, ontological, and etiological lines for ALL (Akkerman & Bakker, 2011; Danforth & Gabel, 2006; Fromm, 1956; Nusbaum, Cowley, Hernández-Saca et al., 2019; Tidwell et al., 2009; Ware, 2004; Wilson, 1998). In this collection, the contributors, individually and collectively, will examine and share their reflection, observations, and world knowledge in engaging within interdisciplinary boundary work within their socio-geographical location(s).

SCOPE OF THE BOOK

Throughout the chapters of the book, each author engages in an intentional conversation around *disability justice radical love meta-critical emotionality consiliencatory boundary* work praxis. Each chapter leans into a different component of the framework we have brought to you. Our introduction is only the beginning of a catalyst that has been bubbling for a long time.

Our volume begins with David Connor's chapter. He reflects upon the field of special education as it relates to disability studies and disability justice. The piece provides a sense of urgency and a call for the field to continue to develop and grow. David I. Hernández-Saca pushes us to imagine beyond what we currently know so that radical love is possible. Sarah Arvey Tov uses radical love and self-study to push the boundaries in teacher education and practice. Amy Peterson, Danielle M. Cowley, Deborah J. Gallagher, and Shehreen Iqtadar take a systemic view of radical love and discuss its potential for school reform. Lydia Ocasio-Stoutenburg (re)centers what is at stake with those who are on the margins—Black and Brown children. Jane Strauss asks us to consider how the tensions between disability studies and special education relate to pedagogy while Nickie Coomer, Ashley Cartell Johnson, Ganiva Reyes, and Brittany Aronson critique the neoliberal nature of special education and call for its transformation so that agentic coalitions for change emerge in the academy and beyond. Martin Musengi engages with the intersections between radical love, Deaf studies, and special education in an African setting, illustrating the need for a global understanding of boundary crossing. Christina Bosch questions the possibilities of ethics of care within boundary work. Shehreen Iqtadar and David I. Hernández-Saca question how self-study can be used as a mechanism for empowerment and change in the academy while Amanda Miller, Chelsea Stinson, and Maria T. Timberlake use poetry to explore how justice-oriented work can be leveraged in the academy and beyond. JPB Gerald asks us to consider how radical love pushes back against oppressive ideologies, whiteness, and ableism while Sarah Schlessinger leverages radical love to question the whiteness of the field of special education.Ananí Vasquez applies the themes of the book to explore how her own identity is shaped by the boundaries work while Gloshanda Lawyer shows us that this work is undoubtedly hard, but also rooted in acts of joy.

Collectively, the chapters provide emotionally grounded critiques, insights, and points of transformation for understanding what boundary work means for the self, for schools, and for the academy. Through the chapters, we can sense, feel, explore, and express the possibilities of a *disability justice radical love meta-critical emotionality consiliencatory boundary work* framework. The book is a beginning and also a call for further critical thinking, feeling, reflection, and action that transcends boundaries between special education and disability studies. It is also a call to push beyond our own fears, insecurities, and vulnerabilities so that radical love and justice become a space for growth and joy, as Gloshanda Lawyer reminds us in her chapter.

REFERENCES

Akkerman, S. F., & Bakker, A. (2011). Boundary crossing and boundary objects. *Review of Educational Research, 81*(2), 132–169.

Artiles, A. J. (2003). Special education's changing identity: Paradoxes and dilemmas in views of culture and space. *Harvard Educational Review, 73*(2), 164–202.

Artiles, A. J. (2011). Toward an interdisciplinary understanding of educational equity and difference: The case of the racialization of ability. *Educational Researcher, 40*(9), 431–445.

Artiles, A. J., & Kozleski, E. B. (2007). Beyond convictions: Interrogating culture, history, and power in inclusive education. *Language Arts, 84*(4), 357–364.

Artiles, A. J., Thorius, K. K., Bal, A., Neal, R., Waitoller, F., & Hernández-Saca, D. (2011). Beyond culture as group traits: Future learning disabilities ontology, epistemology, and inquiry on research knowledge use. *Learning Disability Quarterly, 34*(3), 167–179.

Arzubiaga, A. E., Artiles, A. J., King, K. A., & Harris-Murri, N. (2008). Beyond research on cultural minorities: Challenges and implications of research as situated cultural practice. *Exceptional Children, 74*(3), 309–327.

Ashby, C. (2012). Disability studies and inclusive teacher preparation: A socially just path for teacher education. *Research and Practice for Persons with Severe Disabilities, 37*(2), 89–99.

Baglieri, S., Valle, J. W., Connor, D. J., & Gallagher, D. J. (2011). Disability studies in education: The need for a plurality of perspectives on disability. *Remedial and Special Education, 32*(4), 267–278.

Berne, P., Morales, A. L., Langstaff, D., & Invalid, S. (2018). Ten principles of disability justice. *WSQ: Women's Studies Quarterly, 46*(1), 227–230.

Cheek, J. (2019). Resisting the commodified researcher self: Interrogating the data doubles we create for ourselves when buying and selling our research products in the research marketplace. In D. K. Norman & M. D. Giardina (Eds.), *Qualitative inquiry at the crossroads: Political, performative and methodological reflections* (pp. 141–156). Routledge.

Danforth, S., & Gabel, S. L. (2006). *Vital questions facing disability studies in education* (Vol. 2). Peter Lang.

Fromm, E. (1956). *The art of loving*. Harper Row.

Gerald, J. P. B. (in press). Checklists and merit badges: On whiteness, ability, and the boundary between special education and radical love. In D. I. Hernández-Saca, H. Pearson, & C. Voulgarides (Eds.), Consilience-*ing*, Self-Study-*ing*, Radical Love-*ing* at the Boundary Work of Disability Studies in Education and (Special) Education. *Current Issues in Disabilities and Education Book Series*. Lexington Books.

hooks, b. (1994). *Teaching to transgress: Education as the practice of freedom*. Routledge.

Maxwell, C., & Aggleton, P. (Eds.). (2013). *Privilege, agency and affect: Understanding the production and effects of action*. Springer.

Miserandino, C. (2022). The spoon theory. *But you don't look sick.* https://butyoudontlooksick.com/articles/written-by-christine/the-spoon-theory/

Munoz, J. E. (1999). *Disidentifications: Queers of color and the performance of politics.* University of Minnesota Press.

Nusbaum, E. A., Cowley, D., Hernández-Saca, D. I., Petersen, A., & Smith, P. (2019). These violent [delights] have violent ends: Rising up, pushing back, and possibility of hope. In P. Boda (Ed.), *Essays on exclusion: Our critical, collective journey toward equity in education* (pp. 85–110). DIOPress.

Pearson, H., Cosier, M., Kim, J., Gomez, A. M., Hines, C., McKee, A. A., & Ruiz, L. Z. (2016). The impact of disability studies curriculum on education professionals' perspectives and practice: Implications for education, social justice, and social change. *Disability Studies Quarterly, 36*(2).

Petersen, A., Cowley, D., Gallagher, D., & Iqtadar, S. (2018, April). Teaching in the in between: Opportunities for and resistance to inclusive change in boundary work. In *American Educational Research Association* (AERA), New York City, New York.

Rich, A. (1994). *Blood, bread and poetry: Selected Prose, 1979–1985.* W. W. Norton & Company.

Tidwell, D., Heston, M., & Fitzgerald, L. (Eds.). (2009). *Research methods for the self-study of practice* (Vol. 9). Springer Science & Business Media.

Valle, J. W., Connor, D. J., & Reid, D. K. (2006). Editors' introduction IDEA at 30: Looking back, facing forward—a disability studies perspective. *Disability Studies Quarterly, 26*(2).

Waitoller, F. R., & Kozleski, E. B. (2013). Working in boundary practices: Identity development and learning in partnerships for inclusive education. *Teaching and Teacher Education, 31*, 35–45.

Ware, L. (Ed.). (2004). *Ideology and the politics of (in)exclusion.* Peter Lang.

Ware, L. (2006). Urban educators, disability studies and education: Excavations in schools and society. *International Journal of Inclusive Education, 10*(2–3), 149–168.

Watson, T. J. (2008). Managing identity: Identity work, personal predicaments and structural circumstances. *Organization, 15*(1), 121–143.

Wilson, E. O. (1999). *Consilience: The unity of knowledge* (Vol. 31). Vintage.

Zembylas, M. (2021). The affective turn in educational theory. In *Oxford research encyclopedia of education.* https://oxfordre.com/education/view/10.1093/acrefore/9780190264093.001.0001/acrefore-9780190264093-e-1272

Chapter 1

Practicing Consilience—Thoughts from a Career-long Attempt

David J. Connor

Regardless of whether university professors or classroom teachers are ideological adherents of Disability Studies in Education (DSE), traditional Special Education (SE), or somewhere in the world between, they share concern about the same K-12 students. These concerns include what are the right: labels (if any at all), placements, services, materials, methodologies, and assessments to evaluate and support students academically, socially, and emotionally? Above all, I have found *the* universal guiding concern for teachers under which all other questions fall is: "What is best for my student(s)?" Without wishing to oversimplify a highly complex issue, I have always thought the answer to be, "It depends," because so many considerations have to be weighed. Likewise, as a teacher educator, contemplating *when* and *how* to invoke and utilize DSE and/or SE, the answer has always been "It depends."

I am a gay, white male, of working-class origins and Anglo-Irish ethnicity, who immigrated from the United Kingdom to the United States in the early 1980s. As a humanist, I have always been interested in our diversity in general, including markers of differences such as disability, race, class, sexual orientation, gender, and so on, that influenced my interest in better understanding intersectional identities. As within most families, I have several members with disabilities whose experiences alerted me to how physical and attitudinal barriers exist in society, how absolutely "normal" disability is, and how inclusive practices are naturally enacted every day. In this chapter I share some thoughts and experiences from a career of over three decades teaching children and adults, with and without disabilities. I have previously documented my professional story in the form of an autoethnography (Connor, 2018) as I believe in the value of sharing teacher-to-teacher knowledge through various genres that allow openness, reflection, and reflexivity, including memoirs (Ashton-Warner, 1986; Kohl, 1967; McCourt, 2005; Monroe, 1999), self-studies (Garbet et al., 2018; Grant & Butler, 2018; Kosnick et al., 2006), as well as autoethnographic writing (Smith, 2013; Vasconcelos, 2011),

Over the years I have thought long and hard about the nature of teaching and learning, with the view of how we make classrooms best "work" for teachers and students. My interest in students with disabilities originated in my early teaching experiences in the New York City public schools. During those times, working in self-contained (segregated) classrooms, and then as part of the city's initial, clumsy attempts at inclusion, I witnessed how the well-intentioned phenomenon of SE significantly fell short of promises made about it in both civil rights laws and ideals upheld by academic leaders in the field. While the Education of All Handicapped Children Act (1975) guaranteed placement for all disabled students[1] in schools, they were largely contained in terms of space, cut off from general education curricula, marginalized in school activities, and omitted from accountability measures such as mandated exams. There also existed clear delineations in labels and placements along lines of race, ethnicity, social class, and gender, with more males of color from working class and poor backgrounds comprising the rosters of "special" classes. In regard to Disability Justice as articulated by Berne et al. (2018), I witnessed nonrecognition of intersectional identities and a denial of collective access. In other words, I saw how students with multiply marginalized identities were placed at the lower levels of a hierarchy of worth that is rarely explicitly articulated and sustained within discussions of education, or for that matter, society at large. It meant that most students were contained in separate and unequal parallel schooling practices, removed from the mainstream, symbolizing racial and social class divisions in society.

The discipline of DSE as we know it nowadays did not exist when I taught in the late 1980s/early 1990s, yet I knew the system in which I worked not only looked wrong, it *felt* wrong. A dogged emphasis on generating and maintaining Individual Education Programs (IEPs) seemed to supersede everything else, all kept in meticulous compliance for fear of site inspections by the Board of Education. However, IEPs were rarely read by teachers because they all looked similar, symbolizing a bureaucratic system rather than a humane one. My initial employment, expedited due to a chronic teacher shortage, occurred with a proviso of obtaining a master's degree in Special Education—needed for state certification. So, I taught by day and studied by night. As it happened, the graduate program in SE with a focus on learning disabilities (LD) led by Dr. Kate Garnett at Hunter College was solid. Classes provided the history about why SE existed and, most important to a beginning teacher, contained multiple methods and approaches of how to teach children who did not fit "the norm" in schools. The learning processes of children with LD were framed as mysteries to be solved by special educators who trained in cultivating open, creative minds. Rookie teachers explored possibilities to find whatever it took to "reach" wherever a child was—and then guide the child to their next level in reading, writing, math, organization, social skills, and learning "content." In methods classes, instructors modeled, and we practiced with each other while being observed, reflected in groups, and wrote about our learning. Importantly, we were expected to adapt and modify the methods shared for the children we were teaching.

I came to see what Kate called "the stuff," that is, methods and approaches to teaching, as an essential base from which to build a repertoire. At the same time, I remember thinking: *These teaching methods*[2] *are potentially good for all kids, not just those labeled "special."* Likewise, applying strategies from books like *How to Talk so Kids Will Listen, and Listen so Kids will Talk* (Faber & Mazlish, 1997) demonstrated the benefits of all classroom interactions rooted in empathy and respect. In brief, I saw great value in how the program cultivated students to use research-based methods to become reflective practitioners, expecting them to create their own materials, customizing as needed to meet children's needs. In this process we also learned that research verified practices did not "translate" automatically to all contexts, or even work sometimes (Ferri et al., 2011). Success often depended on reshaped sanctioned practices to meet students' interests and current levels of learning, making them game-like in format to promote engagement by disenfranchised learners. In other words, we did what we needed to do to make teaching and learning work as best we could.

At the same time, while appreciative of the focus on practice within my master's program, I became aware that deficit-based conceptualizations of disability were the bedrock of SE and pervasive throughout the Academy in general. While I dutifully read journal articles, I found them inaccessible in terms of language that was generally teacher-unfriendly. By this, I mean they were filled with jargon, also known as "educationalese," and usually in the format of a controlled scientific experiment, rather than reflective of the complexities of actual classroom life that always buzzed with unpredictability. Quite frankly, the articles were tedious, a problem that unfortunately still exists today, resulting in few teachers reading academic journals, finding them largely incompatible with their world (Connor et al., 2011). Additionally, I did not see representations and discussions in scholarly literature of working class and poor children of color like in the classes I taught. And as much as I liked ideas in Faber and Mazlish (1997), the examples and suggested exercises were all premised on white, middle-class behavioral norms, typifying what I had later found out to be part of the hidden curriculum of schooling (Anyon, 1980). I share these memories to make a simple point: *from the very start of entering the profession I found there were underdeveloped relationships among (a) teachers' lives in schools, (b) teacher education programs,*[3] *and (c) the academic field of Special Education* (see Figure 1.1).

In this chapter I purposefully focus on these three realms in relation to each other, highlighting connections and creating opportunities for deepening our thinking when they come into play with one another. All of this is done with a broad intention of supporting disabled students in schools—while illustrating ways in which DSE and SE have both overlapping and divergent ground.

First, I contemplate the notion of consilience in regard to linking together principles of DSE and SE to contribute in the formation of a comprehensive theory—a goal of this book—that can be useful to new and experienced teachers. Second, I call attention to how conceptualizations of disability have caused what can be perceived as a tug o' war between competing paradigms that can be useful or disorienting, depending upon the context. Third, I discuss how different understandings of disability impact the three overlapping realms of the Academy, teacher education programs, and teaching and learning in K-12 schools. Fourth, I illustrate a selection of issues at the nexus between each realm. Finally, I offer concluding thoughts based upon issues raised, from the specific perspective of working in the field of SE with a DSE disposition.

PLURALIZING PERSPECTIVES

Historically speaking, it is important to note that a handful of career special educators originally came together at various SE conferences to advocate for

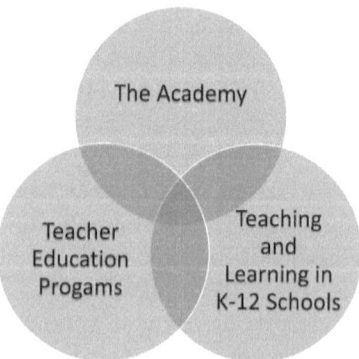

Figure 1.1 **Interrelated Nexuses to Consider When Drawing upon Disability Studies in Education and Special Education.** *Source*: Created by author.

a plurality of perspectives within their field, urging a shift to more inclusive practices. They found little interest in their ideas and a firm reassertion of the field's dominant paradigm. Subsequently, small, separate conferences were held where these critical special educators shared their thoughts, ideas, research, and experiences with a desire to see progressive changes. As a doctoral student during this time, I was fortunate in coming to know such scholars, including Ellen Brantlinger, Scot Danforth, Susan Gabel, Linda Ware, Phil Smith, Deb Gallagher, Phil and Diane Ferguson, among others. I truly felt I was "at the right place, at the right time," and have written about witnessing the establishment, and participating in the growth of DSE as a discipline, because it was professionally life changing (Connor, 2014). It was the first time I had encountered others who cared deeply about the education of students with disabilities but found the field of SE to be extremely limited in its thinking, inhospitable to discussing the concept of disability in multiple ways.

At the beginning, as DSE had yet to be developed, we recognized ourselves as what I later described as "insider-outsiders" (Connor, 2013)—in other words, educators operating within the inescapable institution of SE yet disagreeing with its foundational knowledge, structure, and systems. Furthermore, based upon our experiences, observations, and learnings, we actively sought different ways to broadly engage with the paired concepts of *education and disability* without defaulting to the epistemological monopoly of SE. As a loosely formed network we strove to put forth an alternative framework for thinking about disability, mindful of not wanting to evolve into dogmatic, ultraorthodox ways we had come to associate with SE. Subsequently, once we agreed to develop tenets of DSE, they became forged over a year-long period of online and in-person conversation where we emphasized, among many things, valuing the wholeness of disabled people, cultivating open-ended thinking, engaging with a plurality of paradigms, recognizing eclectic approaches to solving educational problems, and encouraging interdisciplinarity among fields of study (Connor et al., 2008). In developing this framework, we knew it was a "working document," meaning it should be periodically revisited and developed further—something I suggest the new wave of DSE scholars consider taking up. We also knew DSE could never replace the *institution* of SE as we know it, enshrined in laws, structures, systems, professional organizations, teacher certification programs, and so on. However, what DSE did create was a framework for voices historically stifled and silenced by mainstream SE, allowing creative, critical thinking and feeling around how we understand *disability and education.*

Our work as critical special educators who culled heavily from the grassroots interdisciplinary field of Disability Studies was to figure out when and where the two disciplines of DSE and SE were sometimes viewed as distinct, and at other times overlapping. It can be argued that for many of us, our work all along—while not then termed as such—has been a form of consilience, exploring how to negotiate both fields of DSE and SE in our thinking, teaching, and writing. Many of us who identify as DSE scholars have always taught within SE and/or inclusive programs (unfortunately, inclusion still being tightly tied to SE). We recognized then, as we do now, there is no getting away from SE as an institution. However, SE can now be engaged with quite differently than it was in the past because the very existence of DSE has forged a dialog about disability that is far richer and more meaningful than the uni-dimensionality of traditional SE.

While I weave my own methods of navigating the boundaries between DSE and SE throughout this chapter, I believe it useful to the reader to briefly share my understanding of how I conceptualize the three realms addressed by this book—consilience, self-study, and radical love. Generally speaking, as a teacher educator and researcher, consilience means being as open as possible when considering options for resolving problems and improving situations in the four connected areas of interest—theory, research, practice, and policy. Personally, as I iterate several times in this chapter, I have found a DSE approach helps work toward a world that values all individuals and our collective differences. Disability justice, therefore, is an integral part of DSE, and while the framework of Berne et al. (2018) is recent, it is simpatico with the original tenets of DSE (Connor et al., 2008). Unlike DSE, Berne et al.'s work is not limited by its focus on education, but rather articulates a direct challenge to current society as a whole, including its foundational thinking such an unquestioned acceptance of capitalism and individualism. That said, there is also much overlap between the tenets of DSE and those of Disability Justice, including the value of intersectionality, a desire to see greater participation by people with disabilities, recognizing the wholeness of disabled people, a need for cross-disability solidarity, the value of interdependence, and collective access and liberation. Lofty ideals, to some, perhaps, but this is where radical love comes in. We live with ideals. They give us something of value to work toward. Ideals are inextricably entwined with hope, and hope sustains us, motivating us to go on, even in the face of adversity—because we think creating and supporting changes that redefine and respect all human beings is the right thing to do. In sum, we do our best to imagine other possibilities.

That said, even though we are eager and willing to explore possibilities of consilience between DSE and SE, we also have to be mindful that there may be instances in which, at least for now, it may not always be possible—or even desirable. The history of SE—before and after the birth of DSE—reveals instances of seeming irreconcilability. The strange phenomenon exists of DSE and SE as overlapping fields in terms of interests while simultaneously having some profound disagreements. Having both connections and disconnections is part of what we have always grappled with. I believe it therefore worthwhile, in the following sections, to explore the nexuses among the three overlapping realms of the Academy, teacher education programs, and teaching and learning in K-12 schools. In doing so, I illustrate examples of places where consilience can occur and areas where, at least for now, it seems less likely to materialize.

THE CHALLENGE OF CONTEMPLATING DISABILITY DISCOURSE IN MULTIPLE CONTEXTS

In returning to the idea of teachers wanting to do "what's best" for their students, "what's best" cannot be divorced from how educators understand the primary concept of disability. Therein lies the rub. For we all live in a society permeated by a tangle of discourses about disability, continuously in circulation, competing with one another. Among other things, disability can be primarily understood as a human variation, an illness, a natural phenomenon, piteous, burdensome, stigmatized, a tragedy, an aberration, an abnormality, a protected minority status, as culturally defined, as subject to oppression and systematic discrimination. As can be seen from this list, discourses of disability tend to still frame it in a primarily negative way although, thankfully, there are also positive understandings. All of these discourses perpetually assert themselves with, and against, each other, equally inclined to combine or clash in an effort to assert a dominant way to best interpret, and respond to, the concept of disability within any given context—including schools and classrooms.

Every educator is shaped by past and present discourses of disability that all play a role in how students are *perceived*. Conceptualizations of disability are the foundation on which an educator's belief system rests, guiding their words and actions. *A major difference between DSE and SE-oriented scholars is their conceptual understandings of disability*. In the next three sections, I comment upon how differences in understanding disability impact the everyday lives of educators by contemplating what occurs in the academy, teacher education programs, and teaching and learning in K-12 schools.

Differences of Understanding Disability in the Academy

How disability is conceptualized within the Academy varies enormously. Foundational knowledge in SE overwhelmingly draws from Science, and its offspring fields, Medicine and Psychology (Hallahan et al., 2011). These fields are all predicated upon scientific methodology, including experiments in controlled environments featuring objective measures. They also view disability as something to "fix" or "cure," the ultimate goal being a restoration to "normalcy" or "wholeness" or at least as close as possible, as reflected in Wolfensberger's principle of normalization (1972). A scientific lens of understanding disability has historically wielded an epistemological authority that superseded all others. However, a challenge to Science's once unquestionable authority arose when the Social Sciences took a reflexive turn, calling into question the existence of objectivity, including in educational practice (Eisner, 1979). What had been called "objective reality" was now understood as constructed through human interests and interactions (Eisner, 1991). While not negating physical, emotional, intellectual, or sensory differences among humans, Disability Studies scholars argued that society's response to human differences *create* "disability" through processes such as assessing, categorizing, labeling, and placement into specifically designed spaces such as special schools, homes, and institutions.

In line with this thinking, disability rights activists acknowledged their bodily impairments/anomalies while simultaneously asserting that it was society that actively disabled them through attitudes, systems, and inaccessible environmental structures (Linton, 1998). Inspired by the civil rights movement pioneered by African Americans in the 1950s, and later forged by women, and gays and lesbians in the late 1960s, the 1970s saw disabled people create their own movement, demanding full civil rights, including equal access to all aspects of society, including schools (Heumann, 2020). As groundbreaking as these movements were, we must be mindful of using an intersectional lens, too, acknowledging that people at the interstices of different identity markers had qualitatively different experiences in which some benefited far more than others. For example, the women's movement benefited white women more than other racial groups (Breines, 1996) and, initially, the Gay and Lesbian movement has historically been unreceptive—and even hostile—toward trans people (Devor & Matte, 2004). In contrast, Disability Justice recognizes understanding intersectional differences as integral to collective liberation, ensuring no one is left out (Berne et al., 2018), a notion also embedded within the landmark law, the Education for All Handicapped Children Act passed in 1975, guaranteeing a public education for all students, regardless of type and severity of disability. In the subsequent decade, a groundswell of interest about educating students with disabilities caused the field of SE to rapidly expand and gain traction, characterized by leaders in the field as "the Solidification Period" in terms of recognition as a distinct area of study (Hallahan et al., 2014, p. 15).

However, by the mid to late 1980s when I began my teaching career, disability activists, parents and allies, and progressive educators had started the Inclusion movement. This movement had grown in response to disabled students in schools largely being assigned to self-contained classes in separate departments or programs, often in separate spaces (basements, wings, trailers outside, or even in special schools). The push was now for disabled students to be in mainstream classes, learning alongside their nondisabled peers. However, the phenomenon of access to the mainstream—long seen as the goal by disabled people in society—became a highly contentious issue within, and resisted by, the field of SE that had by then established its own separate priorities, interests, and agendas.

In an unprecedented article co-authored by fifteen leading SE scholars, the field eventually acknowledged there was a major paradigmatic "divide" about conceptualizing disability, identifying and placing students, the nature of research, and the purpose of SE (Andrews et al., 2000). While the authors sought broad agreement in a conciliatory manner in order to preserve the field, the foregrounding of philosophical, epistemological, ontological, and methodological tensions indicated, at least to me, that their desire could not come into fruition unless multiple perspectives would become the norm within SE. That said, I respected these scholars' attempts to publicly acknowledge differences in beliefs that existed among them. At the same time, worn down by SE's resistance to plurality, DSE as a nascent subfield of DS began to coalesce, developing alternative ways to conceptualize disability, grounded in civil-rights-based, "grassroots" concerns anchored in lived experiences and identities of disabled people.

What developed as DSE grew in the first decade of the century was its uneasy relationship with SE. As a group of DSE scholars working within the three realms discussed in this chapter, we made earnest attempts to engage the field of SE about different ways of thinking about disability. For example, D. Kim Reid and Jan Valle (2004) described the discursive construction of LD in the *Journal of Learning Disabilities*, inviting a variety of scholars from the field to respond. In another example, building on the work of Andrew et al. (2000) and analyzing growth and tensions in the subsequent decade, Susan Baglieri, Jan Valle, Deborah Gallagher, and I presented "Disability Studies and Special Education: The Need for Plurality of Perspectives on Disability" at the 2010 national conference of the Council for Exceptional Children, later publishing the paper in *Remedial and Special Education* (Baglieri et al., 2011). In a third example, Deb Gallagher, Beth Ferri, and myself co-edited a special double edition of *Learning Disability Quarterly* in which we explored different understandings of LD that are missed and lost if the field only adheres to traditional scientific conceptualizations, presenting this work at the National Council for Learning Disabilities Conference that year (Connor et al., 2011).[4] While sharing our work at conferences we came to notice that special and inclusive educators were genuinely interested in grounding disability in different ways—some "getting it" immediately, reminding us of when we ourselves did not have the words for what we knew and felt. In retrospect, the phenomenon we collectively experienced can be seen as a form of radical love as we were committed to teacher education, and knew there had to be better ways of conceiving human differences and responding to them.

Finally, when the tenets of DSE were developed, formally establishing an alternative voice about disability and education, this triggered anger from some traditional SE scholars. We found this backlash unsurprising, as critical special educators such as Brantlinger (1997), Gallagher (1998), Gartner and Lipsky (1987), and Skrtic (1991), who had previously pointed out SE's hidden ideologies, overconfidence in applying science to knowledge claims, resistance to inclusion, and self-interest in hegemonizing professions, had all been subjected to hostile responses. However, because scholars within DSE work within SE, we endeavored to engage with the field in an exchange of ideas. For example, in "Beyond the Far Too Incessant Schism: Special Education and the Social Model of Disability," we responded to SE's concerns about DSE while providing clarifications and examples that illustrated its value, while again asserting that multiple perspectives were a sign of a healthy field (Gallagher et al., 2014).

Nonetheless, several prominent leaders in SE continued to relentlessly attack DSE, seeing it as an existential threat to their field, stating any knowledge claim that is not scientifically derived is dangerous (see, for example: Anastasiou et al., 2014; Kauffman & Badar, 2018). Unfortunately, this pattern of DSE wishing to engage with SE, and the latter refusing to, can serve to present a polarizing and inaccurate picture. Indeed, because of egregious mischaracterizations of DSE, I felt compelled to write "Why is Special Education so Afraid of Disability Studies?" (Connor, 2019) in which I counter hyperbolic distortions by Kauffman and colleagues, illuminating their flawed logic and challenging SE as a conceptual monopoly. In terms of disability justice (Berne et al., 2018), the stance of traditional leaders verifies why influential fields about disability should be by and/or with people with disabilities, particularly those who are multiply marginalized so that Whiteness and the Patriarchy can be effectively dismantled.

Differences of Understanding Disability in Teacher Education Programs

Like teachers, a professor's belief about disability influences every aspect of teaching about it. When applying for a university position, departmental and program faculty look to see if an applicant is a "good fit," including how that person understands disability. In my own case, on graduating with a doctoral degree, I applied to Hunter College to the "solid" program from which I had graduated thirteen years before. I knew it was a SE department with a strong identity, featuring a number of members not supportive of inclusive practices. I wondered to myself if I would be "good fit" for them? Would my pro-inclusion stance be acceptable? Did it matter that I utilized DSE in my scholarship, and did so in my teaching? As it turned out, as Hunter College is primarily a teaching institution, the main focus was on my abilities to teach methods-based courses, providing teachers with "the stuff" they needed. Once I was working there, some colleagues were interested in talking about my interest in DSE, others not, with one being derisive. To ensure achieving tenure and promotion, I strategically planned venues for publications, aiming at both SE and DSE-friendly journals. This way, I could demonstrate to my department I was professionally connected to "our" field, while also developing DSE writing for other venues. A best-case scenario, and an admitted challenge, is having a publication in an SE journal that allows a DSE lens to be used. This is a form of consilience.

Another interesting challenge was to think of ways I could incorporate a DSE perspective into courses taught. The most strategic one developed was the *Inclusion of Students with Disabilities* as it is a requirement of all general and SE majors. Inclusion can therefore be presented not as a widely believed mandate from on high, but rather framed through a rights-based discourse emphasizing equal access. Throughout the course, conversations based upon the tensions between natural human variation and school structures that attempt to standardize everybody makes for engaging discussions (Connor, 2015). Another course I "made over" with a DSE grounding was *The Study of Learning Disabilities*. Revisions allowed me to go beyond traditional histories, perspectives, laws, and professional organizations by constantly comparing and contrasting personal accounts of LD that often call "traditional" knowledge into question. By having a DSE disposition when teaching this, or any other class, it becomes second nature to share multiple perspectives of disability, and discuss the academic, social, and emotional implications of each framing.

While I did not have it in my power to develop an entire DSE-based program, I did find many ways to incorporate DSE into SE courses via the content taught, resources selected, and assignments given. Graduate students with disabilities in particular valued this approach, as it purposefully sought to address myths, misunderstandings, and stereotypes, to provide equal space for lived experiences of disabled people. Some of the most valuable knowledge in classes is shared by students with disabilities who select to disclose their status. In making changes within courses, I am aware that specific content knowledge must be taught in professional programs leading to state certification. Still, even though teaching such content could be seen as transmitting "set" knowledge (such as laws, key cases, history, and so on), I argue that critical engagement about these topics makes for a good teacher education program (of course, along with "the stuff" of practice). I have found when utilizing DSE, like audiences at SE conferences, it is the first time that most students become aware of it—many immediately seeing Disability Studies' value alongside Gender Studies and Race Studies.

While prepared to be the only DSE researcher within the SE department, I was pleasantly surprised when a significant number of university-wide faculty self-identified as DS scholars. In fact, the City University of New York, of which Hunter College is one of twenty-five campuses, came to develop a system-wide network of DS scholars who meet several times a year. Coming to know so many other scholars and their interests has been both stimulating and gratifying, verifying the value of DS in general—something my SE department gradually became aware of. Just before I retired from full-time teaching, I was asked by my department to present on why DSE, as a special educator, resonated with me. Many colleagues I had worked alongside with for years, including when I was chairperson of the department, were receptive to the ideas I shared. They had grown to know a DSE frame of thinking did not detract from, and very likely deepened, the knowledge of our graduating students who would become career-long educators. I truly believe my experiences as a teacher educator allowed me to use DSE to enhance whatever I taught.

Differences of Understanding Disability When Teaching in K-12 Schools

During their studies at Hunter College, students in special, general, or dual teacher certification programs have to constantly reflect upon what they know about disability and how their beliefs will impact the disabled children and youth they will teach throughout their careers. At the start of the Inclusion course, I provided a graphic organizer titled *Where/How Do Learn About Disability?* for an exercise where I asked students to consider the following different sources: (1) family, (2) personal experience, (3), science, (4) history, (5) religion, (6) psychology, (7) schooling experience, (8) television, (9) law, (10) culture in general, (11) medicine, (12) books, and (13) other. Their responses in these categories were used as a springboard for conversations about multiple messages understood through numerous discourses in constant competition to (re)shape our thoughts about disability.

Some of the things we discussed included how so few knowledge sources are direct accounts of living with a disability, and how nondisabled people's accounts lean heavily toward negative characterization, denying wholeness. The content of the course, I then explain, contains multiple sources directly from people with disabilities. These sources from activists, various grassroots organizations, and research featuring student voices are disability-centric in nature, informative, and insightful, ultimately painting a contrasting picture of disability found in traditional SE literature. Next, we discussed how *schools* teach us about disability, contemplating what we learn through their organizational structures, segregated arrangements, hierarchies of disabilities, certification/professionalization of teachers, and so on. It is important to make teachers aware that they are entering complex school systems that—as microcosms of society—unfortunately are saturated in discourses largely drawn from SE and its claimed basis in science, medicine, and psychology, that have subsequently been inscribed upon legal understandings of disability.

In schools, teachers almost always find themselves expected to "toe the line," and accept existing practices that DSE scholars have claimed as stigmatizing and disempowering (Gabel & Danforth, 2015). In a study about special educators who graduated from a DSE-oriented teacher education program to work in inclusive settings, the authors observed when, where, and how they played their professional cards—including when to frame problems in DSE terms and when to invoke SE discourses in the best interest of students (Narian & Schlessinger, 2018). These moves were termed "agentive maneuverings" (p. 179). Likewise, at IEP meetings, teachers are expected to agree with recommendations made by school teams usually led by psychologists, rather than align with, and authentically engage parents and students, as is the intent of law (Harry & Ocasio-Stoutenburg, 2020). In brief, because SE practices in schools are often mechanistic, compliance-driven, and quite rigid, such contexts make it difficult for individual teachers to push for the larger structural and attitudinal change they would like to see, such as challenging deficit-based understandings of disability, the presumption of competence, and inclusive education as a civil right. Doing so depends upon each instance in its context (Valle, 2009).

CONSIDERING NEXUSES AND RHETORICAL QUESTIONS

In the previous sections I raised numerous issues pertaining to the conceptualization of disability in the Academy, teacher education programs, and teaching and learning in K-12 schools. Each one merited separate consideration as university-based educators operate within these realms and are responsible for engaging with, contributing to, and helping shape each one. As can be seen, each realm contains its own complexities that then come into play at the nexus with others. While limitations prohibit an extensive analysis of interactions, I have articulated some of them in the form of questions in table 1.1, because I see the potential value of promoting conversations at the nexuses among the

Table 1.1 Some Considerations for DSE and SE Scholars at the Multiple Nexus of the Academy, Teacher Education Programs, and Teaching and Learning in K-12 Schools

Nexus 1: The Academy and Teacher Education Programs	Nexus 2: Working with/in K-12 Schools and The Academy	Nexus 3: Teacher Education Programs and and Working with/in K-12 Schools
• What can be gained by including a range of theoretical perspectives about disability in teacher education programs? • In what ways can different theoretical perspectives of disability inform courses on disability history, assessment, inclusive practices, student behaviors, etc.? • In what ways can different theoretical perspectives of disability inform the in-depth study of a specific disability such as autism, behavior disorders, or learning disabilities? • In what ways can different theoretical perspectives of disability inform how methodologies are taught?	• What are ways to center disabled student voices in educational research, and consider them from multiple perspectives of disability? • What are ways to acknowledge and better understand the importance of intersectional experiences of race, class, gender, and disability? • What can be gained by participatory action research to better understand contextual understandings of disability via multiple perspectives? • What can be gained from researching disability in schools via multiple lenses?	• How can diverse theoretical perspectives of disability help inform teachers to make the most informed context-based decisions? • What are ways we can observe (and research) teachers who have learned multiple perspectives of disability—2, 5, 10 years and beyond in their careers? • What are ways university-based educators can engage in-service teachers about students with disabilities from a variety of perspectives? • How can college professors teach preservice teachers to be reflective practitioners who can weigh the pros and cons of different discourses of disability and their ramifications?

three realms. Given that an aim of this book is to explore consilience, I have framed the questions from an open-ended perspective to consider what can be gained. These open-ended questions are intended to help readers explore the intricacies raised when contemplating disability from multiple perspectives.

The final consideration is perhaps the most challenging nexus—that of considering all three realms as they interact simultaneously, bringing an even denser level of complexity to the issues being considered. In a nutshell, the central nexus represents the lives of teacher-researchers focusing on *disability and education*, and the negotiations among discourses to navigate their personal, public, and professional worlds. The center of the three realms serves as the crucible for thinking about disability in terms of what we do and why, the implications our actions have, and how can we best contribute to educating teachers and support them in teaching their students with and without disabilities. In our roles as professionals, we *choose* what we think disability is and how it should be responded to. This choice of how we view other human beings influences everything we do in our teaching and research. We bring our beliefs into classes we teach, presentations made, professional development conducted, programs developed, disability-related scholarship, as well as personal interactions. It is also important to be aware of the historical divide between ivory-tower university perceptions of disability and race evasiveness, including in teacher education programs that tend to resist intersectional approaches that would benefit communities they purportedly serve (Connor, 2017).

PRACTICING CONSILIENCE BETWEEN DISABILITY STUDIES AND SPECIAL EDUCATION

As much we seek to shape and influence others through our beliefs about disability, we must accept the existence of diverse understandings—even those we do not like or agree with—for they are essential to a democracy. Where does that leave us in the sometimes easy, sometimes tense, sometimes seemingly partisan dialogue between DSE and SE when considering the importance of consilience? I hope to have illustrated, by sampling my own experiences as a teacher, teacher educator, and researcher who has always been interested in the paired concepts of disability and education, that consilience is possible. A more difficult question is: Is consilience always desirable—and if not, why? Before I attempt to answer that, I feel compelled to share some thoughts about the notion of consilience in general. As an optimist, albeit rooted in realism and tempered by caution, I view a consilience approach between DSE and SE as a hopeful one. Our fields were never meant to be seen as polar opposites. They are not, and nor can they be entirely divorced from one another—for we are all interested in educating disabled students. Furthermore, there is much to be learned from respectful debates in which contrasting positions should always be examined. Tensions and disagreements, I have almost always found, are productive sites of thinking. In my years teaching at Hunter College with my mentor-turned-colleague Kate, she recognized my DSE perspective brought new angles to look at familiar things and I, in turn, knew her "stuff" for teachers was still essential to their pedagogical confidence and success. She knew changes in thinking about disability were inevitable, and I did not want to "throw the baby out with the bath water" in terms of skills teachers should possess. There is respect in professional compromise, with an understanding it may not be easy, and will always be ongoing.

It must also be recognized that, at times, there are differences in opinion that are not resolvable on the spot. I recall a colleague being uncomfortable when I used the term "educational apartheid" when discussing SE's resistance to inclusive education. While I could appreciate their fears of students with disabilities losing services, I felt my characterization, based on my own experiences and the thinking of many disability activists, was apt. Similarly, a colleague who teaches at a prestigious university shared that his departmental peers ask him to stop using the term "deficit-based" when discussing SE's traditional characterization of students. I share these examples to note that consilience is easier in some realms than others. As can be seen in sustained academic attacks on the field of DSE by leaders in the field of SE, consilience seems less likely, at least until new leadership emerges within SE.

CONCLUDING THOUGHTS

Circling back to the universal question teachers ask, "What is best for my student(s)?" and the answer, "It depends," I cannot help but apply a similar notion to the concept of consilience. In asking, "What's best for consilience to occur?" the answer, too, is "it depends." As educators, we recognize there are not always quick and easy answers to problems, but the context of each situation informs us, allowing us to weigh pros and cons, resulting in pragmatic choices. Exploring consilience between DSE and SE is something I have lived throughout my academic career. I believe it has not only been preferable but actually beneficial, in striving to achieve a sense of harmony among our tri-pronged responsibilities in the Academy, teacher education programs, and supporting teaching and learning in K-12 schools. The work can be incredibly complex, making consilience easier in some realms than others. In other instances, such as engagement with certain leaders in the field of SE, I have not yet found it possible, but hope that may change.

In closing, I reinvoke the term "agentive maneuverings" originally coined by Narian and Schlessinger (2018) to also describe DSE-oriented critical special educators in their daily work in schools. The term strikes me as apt when also applied to university teachers who are in a similar position, strategizing to fulfill their responsibilities in all three realms of the Academy, teacher education programs, and teaching and learning in K-12 schools. This chapter has allowed me to share examples of attempting to enact consilience—without consciously utilizing the term—throughout my career, wherever I could. I commend the co-editors of this book for centering consilience (along with self-study and radical love) for what is a complex, often messy, phenomenon worthy of ongoing focus and debate. I also encourage educators at universities and in schools to actively utilize consilience consciously, proceeding with both hope and caution. That way, arriving at "What's best" for students in specific contexts is through the practice of a thoughtful, deliberative process, culling from multiple perspectives, that should always include students with disabilities.

NOTES

1. I use the terms "disabled students" throughout this chapter. While mindful that some people prefer "students with disabilities" as it denotes people-first language, the use of "disabled students" is in keeping with disability activists that acknowledge bodily impairments exist, but it is society's systems, structures, and attitudes that actually disable people—therefore urging a reclamation of the word "disabled" to be associated with pride (Linton, 1998).

2. For example, the writing process, outlining a five-paragraph essay, using graphic organizers, and so on.

3. One-third of my graduate degree consisted of general education classes that were, by and large, much inferior to my special education classes in terms of content, methods, and history.

4. Ironically, this special edition was secured via a request to the editor pointing out how I, as a reviewer serving for ten years, always had my own work rejected that, when sent to other non-SE journals was published.

REFERENCES

Anastasiou, D., Kauffman, J., & Michail, D. (2014). Disability in multicultural theory: Conceptual and social justice issues. *Journal of Disability Policy Studies, 27*(1), 3–12.

Anastasiou, D., Kauffman, J., & Maag, J. (2017). Special education at the crossroad: An identity crisis and the need for scientific reconstruction. *Exceptionality, 25*(2), 139–155.

Andrews, J. E., Carnine, D. W., Coutinho, M. J., Edgar, E. B., Forness, S. R., Fuchs, L. S., Jordan, D., Kauffman, J., Patton, J., Paul, J., Rosell, J., Rueda, R., Schiller, E., Skrtic, T., & Wong, B. (2000). Bridging the special education divide. *Remedial and Special Education, 21*(5), 258–267.

Anyon, J. (1980). The hidden curriculum: Social class and the hidden curriculum of work. *Journal of Education, 162*(1), 67–92.

Ashton-Warner, S. (1986). *Teacher.* Simon & Shuster.

Baglieri, S., Valle, J., Connor, D. J., & Gallagher, D. (2011). Disability studies and special education: The need for plurality of perspectives on disability. *Remedial and Special Education, 32*(4), 267–278.

Berne, P., Morales, A. L., Langstaff, D., & Invalid, S. (2018). Ten principles of disability justice. *WSQ: Women's Studies Quarterly, 46*(1), 227–230.

Brantlinger, E. (1997). Using ideologies: Cases of non-recognition of the politics of research and practice in special education. *Review of Educational Research, 67*(4), 425–459.

Breines, W. (1996). Sixties stories' silences: White feminism, black feminism, black power. *NWSA Journal, 8*(3), 101–121.

Connor, D. J. (2013). Who "owns" dis/ability? The work of critical special educators as insider outsiders. *Theory and Research in Social Education, 41*(4), 494–513.

Connor, D. J. (2014). The disability studies in education annual conference: Explorations of working within, and against, special education. *Disability Studies Quarterly, 34*(2).

Connor, D. J. (2015). Practicing what we teach: The benefits of using disability studies in an inclusion course. In D. Connor, J. Valle, & C. Hale (Eds.), *Practicing disability studies in education, acting toward social change* (pp. 123–139). Peter Lang.

Connor, D. J. (2017, April). Teaching at the intersection of race and disability: A special education department reflects and (re)acts. *Roosevelt House Faculty Journal.* http://www.roosevelthouse.hunter.cuny.edu/faculty-journal-issues-equity-justice-education-policy/

Connor, D. J. (2018). *Contemplating dis/ability in schools and society: A life in education.* Lexington Books.

Connor, D. J. (2019). Why is special education so afraid of disability studies? Troubling attacks of distain and distortion from leaders in the field. *Journal of Curriculum Theorizing, 34*(1), 10–23.

Connor, D. J., Gabel, S. L., Gallagher, D., & Morton, M. (2008). Disability studies and inclusive education--Implication for theory, research, and practice: Guest editor's introduction. *International Journal of Inclusive Education, 12*(5–6), 441–457.

Connor, D. J., Gallagher, D., & Ferri, B. (2011). Broadening our horizons: Toward a plurality of methodologies in learning disability research. *Learning Disability Quarterly, 32*(2), 107–121.

Devor, A. H., & Matte, N. (2004). ONE inc and Reed Ericson: The uneasy collaboration of gay and trans activism, 1964–2003. *GLO: A Journal of Lesbian and Gay Studies, 10*(2), 179–209.

Eisner, E. (1979). *The educational imagination: On the design and evaluation of school programs.* Pearson.

Eisner, E. (1991). *The enlightened eye: Qualitative inquiry and the enhancement of educational practice.* McMillan.

Faber, A., & Mazlish, E. (1997). *How to talk so kids will listen, and listen so kids will talk.* Harper Publishing.

Ferri, B., Gallagher, D., & Connor, D. J. (2011). Pluralizing methodologies in the field of LD: From "what works" to what matters. *Learning Disability Quarterly, 34*(3), 222–231.

Gabel, S., & Danforth, S. (Eds.). (2008). *Disability and the politics of education: An international reader.* Peter Lang.

Gallagher, D. J. (1998). The scientific knowledge base of special education: Do we know what we think we know? *Exceptional Children, 64*(4), 493–502.

Gallagher, D. J., Connor, D. J., & Ferri, B. A. (2014). Beyond the far too incessant schism: Special education and the social model of disability. *International Journal of Inclusive Education, 18*(11), 1120–1142.

Garbett, D., Ovens, A., & Thomas, L. (2018). Biculturalism 101: A self-study exploring culturally responsive practice. *Studying Teacher Education, 14*(3), 308–319.

Gartner, A., & Lipsky, D. (1987). Beyond special education: Toward a system of quality for all students. *Harvard Educational Review, 57*(4), 367–395.

Grant, M. R., & Butler, B. M. (2018). Why self-study? An exploration of personal, professional, and programmatic influences in the use of self-study research. *Studying Teacher Education, 14*(3), 320–330.

Hallahan, D., Kauffman, J., & Pullen, P. (2011). *Exceptional learners: An introduction to special education* (12th ed.). Pearson.

Hallahan, D., Pullen, P., & Ward, D. (2014). A brief history of the field of learning disabilities. In H. L. Swanson, K. R. Harris, & S. Graham (Eds.), *Handbook of learning disabilities* (2nd ed., pp. 15–32). Guilford Press.

Harry, B., & Ocasio-Stoutenberg, L. (2020). *Meeting families where they are: Building equity through advocacy with diverse schools and communities.* Teachers College Press.

Heumann, J. (2020). *Being Heumann: An unrepentant memoir of a disability rights activist.* Beacon Press.

Kauffman, J., & Badar, J. (2018). Extremism and disability chic. *Exceptionality, 26*(1), 46–61.

Kohl, H. (1967). *36 children.* Plume.

Kosnik, C., Beck, C., Freese, A. R., & Samaras, A. P. (Eds.). (2006). *Making a difference in teacher education through self-study: Studies of personal, professional, and program renewal* (Vol. 2). Springer Science & Business Media.

Linton, S. (1998). *Claiming disability.* New York University Press.

McCourt, F. (2006). *Teacher man.* Simon & Schuster.

Monroe, L. (1999). *Nothing's impossible: Leadership lessons from inside and outside of the classroom.* Perseus.

Narian, S., & Schlessinger, S. (2018). Becoming an inclusive educator: Agentive maneuverings in collaboratively taught classrooms. *Teaching and Teacher Education, 71*(2018), 179–189.

Reid, D. K., & Valle, J. W. (2004). The discursive practice of learning disability: Implications for instruction and parent—school relations. *Journal of learning disabilities, 37*(6), 466–481.

Skrtic, T. M. (1991). *Behind special education: A critical analysis of professional culture and school organization.* Love.

Smith, P. (Ed.). (2013). *Both sides of the table: Autoethnographies of educators learning and teaching with/in (Dis)ability*. Peter Lang.

Vasconcelos, E. F. (2011). "I can see you": An autoethnography of my teacher-student self. *Qualitative Report, 16*(2), 415–440.

Wolfensberger, W. P. (1972). *The principle of normalization in human services*. National Institute on Mental Retardation.

Chapter 2

At the Nexus of Disability Studies in (Special) Education

Toward Consiliencatory Frameworks for Critical Emotion Praxis Liberation

David I. Hernández-Saca

We need a critical emotion revolutionary praxis for liberation (Allman, 2007; Calderón-Almendros, & Ruiz-Román, 2015), the essential coupling of thinking, feeling, reflection, writing, and action (Artiles & Kozleski, 2007) that transcends internal and external boundaries at the nexus of Disability Studies in Education (DSE; Danforth & Gabel, 2006; Pearson et al., 2016; Ware, 2006) and special education (SPED) for individual and societal liberation. This requires vulnerability and transparency, leading to a consiliencatory framework at this nexus and boundary work (Akkerman & Bakker, 2011) of DSE and SPED. Through the use of consilience (Wilson, 1998), self-study (Tidwell et al., 2009) using critical autoethnography (Ellis, 2004; Ellis, & Bochner, 2006; Brandenburg, 2008), and radical love (Fromm, 1956), this study critically examines my experiences as a new assistant professor of DSE within a Department of SPED. As a Latino gay cisgender male with an auditory Learning Disability label, I work within a predominantly white institution (PWI) in the Midwest and face institutional and political challenges that others do not. The imperative of this consiliencatory self-study, critical autoethnography, and radical love work at the boundary of SPED and DSE does not exist in isolation from the historical, social, cultural, spiritual, and emotive dimensions of what counts to be a human being in a global world. The implications for the individualized, societal, systemic, and consiliencatory-disciplinary change and humanization within the academy and educational contexts (Akkerman & Bakker, 2011) for theory, research, policy, practice, and praxis are vital not only for my life chances but for those of other individuals within and outside traditional special education spaces marked by white and ability supremacy.

Within this chapter I first critically chronicle the disciplinary boundaries of traditional special education and DSE. Second, I outline my conceptual framework for this evocative self-study and autoethnography at the boundaries. Third, I ground the research design within a self-study in teacher education theory and practice through the generation of counter-hegemonic lived critical autoethnographic texts. Fourth, I illuminate how I generated themes for this study and how I critically analyzed them. Fifth, I present the following themes at the boundaries of SPED and DSE: *Kids don't learn because their frontal lobes are not fully developed, It's like being in a racist environment, Just get over it,* and *Beyond "Lazy and Unmotivated" Why Parents and Teachers Need to Know about Executive Skills.* Sixth, I end with a discussion, conclusion, and implications that situate my experiences within the larger master narratives and educational system of SPED and LD (Hernández-Saca, 2016) to highlight the need for a critical emotion praxis consiliencatory paradigm shift.

A PERSONAL AND PROFESSIONAL REVIEW OF THE BOUNDARIES

I do not see my personal and professional identities outside of cultural and educational systems, such as special education, general education, and teacher education programs, given my professional role as an assistant professor of DSE within a Department of Special Education (DSpED) at a teaching institution. These systems are not isolated from the historiography of the disciplines. These are the disciplines that I navigate and critically facilitate with my teacher candidates in order to engage in critical and deep understanding. An understanding that moves beyond the technical dimensions of teaching and learning to account for the contextual and critical components of social and emotional justice, practice, and human interaction and development (Rogoff, 2003). In doing so, I ground critical emotion educational praxis at the nexus of general and special education policies and practices (Artiles & Kozleski, 2007). I purposefully frame my work through Critical DSE and an interdisciplinary framework for critical emotion praxis for collaborative and interdisciplinary transformation at the individual and societal levels (Hernández-Saca, 2016).

Since I began my assistant professorship within my DSpED, I have taught courses in the introductory block to our special education minor. I teach: (1) a special education law, assistive technology, and advocacy course, and (2) a transition planning and programming course for students with dis/Abilities[1] at their intersections of power and identities. Within each of these courses, I am intentional with my critical thinking, feeling, and reflection before I act with my colleagues and preservice and in-service teachers about general and special education systems at the intersections of power and privilege such as whiteness and ableism. The current course description for my special education law course reads as follows:

> This course will explore issues in general, special and inclusive education. Specifically, we will focus on law and legal issues, assistive technology, and related educational equity issues centering on identification, assessment, intervention, characteristics, advocacy, and educational implications for teaching strategies and practices for individuals with dis/Abilities. In turn, the course is undergirded from a Critical Theory perspective. Particularly from a DSE paradigm and a consilience interdisciplinary approach that conceptualizes learning and teaching through praxis—the combination of critical reflection and feeling before acting—toward educational equity for ALL students and their families. Nevertheless, with particular attention to historically multiply marginalized youth and students with dis/Abilities at the intersections of power and identities. Given the instructors' operationalization of the course as one where we will survey the law and legal issues, assistive technology, and related current and historical issues we will also focus on advocacy that centers on not only the technical aspects of teaching and learning, but critical issues of social and emotional justice, history and philosophical dimensions to teaching and learning. For example, centering the importance of being a culturally responsive and sustaining pedagogue within educational systems for ALL students who live at the intersections of multiple identities and cultures for individual, societal and systemic transformation and change. Particular attention will be paid to the intersectional experiences of immigrant students (with and without dis/Abilities) and their parents as well as the role of emotion and affect that both afford and constrains people's agency within their sociocultural contexts across time and space. Furthermore, through class readings, lecture, discussion, and critical reflection and action, individually and collectively, we will create an ongoing praxis within our learning community as we continuously become inclusive educators for disability at the intersections of justice! (Hernández-Saca, Fall 2020, Course Syllabus, p. 1)

This course description is the latest articulation of my understanding and inclusion of the critical and contextual dimensions within an introductory course at the boundaries of SPED and DSE. The following is my Fall 2016 co-taught course description:

> This course will explore issues in special and inclusive education, with a focus on law and legal issues, assistive technology, and related educational issues

centering on identification, assessment, intervention, characteristics, advocacy, and educational implications/teaching strategies for individuals with exceptional learning needs. (Hernández-Saca, Fall 2016, Course Syllabus, p. 1)

The juxtaposition of my Fall 2020 course description with that of Fall 2016 illustrates how I reframed the overall foundations of what counts as "special education" for our preservice teachers, mostly able-bodied white, working-class, and middle-class female teachers. Through a DSE paradigm (Connor, 2013), I understand the social and emotional fabric of the special education system from an intersection and interdisciplinary perspective that acknowledges tensions between traditional SPED and DSE. In this chapter, I firmly counter-narrate a consiliencatory disability justice (Berne et al., 2018) frame—the unity of knowledge (Wilson, 1999) across and within disciplines through a *critical self-study* for critical human developmental conflicts and tensions for paradigmatic shifts against global hegemony represented within the traditional SPED system (Rogoff, 2003). Such a framework brings multiple paradigms into conversation to inform my personal and professional core identity, that is, my "self-narrativatization and personal-trajectory" for learning and systems of thought and feelings and "(cross)disciplinary change" within (special) education (Connor, 2017; Foucault, 2000; Gee, 2011). The bottom line, however, is speaking and acting truth to the hegemony of the traditional paradigm of SPED, which has been a mechanism of epistemological violence on the well-being and life chances of Black, Indigenous, and People of Color (BIPOC) at their intersections of power and identities (Hernández-Saca, 2017). I am one of those persons of color at my intersections of traditional SPED and auditory Learning Disability labeling and trauma (Hernández-Saca, 2017).

In understanding my positionality within the U.S. context, elsewhere I have chronicled how I feel, think, and grapple with my label of an auditory LD and SPED trauma (See Hernández-Saca, 2017). I call these LD and SPED emotions. However, these emotions are not a-political, a-historical, or a-cultural but deeply patterned within the literature and in the cultural-social discursive, emotive, and material practices of both LD and SPED. The weight on my body, mind, soul, spirit, and heart has caused psychological trauma, that day to day, through glimmers of hope, love, and transcendence for liberation, emancipation, and freedom against psycho-emotional disablism at my intersections of power and identities, I am able to have post-traumatic growth (PTG; Collier, 2016). Collier (2016) describes PTG as:

> A positive change as well—a new appreciation for life, a newfound sense of personal strength and new focus on helping others . . . a theory that explains this kind of transformation following trauma . . . and holds that people who endure psychological struggle following adversity can often see positive growth

afterward. "People develop new understanding of themselves, the world they live in, how to relate to other people, the kind of future they might have and a better understanding of how to live life . . . refers to what can happen when someone who has difficulty bouncing back experiences a traumatic event that challenges [their] core beliefs, endures psychological struggle, and then ultimately finds a sense of personal growth. It's a process that "takes a lot of time, energy, and struggle." (para 5–7, 9)

When I became aware of having an auditory Learning Disability and heard those words, "You have an auditory Learning Disability," my mind collapsed on itself, and I went into a red and black hole and became terrified. Terror gripped my soul and eclipsed my sense of self, along with my core beliefs about myself, or those I had yet to discover. I felt raped, kidnapped, and alienated. Those old feelings are still there. As I type, they come up and haunt me. These are my contextual and critical components of being an assistant professor of DSE within a PWI. However, glimmers of love continue to sustain me and propel me forward toward PTG. I am also conscious of my personal and professional life at the intersections of traditional SPED and DSE. When I came across the paradigm of DSE, it was life-giving. In contrast, SPED's traditional paradigm felt and continues to feel like an imposition on my epistemic-ontological beliefs and truths. The following history of the disciplines at the boundaries, in turn, is part and parcel of my past, present, and future glimmers of love and PTG. This boundary work, in turn, is about the deconstruction and reconstruction of who I am beyond the boundaries of SPED and DSE for the liberation for all against white and ability supremacy, since that is what has occurred beyond white and ability space.

A History of Disability Studies

Society for Disability Studies

The academic field of Disability Studies emerged within the humanities and social sciences in the United States, Canada, and the United Kingdom in the 1980s. Its founding scholarly organization and society, the Society for Disability Studies (SDS), was first organized in 1982 within the National Social Science Association of the United States (NSSA). At its founding, the organization named its section the Study of Chronic Illness, Impairment, and Disability. In 1986, they renamed themselves to the SDS. Nevertheless, SDS, through its section, the Study of Chronic Illness, Impairment, and Disability within the NSSA, additionally maintains its affiliation status with the International Western Social Science Association (WSSA). Founders of the

SDS were Daryl Evans, Nora Groce, Steve Hey, John Seidel, Jessica Scheer, and Irving Kenneth Zola (1935–1994). The mission of SDS is:

> a non-profit organization that promotes the study of disability in social, cultural, and political contexts. Disability Studies recognizes that disability is a key aspect of human experience, and that the study of disability has important political, social, and economic implications for society as a whole, including both disabled and nondisabled people. Through research, artistic production, teaching and activism, the Society for Disability Studies seeks to augment understanding of disability in all cultures and historical periods, to promote greater awareness of the experiences of disabled people, and to advocate for social change. (Society of Disability Studies, 2021, para 1–2)

Since 1986 SDS has promoted its mission through documenting activities within the SDS journal outlet, *Disability Studies Quarterly*. In 1994, the first DS program was created at Syracuse University. Three years later, in 1997, the *Disabilities Studies Reader* (Davis, 1997) was published. Within the 1997 *Disabilities Studies Reader*, one could find a growing first collection of DS academic papers in the field. Over the next several years, DS continued to grow as a field, and in 2005 the principal professional association for U.S. scholars of language and literature, the *Modern Language Association*, made DS a division of study. As of 2016, there were 42 academic programs in DS across 42 North American colleges and universities (Zubal-Ruggieri, 2016). As chronicled above, SDS, within the academy—in the United States and internationally—has worked toward establishing DS as a legitimate academic discipline.

Disability Studies

Today, DS is an interdisciplinary field of study that conceptualizes "disability" through a social, cultural, and political lens instead of the previous and more commonly used medical, biological, or psychological frameworks. The former way of conceptualizing "disability" has come to be known as the "social model" of disability, while the latter is called the "medical model" of disability. The medical model of disability has been associated with special education, education, medicine, biology, cognitive sciences, and psychology, among others. In contrast, anthropology, sociology, cultural studies, history, critical legal studies, linguistics, philosophy, and cultural and social psychology, among others, have historically been used to foreground the meaning of a social model of disability. The medical model of disability situates "disability" as both deficit and internalized within a person's body, brain, or mind. The social model of disability paradigm challenges the medicalization and location of the "disability" within the individual's body, brain, or mind, and investigates the social construction of both ability and disability, hence, "dis/Ability." By "dis/Ability," some DS scholars indicate that "disability" is open to interpretation and is not a fixed phenomenon, but one that includes both "abilities" and "disabilities." In so doing, DS provides a framework to disrupt the "common sense" assumptions institutionalized within a society. In turn, according to Rice (2007) DS troubles the:

> Singular view of the construct of disability and aims to present a variety of perspectives on disability, both in contemporary society as well as those from a range of cultures and histories. One goal of disability studies is to challenge the idea of the normal/abnormal binary and to suggest and show that a range of human variation is "normal." (p. 466)

DS scholars account for such issues related to disability as a socially constructed phenomenon that is inherently about issues of power, privilege, and difference. In particular, one branch of DS, given DS's nonclinical and instructionist origins, was the development of DSE. DSE focuses on the application of the DS framework within educational contexts.

A History of Disability Studies in Education

Early Cross-pollination between Critical Special Education and Disability Studies in Education

DSE is applying Disability Studies (DS) in educational contexts. Progenitors of the field of DSE included past leadership from the SDS during the 1990s, including special educators by professors Phil Ferguson (past president), Susan Gabel, and Susan Peters (past secretary). SDS leaders particularly focused on issues at the nexus of DS and educational research. By the late 1990s, other DSE members were involved in SDS annual conferences, such as DS scholars Beth Ferri, Linda Ware, and Nancy Rice, among others. They contributed to interdisciplinary beginnings between critical special education and DS related to educational research. It's important to note that critical special education as a form of research and discipline was one of "other forms of education research" applied to the domain of DS scholarship (Connor, 2012) at that time.

Challenging the Hegemony of Positivism

It was during the 1990s that the critical special education community made a turn toward using a postpositivist lens within the traditional special education canon. This was largely done by many of the progenitors of DS, in particular, scholars such as Linda Ware, who moved the conversations to an international stage in New Zealand, Europe, and Australia (Connor, 2012). At the end of the decade, in 1999, Ware gathered the growing DS community of scholars for the first time for an international conference in Rochester, New York (Connor, 2012). At this conference the makings of DSE's conceptual and scholarly community were coming to a theoretical and empirical consolidation, given that several years later foundational texts were being published regarding the field's disciplinary stances such as *Writing, Identity and the Other: Dare We Do Disability Studies?* (Ware, 2001), *Ideology and the Politics of (In) Exclusion* (Ware, 2004), and *Working Past Pity: What We Make of Disability in Schools* (Allen, 2015). Within a Summer Institute held at the University of Chicago in 2004, Ware, David Mitchell, and Sharon Snyder further developed the theoretical and practical applications of DSE (Connor, 2012).

The Coalition of Open Inquiry in Special Education

DSE scholar Scot Danforth submitted a proposal to the national conference of The Association for Severely Handicapped (TASH) entitled, Coalition of Open Inquiry in Special Education (COISE) (Connor, 2012). Danforth and other critical early DSE scholars such as Phil Ferguson, Ellen Brantlinger, Lous Heshusius, and Chris Kliewer further laid the ground to problematize the hegemony of positivism within educational contexts that the traditional special education canon had built. DSE scholars provided a counter-paradigm to "traditional" epistemological, ontological, axiological, and etiological attitudes of special education toward dis/Ability. In his historiography of the field of DSE, Connor (2012) summarized the following "unfortunate developments in disability services":

> the assumption that disability is a primarily bio-physical phenomenon consisting of a deficit condition existing within an individual; the assumption that service professionals know better than persons with disabilities and family members what is best for a served individual; the assumption that diagnosed or labeled individuals should be separated from the mainstream population for purposes of treatment. (para. 3)

This development against the positivist underpinnings of special education leads to a counter-disability or a non-positivist discourse, which has had less influence and power within the academy (Connor, 2012) than the hegemonic zeitgeist of special education. Danforth and the other panelists:

> explored alternative ways of envisioning, writing about, and talking about the lives and possibilities of persons with disabilities including many traditions of

scholarship (social science, humanities, arts, spiritual traditions, etc.) and the numerous voices that have something to say about disability issues. (Connor, 2012, para. 4)

DSE-SIG-AERA

In the aftermath of the 1999 "Open Inquiry" panel, the growing field of DS and a specific group of scholars within the DS community concerned with educational contexts decided to name themselves DSE and, after deliberation, applied to become a Special Interests Group within the American Educational Research Association (AERA) in 2000. The DSE community within the AERA continued to grow throughout the 2000s and 2010s with the creation of the DSE-SIG of AERA Award for Emerging Scholar in DSE to David J. Connor in 2006. Through a vote in 2009 the title of this award was changed to the Outstanding Dissertation Award in order to make a distinction with the Junior Scholar Award in DSE given at the Second City DSE conference.

Disability Studies in Education and Intersectionality

Throughout the history of DS and DSE, attention to people's intersectional lives with disabilities was not the norm. In other words, the emerging field was at risk of reproducing the larger hegemonic and white supremacist order that surrounded it (in this case, perpetuating a narrative of disability as non-intersectional). Nevertheless, Connor's 2005 dissertation and 2006 Emerging Scholar in DSE award, which eventually became his book, *Urban Narratives: Portraits-in-Progress: Life at the Intersections of Learning Disability, Race, & Social Class* (2008), was an exception. Moreover, leading scholars Subini Annamma, David Connor, and Beth Ferri (2013) have pushed the field of DSE and Critical Race Theory to account for both disability and race, and more specifically, to examine how racism and ableism mutually constitute educational spaces and major social institutions, the former due to Western cultural norms.

The National Black Disability Studies Coalition

The work of the National Black Disability Studies Coalition (NBDC) centers knowledge about the experience of disability while Black, within the African Diaspora and the United States. The mission of NBDC is:

> to create a space for inquiry within universities that brings together faculty and students . . . to consider Black disability issues within broad-based social, cultural and historical contexts . . . to put out a call to action to Black students with disabilities, so that they can lead the next wave of change. This collection

of writings is offered in the spirit of that call, and includes a collaboratively-authored Black disability studies (hereafter Black DS) syllabus, as well as reflections from members of the Coalition on their experiences of teaching and learning in Black DS classrooms. (Dunhamn et al., 2015, para. 1)

Furthermore, Dunhamn et al. (2015) articulate that a Black DS framework wishes "to give educators and students a sense of how they might begin to incorporate some of the principles of Black DS, and disability justice more broadly, into the learning spaces they inhabit" (para. 2). In Dunhamn et al.'s articulation of what counts as a Black DS, they push back on how Disability Studies in general has been treated in society and in education. For example, they challenge special education's dominance and the idea that Black DS should not be considered an add on or "marginalized special-topic course, but rather a crucial part of all disability studies courses and pedagogies, as well as all Black and Africana Studies courses" (para 3). Therefore, Black DS is about "paradigm-shifting change" in contexts of education and society given the legacies of white and ability supremacy (Dunhamn et al., 2015, para. 3).

The National Black Disability Coalition centered counter-hegemonic theory, research, policy, practice, pedagogy, and praxis within higher education courses that would traditionally ignore the intersectionality of both disability and race. In other words, they urged cultural practices within higher education to center historically multiply marginalized identities, such as disability with race or race with disability, as part and parcel of the generative and liberatory language of an NBDC against the hegemonic order that benefits white and able-bodied people.

Personally and professionally, I am humbled and grateful for the shoulders we are standing on as it relates to the meaning of dis/Ability at the intersections of multiple forms of difference. In other words, for the epistemological, ontological, axiological, and etiological lines of what counts as intersectional dis/Ability that the aforementioned history at the boundaries of traditional special education and DSE has created. This development is generative of growth for the full range of human variation given the salience of disability at the intersections of power and identities. The experience of multidimensional dis/Abled students and people in education and society are not singular. There is danger in a single story (Adichie, 2009) or representation about how youth and everyone in educational communities experience dis/Ability at the intersections of power, identities, and pain. Given the opposing paradigm of traditional special education of DSE, DSE has contributed to shifting perceptions and actions that systematically take place within and outside teacher education programs for preservice and in-service teachers.

However, who benefits? Who does not benefit from our past history of critically studying dis/Ability at the intersections of power and identities?

How are the current nomenclature and language, policies and practices, and disciplinary knowledge base affording and constraining agency within and across systems? But more importantly, what about individual well-being and social and cultural transformation that relate to intersectional dis/Ability? For a very long time, I have felt and continue to feel the weight of white and ability supremacy on my psyche. Feminist DS scholar, Carol Thomas (1999) described this as the psycho-emotional disablism model of dis/Ability. Psycho-emotional disablism bridges the medical and social model of dis/Ability and accounts for the impacts of social barriers on the agency of people with impairments by accounting for the personal experiences of people with impairments. This complements the tenet of centering the voices of people with dis/Abilities in reading and writing their world (Freire, 1970) and its generation of new intersectional dis/Ability counter-hegemonic for individual and societal transformation, freedom, and liberation given the hegemonic forces at play on our psyches at the personal, interpersonal, structural, and political levels of society (Crenshaw, 1991). This historiography of the boundaries of traditional special education and DSE is my way of freeing myself from the epistemological violence that behaviorist and traditional positivist paradigms have inculcated on my mind, heart, body, soul, and spirit (Cannon & Hernández-Saca, 2021; Hernández-Saca, 2021; Hernández-Saca & Cannon, 2019).

Furthermore, the historiography of DSE in relation to the traditional special education system has consisted of a critical self-study in teacher education project. From the gathering of critical special educators to the establishment of special interest groups within national and international educational associations such as the AERA, and the training of professors and creation of professional networks of critical special educators and advocacy and activism, inside and outside of the academy, such movements and developments contributed to the creation of DSE. The purpose and function of this chapter is descriptive as opposed to prescriptive to not only understand the boundary work between traditional special education and DSE, but to propose a way forward through consilience-interdisciplinarity, self-study in teacher education, Disability Justice, and hence liberation through radical love—care, respect, knowledge, and responsibility. The tools and strategies of Disability Justice are emergent, however, and situated in local contexts in order to transcend positivist and postpositivist structures from traditional special education anchored in the medical-psychological model of dis/Ability, which in turn erases the intersectional lives of people with dis/Abilities and students. Personally, professionally, and programmatically, in turn, as an Assistant Professor of DSE within a DSpED, I navigate the boundaries between traditional special education and DSE, in order to orient future general and special educators to critically think, feel, and reflect before they act personally, professionally, and programmatically in their future careers and responsibilities (Kosnik et al., 2006).

CONSILIENCATORY METHODOLOGIES: *SELF-STUDY IN TEACHER EDUCATION AND AUTOETHNOGRAPHY*

The methods include constructs from self-study and consilience methodologies (Tidwell et al., 2009; Wilson, 1999). The following self-study quality indicators were used:

1) Thorough description of the context, data collection, and analysis
2) Thoughtful problematization of the researcher and their practice
3) Indications for how the study changed the researcher's practice
4) Description of how it might contribute to the knowledge base for teaching (Schulte, 2015)

Complementally, consilience provided me the interdisciplinary eclecticism to critically examine the complexity I experience on a daily basis, relating to the fear, vulnerability, and eventual bullying as a first-year assistant professor of special education at the boundaries.

Self-study Methodology Through Autoethnographic Texts and Methods

Self-study is not autoethnography (Ellis & Bochner, 2006); however, self-study includes autoethnographic methods. The purpose of self-study is to gain self and situated knowledge about how one's identity impacts and informs one's practice and vice versa. A successful self-study may include professional and personal improvement about the inquiry topic and the research questions.

Autoethnography is about studying the culture one lives in to create emic—insider—understanding of the problem of practice that is under study. Ever since I became aware of my auditory Learning Disability (LD) diagnosis, I have, in retrospect studied myself—my thoughts, feelings, and actions—to the point where what I discovered about myself has caused me deep traumatic scars in my heart, soul, spirit, mind, and body due to the direct and indirect impact of being labeled and stigmatized. However, recently, through the development of critical emotion praxis friendships within the academic community (Boskovich et al., 2019), I have come to ground my work within a spiritual paradigm that helps me be myself even though I still wake up and live and go to bed with the damaging effects of the traditional special education and their direct and indirect consequences on my body and mind. DSE scholars and their counter-paradigm have helped trouble and dispel the hegemonic forces of whiteness and ability supremacy in the paradigmatic apparatus of special education. I am tired of being sick and tired (Cannon & Hernández-Saca, 2021), and only very recently I have come to realize I am not alone (Hernández-Saca & Cannon, 2019). I am also gay, have deep connections to the LGBTQIA community, and have a strong gay identity as well as El Salvadorian and Palestinian identities and other historically multiply marginalized identities. However, my disability identity or experiences with psycho-emotional disablism still haunt me (Hernández-Saca, 2021; Yoon, 2019). Given my personal connection to the ways in which I move and am part of the world, for how special education and intersectional life at the nexus of language, an auditory Learning Disability, special education and LD, and special education trauma have shaped and continue to shape my lived realities on the ground as a human being, I turn to autoethnography as a teacher educator for self-study in teacher education sake.

Elsewhere, within a collective autoethnography, my critical friends and I summarized the following principles of autoethnography that I also anchor in this self-study of my teacher education practice:

1) Autoethnography is both the research process and a writing genre, that privilege "concrete action, emotion, embodiment, self-consciousness and introspection" and the writing of autoethnographic texts that are "partial, situated and incomplete" in the autoethnographic process of further understanding self in context and culture and culture in context and self. In so doing, creating, knowing, and discovering who you are in relationship to an audience and hence it is purposeful (Jones et al., 2013).
2) The personal is sociocultural and political, that is, self-reflection represents my social realities.
3) These social realities are constructed to and through narratives that "stick" and are often institutionalized.
4) In naming my social realities, I continue to radically (re)name to counter with new narratives about dis/ability at my intersections of historicity, power, and identities (Ellis, 2004, p. xix, as cited in Douglas & Carless, 2013, p. 85).

Through the above tenets and the research and writing methods for autoethnographic texts (Allen, 2015) we enter into a process of becoming more fully human (Freire, 1970).

Data Collection and Analysis

The data sources were documentation of my experiences being bullied as a first-year assistant professor. Specifically, these included critical reflections in the form of journal entries about my experiences and a year-long course syllabus that was related to the social and professional context in which the bullying occurred. Both were analyzed using the constant comparative method and reflexive, retrospective analysis (Brandenburg, 2008; Glaser & Strauss, 1967; Samaras et al., 2004). Bullough and Gitlin (1995) posit "to know the past is to know oneself as an individual and as a representative of a socio-historical moment in time; like others each person is a victim, vehicle, and ultimately a resolution of a culture's dilemmas" (p. 25). Analytically, I used critical reflection and retrospective analysis (Brandenburg, 2008) and relied on critical friends to help me unpack my experiences and responses to the boundaries of the traditional canon of special education and DSE given my personal and professional history being labeled with an auditory LD and receiving K-12 special education and Disability Student Services while in higher education (Hernández-Saca, 2017). Authentic problematization of one's practice can occur through dialogue with one or more persons and/or through the reading of research to perpetuate the modification of ideas (Costa & Kallick, 1993) for more critical friends. The critical friend tenet of multiple perspectives is complementary to a consilience interdisciplinary approach. Lastly, the historiography of the field of DSE has also served as a data and analysis for this self-study in teacher education in that it provides the foundational knowledge at the boundary between traditional special education and DSE. The trustworthiness of a self-study is the verisimilitude in one's believability, humility, authenticity, and vulnerability that leads to a high level of self-awareness to inform constructivist new knowledge for one's practice and to inspire change in one's practice.

MY RACIST AND ABLEIST STRUGGLE AS A NEW ASSISTANT PROFESSOR OF DSE AT THE BOUNDARIES

I was bullied due to the sociocultural milieu related to special education boundaries and DSE working to and through each of us. The conflicting paradigms that create discord and bullying behavior stem from not only individuals themselves but from historical-material and discursive perspectives at the nexus of special education and DSE. With such perspectives, the following themes emerged: "Kids don't learn because their frontal lobes are not fully developed"; "It's like being in a racist environment"; "Just get over it"; and "Beyond 'Lazy and Unmotivated': Why Parents and Teachers Need to Know about Executive Skills." These themes correspond to racist and ableist practices I experienced during my first year as an assistant professor of DSE in a historically white institution. They relate to the cultural and social contexts that I needed to navigate and from which I needed to liberate myself. According to the master narratives of LD, I was the problem in these traumatic events; nothing could be further from the truth. However, institutionally and politically, this felt as if it were so. I now turn to describe each theme.

"Kids don't learn because their frontal lobes are not fully developed." After graduate school, I was excited as a new assistant professor to begin my new career. I came from a rigorous PhD program that was critical of special education and was advised not to demonize traditional special education. As an undergraduate and master's student, I began to question many of my life experiences within special education from K-12 and higher education. Even though I did not know what those words meant or even knew they existed at the time, the scientism and positivism of special education represented the stripping of my self-determination deep down in my soul of souls and hearts of hearts. As a 39-year-old human and spiritual being, I still carry the scars and trauma that caused my body and mind to shatter. Previously, I called myself a "wounded bird" or a "wounded soul" due to the internal ableism that I know did not originate inside me but manifested due to material, emotive, and discursive associations with and consequences of being a person of color, an immigrant, an English Language Learner labeled with an auditory LD and placed in special education for most of my educational career (Hernández-Saca, 2019). This historicity based on whiteness, ableism, and the desire to be "objective" is a species of positivism and scientism that silences people with impairments and erases their lived experiences. As a new assistant professor I was partnered with a new colleague who kept saying, "Kids don't learn because their frontal lobes are not fully developed." I could not hear and not be affected by this authoritative and uncritical statement as a human being with a deep respect for children and the care for their well-being. This statement harkened back to the power of special education—defining and making sense of children without questioning those knowledge claims and where they came—as it relates to issues of white and able-bodied and minded representations, power, and privilege against those identified, measured, classified, and found wanting. "Kids don't learn because their frontal lobes are not fully developed" is based on a medical-psychological model of dis/Ability, and this statement would never come out of the voice of a student so labeled or their parent. A reductionist argument, it essentializes ableist and deficit thinking and language (Patton Davis & Museus, 2019).

"It's like being in a racist environment." When I sought consolation from a senior scholar of DSE, I was grateful that I was not "making up" how horrible it felt when I heard the words, "Kids don't learn because their frontal lobes are not fully developed." I was immediately affirmed and reassured. I was also reassured by another mentor, critical friend, and colleague in my Department. It was not me. I am not the problem. Our emotions, bodies, energies, and institutions matter for the epistemological, ontological, axiological, and etiological worldviews that are structured within traditional paradigms about dis/Ability. I needed to be brave and to speak back and be an unruly bodymind so that I could resist further damage from the system of special education. The traditional educational psychology paradigm might have labeled me as the "problem," but no! My colleague expressed it precisely when she stated: "It's like being in a racist environment." Yes! A racist and ableist environment. This was the social model in action. Thank you for your saving energy and counter-narrative about students labeled with disabilities, compared to my co-teacher. How can someone labeled from the special education system develop a healthy sense of self when an entire system of special education hunts for something wrong within me? Or us? We did not create this system, but its deconstruction and critique is well overdue. For liberation's sake, we should not give power to such a machine that presumes to "know" us, how we learn, or how we do not learn. This is a racist, eugenicist colonization of the mind, body, soul, spirit, and heart. For too long the hegemony of what counts as dis/Ability has been in the hands of the special education system, which is not divorced from historical oppressions on the consciousnesses of those labeled and "found" to have highly subjective categories of dis/Ability. This problem of practice must be deconstructed to reimagine education otherwise since our human spirits are being destroyed and oppressed.

"Just get over it." Some messages, however, that I also received were to "just get over it." This is endemic in our European-American culture that privileges the mind over body, feelings, and emotions. The hegemony of rationality (Calderón-Almendros & Calderón-Almendros, 2016) is a species of our culture that tells us to just "man up" and get over it. Who benefits? Who does not benefit from such responses or a lack of responses to the crying in our souls at the intersections of power and privilege? Why do we ignore our emotions? Why are we told repeatedly that we are "too emotional" or "too sensitive," that "we don't have time to feel" and "we have to focus," and "let's move on" and "feel it, name it, and let go." The Buddhist in me is happy to let go, but is that just? What do we do when we are systematically oppressed at the intersections of power and privilege based on the social construction of what counts as special education and Learning Disabilities? How can we let go, when they do not let go of the current paradigm that quantifies, labels, rationalizes, classifies, and ultimately imposes a regime of truth on our psyches, spirits, souls, bodies, and minds? How can we let go and get over it?

This is the mental gymnastics that I awake to every day. The post-traumatic and chronic stress created by a system of special education weaponized by the ideology of normal as racist and ableist practices across K-16 and beyond (Cannon & Hernández-Saca, 2021) have influenced my personal, interpersonal, structural, and political life (Crenshaw, 1999). In turn, when such phrases are suggested with the intention of "helping," they are deeply under-theorizing the extent to which mechanisms of racist and ableist practices shape many lives (including my own) at the intersections of power, identities, and well-being. The technical processes that we experience are not isolated from the contextual and critical components of human practice. Nevertheless, resistance to the construction of new knowledge at the paradigmatic levels, shaped by what can be said and what cannot be said, is a matter of power, privilege, and positionality, that is, who can frame the problems of practice. To let go of pain or be told to let go is inhumane and deeply problematic, as the origins of such emotions and thoughts within social and cultural contexts and practices that might benefit some versus others might go unexamined. Freire (1970) called this a culture of silence and a negation of dialogue and hence praxis. In turn, justice in practice is disrupted and there is a lack of critical emotion praxis that can lead to liberatory and conciliatory change.

"Beyond 'Lazy and Unmotivated': Why Parents and Teachers Need to Know about Executive Skills"

I had never heard of transition before the Fall of 2016. Transition is a subfield of special education that focuses on preparing students with special education disability labels for the world of higher education or world of work, in other words, becoming adults. At a state conference on transition, a colleague and I attended a keynote titled "Beyond 'lazy and unmotivated' why parents and teachers need to know about executive skills." When the speaker got to an explanation of why we should not confuse student's lack of motivation with laziness, the speaker referred to picture comparisons of the limen insulae in the frontal lobe for students with executive functioning and students with executive functioning deficits. The limen insulae:

> indicates the band of transitional cortex that extends along the sylvian stem between the anterior perforated substance medially and the gray matter at the pole of the insula laterally. Since this band lies at the inflection point of the sylvian stem, the term limen insulae is also used to indicate the peak of the falciform fold between the frontal lobe superiorly and the insula-temporal lobe posteroinferiorly. The new term pole of the posterior lobule is introduced to indicate the anteriormost extent of the posterior lobule of the insula where the two long gyri converge to form the posterior wall of the limen insulae. (Naidich et al., 2004, para 5)

The air of benevolence, scientism, and certainty grounded in positivism overwhelmed me and made me so angry that my colleague and I walked out. We then debriefed the racist and ableist ideology about children's capacities being rationalized as existing inside them and their brain. I was taken aback. Being cognizant of our emotions or our emotion boundary work is critical for individual and systemic change regarding the knowledge base that informs our practices, but more importantly, what we think we know about students and their capabilities. This social, cultural, political, economic, material, and discursive construction of dis/Ability is a deficit model, in which we situate something wrong with our students and use the cloak of benevolence and science against our children. These racist and ableist categories continue to misguide efforts toward truly engendering a culture of liberation through critical thinking, feeling, and reflection against racist and ableist hegemonic orders about dis/Ability at the intersections of power and identities.

Toward a Critical Consilience Emotion Praxis at the Boundaries

This chapter on understanding the boundary work between traditional special education and DSE, from consilience, self-study, radical love, and Disability Justice at the historical, contextual, and critical levels of everyday practices of students, parents, special and general educators, other general and special educational personnel, stakeholders, critical special educators, teacher educators, and educational equity researchers, is important for the future of both fields and their (inter)relationships. Through critically knowing, reflecting about a field's past, present, and future all agents in the field can engage in critical emotion praxis—critical thinking and feeling before we engage in the (re)production of the intersectional dis/Ability politic for the benefit of students and families, especially BIPOC and youth and their families at different paradigmatic levels of being human for radical love, healing, and liberation for ALL.

This chapter provided a critical review of the fields of traditional special education and DSE. I did so by engaging in a self-study of my teacher education work that critically examines my experiences as a new assistant professor of DSE within a DSpED at the boundaries that generated the following themes: *Kids don't learn because their frontal lobes are not fully developed, It's like being in a racist environment, Just get over it*, and *Beyond "Lazy and Unmotivated" Why Parents and Teachers Need to Know about Executive Skills*. The history of the boundaries between traditional special education and DSE chronicled above provided me with hope. Especially, where the fields of DS and DSE have been, what they have currently established for a junior faculty member like myself and my colleagues and mentors in order to contribute to critical special education and DSE theory, research, and praxis. With the theoretical, methodological, and pedagogical framework established within this chapter and book, I am hopeful that I can engage in self-study about the field, and more importantly engage future general and special educator teacher education. Existentially, then, what, how, and why I learn about myself personally and professionally matters to what, how, and why I act, broadly defined at the boundaries of special education and DSE. For me, where this not only becomes relevant is with my role as an Assistant Professor of DSE with my future general and special educators, but personally and professionally and programmatically across all of my responsibilities within and outside of the academy. For example, how I structured the purpose and overview of my courses is an example of the curriculum I frame for my students and myself as well at the boundaries between traditional special education and DSE in their orientation to the profession. Within this book and chapter, in turn, we explored the faultline between and within the fields, so that we do not confuse the purpose and function of education for ALL students, in ways that allow for all of our humanity beyond the medical-psychological model of dis/Ability for humanization and liberation sake in (un)learning educational contexts.

NOTE

1. By "dis" slash "Abilities" (i.e., dis/Abilities) or "disability" and "Abilities," I foreground the social, emotional, cultural, and political construction of both "disability" and "abilities" in educational contexts.

REFERENCES

Adichie, C. N. (2009). *Chimamanda Adichie: The danger of a single story.* TED. https://www.tcd.com/talks/chimamanda_ngozi_adichie_the_danger_of_a_single_story?language=en

Akkerman, S. F., & Bakker, A. (2011). Boundary crossing and boundary objects. *Review of Educational Research, 81*(2), 132–169.

Allen, D. C. (2015). Learning autoethnography: A review of *Autoethnography: Understanding qualitative research. The Qualitative Report, 20*(2), 33–35. http://www.nova.edu/ssss/QR/QR20/2/allen1.pdf

Allman, P. (2007). *An introduction to the revolutionary intellect of Karl Marx.* Brill Sense.

Annamma, S. A., Connor, D., & Ferri, B. (2013). Dis/ability critical race studies (DisCrit): Theorizing at the intersections of race and dis/ability. *Race Ethnicity and Education, 16*(1), 1–31.

Artiles, A. J., & Kozleski, E. B. (2007). Beyond convictions: Interrogating culture, history, and power in inclusive education. *Language Arts, 84*(4), 357–364.

Berne, P., Morales, A. L., Langstaff, D., & Invalid, S. (2018). Ten principles of disability justice. *WSQ: Women's Studies Quarterly, 46*(1), 227–230.

Boskovich, L., Cannon, M. A., Hernández-Saca, D. I., Kahn, L., & Nusbaum, E. A. (2019). Self-study of intersectional and emotional narratives: Narrative inquiry, Disability Studies in Education, and praxis in social science research. In S. E. Green, Loseke, B. M. Altman, & S. N. Barnartt (Eds.), *New narratives of disability: Constructions, clashes, and controversies research in social science and disability* (Vol. 11, pp. 215–230). Emerald Publishing.

Brandenburg, R. T. (2008). *Powerful pedagogy: Self-study of a teacher educator's practice* (Vol. 6). Springer Science & Business Media.

Bullough, R. V., & Gitlin, A. D. (1995). *Becoming a student of teaching: Methodologies for exploring self and school context*. Garland Publication.

Calderón-Almendros, I., & Calderón-Almendros, R. (2016). "I open the coffin and here I am": Disability as oppression and education as liberation in the construction of personal identity. *Disability & Society, 31*(1), 100–115.

Calderón-Almendros, I., & Ruiz-Román, C. (2015). Education as liberation from oppression: Personal and social constructions of disability. In F. Kiuppis & R. Sarromaa Haussätter (Eds.), *Inclusive education twenty years after Salamanca* (pp. 251–260). Peter Lang.

Cannon, M. A., & Hernández-Saca, D. I. (in press).The gift of disruption: Feeling and communicating subverted truths at the intersection of identity and ableist practices. In C. A. Mullen (Ed.), *Handbook of social justice interventions in education*. Springer.

Collier, L. (2016). Growth after trauma: Why are some people more resilient than others—and can it be taught? *American Psychological Association, 47*(10), 48. https://www.apa.org/monitor/2016/11/growth-trauma

Connor, D. J. (2005). *Labeled "Learning Disables": Life in and out of school for Urban black and/or Latino (a) youth from working class background* (Doctoral Dissertation). Teachers College, Columbia University.

Connor, D. J. (2008). *Urban narratives: Portraits in progress, life at the intersections of learning disability, race, & social class* (Vol. 5). Peter Lang.

Connor, D. J. (2012). *History of disability studies*. Hunter College. http://www.hunter.cuny.edu/conferences/dse-2012/history-of-disability-studies-in-education

Connor, D. J. (2013). Who "owns" dis/ability? The cultural work of critical special educators as insider–outsiders. *Theory & Research in Social Education, 41*(4), 494–513.

Connor, D. J. (2017). Who is responsible for the racialized practices evident within (special) education and what can be done to change them? *Theory into Practice, 56*(3), 226–233.

Costa, A., & Kallick, B. (1993). Through the lens of a critical friend. *Educational Leadership, 51*(2), 49–51.

Crenshaw, K. (1991). Mapping the margins: Identity politics, intersectionality, and violence against women. *Stanford Law Review, 43*(6), 1241–1299.

Danforth, S., & Gabel, S. L. (2006). *Vital questions facing disability studies in education* (Vol. 2). Peter Lang.

Davis, L. J. (1997). *The disability studies reader* (1st ed.). Routledge.

Dunhamn, J., Harris, J., Jarrett, S., Moore, L., Nishida, A., Price, M., Robinson, B., & Schalk, S. (2015). Developing and reflecting on a Black disability studies pedagogy: Work from the national black disability coalition. *Disability Studies Quarterly, 35*(2).

Ellis, C. (2004). *The ethnographic I: A methodological novel about autoethnography* (Vol. 13). Rowman Altamira.

Ellis, C., & Bochner, A. (2006). Analyzing analytic autoethnography: An autopsy. *Journal of Contemporary Ethnography, 3*(4), 429–449.

Foucault, M. (2000). So is it important to think? In J. Faubian (Ed.), *Essential works of Foucault 1954–1984. Volume 3, Michel Foucault: Power*. Penguin Books (Interview conducted 1981).

Freire, P. (1970/2000). *Pedagogy of the oppressed*. Continuum.

Fromm, E. (1956). *The art of loving*. Harper Row.

Gee, J. P. (2011). *An introduction to discourse analysis: Theory and method*. Routledge.

Glaser, B. G., & Strauss, A. L. (1967). *The discovery of grounded theory; strategies for qualitative research*. Routledge.

Hernández-Saca, D. I. (2016). *Re-framing the master narratives of dis/ability through an emotion lens: Voices of Latina/o students with learning disabilities* (Doctoral Dissertation). Arizona State University, Tempe, AZ.

Hernández-Saca, D. I. (2017). Reframing the master narratives of dis/ability at my intersections: An outline of an educational equity research agenda. *Critical Disability Discourses/Discours critiques dans le champ du handicap, 8*. https://cdd.journals.yorku.ca/index.php/cdd/article/view/39723

Hernández-Saca, D. I. (2019). Transitioning through an inclusive model of dis/ability at the intersections: It takes an inclusive village and spirit. In J. W. Valle & D. J. Connor (Eds.), *Rethinking disability: A disability studies approach to inclusive practices* (pp. 265–266). Routledge.

Hernández-Saca, D. I. (2021). Recovering the spirit. In D. J. Connor & B. Ferri (Eds.), *How teaching shapes our thinking about disabilities: Stories from the field* (pp. 263–276). Peter Lang.

Hernández-Saca, D. I., & Cannon, M. A. (2019). Interrogating disability epistemologies: Towards collective dis/ability intersectional emotional, affective and spiritual autoethnographies for healing. *International Journal of Qualitative Studies in Education, 32*(3), 243–262.

Jones, S. H., Adams, T. E., & Ellis, C. (Eds.). (2013). *Handbook of autoethnography*. Routledge.

Kosnik, C., Beck, C., Freese, A. R., & Samaras, A. P. (Eds.). (2006). *Making a difference in teacher education through self-study: Studies of personal, professional and program renewal* (Vol. 2). Springer Science & Business Media.

Naidich, T. P., Kang, E., Fatterpekar, G. M., Delman, B. N., Gultekin, S. H., Wolfe, D., Ortiz, O., Yousry, I., Weismann, M., & Yousry, T. A. (2004). The insula: anatomic study and MR imaging display at 1.5 T. *AJNR. American Journal of Neuroradiology, 25*(2), 222–232.

Patton Davis, L., & Museus, S. (2019). What is deficit thinking? An analysis of conceptualizations of deficit thinking and implications for scholarly research. *Currents, 1*(1), 117–130.

Pearson, H., Cosier, M., Kim, J., Gomez, A. M., Hines, C., McKee, A. A., & Ruiz, L. Z. (2016). The impact of Disability Studies curriculum on education professionals' perspectives and practice: Implications for education, social justice, and social change. *Disability Studies Quarterly*, *36*(2).

Rogoff, B. (2003). *The cultural nature of human development*. Oxford university press.

Rice, N. (2007). Disability Studies. In G. L. Anderson & K. G. Herr (Eds.), *Encyclopedia of activism and social justice* (Vol. 1, pp. 466–466). SAGE.

Samaras, A. P., Hicks, M. A., & Berger, J. G. (2004). Self-study through personal history. In J. Kitchen, A. Berry, S. M. Bullock, A. R. Crowe, M. Taylor, G. Hafdis, & L. Thomas (Eds.), *International handbook of self-study of teaching and teacher education practices* (pp. 905–942). Springer Netherlands.

Schulte, A. K. (2015). Presentation to the collaborative reflective experience and practice in education (CREPE) group at Deakin University, Australia. [PowerPoint slides].

Tidwell, D., Heston, M., & Fitzgerald, L. (Eds.). (2009). *Research methods for the self-study of practice* (Vol. 9). Springer Science & Business Media.

Ware, L. (Ed.). (2004). *Ideology and the politics of (in)exclusion*. Peter Lang.

Wilson, E. O. (1999). *Consilience: The unity of knowledge* (Vol. 31). Vintage.

Yoon, I. H. (2019). Haunted trauma narratives of inclusion, race, and disability in a school community. *Educational Studies*, *55*(4), 420–435.

Zubal-Ruggieri, R. (2016). *Academic programs in disability studies*. Syracuse University. http://disabilitystudies.syr.edu/programs-list/

Chapter 3

Anti-ableism in Teacher Education

Celebrating Disability Identity Through Self-study and Radical Love

Sarah Arvey Tov

> What I've experienced is people saying that I can't do things because I have a disability. The grown-ups at my school wouldn't do anything about it. It just really hurt me . . . I can do things even if you think that I can't. (AJ, 2018)

In the United States, one out of five people identify as having a disability (U.S. Census Bureau, 2012) and there are 6.7 million students classified with disabilities, making up about 14 percent of total public-school enrollment (U.S. Department of Education, 2020). Yet, teachers remain largely unprepared to talk about disability in their classrooms (Bacon & Lalvani, 2019; Lalvani & Baglieri, 2020). To address the lack of resources attending to disability identity in teacher education and classroom curriculum, a collective of disabled[1] activists, filmmakers, and educators created the One Out of Five (OO5): Disability History and Pride Project. The cornerstone of the OO5 curriculum was student voice videos featuring disabled youth, such as AJ (Office of Education Ombuds, 2018). Disabled students' authentic storytelling was paired with lesson plans and curricular resources discussing disability identity, intersectionality, disability history, and allyship and solidarity.

Throughout this chapter, I use quotes from the youth featured in the OO5 student voice videos to exemplify how disabled youth theorize through their lived experiences and align with disability activism and academic research. Furthermore, "student voices offer opportunities for critical self-reflection" as educators and scholars (Peters, 2010, p. 592). As educational research is designed to support innovative teaching practices and student well-being, it is essential that youth be at the forefront of our theory-building and transformative teaching practices.

Aligned with disabled activists' and youths' call for disability representation in school curriculum, there is an increasingly urgent call for research on teachers' conceptions of disability and their understanding and application of anti-ableist practices (Annamma & Morrison, 2018; Baglieri & Lalvani, 2020; Connor & Gabel, 2013; Lalvani, 2015). In response to the well-documented pathologization of students with disabilities, particularly students of color with disabilities (Annamma, 2018; Artiles, 2019; Connor, 2017; Voulgarides & Tefera, 2017), teachers and researchers have a collective responsibility to support, document, and expand classroom practices centering the experiences of youth with disabilities. This is particularly crucial in disrupting deficit views of disability that are disproportionately experienced by queer, immigrant, Black, Indigenous, and People of Color (BIPOC), and multiply marginalized students with disabilities (Annamma et al., 2013; Connor, 2017). As such, I situate anti-ableist practices in the intersectional[2] movement for educational justice and specifically consider OO5 as a boundary object that serves to facilitate dialogue about disability across educational settings (Akkerman & Bakker, 2011).

Importantly, I incorporate self-study, examining the ways that this collaborative project contributed to "living educational theory" (Pinnegar & Russell, 1995), considering the ways that we aligned our beliefs and practices, as well as personal reflexivity. I discuss how diving into disability history and culture transformed my identification as a disabled educator and scholar, and supported me while navigating qualitative research utilizing arts-based methods as an embodiment of disabled epistemologies (Johnson & McRuer, 2014).

This chapter addresses the importance of representation of disability in school curriculum and the movement toward critical asset pedagogies celebrating disabled brilliance. First, I explore theoretical framings of disability and ableism in schools, including the boundary work between special education, Disability Studies in Education, and general education. I then elaborate on the collaborative development of OO5 and design of a teacher education course that used OO5 to exemplify consilience, the unified nature theory and practice (Wilson, 1999). With attention to self-study, I present accompanying qualitative research of the teacher education course documenting how OO5 was taken up by general education teachers in shifting their conceptions of disability, pedagogical practice, and classroom culture. Finally, I discuss the ways that anti-ableist classroom practices contribute to radical love in schools.

DISABILITY AND ABLEISM IN SCHOOLS

> I was struggling with how to write and process thoughts when I would become overwhelmed stressed out like too overwhelmed, too stressed, I would just start crying . . . What my disability gives me it just makes me stressed out more it makes me overwhelmed, and it just makes it so I can't process the information fast enough. (One Out of Five, Warren, 2018)

Traditionally, discussions of disability in educational research and schooling practices have focused on special education with the aim of "fixing" and assimilating students with disabilities into normative constructs of intelligence and productive value (Baglieri et al., 2011). Through that lens, one may argue that Warren's statement positions his disability as a deficit and an individualized problem (Shakespeare, 2010). Disability Studies in Education (DSE), on the other hand, examines the roles that schools play in defining "normality" and marginalizing students who fall outside of those definitions (Baglieri et al., 2011; Shakespeare, 2010; Skrtic, 1995). DSE would not place the blame on Warren's disability, but instead the ways that the educational system, school, and classroom created an inaccessible learning environment that caused the stress and overwhelm that Warren describes. These opposing perspectives contribute to the importance of boundary work between special education and DSE to address the "sociocultural difference leading to discontinuity in action and interaction" (Akkerman & Bakker, 2011). This boundary work reaches beyond special education to engage general education in grappling with the long history of ableism in schools and ways to collectively work toward educational justice across educational settings.

Theorizing DSE followed the Disability Rights Movement and broader critical theory of Disability Studies, which rejected deficit notions of disability and instead attended the ways that disability is socially constructed as a product of inaccessible environments and cultural narratives of inadequacy (Oliver, 1990, Linton, 1998). The original applications of DSE suggested a pivotal shift in the goals of special education (Skrtic, 1986). While recognizing the importance of disabled students' civil rights, DSE went beyond a legal framework to one that directly addressed the underlying "beliefs about the nature of disability" in school (Skrtic, 1986, p. 5). DSE may be mistaken for a progressive vision of special education, when in fact DSE imagines an entirely alternative framework for schooling. In schools, "disrupting ableism can only be achieved if teachers position disability as a valued form of human diversity, create spaces for rethinking the constructs of disability and normalcy, and teach their students to embrace differences without stigmatizing them" (Lalvani & Bacon, 2018). In recent years, there has been particular attention to the ways that disability is constructed alongside race in schools, resulting in disproportionate classifications, segregation, and reductive remedial instruction (Artiles, 2019; Annamma et al., 2013; Kulkarni, 2020). Without addressing the intersectional construction of disability, schools continue to be places where disabled students' creativity, ambitions, and cultural heritage are stifled in lieu of a desire to assimilate them into a standardized white nondisabled educational system.

Normative schooling practices, deficit narratives, and inaccessibility in our schools are examples of ableism in the educational system. In this chapter, I utilize Disability Justice activist Lydia X.Z. Brown's (2014) definition of ableism:

1. Oppression, prejudice, stereotyping, or discrimination against disabled people on the basis of actual or presumed disability.
2. The belief that people are superior or inferior, have better quality of life, or have lives more valuable or worth living on the basis of actual or perceived disability. (para. 4)

In this definition, it is particularly important to note that ableism is not solely experienced by people with disabilities but also by those with presumed and perceived disabilities. This considers the ways that ableism manifests in the United States through anti-Blackness, eugenics, English monolingualism, anti-transgenderism and homophobia, colonialism, and capitalism, which socially construct hierarchies of intelligence that permeate the foundations and ongoing practices of teaching and learning (Annamma et al., 2013; Lewis, 2020). In schools, ableism may dictate who deserves a quality education, whose knowledge and learning is most worthwhile, and what is defined as "smart" (Leonardo & Broderick, 2011)

Ableism occurs at an *individual* (e.g., personally held beliefs and interpersonal interactions), *cultural* (e.g., social and cultural norms upheld through language and media representation), and *institutional level* (e.g., environmental and structural policies and practices) (Lalvani & Baglieri, 2020; Valle et al., 2006). In schools, these levels of ableism interact and inform one another and disproportionately impact students of color because of the collusive nature of racism and ableism (Annamma et al., 2013; Artiles, 2019; Kulkarni, 2020). On an individual level, teachers may pity students with disabilities. In turn, students may internalize ableism as if their disability is something "wrong" with them and distance disability from their other personal and social identities (Connor, 2008). That is only reified by ableism on a cultural level through narratives of "normalcy" and negative associations with disability as it intersects other marginalized identity markers (Annamma et al., 2013). Teachers dole out cultural constructs of "smartness" for ways of behaving and learning that exclude and isolate disabled students, especially those who are multiply marginalized (Leonardo & Broderick, 2011). This is further perpetuated by institutional barriers and policies segregating disabled students from their peers, particularly as it is used for de facto racial segregation (Kulkarni, 2020).

One way that ableism and intersecting systems of oppression continue to infiltrate our schools is through curriculum that perpetuates cultural narratives of normality and lacks representation of multiply marginalized disabled people (Annamma & Morrison, 2018; Erevelles, 2005; Lalvani & Baglieri, 2020, Valle et al., 2006). Students with disabilities entering the general education setting are expected to shed their disability identity and mannerisms (Lalvani & Bacon, 2018). The exclusion of disability representations, histories, and culture in curriculum can lead to a sense of isolation and lack of belonging for disabled youth (Lalvani, 2015). Disrupting ableism in schools comes with the important recognition of disability as a social and political identity constructed through collective struggle and resistance (Kafer, 2013; Linton, 1998). Inclusion practices must be grounded in teachers' and institutions' commitment to meaningful learning through embracing and celebrating difference and multiple ways of knowing and being (Baglieri, 2017). Wade (1994) shares:

> Culture. It's about passing the word. And disability culture is passing the word that there's a new definition of disability and it includes *power*. . . . Culture. It's finding history, naming and claiming ancestors, heroes. As "invisibles," our history is hidden from us, our heroes buried in the pages, unnamed, unrecognized. Disability culture is about naming, about recognizing. (p. 15, italics in original)

Schools are not "passing the word." Students with disabilities are not given space or time to build a sense of community and pride in their disability identities. They are confined to labels that are placed upon them, as opposed to having the opportunity to name and claim disability for themselves.

DISABILITY REPRESENTATION IN CURRICULUM

> The biggest part of my disability is that it makes it really hard to connect with people, and to have, like, a normal social life, so I think it's more of a social disability than a physical disability. I really don't have too many friends with disabilities, there's really not a lot of disability representation at my school, which makes it even harder, because people just don't understand, right? They don't see a lot of people with disabilities, which is why I think it's so important to spread the word. (One Out of Five, Anna, 2019)

> When I was younger, at my old school, I felt left out a lot of the time . . . Pride, to me, it's like having a sense of love for yourself, the ability to believe in yourself that you can do it, and that means that I can do things ongoing. (One Out of Five, Julian, 2019)

One way to cultivate students' pride is through curriculum that authentically represents students with disabilities' lived experiences and celebrates disability wholeness and community. As Anna indicates in the quote above, disability representation is considerably lacking, which contributes to misunderstandings about disability identity and culture (Lalvani, 2015). On the other hand, infusing curriculum with authentic discussions about disability and positive disability representation can provide the sense of pride that Julian speaks to, "having a sense of love for yourself, the ability to believe in yourself."

In Washington State (where I live and collaborated on this project), students with disabilities came together to advocate for disability history to be mandated in school curriculum. As a result of their advocacy, in 2008 the Washington State legislature passed the Disability History Act (RCW 28A.230.158) to "increase awareness and understanding of the contributions that people with disabilities in our state, nation, and the world have made to our society . . . and inspire students with disabilities to feel a greater sense of pride, reduce harassment and bullying, and help keep students with disabilities in school." While this policy was written with the best intentions, it was an unfunded mandate and there were no materials or training provided to make it a reality. Disappointed by the lack of resources, in 2018 disabled activists, youth, and educators came together to ensure that the mandate would be fulfilled and aligned with the disability rights movement slogan "Nothing About Us, Without Us."

So started the cross-disability collaboration to express radical love and representation for the disability community through the development of OO5. Carrie Basas, director of the Office of Education Ombuds, and Clarke Matthews, co-creative director of Rooted in Rights, a multi-media disability story-telling branch of Disability Rights Washington, came together with the determination to create media and curriculum amplifying disabled stories and experiences. To highlight the experiences of students with disabilities through authentic storytelling, Rooted in Rights created six student voice videos featuring disabled students with varying disabilities and intersectional identities. In each short video, disabled youth share their interests and aspirations along with the ways that they navigate their schools and communities with a disability and the role that disability plays in their lives and identity. To accompany the videos, Adina Rosenberg, a high school special education teacher, and I designed five lessons about disability identity and history: Introduction to Disability, Intersectionality, Disability History in the United States, Disability History in Washington State, and Allyship and Solidarity.

The OO5 resources work at the boundaries of disability pride and institutional schooling practices, disrupting ableist assumptions about disability through its leadership, design, and content. There was disabled leadership at every level of the project, which provided a space for cross-disability solidarity and mentorship. As opposed to the stifling of disability discussions in school, counternarratives of disabled creativity, resilience, and community were at the heart of each component of the learning resources. In our design process we had a consilience across disciplines as we came together from our respective personal and professional expertise. Consilience as defined by Wilson (1999) is "Literally a 'jumping together' of knowledge by linking the facts and fact-based theory across disciplines to create common groundwork of explanation" (p. 8). We were developing a common groundwork for the ways that disability can be talked about through classroom curriculum. In doing so, we used the arts, archival research, academic theory, and grassroots activism. This range of entry points shines through in the final products, as teachers and students are provided multiple ways to engage and connect with the content.

The OO5 resources are designed to be used across educational settings, breaking the notion that disability is a topic confined to special education. They serve as a boundary object as they are "doing the [boundary] crossing by fulfilling a bridging function" (Akkerman & Bakker, 2011, p. 133) to "articulate meaning and address multiple perspectives" (Akkerman & Bakker, 2011, p. 141). The resources are robust enough to stand on their own, while allowing flexibility for teachers to adapt them to their class context (Star & Griesemer, 1986). OO5 offers space to deconstruct, learn about, identify with, and celebrate disability.

SELF-STUDY CELEBRATING DISABILITY IDENTITY

Within the boundary work of OO5 was the deepening of a self-study process as my exploration of disability history and identity contributed to personal transformation as well as shifts in scholarly and pedagogical practice as a white, queer, Jewish, disabled educator and scholar. In my eight years as a special education teacher, I engaged in anti-racist activism and solidarity in movements for racial justice in education, especially as they intersect with expansive views of inclusion and special education. I worked against racialized and ability-based tracking and centered culturally relevant curriculum and practices as a central tenet of inclusive classrooms. In my personal identity work, my whiteness is more apparent than my disabilities, which contributes to the social assumption of competency and grants me unjust power. Regardless of the immense impact that my disabilities have on my life, I did not always consider disability as a prominent identity marker. Until working on OO5, I had primarily medicalized my bipolarity and traumatic brain injury (TBI), despite their social, professional, and political implications in my life. Working on OO5 and feeling in connection with the disabled community, my disability identity shifted toward wholeness as I continued to work against intersecting systems of oppression. Furthermore, learning alongside youth for OO5 affirmed the importance of inter generational learning in transforming my own misconceptions of disability identity.

Self-study included intentional moves to link human action and knowledge growth, engagement of oneself alongside others in teaching and learning by "storying" experience, and the process of implicating one's identities toward meaning making and the construction of knowledge (Craig, 2009). The collaborative nature of OO5 and co-design of the subsequent teacher education course, notably called on consilience centering the importance of shifting pedagogical moves while learning about disability theory, identity, and history. This process included both inner personal and interpersonal reflections that utilized storying to express connections with disability and our intersectional experiences. Working within the vulnerability of our identities contributed to emerging and expansive notions of radical love (Freire, 1996). As such, we worked toward an individual, cultural, and institutional understanding of how ableism shows up in our mindsets, classrooms, schools, and community and co-constructed knowledge between students, teachers, and teacher-educators with the goal of recognizing incongruences between our beliefs and practices (Freire, 1996).

As I moved into a position to design teacher education coursework and research, I engaged in collaboration and reflexivity while planning curriculum, coursework, and methods. Self-study became a tool for me to identify "the construction of an explicit pedagogy of teacher education and growth in practice that follows from [self-study as] critical self-examination" (Vanassche & Geert, 2015, p. 509). It was also an opportunity to disrupt my own normalizing curriculum and shift toward curriculum *for* and *by* disabled peoples. Overall, my work aligns with the goals of self-study to simultaneously impact pedagogical intervention, uncover living contradictions between our beliefs and practice, work toward social justice in and through education, and expand broader philosophies and theories of practice (Vanassche & Geert, 2015).

CENTERING DISABLED PERSPECTIVES IN TEACHER EDUCATION

Hang in there. Just because we learn differently doesn't mean like we're not able, and I'm not saying it like all neurotypical people believe that, but I'm just leaving a message for the ones that maybe are naive to that point you know just be patient and you know we'll get the hang of things. There's still a community out there for [disabled youth] and don't give up. (One Out of Five, Kenassa, 2019)

The ways that OO5 centers disabled voices in curriculum, particularly those of youth with disabilities, flips the script on ableist conceptions of knowledge construction and production. After developing OO5, I was approached by a two-year alternative route program for in-service teachers at a large university that prides itself on social justice teaching practices. However, their program did not address disability as a component of student identity, aspect of diversity, nor an issue of social justice. To address that gap, they asked to collaborate on a DSE course during which their in-service teachers would pilot the OO5 resources in their respective classrooms. The new course, DSE in Pedagogy and Practice, was an important replacement for the previously used introduction to special education that focused solely on classification and compliance.

I collaborated with another instructor who had strong personal connections to special education and disability. We both had extensive experience teaching special education, as well as personal experience with disability. The other instructor had been placed in special education upon immigrating to the United States due to his limited English vocabulary, and experienced the deficit narratives associated with being classified with a disability in school, as well as the intersection of immigration, language, and disability. While our experiences are very distinct, they informed our work as teacher educators.

In the 10-week DSE in Pedagogy and Practice course, stories and self-study were essential to learning and grounding anti-ableist practices with explorations of intersectionality. The course objectives were to provide (1) space and time for personal reflections on teachers' experiences and understanding of disability in their lives, (2) a DSE framework with shared reading and common definitions to support dialogue about disability and ableism in schools, and (3) tools to support DSE in classroom practice. The course project was the implementation of a modified OO5 lesson used to enhance their curriculum, not simply used as a disconnected one-off lesson.

In addition to the collaborative facilitation of the DSE in Pedagogy and Practice course, I designed a qualitative research project exploring how OO5 mediated teachers' conceptions of disability and the application of DSE to their classroom practices. This research attended to the gap in empirical research addressing the interplay between DSE theory and curriculum in practice in K-12 settings. Recruiting in-service general education teachers was optimal for the study because it afforded the opportunity to consider tangible, as opposed to hypothetical, applications of disability into classroom curriculum and the implications of incorporating disability representation in classroom practice. The DSE in Pedagogy and Practice course included 20 teachers, all of whom chose to participate in the research project, spanning a range of grade levels K-12 and content areas, which afforded the opportunity to explore how disability-centered lessons can be taught across educational settings.

DISABILITY AS INSIGHT IN RESEARCH METHODOLOGIES

Throughout DSE in Pedagogy and Practice, I was a participant observer, engaging in dialogue and instruction while recording data, taking field notes, and writing memos (Merriam, 2016). I collected data through course session observations and course-generated documents.[3] Getting to know the teachers throughout course sessions and discussing their classroom practices created a sense of collaborative learning. I was also able to gain a more holistic understanding of teacher practice by watching recordings of teachers' creative implementation of the OO5 lessons. In my data analysis, I chose to ultimately focus on teachers' written reflections to capture their experiences as described in their own words.

Throughout the research that accompanied the DSE in Pedagogy and Practice course, I felt consistently up against ableist notions of what it means to collect, analyze, and present findings. I was intensely frustrated due to the ableist limitations of what is considered rigorous research methodology because my disability did not allow me to go about "research as usual." After hours and hours of staring at data and experiencing agonizing self-doubt, I noticed I was up against my own internalized ableism. Therefore, I turned toward expansive notions of research and inquiry that uplift cripistemologies celebrating disabled ways of knowing and being (Johnson & McRuer, 2014). I mapped out my research process incorporating traditional methods of qualitative research (Miles et al., 2014, Saldaña, 2009, Strauss & Cordin, 1990) alongside arts-based research (Barone & Eisner, 2014; Butler-Kisber, 2018) to support multiple methods of engagement, representation, and expression (Meyer et al., 2014).

For the purposes of this chapter, I will focus on my arts-based methods because I used them as a personal tool to combat internalized ableism that I experience in the academy. I dove into a self-study of arts-based research to interrupt normalized conceptions of research and invite an expansive analysis of data that deepens our understanding of the world (Barone & Eisner, 2014; Leavy, 2015). Furthermore, it empowered me as a disabled researcher to think, learn, and grow on my own terms. I chose to use two arts-based methods, collage and found poetry. Both of these methods invite the research to break up the text in ways that reveal aspects of the data that might otherwise go unnoticed, as well as draw connections within and across cases (Butler-Kisber, 2018).

I primarily used data collages as memos to track my interpretations of the ways that teachers were making sense of DSE in relation to their personal experiences. Data collages "counteract the hegemony and linearity in written text, increase voice and reflexivity in the research process, and expand possibilities of multiple and diverse realities and understandings" (Butler-Kisber, 2018, p. 5). I found images that represented my coding methods and analysis and then juxtaposed image fragments and direct quotes to create meaning (Butler-Kisber & Poldma, 2010). For instance, while creating the data collage for Pablo's written reflection, I used primarily architectural images with intersecting lines to capture the shifting constructions of disability that one teacher, Pablo, wrote about. The most central image was an upward perspective of architectural artwork coming together in such a way that the black poles appeared to be converging in front of a gradation of yellows, pinks, and purples in the sky at dusk. At the base of the image was Pablo's quote, "I think of disability studies in terms of identity, intersectionality, and a system of oppression. For example, I think of how people's lived experiences are different and how my actions and words contribute to greater systems of oppression towards people with disabilities." The image served as visual analysis of the quote by capturing the converging concepts that contributed to Pablo's understanding of DSE. I used visual representation of individual reflections like Pablo's, and I looked across data collages to find new meanings and relationships between teacher experiences.

In addition to visual analysis, I also found value in playing with word structures. I was interested in the ways that words, grammar, and sentence structure contribute to meaning. Overwhelmed by staring at full pages of text that seemingly all ran together, I used found poetry as a tool to pull out key words and phrases found directly in the teachers' reflections to create a poem. Found poems provided a method of identifying and capturing heightened moments and feelings described by participants in a way that formulated research writing techniques cannot (Faulkner, 2018). Defining found poetry, through the construction of a found poem of her work, Patrick (2017) explains:

Definition of terms: A Found Poem
Research poets
refashion and reorder data,
presenting it as a poem . . . crafting original poetry
in the voice of the researcher,
crafting found poetry
in the voice of the participant.
(p. 65, italics in the original)

All poems I constructed were participant-voiced, meaning they are written directly from quotes by participants (Prendergast, 2009) and "'untreated' (conserving virtually the same order, syntax and meaning as in the original)" (Butler-Kisber, 2019, p. 3). I did two rounds of found poems, one focusing on each teacher's individual reflections, and the second constructed from data across teachers' reflections. The individual found poems were used as analytic memos and the cross-reflection data poems are used as expressions of my findings.

Through coding and arts-based analysis, three themes arose: (1) DSE contributed to teachers' shifting definitions and conceptions of disability on a personal level, (2) One Out of Five served as a mediational tool to enact anti-ableism on a cultural level in their classrooms, and (3) the interplay of theory and practice contributed to teachers' envisioning anti-ableist practices on an institutional level. In this chapter, I focus on the second finding because of the ways that teachers experienced consilience in their classrooms through a co-construction of disability knowledge alongside their students that captured radical love and solidarity through anti-ableist classroom culture and curriculum.

ANTI-ABLEISM IN CLASSROOM CULTURE AND CURRICULUM AND CLASSROOM CULTURE

Through the DSE in Pedagogy and Practice course and use of OO5 curriculum, teachers used self-study to reflect on their agency to interrupt ableism in their classroom culture and curriculum. In this process, teachers grappled with their ability to thoughtfully teach about disability, particularly when it was a new topic for them. OO5 proved to be a meaningful tool to scaffold teachers into conversations about disability and created space to co-construct knowledge alongside their students. The OO5 student voice videos, as well as students' voice and perspective in their classrooms, contributed to new ways of naming injustice, enacting change, and promoting positive identity development (Peters, 2010).

In course sessions and written reflections, teachers shared concerns that they would pass down their ableist cultural inheritance if they tried to talk about disability in their classroom. As Margot wrote:

> preparing to teach about disability to my students revealed personal assumptions and misunderstandings . . . Even with such awareness about the meaning of the label "disability," I found that I still took a fairly deficit minded approach to the application and practice of my ideas in my life. As a person without any visible or invisible disabilities I could learn about disability all I wanted, and yet remain part of the problem in supporting change in everyday experiences and realities around me.

Reflecting on her unjust power as a nondisabled person, Margot brought up the important distinction of awareness and action. While she identified the ways in which her awareness has grown, she continued to grapple with how to put that into practice. Later, she said that using OO5 was a "powerful experience for me as the teacher and students alike. I found that conversation was not 'scary' or 'difficult' because it was supported within a framework that was intentionally designed and build in collaboration with [disabled people]." Providing a framework that centers the voices of disabled youth and activists, and educational tools to support anti-ableist curriculum, created a bridge from theory to practice.

Disability in the curriculum also disrupted the cycle of silence about disability in schools. Eleanor, a teacher with a disability, shared that:

> My students were very open to talking about the idea because they had never talked about it before. Just like me, they had assumptions about disability, but there was never a time for clarification or an opportunity to learn more about it.

When given space and time to discuss disability, students were engaged and curious. Eleanor brought disability history in the United States to her unit on the Constitution through "examples of activism and using your 1st amendment to speak out for what you believe in and value. I think that this was a great way to peak the interest of my students and hook them to the task." OO5 was a first step toward incorporating disability meaningfully into the curriculum. In addition to curriculum content, Eleanor noticed the importance of talking about disability in shifting classroom culture. She said,

> Another thing that I felt was successful was me giving examples of my own disabilities with ADHD, Depression, and Anxiety. It allowed for open communication, relationship-building and destigmatizing those illnesses/disabilities for my students and gave them a space to feel safe and open up about the topic.

Creating an anti-ableist culture in her classroom included a meaningful curriculum, learning through curiosity, and relationship building.

In addition to reflections of generally destigmatizing disability through counternarratives, teachers discussed tangible ways that they saw classroom culture shift as a result of talking about disability explicitly in curriculum. After watching warren's student voice video, Kevin wrote that "I even had a student that had an iPad for the same reason as the boy in the video. He waved the iPad proudly and was eager to share his tool with the class." Disability representation opened up space for students to share knowledge and expertise from their personal experiences. Pablo noted that in his class

> There is less "secrecy" around who gets what and why. Students have been talking about invisible disabilities—those that affect learning in school. This has demystified why classroom tools like audio books, text-to-speech, augmented text are used in class. Students that use these tools are able to advocate for themselves and explain why it helps them.

This transformation served to create a classroom culture focused on collective accessibility. Students were not only able to express their access needs but also learn how to best support one another.

Looking across teachers' reflections, positively representing disability in curriculum and classroom culture created opportunities for students to explore history and identity to new depths. This cross-reflection found poem begins with excerpts based on teachers' initial concerns, followed by their learning with students, and cultural shifts they witnessed on a classroom level:

Disability
Previously taboo
Would they take it seriously?
Will my own biases show?
I was pleasantly surprised
by the wealth of knowledge.
I saw their participation rise,

allowed for relationship building,
a starting point to destigmatize.
Learning with my students.
Learning from my students.
New words to describe ideas,
language to talk about identity.
Time for clarification.
Defining disability,
not just visible,
invisible too.
Ableism, allyship, inclusion.
Discourse was not diminished
but increased.
Less "secrecy"
about who gets what and why.
Students told not to talk about disability
had many questions,
curious about the world around them.
Why do we have the word disability?
What else is important in disability history?
What needs to change?
Is it okay if I call something dumb?
Or is that hurting people with disabilities?

Emotions, change, relationships,
complexities that encompass disability.
Day-to-day experiences at school
connected back to disability.
Critique what currently exists,
constructs of disability.
Think of an interest
intersected with disability.
Space to feel safe,
he waved his iPad proudly
eager to share.
Made connections between
assistive technology her friends use.
They receive speech services,
did not see any shame.
New attitude and mentality,
advocating for themselves.

DISABILITY STUDIES IN EDUCATION AS RADICAL LOVE

The findings from this qualitative study suggest the importance of teacher training grounded in the perspectives and experiences of disabled youth and activists. Teacher education appeared to be enhanced through personal reflection, theory, and practical tools encouraged processing, embodying, and imagining DSE on individual, cultural, and institutional levels. Teachers were then able to weave practices that disrupted ableism through curriculum and asset-based pedagogies for disability. Teachers' knowledge and practice were informed interchangeably at theoretical and practical levels.

Across the OO5 collaboration, the DSE in Pedagogy and Practice coursework, and my research methods, there was a reciprocity of theory and practice. Within and across them were glimpses of the radical love possible in intersectional disability representation. Radical love is an assertion of presence and wholeness in the midst of a world that oppresses people labeled as "other" across social identities. As Mingus (2018) shares:

> It shouldn't be that we have to go to the margins of the margins of the margins of the margins. And don't get me wrong; I love living out there. There are amazing things and people out there. *And* it shouldn't be that that's the only place where we can be whole. (italics in original, para 19)

Radical love in educational justice requires representation that affirms disability identity and intersections with the many dynamic aspects of our identity that make us whole.

Self-study methods also hold space for radical love as they exist in "open, collaborative, and reframed practice" that provide opportunities to engage with one another as collaborators to understand and evolve our discourse and practice and the ways that they inform one another (Samaras & Freese, 2009, p. 7). Each collaboration described in this chapter, those among the OO5 team, between co-instructors, and alongside classroom teachers and their students, contribute to surfacing and dismantling ableist assumptions that underlie our practices. While I took on multiple roles across the span of this project with seemingly varied purposes; I did not experience them as mutually exclusive. To the contrary, I found that my personal and professional roles were enriched. A self-study lens "focused on our purpose and whether we were aligning our beliefs with our practice" (Samaras & Freese, 2009, p. 12) allowed for radical self-love and community care i hadn't previously experienced as a disabled student graduate.

Curricular collaborations and radical love bring excitement into teaching and learning. hooks (1994) wrote, "*Excitement* in higher education was viewed as potentially disruptive of the atmosphere of seriousness assumed to be essential to the learning process" (italics in original, p. 7). We are taught that to learn we need to maintain seriousness and uphold ableist assertions of rigor. However, that stifles the expansive ways we could be connecting with one another and advancing innovative theory and practice. Breaking the culture of silence about disability in schools requires respect and appreciation of disabled experiences and the co-construction of knowledge toward a liberatory education (Freire, 1996; Gibson, 2006). Curriculum can serve as a method of problem-posing, taking action against injustice, and collective dreaming (Reed et al., 2015). Wong (2020) wrote, "Collectively, through our stories, our connections, and our actions, disabled people will continue to confront and transform the status quo. It's who we are" (p. xxii). The work is always growing, changing, and evolving. Curricular resources, classroom practices, and teacher training must center the knowledge and experience of disabled youth, particularly those at the intersections of marginalized identities, with radical love in order to confront and transform the status quo in schools.

NOTES

1. In the disability community there has been a movement to reclaim language such as "disabled," "mad," and "crip." Reclaiming these terms serves to destigmatize the labels and leave space to self-identify with critical aspects of their lived experiences. There is discussion of person-first (person with disabilities), indicating the importance of recognizing that a person is not solely defined by their disability, and identity-first language (disabled person), with disabled scholars and activists foregrounding the importance of their disability identity. When known, I use the terminology that a particular person, group, or community prefers. Otherwise, I use person-first and identity-first language interchangeably. I personally use person-first, identity-first language, and the terms Mad and disabled when referring to my personal identity and community.

2. The term intersectionality was originally coined by Crenshaw (1989) in reference to the distinct experience of multiple marginalization of Black women. Crenshaw (1989) states that the goal of an intersectional framework "should be to facilitate the inclusion of marginalized groups for whom it can be said: 'When they enter, we all enter'" (p. 167). I use Discrit (disability studies/critical race theory) to inform my understanding and analysis of intersectionality in education (Annamma et al., 2013).

3. I chose to prioritize written reflections as my focal data as it was a common piece of data across the teachers. I had four teachers participate in optional interviews;

however, I noticed that my interviewees did not have disabilities and each discussed disability as a new consideration for them. Close analysis of the optional interviews may have yielded insights as to nondisabled educators' analysis of their unjust power and learning from disabled students' and activists' stories but did not capture the range of experiences across all 20 participants, particularly those with direct personal connections to disability.

REFERENCES

Akkerman, S. F., & Bakker, A. (2011). Boundary crossing and boundary objects. *Review of Educational Research, 81*(2), 132–169.

Annamma, S. A. (2018). *The pedagogy of pathologization*. Routledge.

Annamma, S. A., & Morrison, D. (2018). Identifying dysfunctional education ecologies: A DisCrit analysis of bias in the classroom. *Equity & Excellence in Education, 51*(2), 1–18.

Annamama, S. A., Connor, D., & Ferri, B. (2013). Dis/ability critical race studies (DisCrit): Theorizing at the intersections of race and dis/ability. *Race, Ethnicity & Education, 16*(1), 1–31.

Artiles, A. J. (2019). Fourteenth annual brown lecture in education research: Re-envisioning equity research: Disability identification disparities as a case in point. *Educational Researcher, 48*(6), 325–335.

Bacon, J. K., & Lalvani, P. (2019). Dominant narratives, subjugated knowledges, and the righting of the story of disability in K-12 curricula. *Curriculum Inquiry, 49*(4), 387–404.

Baglieri, S. (2017). *Disability Studies and the inclusive classroom.* Routledge.

Baglieri, S., Valle, J. W., Connor, D. J., & Gallagher, D. J. (2011). Disability Studies in Education: The need for a plurality of perspectives on disability. *Remedial and Special Education, 32*(4), 267–278.

Barone, T., & Eisner, E. W. (2012). *Arts based research.* SAGE Publications.

Berne, P. (2015, June 10). Disability justice—A working draft. Sins Invalid: An Unashamed Claim to Beauty in the Face of Invisibility [Blog post]. http://sinsinvalid.org/blog/disability-justice-a-working-draft-by-patty-berne

Brown, L. X. Z. (2014). Definitions. Autistic Hoya [Blog post]. https://www.autistichoya.com/p/definitions.html

Brown, L. X. Z. (2017). *All the weight of our dreams: On living racialized autism.* Dragonbee Press.

Butler-Kisber, L. (2018). *Qualitative inquiry: Thematic, narrative and arts-based perspectives* (2nd ed.). SAGE Publications.

Connor, D. J. (2008). *Urban narratives: Portraits in progress, life at the intersections of learning disability, race, & social class.* Peter Lang.

Connor, D. J. (2017). Who is responsible for the racialized practices evident within (special) education and what can be done to change them? *Theory into Practice, 56*(3), 226–233.

Connor, D. J., & Gabel, S. L. (2010). Welcoming the unwelcome: Disability as diversity. In T. Chapman & N. Hobbel (Eds.), *Social justice pedagogy across the curriculum* (pp. 201–220). Erlbaum.

Craig, C. (2009). Trustworthiness in self-study research. In C. A. Lassonde, S. Galman, & C. Ksnik (Eds.), *Self-study research methodologies for teacher educators* (pp. 21–34). Sense Publishers.

Disability history month act, RCW 28A.230.158 (2008). app.leg.wa.gov/rcw/default.aspx?cite=28A.230.158.

Erevelles, N. (2005). Understanding curriculum as normalizing text: Disability studies meet curriculum theory. *Journal of Curriculum Studies, 37*(4), 421–439.

Faulkner, S. (2018). Crank up the feminism: Poetic inquiry as feminist methodology. *Humanities (Basel), 7*(3), 85.

Freire, P. (1996). *Pedagogy of the oppressed* (revised). Continuum.

Gibson, S. (2006). Beyond a "culture of silence": Inclusive education and the liberation of "voice". *Disability & Society, 21*(4), 315–329.

Gonzalez, T. E., Hernandez-Saca, D. I., & Artiles, A. J. (2017). In search of voice: Theory and methods in K-12 student voice research in the US, 1990–2010. *Educational Review, 69*(4), 451–473.

hooks, bell. (1994). *Teaching to transgress: Education as the practice of freedom.* Routledge.

Individuals with Disabilities Education Act, 20 U.S.C. § 1400 (2004).

Johnson, M., & McRuer, R. (2014). Cripistemologies: Introduction. *Journal of Literary & Cultural Disability Studies, 8*(2), 127–147.

Kulkarni, S. S. (2020). Racial and ethnic disproportionality in special education programs. In *Oxford Research Encyclopedia of Education*. Oxford University Press.

Ladau, E. (2015, July 20). Why person-first language doesn't always put the person first. Think inclusive [Blog post]. https://www.thinkinclusive.us/why-person-first-language-doesnt-always-put-the-person-first/

Lalvani, P. (2015). "We are not aliens": Exploring the meaning of disability and the nature of belongingness in a fourth grade classroom. *Disability Studies Quarterly, 35*(4), Doi: 10.18061/dsq.v35i4.4963. https://dsq-sds.org/index.php/dsq/article/view/4963/4107

Lalvani, P., & Baglieri, S. (2020). *Undoing ableism: Teaching about disability in K-12 classrooms.* Routledge.

Leavy, P. (2015). *Method meets art: Arts-based research practice* (2nd ed.). Guilford Press.

Leonardo, Z., & Broderick, A. (2011). Smartness as property: A critical exploration of intersections between whiteness and disability studies. *Teacher College Record, 113*(10), 2206–2232.

Lewis, T. A. (2020, January 1). Ableism 2020: An updated definition. Talia A. Lewis [Blog post]. https://www.talilalewis.com/blog/ableism-2020-an-updated-definition

Linton, S. (1998). *Claiming disability: Knowledge and identity.* New York University Press.

Lynn, B.-K., & Poldma, T. (2010). The power of visual approaches in qualitative inquiry: The use of collage making and concept mapping in experiential research. *Journal of Research Practice, 6*(2), M18.

Merriam, S. B., & Tisdell, E. J. (2016). *Qualitative research: A guide to design and implementation.* Jossey-Bass.

Meyer, A., Rose, D. H., & Gordon, D. T. (2014). *Universal design for learning: Theory and practice.* CAST Professional Publishing.

Miles, M. B., Huberman, A. M., & Saldaña, J. (2014). *Qualitative data analysis: A methods sourcebook* (3rd ed.). SAGE Publications.

Mingus, M. (2012, May 8). Feeling the weight: Some beginning notes on disability, access, and love. Leaving evidence [Blog post]. https://leavingevidence.wordpress.com/2012/05/08/feeling-the-weight-some-beginning-notes-on-disability-access-and-love/

Mingus, M. (2018, November 3). "Disability justice" is simply another term for love. Leaving evidence [Blog post]. https://leavingevidence.wordpress.com/2018/11/

Mooney, J. (2013). *The gift: LD/ADHD reframed* [YouTube video lecture]. https://www.youtube.com/watch?v=r5n8iUi1w08

Patrick, L. D. (2016). Found poetry. *Literacy Research, 65*(1), 384–403.

Peters, S. J. (2013). The heterodoxy of student voice: Challenges to identity in the sociology of disability and education. In M. Arnot (Ed.), *The sociology of disability and inclusive education* (pp. 69–80). Routledge.

Pinnegar, S., & Russell, T. (1995). Introduction: Self-study and living educational theory. *Teacher Education Quarterly, 22*(3), 5–9.

Reed, J., Saunders, K., & Pfadenhauer-Simonds, S. (2015). Problem-posing in a primary grade classroom: Utilizing Freire's methods to break the culture of silence. *Multicultural Education, 23*(1), 56–58.

Saldaña, J. (2009). *The coding manual for qualitative researchers.* SAGE Publications.

Samaras, A., & Freese, A. (2009). Trustworthiness in self-study research. In C. A. Lassonde, S. Galman, & C. Ksnik (Eds.), *Self-study research methodologies for teacher educators* (pp. 3–19). Sense Publishers.

Shakespeare, T. The social model of disability. In. L. J. Davis (Ed.), *The disability studies reader* (pp. 266–273). Routledge.

Sins Invalid. (2019). *Skin, tooth, and bone: The basis of movement is our people* (2nd ed.). Sins Invalid.

Skrtic, T. M. (1986). The crisis in special education knowledge: A perspective on perspective. *Focus on Exceptional Children, 18*(7), 1–16.

Star, S. L., & Griesemer, J. R. (1989). Institutional ecology, translations' and boundary objects: Amateurs and professionals in Berkeley's Museum of Vertebrate Zoology, 1907–1939. *Social Studies of Science, 19*(3), 387–420.

Strauss, A., & Corbin, J. M. (1990). *Basics of qualitative research: Grounded theory procedures and techniques.* Sage Publications.

U.S. Census Bureau (2012). *Americans with disabilities: 2010.* https://www.census.gov/library/publications/2012/demo/p70-131.html

U.S. Department of Education. Institute of Education Sciences, National Center for Education Statistics. (2020). *Students with disabilities.* https://nces.ed.gov/programs/coe/indicator_cgg.asp

Vanassche, E., & Geert, K. (2015). The state of the arts in self-study of teacher education practices: A systematic literature review. *Journal of Curriculum Studies, 47*(4), 508–528.

Voulgarides, C. K. (2018). *Does compliance matter in special education?: IDEA and the hidden inequities of practice.* Teachers College Press.

Wade, M. W. *(1994).* Disability culture rap. In B. Shaw (Ed.), *The ragged edge: The disability experience from the pages of the first fifteen years of the disability rag* (pp. 15–18). Avocado Press.

Wilson, E. O. (1999). *Consilience: The unity of knowledge* (Vol. 31). Vintage.

Wong, A. (2020). *Disability visibility: First-person stories from the twenty-first century.* Vintage.

Chapter 4

Teaching in the In-Between

Opportunities and Factors Informing Inclusive Reform in One School District

Amy J. Petersen, Danielle M. Cowley, Deborah J. Gallagher, and Shehreen Iqtadar

The notion of inclusion and inclusive schooling is deeply rooted in historical and political contexts informed by diverse perspectives, definitions, and paradigms (Artiles et al., 2006). Drawing on conceptions of justice, Waitoller and Kozleski (2013) describe inclusive education as:

> A continuous struggle toward (a) the *redistribution* of quality opportunities to learn and participate in education programs, (b) the *recognition* and value of differences as reflected in content, pedagogy, and assessment tools, and (c) the opportunities for marginalized groups to *represent themselves* in decision-making processes that advance and define claims of exclusion and the respective solutions that affect their children's educational futures. (p. 35)

While most educators claim allegiance to inclusive schooling as an ideal, its actual enactment continues to be resisted and contested (Croll & Moses, 2010). The opportunity for students with disabilities to learn with and alongside peers in general education settings continues to be elusive (Artiles & Kozleski, 2016).

This chapter examines educators' learning about inclusive pedagogy during a three-year university-school district partnership focused on inclusive reform at Rolling Prairie Community School District[1] (RPCSD). Inclusive reform was defined as the intent to improve the lived and educational experiences of students labeled with a disability through professional development focused on creating welcoming and inclusive spaces and pedagogy that supported all students through universal design, differentiation, and constructivist learning principles. Using a disability justice consilience lens (Berne et al., 2018; Wilson, 1999), in conjunction with the theoretical framework of Cultural Historical Activity Theory (CHAT), this chapter explores the sociocultural-historical contexts affecting various stakeholders in the school and community as well as the constructed boundaries within which general and special educators carried out their work. To understand these reform efforts, the school district's learning context (including the historical norms within the school and community shaping various stakeholders' perspectives) is explored within the special education settings where educators delivered services to students labeled with disabilities. A detailed description of educators' motivation to learn, what they learn, and how they subsequently navigate and negotiate their new identities and knowledge is described.

METHODS

We employed qualitative methodology (Bogdan & Biklen, 1998; Glesne, 2006) to explore RPCSD's change process as they learned about and implemented inclusive schooling for all students. The design and enactment of qualitative inquiry typically focus on in-depth, long-term relationships with individuals and locations or sites of interest. Such research entails "understand[ing] some social phenomena from the perspectives of those involved, to contextualize issues in their particular socio-cultural-political milieu, and sometimes to transform or change social conditions" (Glesne, 2006, p. 4). Thus, we used ethnographic methods (Bogdan & Biklen, 1998) to focus on the experiences and perspectives of educators. Ethnography was well-suited to gauge the broader context of RPCSD while also facilitating deep relationships and connections among various stakeholders. Underlying this approach assumes that all human interaction is a story filled with multiple and often conflicting vantage points (Foot, 2014; Smith, 1989, 1993). As researchers, our goal was to gain a nuanced understanding of a variety of stakeholders' perspectives and experiences while capturing the complexity of creating inclusive communities (Gallagher, 1995; Glesne, 2006; Smith, 1989, 1993).

Researchers Positionality

Our interest in carrying out this research emerges from long-standing values about difference and belonging and our hope for spaces and communities that unconditionally accept and honor human difference. As researchers doing disability justice (Berne et al., 2018) work, we recognize the importance of our positionality and acknowledge that each of us embraces and enacts multiple and often conflicting identities. Depending on a given context, interaction, or environment, our identities both marginalize and privilege. We are university professors and instructors. Some of us are white, and some of us are recent immigrants. Two of us are mothers, and one a mother of a child with a disability. We are women. We all come from low social-economic backgrounds; three of us are first-generation college graduates. We carry these backgrounds and experiences with us as we seek to understand and strive to recognize how these lenses shape our understanding of the world.

Participants

Approximately 2,100 students served across four elementary schools, a middle school, a high school, and an alternative high school comprise RPCSD. Sixteen educators, including seven general education teachers, seven special education teachers, one counselor, and one administrator, agreed to participate in the research study. Of these teachers, six special educators served elementary students, one special educator served secondary students, and there were four elementary general educators and three secondary general educators.

We recruited participants from a group of RPCSD educators who participated in a 15-credit hour *Inclusive Educator Certificate Program*. The certificate program included five courses centered on inclusive reform's philosophical, legal, historical, and pedagogical aspects. It challenged educators to explore new ideas and understandings related to human diversity and ability, schooling structures, and inclusive education. In addition to this coursework, these educators received instructional coaching support from university faculty and participated in district-wide professional development on inclusive reform and pedagogy.

Data Collection

We obtained permission to carry out this research through the university Institutional Review Board (IRB) and obtained consent from all participants. Data collected included interviews, observations, documents, and artifacts. Observations included classroom, in-service professional development meetings, and informal interactions. Interviews included fifteen semi-structured interviews as well as informal interviews and conversations. These interviews were audio-recorded and transcribed. Throughout the three-year project period, approximately seventy-two classroom observations, four professional development trainings, and multiple school and community meetings were observed. In addition, upon completion of the coursework, participants consented to the use of their reflective discussion board postings as data. A total of 793 reflective discussion posts were collected.

Data Analysis

Conceptualizing methods of analysis as iterative tools to facilitate understanding (Gallagher, 1995), the process of data analysis was ongoing and we relied on many general strategies to aid analysis and understand the change process as we sought to implement inclusive reform. These strategies included, but were not limited to, immersing ourselves in the data, sketching ideas, taking field notes, journaling, playing with metaphors, listening to the transcribed interviews, sorting information, and analyzing documents (Bogdan & Biklen, 1998; Janesick, 2004). We also kept a detailed audit trail in the form of a methodological log (Gallagher, 1995). This log served as a tool of analysis and also created an "audit trail," providing documentation of our thinking and decision-making throughout the study (Glesne, 2006, p. 167).

We debriefed, discussed, and further analyzed the data in research meetings where our logs served as referent points and catalysts for our conversations. The records became a tool to cross-reference our understandings with the multiple sources of data in our effort to "increase the likelihood that they [we] gathered the information as accurately as possible, reflected the participants' points of view, and considered as much as possible of the whole topic/setting/phenomenon" (Ferguson & Ferguson, 2000, p. 183). By moving back and forth between our methodological logs, research conversations, and other data sources, we were able to compile from several sources of data (i.e., field notes, transcripts, discussion posts, and reflections maintained in the log) a richly nuanced, coherent, and well-reasoned picture of the process of inclusive reform and the experiences of educators within RPCSD. Our choice of methodology and methods was significant in that we acknowledged reality as constructed with multiple and conflicting perspectives, and in doing so, our methods facilitated a complex understanding of the process of inclusive reform that aligned with the concepts of disability justice, consilience, and boundary work.

THEORETICAL AND CONCEPTUAL FRAMEWORK

CHAT. Cultural historical activity theory (CHAT) and a theory of expansive learning were used as analytical tools to understand the factors informing inclusive reform (Akkerman & Bakker, 2011; Engestrom, 2001). CHAT is a theoretical framework that helps to illuminate how individuals learn and act within broader cultural and social contexts. It serves as a tool to examine both the macro structures that inform learning and individual or micro experiences informed by macrosystems. Moving between the macro and micro allowed for a nuanced analysis that illuminates the complexities of inclusive reform and change.

The primary unit of analysis in CHAT is the activity system(s). An activity system represents complex social organizations that include subjects (i.e., educators), communities (i.e., school board), tools (i.e., curriculum), outcomes (i.e., learning to be inclusive teachers), division of labor (i.e., who does what), and rules (i.e., school and district policies that reflect underlying beliefs about students). Taken together, activity systems are composed of individuals and organizations that are diverse and represent multiple points of view or voices, traditions, and interests (Foot, 2014). Activity systems take shape and are transformed over lengthy periods and can be understood by examining the historical context, multiple perspectives, and contradictions that emerge and lead to new tools, division of labor, and rules as learning occurs.

Expanding on the CHAT framework, Engestrom (2001) proposed a theory of expansive learning to account for and describe the process of learning. A theory of expansive learning seeks to understand how new knowledge emerges resulting in change while recognizing that learning is a dynamic process that is difficult to articulate or define a priori. A theory of expansive learning examines both the broad social contexts and individual experiences by exploring four central questions: *Who is learning? Why do they learn? What do they learn? And, how do they learn?* In this study, to understand the factors that informed inclusive education reform, we describe the learning context within which the inclusive reform project was enacted and focus on three questions: *Who is learning? Why do they learn? And, what do they learn?*

Consilience. In addition to the CHAT theoretical framework, we also drew from a consilience lens (Artiles, 2009; Berne et al., 2018; Wilson, 1999) to understand the "realities" of inclusive reform. Specifically, using the three consilience domains of *context*, *history*, and *power*, we sought to understand how we do intersectional work aimed at inclusive reform. We understood context as the social, political, and structural conditions or circumstances that impacted the inclusive reform project. The history domain was defined as the past events and or traditions that influenced the project. Last, we used the domain of power to understand interactions between and among various stakeholders. A few guiding questions guided our use of these domains. *What contexts inform such work? How does the history of special education impact reform? How is power enacted and negotiated to bring about change? Finally, as teacher educators, how does our learning guide our practice and continued efforts toward reform?*

Disability Justice. Last, from a lens of Disability Justice (Berne et al., 2018) this work was framed by a number of underlying principles. From the outset, we acknowledged that individuals have multiple identities that may intersect, be shaped, and matter more or less depending on the context. We also understood individuals as whole and their value and worth not dependent on what they may produce. We worked to honor the needs, insights, and participation of diverse individuals and groups, recognizing our interconnectedness and interdependence, with the intent of working for collective liberation. Finally, we understood the work as slow and the need to sustain it over time.

THE LEARNING CONTEXT

Like all school districts, RPCSD was situated within a community and therefore also within cultural, political, and historical norms. Historically, RPCSD was located within a rural, close-knit community with a long and firmly established tradition of providing segregated special education services and supports. As we attempted to understand the various factors that influenced reform, the historical context, coupled with the diversity of perspectives among educators, community members, administrations, and the school board, provided a rich and complex backdrop for change and disability justice work. As we approached the learning context, the notion of a *consiliencatory turn* guided our work. *How do we do intersectional work aimed at inclusive reform, and what contexts inform such work?*

"Rocky from the Start"

As many participants readily acknowledged, our project was far from being warmly embraced by the whole of the RPCSD. In fact, it was actively (though covertly) opposed both within the school district and among the most politically conservative and powerful voices in the community. When asked to reflect on inclusive reform's overall process, a common theme dominated educators' responses. Educators described the partnership and project as "rocky from the start," as those in opposition to inclusive reform ranged from the vociferously opposed to the mildly disapproving. Consequently, our participants found themselves distinctly marginalized in what became a politically divided environment. Certainly, a lack of widespread understanding of the project's goals, outcomes, and rationale stemming from the district's administrative partners dismissal of the need for thoroughgoing communication certainly contributed to this confusion and discord. That said, the more significant pushback came from those who simply rejected the underlying values and goals of inclusive education—including, and perhaps especially, from those who felt that they or their children stood to relinquish a measure of privilege if inclusive education reform was actually achieved.

Jackie, the director of special education, elaborated on the political landscape overshadowing the project. She shared that the school board, pressured by a politically conservative group known as SOS (Save Our Schools), hired a new superintendent, Dr. White, to make significant changes. The SOS group felt educators held too much power, and they desired to hire a superintendent who would make teachers "tow the rope." One teacher recalled:

> Dr. White was hired because he was not afraid to come in and say, "Quit dressing like a slob and come to work every day."

While Dr. White fulfilled the school board's expectations related to "reining in" the teachers, he aspired for other changes that the district's conservative elites had not anticipated. He wanted to create more inclusive schools and classrooms; however, when he challenged the "way things had always been done" by initiating the inclusive reform project, a strong division within the community became evident. As it turned out, Dr. White's political and ideological leanings were not quite what SOS leaders had in mind. On the one hand, Dr. White fulfilled the school board's expectations and SOS by "reigning in" the teachers in a decidedly heavy-handed manner. On the other hand, his far too communitarian and egalitarian support for inclusive education disrupted the norms of enforcing the social class order in Rolling Prairie (Brantlinger, 2003).

Jackie described the overt and covert power that the SOS group exerted on the school board in no uncertain terms. "There's a real right-wing conservative group. They run the show. If you don't go their way, then they create fear," she explained. Implying that individuals were explicitly threatened with the potential loss of business or harm to their career, Jackie shared that many community members were reluctant to support Dr. White's vision for change. The pressure to conform was so intense that one school member who served on the local police force resigned from the board when his aspirations to become chief of police were threatened.

This learning context set the stage for later negotiations of power among educators and other stakeholders working toward disability justice (Berne et al., 2018). The setting's contextual elements, including the stakeholders, educators, and community, intersected with its historical norms and challenged the "ways in which things were always done." The challenging nature of this context immediately positioned educators at the boundaries of change.

"Caught in the Middle"

Initially unbeknownst to us as the university partners, educators who participated in the inclusive certificate coursework soon found themselves caught in the middle. Special educators described feeling fear that they would lose their jobs if they did not participate. As Jackie explained:

> He [the superintendent] had a vision about having more general education teachers having more training to work with kids with disabilities. Yet, special educators misunderstood this vision and worried the goal was to put special education teachers out of a job.

Jill, a general education high school history teacher, recounted:

> The thing that irritated a lot of people was that he claimed that what would happen was that we would have these general education teachers who would take these classes to be certified to teach special education. Then we wouldn't need as many special education teachers.

Coupled with the fear of losing one's job, a lack of clear communication compounded the situation—including the administration's lack of communication with us as university partners. Educators later commented that they did not fully understand the purpose or direction of the inclusive reform project as a result of the lack of coherent communication.

Educators quickly found themselves in a thorny situation as they were accused of gaining unwarranted advantages through their participation in the inclusive reform project. Dana, an elementary special education teacher, explained, "The perception was that we were getting a really great deal and it [the coursework] was free to us, and we were privileged." Yet, there were also consequences related to participating. Describing the broader political context, Dana continued: "He [the superintendent] was not well-liked at the time. So, I remember there being backlash even at the beginning." That backlash continued throughout the three years of the project and had a lasting impact. As Jill put it:

> I think that maybe it [the backlash] has affected how people perceive those of us who stuck with it [the project]. I think there's definitely some distrust. I was sitting in a meeting with my department, and one of my colleagues said, "You took all those classes that Dr. White set up, so you must be buddies with him."

Such direct affiliations with the project (and therefore conspicuous tie to Dr. White) resulted in a district divided by those who had participated in the project's inclusive certificate component and those who had not. Dr. White, however inadvertently, managed to offend the school board, SOS group, and educators—apparently by having the naïveté to assume that inclusive values both were and should be widely shared among the districts' educators as well as the community at large. This assumption, and consequent sense that careful communication was not needed, thus set off a series of conflicts that almost fatally doomed the inclusive partnership. Heather shared:

> I almost felt like a traitor being in this class that everyone else was saying, "This is a Dr. White thing. He started it. I'm not going to finish it." It was kind of awkward. Then anytime you said anything about inclusion, people would be upset. It was such a hot word that I was almost afraid to share anything with anyone that wasn't in the class.

This politically charged context served as the backdrop for the learning and reform efforts. It also delineated a boundary where power would play out as new understandings emerged on the part of educators. Participation in the project came at significant costs, as those in the university-school partnership were in a unique, marginalized, and, at times, even ostracized position within the school and wider community. They were becoming disability justice educators. They were beginning to recognize the context and structures with which they existed as educators and the interplay of power in maintaining "the way things had always been." As they moved forward with the project, they were willing to make themselves vulnerable in ways that led to deep reflection and change.

WHO IS LEARNING?

In this project, general and special education were identified as separate but related activity systems. While general and special education activity systems operated within the shared political landscape described above and shared the goal of educating students, each system otherwise operated independently of one another. General and special education activity systems used unique and specific curricula, tools, and rules.

In our efforts to support inclusive reform, we continually wondered how the tradition and field of special education, with its historical norms, impacted teachers' daily practice, how such traditions were counter to inclusive reform, and how they might be reimagined.

The general education activity system included general education teachers who used general education curriculum and standards. General education teachers were organized by grade level and adhered to school rules and policies. While general education teachers collaborated with grade-level colleagues for curricular planning, they generally worked in isolation, teaching behind closed doors. When concerns arose about students' progress, an intervention model was followed wherein students were identified for additional, intensive, and targeted supports. Students who failed to make sufficient progress during the intervention period were identified as eligible for special education services and supports. General education teachers operated from the notion that students were no longer their responsibility once they were identified for special education supports and services.

The special education activity system was governed by the Individuals with Disabilities Education Act (IDEA) legal framework and included special education teachers and special education curriculum and pedagogy. These curricular tools included a specialized curriculum designed to break down and target specific skills. Instruction often entailed sequenced direct instruction lessons that required the mastery of rote, isolated skills (Heshusius, 1982, 1984; Iano, 1990, 2004). Essential tools of special education teachers were accommodations and modifications to support students with disabilities. Special education teachers assumed full responsibility for students identified as needing special education services. Students were grouped by common disability categories and provided services in pull-out and self-contained special education classrooms. Special education teachers often served multiple grade levels, sometimes spanning K-6 or 9–12.

Although general and special education systems carried out their respective functions largely in isolation of each other and operated using different tools and rules, they shared a philosophical orientation about students with disabilities. At the outset of the project, both general and special education teachers viewed special education students through the medical model of disability framework. The medical model of disability understands disability as a reified and inherent condition—a deficit—that is need of curing or fixing so that the person might be "normal" or, as often described in schools, "average" (Pfeiffer, 2002). From this perspective, students determined eligible for special education services were perceived as possessing a deficiency in need of "fixing" or remediating so that they may be "normal" or "average" (Brantlinger, 2006; Iano 1990). In accepting this responsibility, special education teachers also accepted the division of labor that designated students as "your students/my students."

WHY DO THEY LEARN?

Within any activity system, contradictions exist that serve as sources for potential learning and change. When activity systems move through periods of transformation, these contradictions are aggravated and result in individuals deviating from the norm and enacting change. As project participants began to explore alternative understandings of difference (i.e., medical model vs. social model) and the purpose of schooling they began to weigh these new understandings with their personal experiences and background. In short, the professional became personal as they made sense of their own experiences and identities within the context of their professional lives. In doing this, contradictions emerged that resulted in feeling morally and ethically compelled to change their practices and continue learning and participating in the project (Gallagher et al., 2019). These educators were beginning to assume a radical love (Fromm, 1956) for themselves and the students they served. That is, they had developed a deep care and responsibility for one another through listening and seeking to deeply understand without judgment. They respected the lived experiences of their students, were able to situate those experiences within the broader contexts, recognize the connections and use their newly emerging positionality of critical special educators to honor students' voices and needs (Lake, 2016). Through engaging in critical dialogue about their positionality and how their experiences influenced their understandings and interactions with their students labeled as disabled, they were able to begin to question the tenets of the field of special education. For example, they began to understand the nature of disability not as a medical condition in need of remediation, but as a social construction. Similarly, they began to redefine their roles as educators not as technicians who worked to remediate or bring students up to some mythical average, but rather as educators who viewed students holistically and worked to facilitate deep, meaningful learning that honored student differences. Below, we focus on two prominent contradictions that served as impetus and motivation for change.

Reconsidering Normal, Dis/ability, and Difference

The first contradiction that emerged illuminated the problematic relationship between general and special education and how students were labeled as disabled. Not surprisingly, the issue of labeling, and subsequently how participants understood their students, turned out to be a provocative one. The issue predominantly centered on the "accurate identification" of students with disabilities (Gallagher et al., 2019). Joy, a special education teacher whose own daughter was labeled with a disability, grappled with the issue:

> there can be a time and place where labeling can be helpful. If we are accurately labeling and using the information to improve the situation, then labeling can be meaningful.

And, then, immediately, she questioned:

> It used to be politically correct to label [a student] "mentally retarded." Now, we say, "intellectual deficit." Is that really any better? Maybe outwardly labeling someone based on their cognitive intelligence is wrong . . . and not just the label we use?

An alarming contradiction emerged as project participants explored the meaning of disability through the medical and social models. They came to understand that at its core, the difference between the medical model of disability (which predominates in educational practices, informs traditional special education scholarship, and serves as the basis of federal special education law) and its social model contender boils down to whether disabilities *exist* as epistemologically *real* conditions in the sense that they are intrinsic to the individual, can be quantified, and are properly grounded in the logic of ability as normally distributed (Dudley-Marling, 2010).

The medical model affirms this perspective, while the social model holds that disabilities are the product of culturally mediated interpretations of various human differences—subjective appraisals rather than objective observations. Simply put, the social model supports the position that disability is a social construct or an *idea* about the nature of certain kinds of human variation (Kliewer & Biklen, 1996). In contrasting these two frameworks, project participants realized that viewing students through a medialized lens had consequences that they had not previously considered. Illuminating the contradiction, one teacher stated:

> Everything about special education is constructed (or made up if you will). Many of the methods and practices used in education today are starting to seem like fallacies to me: the bell curve, the idea of normal, the notion that IQ tests accurately measure intelligence, the idea that intelligence is a 'thing' that could be measured, the category of learning disabilities, the thought that standardized testing of children reflects their knowledge and understanding . . . The sum total of these practices is that we have a field of kids we have deemed "broken," "underachieving," and/or "disabled."

How normal is defined, educators concluded, was always a social construction that emerged from social, historical, cultural, and economic contexts. They realized that the concept of normal was intricately linked to the labeling, identification, and diagnostic process that they found themselves inevitably a part of in their role as an educator within the larger context of schooling. Project participants felt empowered to understand students from a social model framework that did not perceive students as broken and in need of fixing and recognized they could transform the learning conditions and physical environments to ensure inclusion for all students. This new construction of knowledge represented a consilience of redefining difference from a socially constructed lens.

Reconsidering the Purpose of Schooling

Through the coursework, project participants also explored and examined their personal experiences within the broader schooling context. These explorations entailed conversations about ability, race, and class and how each discourse intersects in ways that perpetuate inequality for individuals labeled with one or more marginalized identities. These rich conversations lead project participants to examine their own identities closely. Although RPCSD educators and students were overwhelmingly white, there were unambiguous community divisions along social class lines. Thinking about these issues and their positionality within the intersecting discourses of race, class, and ability lead to a second contradiction.

Before the coursework, participants admittedly adhered to the belief that if an individual worked hard enough, they would be rewarded with success. Conversely, if an individual was not successful, conventional logic followed that the individual had not worked hard and was not deserving of success. This meritocratic hegemony was a commonly held value on the part of project participants. The majority of them were first-generation college graduates and had, by most accounts, pulled themselves out of a life of poverty through such hard work. Thus, participants struggled with social class issues because such issues inevitably caused them to critically question the nature of their success and, consequently, their identities. Participants began to understand the mythology of meritocracy as problematic in that the concept failed to acknowledge the complexities that inform a person's opportunities, and thereby success. They began to examine their successes and experiences, questioning their position and role within larger structural inequalities.

For this reason, the issue of social class stereotypes captured their collective interest and ambivalence surrounding the issue of merit. Participants grappled with the nuanced nature of class stereotypes. As Julie worked to process issues of social class stereotypes, she shared:

> During last week's discussion, I could not help but think about specific families I have worked with who lived in free and reduced housing but dressed in more name brand clothing than I could ever afford myself, or who wanted their child to have a disability so that they could receive more government handouts, among other stories. But then, on the other hand, I also agree that there are those who, no matter how hard they try to better their lives, seem always to get dealt a bad hand and are unfortunately looked down upon because of those who give them a bad name, but do not deserve the labels they receive.

With growing uneasiness, educators began to make connections and draw parallels among marginalized groups. For example, Lisa identified the influence of class related to one of her students labeled as having a moderate/severe disability. She indicated that the student had been segregated based on her disability label (and appearance) and the student's social class background. She reflected on the student: "The potential was there. It just was never tapped because there were some assumptions made about her ability based on a kind of look and a family situation."

Despite the difficult nature of these issues, continued conversations illuminated contradictions between educators' beliefs and practices. Educators began to acknowledge how stereotypical assumptions grounded in realist notions of ability, race, and class informed educators' practices and students' experiences in the classroom. They also began to understand schooling's purpose from a new perspective, resulting in an uneasy awareness of schools as inherently inequitable. These contradictions gave way to new understandings that resulted in more deeply committed participants and motivated them to transform their schools and classrooms.

WHAT DO THEY LEARN?

As described above, educators experienced a profound shift in their thinking about students with disabilities and the nature of schools. To reconcile the contradictions and their new learning, educators welcomed new rules and a new division of labor to implement inclusive practice. Yet, as they implemented new practices, they continually struggled to negotiate the multiple perspectives and political and historical contexts surrounding their efforts. These struggles represented disability justice work and the power at play when new understandings emerge and lead to new pedagogy and practice. Below, we consider how power is enacted and negotiated to bring about change. We recognized a seemingly intrinsic dominant power at work within the traditional special education and general education activity systems that seemingly appeared rationale and legitimate and as a result of long-held structures and beliefs that were couched within a political and social context. As our project participants grew in their knowledge and thereby questioned these structures, they used their power to initiate change in ways that threatened these dominant power structures.

New Division of Labor and New Tools

As educators shifted from a medicalized understanding of their students' differences to a social understanding, the rules relating to who was responsible for and could provide instruction to students with disabilities changed. For example, Jill explained that her involvement in the inclusive partnership as a secondary history teacher provided her with, for the first time, a realization that she could work successfully with special education students. This insight marked a momentous conceptual breakthrough for her as a teacher. Previously, she had always considered teaching *those* students to be her special education colleagues' job. She recounted such logic as:

> I think in your first few years of teaching, you just assume that's not my job. That's a special ed. teacher's job. All of a sudden, the last couple of years, going through these classes and stuff, it's like, oh my gosh. No, here's the deal! We can co-teach, and we can make this a stellar room.

This shift in her thinking immediately impacted her practices and her desire to educate students with disabilities. Through an inward turn, her outward practice began to reflect principles of disability justice such as interdependence, sustainability, and wholeness (Berne et al., 2018). Her inclusive history classroom was sustained through co-teaching, while autistic students and others in her classroom began learning in interdependent ways (i.e., collaborative learning, project-based instruction) that honored their wholeness (learning activities that sustained and were responsive to sensory diversity and neurodiversity).

As educators began to take responsibility for all students, they recognized the value of understanding their students profoundly and in ways that informed their practices, particularly relating to differentiated instruction. As Joy described:

> Every student has different background knowledge, preferences, interests, and learning styles. The label that a student may (or may not) have is only a small piece to the puzzle. And, even within that puzzle, not all students exhibit the same symptoms when it comes to a diagnosis. I feel that the most important piece to teaching any student is developing that relationship with your students! Taking the time to get to know your students is going to help you determine your best approach to teaching them.

Thus, co-teaching and differentiated instruction became a sustainable means to share responsibility for educating all students.

Negotiating the Boundaries

Upon completing the coursework, educators, in particular, special educators, were motivated to initiate larger-scale change in their school buildings.

However, initiating such change was a formidable challenge with colleagues who had not participated in the coursework. Special educators found themselves attempting to persuade general educators to view themselves as the actual, bona fide teacher of students with disabilities. These general educators had not had the same opportunities to reflect, critically examine, and learn about inclusive practice in ways that motivated them to transform their classrooms and change their practices. Subsequently, they did not understand their roles or responsibilities within the newly proposed division of labor. They were not receptive to new tools, such as co-teaching or differentiating instruction for all students.

Non-project participants lacked a desire to co-teach or implement differentiated instruction. As Dave, the high school guidance counselor explained, many teachers felt, "this is how I've taught for 15 years. I do my thing by myself; I know what I'm doing. I don't want anybody else in here." Joy echoed this sentiment about the elementary teachers with whom she attempted to build relationships: "I didn't feel like they understood. I was trying to help them. I would try to send them materials, and they would say, 'don't tell us what to do in our classroom.'" These interactions led Joy and other project participants to feel frustrated.

Navigating the shared classroom space, using one another's expertise, and sharing responsibility for all students were difficult and threatened a desperately guarded sense of professional autonomy. Special education teachers felt strongly that non-project general education teachers did not value their expertise or accept special education students as their responsibility. Holly explained: "They didn't really know how to modify things or make any changes or adjustments. In their eyes, this was my student, not their student."

Joy further expressed frustration with her non-participating general education counterparts who were unwilling to consider or learn how to support students with disabilities in their classrooms. She recounted one such conversation:

> I had a teacher telling me one day this week . . . how am I supposed to do my job when I have kids in my room that are on like the first-grade level, the second-grade level, the third-grade level?

For Joy, it was inexplicable how this teacher *could not do her job* as she declared, "like you are a teacher, it is fine," implying that a teacher's responsibility was to teach all kids. In short, special education teachers mostly felt that it was a no-win situation. They struggled in building necessary relationships to co-teach and support students with disabilities because their non-project general education counterparts were often unwilling or lacked the knowledge to support students with disabilities in their classrooms.

DISABILITY JUSTICE AND CONSILIENCE: THE WORK OF EDUCATORS

Disability justice work and the notion of consilience provide both a frame to understand the work of inclusive reform and important implications. As RPCSD partner educators worked to enact inclusive reform, their learning and practices were informed by the experiences, background, and contextual elements, including the history of the community, its school district, and the field of special education. The work of disability justice and inclusive reform was challenging in that these various contexts and elements intersected at the boundaries of traditional systems of special education and reform efforts. Power emerged at these intersections as educators developed new understandings, turned away from traditional ways of knowing, and shifted to radical love as a way to understand one another and their students. Such work had its costs, as many educators experienced isolation and pushback; however, the work also led to unity and a newly constructed community and culture of educators who no longer viewed their students as "broken" or "in need of fixing." These educators cared deeply for their students—and we would venture to say that they came to know what it was to unconditionally, radically love their students. When provided new learning that engaged critical exploration of the contexts and histories informing the tradition of special education, they made themselves vulnerable to change and were empowered with new understandings that they translated into practice. In short, they learned to recognize the contexts at play, the intersecting web of power and privilege, and the ability to use their inclusive pedagogy as a means of resistance. Their shift to understanding their students as whole with multiple identities and their commitment to collective access and liberation access illuminated inclusive pedagogy as a means of resistance.

As teacher educators who engaged with these educators, we were in awe of their willingness to question and challenge long-held beliefs and ideas through new learning and ways that resulted in newly constructed identities. As they grappled with tough questions about difference, equity, and inclusive schooling, we, too, found ourselves emerged in the contexts, histories, and power at work at the boundaries. We recognized this work as disability justice work, and we reflected on how this work would shape our roles as teacher educators. As teacher educators, we must continue to challenge students to redefine the meaning of difference and do so from an intersectional approach (Crenshaw, 1990). We must prepare educators in disability justice work and that of boundary-crossing.

Just as the teachers in this project assumed the role of a boundary worker, advocating for change within and across the boundaries of general and special education activity systems, we must prepare preservice educators to do the same. To do this, we must emphasize an interdisciplinary curriculum that is theoretically strong with ample opportunities to apply theory to practice. We must focus on multiple ways of knowing and challenge deficit understanding of disability in favor of disability as a socially constructed and therefore moral/political category. We must also explicitly teach how educators might engage to bridge, transform, or overcome boundaries. We must articulate connections between the practices of overlapping communities (i.e., general and special education) and facilitate new pedagogies. When we can prepare future teachers with the space to explore their identities, experiences, and professional desires in relation to the contexts and histories underlying the field of special education, we can do the work of disability justice and consilience.

CONCLUSION

This chapter focused on the factors that informed general and special educators' learning during a three-year school-university partnership project. Using the domains of disability justice and consilience, including the intersections of contextual, historical, and power work, this chapter describes the school district's learning context, including the school and community's historical norms and the various stakeholders. Working within and across general and special education activity systems, participants experienced a profound shift in how they understood the nature of difference and structural inequalities. This resulted in a desire to transform their classrooms and instructional practices. Through the lens of disability justice, they navigated multiple and intersecting histories and contexts using their power to build bridges across general and special education and enact reform.

NOTE

1. Pseudonyms were used throughout the chapter.

REFERENCES

Akkerman, S. F., & Bakker, A. (2011). Boundary crossing and boundary objects. *Review of Educational Research, 81*(2), 132–169.
Artiles, A. J. (2009, Summer). From the vice president. *Division G: Social Context of Education, Newsletter.*
Artiles, A. J., & Kozleski, E. B. (2016). Inclusive education's promises and trajectories: Critical notes about future research on a venerable idea. *Education Policy Analysis Archives, 24*(43), 1–25.

Artiles, A. J., Kozleski, E. B., Dorn, S., & Christensen, C. (2006). Learning in inclusive education research: Re-mediating theory and methods with a transformative agenda. *Review of Research in Education, 30*(1), 65–108.

Berne, P., Morales, A. L., Langstaff, D., & Invalid, S. (2018). Ten principles of disability justice. *WSQ: Women's Studies Quarterly, 46*(1), 227–230.

Bogdan, R. C., & Biklen, S. K. (1998). *Qualitative research in education: An introduction to theory and methods*. Allyn & Bacon.

Brantlinger, E. A. (2003). *Dividing classes: How the middle class negotiates and rationalizes school advantage*. Routledge.

Brantlinger, E. A. (Ed.). (2006). *Who benefits from special education?: Remediating (fixing) other people's children*. Routledge.

Crenshaw, K. (1990). Mapping the margins: Intersectionality, identity politics, and violence against women of color. *Stanford Law Review, 43*(6), 1241–1299.

Croll, P., & Moses, D. (2010). Ideologies and utopias: Education professionals' views of inclusion. *European Journal of Special Needs Education, 15*(1), 1–12.

Dudley-Marling, C., & Gurn, A. (Eds.). (2010). *The myth of the normal curve* (Vol. 11). Peter Lang.

Engrestrom, Y. (2001). Expansive learning at work: Toward an activity theoretical reconceptualization. *Journal of Education and Work, 14*(1), 133–156.

Ferguson, D. L., & Ferguson, P. M. (2000). Qualitative research in special education: Notes toward an open inquiry instead of a new orthodoxy? *JASH, 25*(3), 180–185.

Foot, K. A. (2014). Cultural-historical activity theory: Exploring a theory to inform practice and research. *Journal of Human Behavior in the Social Environment, 24*(3), 329–347.

Fromm, E. (1956). *The art of loving*. Harper Row.

Gallagher, D. J. (1995). In search of the rightful role of method: Reflections on my dissertation experience. In T. Tiller, A. Sparkes, S. Karhus, & F. Dowling-Naess (Eds.), *Reflections on educational research: The qualitative challenge* (pp. 25–42). Kasper Forlag.

Gallagher, D. J., Petersen, A., Cowley, D., & Iqtadar, S. (2019). A sentimental education: Insights for inclusive reform from a university/school district partnership. In M. J. Schuelka, C. J. Johnstone, G. Thomas, & A. J. Artiles (Eds.), *SAGE handbook of inclusion and diversity in education* (pp. 146–158). Sage.

Glesne, C. (2006). *Becoming qualitative researchers: An introduction* (3rd ed.). Pearson Education.

Heshusius, L. (1982). At the heart of the advocacy dilemma: A mechanistic world view. *Exceptional Children, 49*(1), 6–13.

Heshusius, L. (1984). Why would they and I want to do it?: A phenomenological theoretical view of special education. *Learning Disability Quarterly, 7*(4), 363–368.

Iano, R. P. (1990). Special education teachers: Technicians or educators? *Journal of Learning Disabilities, 23*(8), 462–465.

Iano, R. P. (2004). The student and development of teaching: With implications for the advancement of special education. In D. J. Gallagher, L. Heshusius, R. P. Iano, & T. Skrtic (Eds.), *Challenging orthodoxy in special education: Dissenting voices* (pp. 65–88). Love Publishing.

Janesick, V. J. (2004). *"Stretching" exercises for qualitative researchers.* Sage.

Kliewer, C., & Biklen, D. (1996). Labeling: Who wants to be called retarded. In W. Stainback & S. Stainback (Eds.), *Controversial issues confronting special education: Divergent perspectives* (2nd ed., pp. 83–95). Allyn & Bacon.

Lake, R. L. (2016). Radical love in teacher education praxis: Imagining the real through listening to diverse student voices. *The International Journal of Critical Pedagogy, 7*(3), 79–95.

Pfeiffer, D. (2002). The philosophical foundation of disability studies. *Disability Studies Quarterly, 22*(2), 3–23.

Smith, J. K. (1989). *The nature of social and educational inquiry: Empiricism versus interpretation.* Ablex.

Smith, J. K. (1993). *After the demise of empiricism: The problem of judging social and educational inquiry.* Ablex.

Waitoller, F. R., & Kozleski, E. B. (2013). Working in boundary practices: Identity development and learning in partnerships for inclusive education. *Teaching and Teacher Education, 31*(2013), 35–45.

Waitoller, F. R., Kozleski, E. B., & Gonzales, T. (2016). Professional inquiry for inclusive education: Learning amidst institutional and professional boundaries. *School Effectiveness & School Improvement, 27*(1), 62–79.

Walker, D., & Nocon, H. (2007). Boundary crossing competence: Theoretical considerations and education design. *Mind, Culture, & Activity, 14*(3), 178–195.

Wilson, E. O. (1999). *Consilience: The unity of knowledge* (Vol. 31). Vintage.

Chapter 5

On the Margins of the Marginalized

Protecting and Loving on Black Children with Intellectual Disability and Emotional and Behavioral Disturbances

Lydia Ocasio-Stoutenburg

I open this chapter with a quote by author and activist James Baldwin from "My Dungeon Shook: Letter to My Nephew on the One Hundredth Anniversary of the Emancipation," the opening excerpt from *The Fire Next Time*, a political essay first published in 1963. Baldwin's words are striking and powerful, awakening his nephew to the experience of being Black in a racialized society, where identity sets the parameters for opportunity, expectation, and mobility through social class.

> You were born where you were born and faced the future that you faced because you were black and for no other reason. The limits of your ambition were, thus, expected to be set forever. You were born into a society which spelled out with brutal clarity, and in as many ways possible, that you were a worthless human being. (Baldwin, 1993, p. 7)

The subjective determination of one's worth has manifested in a material reality for people of color in the United States, reproduced across generations and systems. Dis/ability has followed a similar trajectory of discrimination and exclusion based on how people are assessed and categorized, inextricably linked to racialization. Rather than embracing the range of people's presentations as part of the full expression of humanity, it is used as an instrument for limitation. What an irony, that realities have been constructed based on the constructs of race and dis/ability.

The word *normal* is used so frequently as a descriptor in our world, transcending time, cultures, and domains. It is a part of medical jargon, for example, "this is part normal or abnormal development." It is used in our educational assessments, as in "this child's performance falls within this part of a normal curve." It is a used in economics, as in "These are normal fluctuations." Even meteorologists describe how the temperatures range, relative to "normal." In reponse to the shelter-in-place orders at the outbreak of the COVID-19 pandemic, which mandated school closures, remote work, and social distancing, a commonly asked question was, "When will we get back to normal?" Normal is a construct, yet the word normal constructs meaning about conditions, experiences, and people that leave little room for variation. Much more than an adjective, normal is relational, very much like the word "power," as theorized by Bourdieu.

According to Merriam-Webster's dictionary, the second definition of power is "having authority or influence over another," which means that power does not exist on its own but is given meaning through this differential. Bourdieu further illustrates the relationship-derived symbolism of power, describing "a determinate relationship between those who exercise power and those who undergo it" (1979, p. 83). Normalcy gleans its meaning in the same way, dependent upon the relationship between those who are considered normal, according to a set of constructed standards, and those who are not. Therefore because of the polemic nature of relational terms such as normal, falling below the standard becomes problematized, pathologized, and classified as deviance. It is important to think of this not as a theoretical concept but to examine evidence of how this is operationalized, codified, and redefined across disciplines, such as medicine, psychology, and education (Artiles, 2011; Dudley-Marling & Gurn, 2010). Scholars have noted how these ideologies have not only been used to gauge children's proximity to the standards of normal, but they have taken on the function to determine their access, opportunities, placements, resources, treatments, and belonging in schools.

Scholarship has also long described a "dilemma of difference" when it comes to children in dis/abilities in educational settings. While special education has provided a set of services for children who may need greater individualized support, its context also relies heavily on their very categorization; children would need to be outside of a "normal" parameter in order to qualify for such services (Minow, 1990). But how are these parameters set? And by whom? Though arbitrary, the abled-dis/abled binary has been constructed and reconstructed throughout history in ways that marginalize individuals. Trent (2016), for example, described how the abrupt decision to change the criterion for intellectual dis/ability from one standard deviation below the I.Q. norm to two standard deviations below the norm resulted in many individuals no longer being categorized as such. Dudley-Marling and Gurn (2010) described how the normal curve has been erroneously used as a tool as used to define parameters of what is deemed intelligence, emphasizing its pseudoscientific origins that centralize a white and middle-class standard. Fields such as Disability Studies in Education (DSE) continue to challenge the ideologies of normalcy rooted in the medical-psychological and eugenic models, only not framing dis/ability as part of human difference but also noting the arbitrary nature of the instruments of assessing intelligence through standardized testing (Gallagher, 2010). Annamma et al. (2013) described how the constant reification of normal problematizes dis/ability, noting, "normal as a phenomenon desired by these powerful disciplines maintains that difference is conceived as deviance, an analogy that is fundamentally problematic" (p. 1278). Although the dilemma of difference described is a reality that impacts *all* children, especially for children with dis/abilities, it is important to underscore the particular ways in which the bounds of normalcy have been constructed for Black and Brown children within the educational system. Special education scholar Alfredo Artiles (2011) has furthered the work of Minow (1990) on this dilemma to describe the "paradox" of the very intent of special education and its reality for children of color. Decades of data have presented the reality of disproportionate number of referrals of Black and Brown children from working-class families to special education and an overrepresentation in dis/ability categories, particularly for intellectual disability (ID) and emotional and behavioral disturbance (EBD) (Artiles & Trent, 2004; Artiles, 2011; Donovan & Cross, 2002; Harry & Klingner, 2022; Losen & Orfield, 2002). Though the argument still echoes how concepts like race, ability, and social class are socially constructed, danger lies in remaining ignorance of its eugenic roots (history) and systemic manifestations (history and present).

POSITIONALITY OF THE BRICOLEUR

It is not ironic that I found myself teaching on two campuses of the same university—the clinical/medical campus and the academic campus, which houses the school of education. In education, I taught and mentored a range of doctoral students, many of whom were preservice and in-service educators, in the clinical and counseling psychology professions or in the business of developing course tools and technologies. I also served as the faculty mentor and facilitator for dis/ability advocacy and understanding family-professional partnership training sessions for a Leadership in Neurodevelopmental Disabilities (LEND) training program. These students were seeking to better understand the world of families and children with dis/abilities. Trainees represented multiple disciplines and life experiences—family/community, medicine, psychology, and speech language pathology were some examples. For the most part, being an instructor at both campuses had distinct roles with separate requirements. However, I recognized myself as Denzin (1994) described, ever the qualitative researcher, the "bricoleur" whose "labor is a bricolage, a complex, dense, reflexive, collage-like creation that represents the researcher's images, understandings and interpretations of the world or phenomenon under analysis" (p. 10). I took time to weave and observe the common threads across my experiences in a reflexive process. Many of the educators, therapists, residents, and family members who came to further their education or training were shocked by the rift between their own good intentions and the injustice that they were often not aware of, that was perpetuated by their fields, clinicians, mentors, or community leaders. Certainly, some entered their respective professions with a desire to heal or to fix. It, therefore took them to a personal and professional crossroad when I asked them whether it was the children or the systems that needed fixing.

As the Black mother of a child with a dis/ability and advocate, I put forth my own positionality, knowing that a often play a substantial role in the formation of students and trainees, and how they will engage with families and children in the future. I am often asked what brought me into the field of special education and the short answer is my son, to know everything I needed to know in how to fight for him. Often I am asked why I did not pursue law or psychology and I legitimize these questions, as the former would have provided me with the legal knowledge and the latter perhaps some clinical insights. However, I understood the limitations of the law, especially under IDEA (2004) as it cannot shield families from the bureaucracy and inequities within the systems of care purported to serve children. Secondly, I found psychology to be much too prescriptive and un/intentionally pathologizing to understand the complexity and marvel that I have come to know in my son. Ironically, I have come to encounter and re-encounter the word normal in the very context of special education that I presumed to be "safe" and understanding of human difference, admittedly in ways that have been hurtful to me and to those who have come under my service and care.

RECONCILIATION AND CONSILIENCE

In this chapter, I assert that both reconciliation and consilience are tools needed to redress the indebtedness described by Ladson-Billings (2007) accumulated by the educational system toward generations of Black and Brown children. I have come to understand how my experiences of people and communities have called for a reconciliation of the word normal, especially when we consider children who happen to fall under the categories of intellectual disability (ID) and emotional and behavioral disturbance (EBD) for whom Black and Brown children have been disproportionately assigned

(Artiles, 2013). This work is one of considering a consilience between the traditions of special education (SpEd) and disability studies in education (DSE). Though their foundations and orientations are typically opposed, we have the potential to support our children with the best that these fields have to offer them. In doing so, my hope is not only to advance the conversation but to also advance our outward and inner actions, reframing our work in love. As illustrated through case studies of children representing these identities, this work proposes a rationale for novel approaches that educators can take toward supporting children that are subtractive of the systemically embedded ableist, racist, and classist ideologies.

This chapter is also constructed in ways that also push past typical boundaries. Woven throughout this work is a search of the literature, the qualitative research genres of narrative inquiry and critical autoethnography as well as the departure from academic writing into poetic expression. In many ways, this work is liberatory; I borrow the expressive language of scholar David Hernández-Saca, that loosening the restrictions in this manner is also "making sense of my own emotions, which institutionalized ways do not allow for" (2019, p. 428). I acknowledge the limitations of my own lens; though I am a mother of a child with a dis/ability diagnosis, this is not the same as the person presenting with a dis/ability. Even my convention of dis/ability is a choice which reflects a movement to center ability. Inasmuch as my intention is not to erase the beauty and full human expression of what it is to be dis/abled, some would argue that this convention does just that. It is important for us to understand how even just one degree removed, our perspective is never perfect, and we must do as much as we can to center individuals who are experiencing the phenomena firsthand. I also put forward my positionality as the mother of a child who hopes one day that her child, a young Black man with a dual dis/ability diagnosis, can one day speak for himself. In the time being, however, I speak for him, knowing I have a limitation: I am still not his voice.

In the following three excerpts, I invite you to explore the nuances of normal across the cases of three children and youth with dis/abilities. Each of these cases represents a young person, who happens to carry a stigmatized dis/ability label in addition to belonging to a historically disenfranchised racial and ethnic identity group. Each of these children has been failed in some way by the systems they are reliant upon, simply because of their social proximity to what society has deemed "normal."

MARTIN: "I'M NOT SLOW"

Martin is a bright, Black boy of twelve years of age who is dreaming about a career in railroad engineering. Martin loves the intricacies of things, his mind always focusing on how things fit together and then function. If you sat with him for long enough, Martin could pull apart a few Styrofoam cups and reconstruct them into a model building, all while holding a conversation. And Martin can hold a conversation for a while.

Martin had been oscillating between a foster care placement and the custody of a biological family member for years. Instead of receiving love consistently, Martin was caught in an ongoing battle between systems, schools that did not understand him. There were people in and out of his life, case workers, teachers, and support personnel. The first label Martin received was Attention Deficit Hyperactivity Disorder (ADHD), determined by a clinician affiliated with the foster care system, which he used to justify medicating him. Martin clearly expressed to his case managers how the medications made him feel sad, tired, and "weird" which were often shared in both his IEP meetings and therapy sessions, but were quickly dismissed as insignificant. Martin had been doing well in school, but the side effects of the medications began to impact his academic performance, as suggested by his grades. Scholars have long described how grades—through continuous and periodic standardized testing—are the metrics by which academic ability and intelligence are assessed. These have been investigated and unpacked by both critical race scholars and DSE scholars. In her 2006 Presidential Address for the American Educational Research Association, scholar Gloria Ladson-Billings (2007) described the dangerous yet recursive process of decontextualizing the academic experiences of Black and Brown children. Billings' point is that the so-called "achievement gap" between children of color and their white counterparts continues to perpetuate the narrative that there are intrinsic deficits within Black and Brown children that are not found in their white counterparts while "objective" evaluators and education policymakers remain ignorant of the processes by which standardized testing, a lack of investment in quality teaching, and differentials school resources create inequities from the starting block. DSE scholar Deborah Gallagher (2010) provided a parallel argument on the inequitable educational environments created for children with dis/abilities, noting how reliant the field of special education is upon the very same assessment-driven pedagogies that become the instruments for categorizing and labeling children, distancing them from the very individualized investments they need to help them thrive. It is of no surprise that children like Martin, who find themselves at the junction of these realities based on the multiple, intersecting identities they hold, are the subjects of and subjected to the testing culture. In the following paragraphs, we will see how purposive these instruments were.

School administrators used the assessment and referral process to justify Martin's placement at another school, a school that they felt could better serve children "like him" even though they gave no explanation to what this might mean. In their data collection, the legal interns who I supervised at the time, spoke of a "Mr. M." who was playing somewhat of a significant role in Martin's daily interactions at the school. "Who is Mr. M?" I asked. He was not Martin's teacher, coach, or a part of his day in any way related to academics or related services. "Mr. M," we had come to discover, was a tall, Black man who had the title of "counselor" at the school, often called upon to handle disciplinary actions across classrooms, even for students who were not serving an indoor suspension. In discussing this further with the special education coordinator, I learned that "Mr. M" was somehow tasked with the responsibility for the execution of Martin's behavioral plan, although no one seemed to be able to find the functional behavioral assessment when we requested it. This was to no avail, however; collecting data from teachers, the school psychologist, and other school staff, including a "Mr. M," a case was building, not for Martin, but against him.

Martin's foster caregiver, a kind man in his late 20s by the name of James, was doing his absolute best to create what I would call a "love counternarrative" by continually sharing just how well Martin was doing with some structure, high expectations, and downright love with whomever would lis- ten. He provided a home and the consistency that Martin needed. He was the point of contact, as was his guardian-ad-litem, who was assigned to manage his educational decisions. However, bypassing these key individuals and without fully explaining what the consequences might be for Martin, the school contacted Martin's biological mother, Nicole, to tell her that they were administering his assessments. Nicole agreed, of course, believing that this was in the best interest of her child. Nicole certainly did not even know that the tests would result in Martin receiving a second label of EBD.

Martin's performance at the new school was severely impacted by his environment. Martin had a teacher who was "trained in EBD," yet had no tolerance or skills to support student behaviors. She taught without an understanding of Martin's trauma, or the resistance he sometimes exhibited in the classroom to get some agency and control of his life. Since under IDEA, Martin's current three-year eligibility had ended, it was time to reassess Martin, this time, to rule out intellectual ability. The evaluation team used Martin's current school performance to raise questions about his intellectual ability, for the purpose of the placing him at a new school. The new school was the most segregated setting, one which served students with ID, which a focus on vocational training. Martin protested, recalling the history of his own identification process and the consequences of such. Martin's statements were descriptive of his own self-perceptions against those imposed upon him:

> I know they say I'm dumb, but I'm not. I don't even belong in this class. I need to be with the normal kids. And now they 'bout to send me to the school with the slow kids. I'm not slow. I just hate being here.

Martin's word choices, which polarize "normal" vs. "slow," reflect just how he constructs the meaning of dis/ability, how students with dis/abilities are perceived, and the stigma attached to attending this school. Researchers have described how students are both socially and emotionally impacted by the labels they receive and ability grouping, although this is often perceived through a deficit lens (Hernández-Saca, 2019; Hudak & Kihn, 2001). Hernández-Saca (2019) illustrated a powerful example of the impact of labeling in the lived experience of a Latina student named Sophia with a learning disability (LD). Much like Martin, Sophia had internalized negative messaging about dis/ability in her own use of the word slow, as she compared herself with other students, "probably I am like slow or something, I don't know" (2019, p. 442). Hernández-Saca (2019) emphasized the dis/ability labels affixed to students have an impact on their emotions adding, "students don't experience the positionality of LD divorced from emotion, affect, culture, and other social categories of difference" (p. 425).

Martin, as a student with EBD, showed a resistance to the label and placement which was the likely result of what Iqtadar et al. (2020) described as "internalized disablism," the emotional impact of the multiple processes of racism, ableism, classism, and other forms of social oppression restricting Martin's own agency as a student. On one level, his rejection of the school is an indicator of just how Martin had internalized the societal messages about dis/ability that are laden with deficits. On a deeper level, however, Martin, though having the EBD label, was resisting the ID label for himself. The next excerpt further describes the experiential and opportunity consequences of dis/ability labeling for children with ID.

ISAIAH: THE RIGHT TO PLAY

It was April of 2020 and I had just completed the presentation portion of my dissertation. It was time for the defense. In my mind, I had done the hardest part. I had done the impossible, having gone through all of the intense study, keeping up all of my assistantships, teaching, supervising, and running all over the district to advocate for students in schools, advocating for Isaiah as well as my other children in their schools as well. I was living more than a double consciousness, as powerfully illustrated by DuBois (1994), the reality of always looking at myself through the lens of others, recognizing how many would have contempt for me because of the color of my brown skin and yet moving myself forward as the fulfillment of my ancestors' hopes and sacrifices. I was a doctoral student, a Black woman, a mother of five, and the mother of a child with a dis/ability lacking extensive resources and networks of support. It was important for me to keep my collected countenance for a few more minutes.

One of my attendees, Dr. David Connor, a scholar whose work I greatly admired, asked me about some of the statements one of my study participants had made about being "normal." Althea was the Black mother of a child with Down syndrome like me, whose experiences with her son in the healthcare, school, and community settings were so shockingly disappointing that she began to wonder if the so-called "experts" really understood her child's needs. In one of our interviews, Althea spoke about the administrators at her son's previous school:

> Because of this person there, the principal of the school. She was dealing with the *normals* and she had no idea how to deal with the children that had Down syndrome and how to work with the children that don't work the way the *normals* work. . . . These children have respiratory problems. They have all types of problems. And you have them cooped up in this musty, stinking thing. And they have to walk out in the rain to get from the main school to the portal . . . she just hated me.

None of us had to dig very deep to understand the meaning of Althea's statements. Yet his question was not to clarify Althea's meaning, but rather to uncover my own reaction to what she said about normalcy. It was a moment that unearthed me.

What derailed me in that moment was that I had been working on this research and yet I remained detached from it. I did not realize that I was protecting myself from my own emotions, from revisiting moments that had traumatized me. His words had transported me to a memory that I tucked away neatly and had chosen not to revisit. I remembered being on my way home after dropping off something at the high school for one of my older children and passing by the elementary school. It was just about noon and the children were coming outside to have recess. They were just about my Isaiah's age, the Kindergarten classes. I watched and I waited in my car. I watched them playing, screaming, falling, crying, laughing, and doing what children do. I watched them then go back into the school as the older children started coming out. It suddenly occurred to me that what I was waiting for was not going to happen. Isaiah was not coming out to play. I felt the tears rolling down my cheeks before I even could even feel the impact of my own sorrow. I sat in my car and I wept. I did not cry. These sobs came from deep within, from my soul. I made a sound I did not even know I knew how to make. But what was I weeping for?

In that moment, I wept for his right to play, something so definitive of childhood, that was taken from him. The school had not repaired the gravel on the playground, which made it harder for the ID class, a class so named for children with the label of intellectual disability, to push the wheelchairs out there. Some kids in his class could not go out, so no one went out. They had recess in the classroom, but they did not hear any complaints from the children because no one could speak yet. And they did not hear the complaints from the parents because we did not know. That was what I grieved for, these experiences of joy that the world would take from him as they had taken them from me.

I insert this critical autoethnography here as it turns the lens inward, forcing me to examine the parts of how I have encountered intellectual dis/ability in my family experience. Bochner and Ellis (2016) described how the standardized format of writing may provide restrictive boundaries for exploring more nuanced concepts, particularly around social and cultural identity. The exploration of one's own multiple identities is a hallmark of critical autoethnography, as I explore my emotionality, presence, privileges, marginalization, fears, experience of parenting a child with a dis/ability, social isolation, and resistance. Boylorn and Orbe (2016) note how social tensions often coexist and are captured in the personal narrative, adding "We write as an Other, and for an Other" (p. 5). Finally, the reflexivity that is invoked in the writer through autoethnography is essential for drilling into deeper concepts. *What is it about my participant's testimony that gave me a message about normal? Do I agree with her as a mother of a child with Down syndrome? What message in my own personal history gave me the message that my son was not normal?* These questions are not exclusive to me as a parent, as evidenced in the next excerpt. While the interrogation and reflection of self and one's own positionality is something I continue to do, it is also something that I assign my students across disciplines to do. Within the school of education at my institution, there is no distinction between general education and special education teacher preparation, as educators are expected to leave with the skills prepared for every individual student in their classrooms. My transition supports course involves a field-based component to develop assistive technology to support transitioning high school students. There is typically a great deal of sociocultural dissonance, as the majority of the undergraduate students are white from upper- to middle-class families and do not require any accommodations, while the students they are paired to work with are Black or Latinx and have the label of ID or EBD. As part of this course, I weave in Harry and Kalyanpur's (2012) culturally reciprocal approach to practice, requiring my undergraduates to interrogate their own macro- and microcultural identities and lenses before they interact with students. I ask them to maintain reflective journals throughout the course and prompt them with similar queries. *What are your own ideas about normal? What messages do you receive from your field, your family, your community, and society about normal and how does this impact your expectations with your student?* In their initial reflections, many share how they have never encountered a student with a dis/ability or a student of color and certainly not any student who had experienced intersectionality. By the end of the course, I am never surprised when they produce their students' multimedia portfolios, celebrating all of the strengths and talents they did not expect to encounter. The inner work, before the outer work, is critical for practitioners, considering the ways in which children are so often marginalized.

RHONDA: "THEY LEFT WITHOUT US"

In our book, *Meeting Families Where They Are* (2020), and its case study companion book, *Building Equity through Advocacy in Special Education* (2021), Dr. Beth Harry and I share the story of our participant, Rhonda and her daughter Amira. Amira is a beautiful eighteen-year-old Black girl who is a cheerleader, loves to roller skate, and whose favorite R&B singer is Charlie Wilson. Amira has a dis/ability which to this day remains relatively undetermined, though there may be several IEP documents that read EBD, ID, visual impairment (VI), or some combination of all three. Several practitioners have even suggested that she might have a "touch" of autism spectrum disorder (ASD). Even after subjecting Amira to batteries of tests and diagnostics, Rhonda still does not have a definitive diagnosis for her daughter. Though this may be shocking or confusing to many, it highlights both the ambiguity and power of categories that have done a dance around Black parents like Rhonda since the birth of her child. Rhonda had been told frequently: "We just have to wait and see" (p. 48). The consequences of this vagueness have manifested in Rhonda's fifteen-year battle with the schools, healthcare system, and communities to provide adequate treatment and equitable opportunities for her daughter.

Rhonda is a Black, college-educated single parent, whose family members have left her with a strong legacy of advocacy. Her mother was an educator in the South, and her father a hardworking retired veteran. Both were active in the Civil Rights movement, and though they did not have any experience with dis/ability, they did not see the type of barriers that Rhonda was enduring with Amira as very dissimilar from the struggles for equity they had witnessed and been a part of. Rhonda's two sisters, one of whom she affectionately calls "Big Mama" as she took on the role of encouraging Rhonda in her advocacy for Amira when their mother passed away, have both been continually present at IEP meetings or promoting inclusive but transitioning opportunities on their own. Rhonda has harnessed two very key strategies from the collective strengths, values, and everyday actions of her family members that have served to support her advocacy for Amira. One is her commitment to maintaining a steady economic means to support her two daughters, which she felt were essential in accessing opportunities for enrichment in schools and in the community. Finances not only determine what school one can attend and what resources that school has, but it also designates the recreational activities available in those schools. Finances also play a strong role within the supports for people with dis/abilities; Rhonda shared the impact of the assumptions people even within the dis/ability community as "on services"—that is receiving supplemental support based on income, so often associated with being a person of color. She distinguished herself from this stereotype, though it did not stop the assumption from being made about her or others she encountered. A second point is that it became inconsequential for Rhonda and her family to attach any meaning to a label for Amira, whether she received one or not. She shared how the reading of a book, *Learning without Labels*, changed her life and directed her battle for Amira to be included in every setting.

In the school system, Rhonda's requests for exposure to the general education classroom have been met with the overtures for compliance rather than allowing Amira the opportunity to take advantage of the education that her same-aged, "typically" developing peers were receiving. The process became so frustrating to Rhonda as a mother, she expressed, "There were days when I was breaking down. . . . I was breaking down because you start losing hope. You start feeling like nobody knows or nobody cares, or maybe you're not saying the right words." Though agonizing, Rhonda continued to endure the fight for Amira, advocating really for her to have the "normal" high school experiences that her elder daughter had years prior. She followed the prescribed protocol, using the IEP to voice her requests and document them, a routine she had been reminded to do for years. However, she discovered this process to be superficial, as Amira was placed in EBD classes before even receiving an assessment for behavior. This continued, as Amira remained in self-contained settings throughout her schooling.

In the transition planning meeting held in the summer just prior to the start of Amira's senior year, Rhonda advocated for Amira to have at least one course in a general education classroom, insisting that it be something meaningful to prepare and support her transitioning out of high school. The school personnel resisted, telling her that she would need too much hands-on support and that they were going to "cut out" the in-class paraprofessional supports (Ocasio-Stoutenburg & Harry, 2021). Though Rhonda's efforts were successful in having this documented on Amira's IEP, the reality of its implementation took Rhonda by surprise. In fact, she referred to the circumstances of the COVID-19 pandemic as a "blessing and a curse" as it resulted in transparency with what was truly happening at the school. While the IEP meeting was held in August, it was not until January of the following year for the selected class to be put on Amira's schedule. Furthermore, Amira was told that she would have to "wait for someone" to bring her to the class even though she had attended the same school for four years and went to classes on her own. This school-imposed reliance led to there being only a few times where she actually attended the class before in-person schooling ceased altogether. Amira shared with Rhonda how the staff would say to her, "I'm tired of taking you" (p. 64). Incidents such as this which were peppered throughout Amira's schooling experience led Rhonda to call the IEP, "just a piece of paper" (p. 54).

Rhonda and Amira's experience with school speaks about the limitations of special education and its legislation. There is the expectation that incorporation (parent and/or student input at the IEP meeting) translates into implementation (carrying out the IEP goals, as written) when the reality may be much different. Studies have captured a glimpse of what so many parents endure on a yearly basis, and how this process is mediated by the underlying bureaucracy and hidden rubric of schools. In her study of schools, Voulgarides (2018) underscored the stark difference between compliance with procedures and fidelity.

INTENTIONAL LOVE AND BLACK CHILDREN WITH ID AND EBD

The previous cases describe a snapshot of three different children, at three different ages, who carry the labels ID, EBD, or both. All of these children are Black with African American, Caribbean, or Latinx ethnicity. All of them, throughout the course of their schooling, have been given the message that they are in some way of "less value," "less worthy" of what children are deserving of, based on their dis/ability label or the ambiguity of such. Their experiences are magnified at the intersection of their dis/ability label with their other identities, such as their race or in Martin's case, also being in the foster care system without the permanency, supports, and other advantages that other families might provide children with. Decades of research studies have supported how children of Color as well as whose families are experiencing greater socioeconomic barriers have been disproportionately represented in the categorical labels of ID and EBD. Yet, such labels carry a greater stigma compared to other dis/ability labels, marked by a fixed, deficit-focused perception of difference (Ong-Dean, 2009). Kittay (2019) noted how one of the issues is how much moral value is assigned to cognitive ability, thus devaluing those who are classified as lacking. In addition, reports have also described how children in these categories have been subjected to greater numbers of discriminatory and punitive practices within school settings (Epstein et al., 2017). At the intersection of these social identities, these children may then be considered to be on the margins of already marginalized categories.

As illustrated through these narrative texts of children representing these identities, this work proposes a rationale for novel approaches that educators can take toward supporting children that are subtractive of the systemically embedded ableist, racist, and classist ideologies. Though DSE and SpEd have had distinct trajectories, each field has contributed to the redress of educational injustices experienced by children with dis/abilities throughout history. Simultaneously, these fields have either disrupted or reinforced the conceptualization of normalcy. Borrowing from the collective strengths of these two traditions, this chapter calls for a consilience between these two fields, using love as a centerpiece and intentional practice for children who are further marginalized based on their intersecting identities and dis/ability labels. *What would it mean to love on Black and Brown children with ID and EBD? What if we used this as a framework?* We can use this as a beginning point to empower teachers, caregivers, support personnel, and other stakeholders toward recognizing students' individual support needs, removing the social and environmental barriers that children face, and turning our attention toward revisionist thinking and practices.

"NORMAL" AS PROPERTY: HISTORICAL FOUNDATIONS

With regard to both identity and ability, an expectation has been historically created, a range of normal, indoctrinated in the early practices of eugenics. Gould (1996) described at length how the misuse and interpretations of the scientific method were used to create norms which rendered people outside of the range of "normal deviant" or "abnormal." Such categorizations, corroborated by scientists and medical practitioners, justified discriminatory practices at multiple points in history. Examples of such practices in early American history were the phrenology and craniology experiments on Black men and women. Such experiments were used to render people "inferior," "abnormal"—or even "subhuman"—by scientists' determination in order to be enslaved. In a similar vein, the administration of I.Q. tests could render individuals with disability "abnormal," as Binet (1903) and others sought to prove who was worthy of a public education and henceforth, a place in the world. Gould (1996) in fact, described this shift:

> Craniometric arguments lost much of their luster in our century, as determinists switched their allegiance to intelligence testing—a more "direct" path to the same invalid goal of ranking groups by mental worth—and as scientists exposed the prejudiced nonsense that dominated most literature on the form and size of the head. (p. 140)

Sir Francis Galton's creation of a "social Darwinism" would generate theories about genetic fitness that excluded people who fell outside of these norms (Dudley-Marling & Gurn, 2010).

Certainly, pathologizing persons with dis/abilities was problematic on its own, but consider the wielding power of justifying decisions on what to do with and about them (Artiles, 2011). Exclusion from schools and communities was at the discretion of the gatekeepers, who were both administrators and parents. Their criminalization, based on their "deviance" however, could potentially serve broader economic and social purposes (Artiles, 2013; Carey, 2009). For one, it could remove the "abnormal" and "undesirable" persons from the public which could be viewed as protective. Second, it could justify the creation of institutions, advertised as places of care. The medical and psychological communities were aligned with this movement, rendering parents unable to make decisions and placing the care of children with dis/abilities in the hands of qualified professionals. C. Anderson Aldrich, a renowned physician, outlined the practices of removing children with Down syndrome from their mothers shortly after birth to be placed in institutions. The quotation below reflects the eugenic, deficit-laden attitudes toward people with Down syndrome:

> From the standpoint of the child's living an adequate social life, the prognosis is worse. I have often remarked the better they were, the worse off they were. The inadequacy which is inevitable in mongolism is not so noticeable if the child is an evident idiot and if he is treated appropriately. But if he "almost makes the grade" and tries to enter freely into the competition of civilized living, his experience is usually devastating and may lead to serious social situations. (Aldrich, 1947, p. 127)

Though disturbing, this quote represented standard medical practice at the time, as renowned physicians such as Aldrich and Dr. Benjamin Spock would encourage the institutionalization of children with Down syndrome very shortly after birth. Because they were respected in their fields, such framing contributed to the social stigma toward children. What is remarkable, however, is how little this had to do with medical science or even ability; for Aldrich was clearly describing graver "social situations" for persons with Down syndrome whose features were more similar to individuals without dis/abilities. The use of language, the "civilized" is purposely juxtaposed to underscore the lack of civility of the person with Down syndrome.

The Intersectional Lens

It is important to look at the history of normalcy, as it sets the foundation for examining how normalcy is constructed for students with dis/abilities and other intersecting identities. I emphasize an understanding of intersectionality as intended by critical legal scholar Kimberlee Crenshaw (1991) viewing it as a confluence and duality of oppression rather than separate experiences in tandem. The first consideration is the phenomenon of within-disability marginalization, that is, the experience of being further marginalized within an already marginalized group of dis/ability (Ong-Dean, 2009). Though it is hard to imagine these hierarchical patterns being reproduced within a disenfranchised group, even dis/ability labels are rank-ordered based on their proximity to what is deemed normal, as Thorius (2019) noted "normalcy operates to maintain positions of superiority for some and inferiority for others" (p. 211). In our book, *Meeting Families Where They Are*, one of our participants, Patty, the grandmother of a young boy named Richard with Williams Syndrome, so powerful described ID as the "underprivileged dis/ability" because of its ambiguity, lack of supports, and lack of power among those who advocate for it. Down syndrome is one such example of a stigmatized dis/ability associated with ID. Despite the decades of both research and media supporting the strengths and potential of people with Down syndrome, for example, ableism persists even before these children are born. Advancements in prenatal screening have resulted in doctors pressuring mothers to terminate their children based on the likelihood and/or confirmation of diagnosis (Skotko, 2005; Lalvani, 2008; Sheets et al., 2014; Marshall et al., 2014; Ocasio-Stoutenburg, 2020). Moreover, studies have reported how women who have chosen to forgo further testing and/or abortion and keep their children have experienced othering by the healthcare professionals and community members (Gabel & Kotel, 2015; Lalvani, 2008; Ocasio-Stoutenburg, 2020). In a third layer, research has reported the limited opportunities of children with ID in schools, associating this label with a "fixed" status and offering fewer opportunities and access to the general education curriculum (Gabel et al., 2013). These experiences are in stark comparison with the less stigmatizing LD, a category that scholars have noted that was advocated for by many white and middle-class parents sought to create and justify in order for their children to maintain access to both learning preferences and social status. (Sleeter, 1987; Ong-Dean, 2009). In contrast, with LD, Ong-Dean (2009) adds, "some causes, such as Down syndrome, which is defined by readily identifiable chromosomal abnormalities, are seen as inevitably tied to mental retardation, or, at least, to low-average cognitive ability" (p. 79).

A second exploration involves probing the magnification of marginalization that occurs at the conjunction of dis/ability and race. Disability critical race theory (DisCrit) by Annamma, Connor, and Ferri (2012) has been particularly useful in conceptualizing how racism and ableism operate to maintain the dominance and supremacy of being white, middle class, and able throughout history. Artiles et al. (2016) provided a powerful description of how this has been historically and pervasively operationalized in schooling:

> Since the post-World War II civil rights legislation, intersectionality around disability and difference has played havoc with the concept of student rights as a primary reform mechanism in public education. If intersectionality is not the only barrier to an effective education for diverse populations, it is an important complicating factor. (p. 791)

The Intent of Special Education

The field of special education was a product from the concerted efforts of policymakers, disability rights activists, and the majority of white middle-class parent activists as a redress to the exclusion of children with dis/abilities from schools (Ong-Dean, 2009). The intent was to codify their rights and to guarantee the provisions of education and related services, to push back on the static, deterministic view of children while placing greater emphasis on their potential (Turnbull et al., 2011). The momentum and legislative success of the Civil Rights Movement helped to propel these movements forward. Using the arguments of the 14th Amendment, which had already secured the landmark legislation of *Brown vs. Board of Education of Topeka (1954)* rendering the segregation and exclusion of children from schools on the basis on race unconstitutional, the white middle-class parent advocacy movement followed suit in securing the rights for their children with dis/abilities under Public Law 95-145, The Education for all Handicapped Children (EHA) in 1975, which became what we know today as the Individuals with Disabilities with Education Act (IDEA, 2004). As the children of these white middle-class parents reached adulthood, a divergence of these movements occurred, as young adults with disabilities lobbied for their own rights to decide how and where they want to live, thus the mantra "nothing about us without us" (Charlton, 1998).

Labeling without love leads to dehumanization
They took away our ancestors' names
Gave them a new one
Told them, "This is what we'll call you now."
Their real names we'll never know.
Now they take our children's names
Give them a label
Tell them, "This is who you are now."
But I say their names
Cuz who they are they'll never know.

One foundational underpinning of special education hinges on the belief in intrinsic differences in children, based on a standard distribution, a "normal" curve for intelligence, behaviors, and even social and emotional skills through the medical-psychological model of disability. Hudak and Kihn (2001) described the "staying power" of labels in schools and how it predisposes practitioners' thinking and practices about children before even encountering them. This is especially evident in a forum where assessments and evaluations are ongoing and have the power to make decisions about where and how children are educated.

One of the consequences of *labeling without love* is that it creates categories that describe children according to a standard or norm, to focus on their deficits and little attention to their strengths, capabilities, and potential: hence, *dis*-dash (/)-*abilities*. In addition, *labeling without love* tends to operate along a framework that emphasizes supposed "neutrality" in a world of social hierarchies that has racializes, stigmatizes, and discriminates. To examine what this looks like, we need to include the historical experiences of Black and Brown children with dis/abilities in schools.

Four decades of scholarship reported on the parallel movements that emerged post desegregation based on Color and ability. The exodus of white middle-class families from public schools, known as the "white flight" was a consequence of racism and ableism, as many white middle-class women parents believed their children's education would be negatively affected by the presence of children in schools who held more socially stigmatized identities (Eitle, 2002; Blanchett et al., 2005; Ong-Dean, 2009). Blanchett et al. (2005) described the response to desegregation as *a resegregation into special education categories*. Scholars reported on the inequities in special education identification and practices, as Black, Brown, Indigenous children, and children experiencing challenges in socioeconomic status were disproportionately funneled into the categories of "mental retardation" (now known as intellectual disability), emotional and behavioral disturbance, and tracked into nonacademic classes in spite of the capabilities they displayed outside of school settings (Artiles, 2011; Artiles & Trent, 2004; Losen & Orfield, 2002; Harry & Klingner, 2014; Mercer, 1973).

What then could have been the response of advocates to combat these unjust practices? Castles (1994) described how important the social movement away from the very stigmatized label of "mental retardation" was for white Americans, to hold on to the conceptions of normalcy. In many ways, normalcy could be perceived as white property, a type of capital to be acquired and protected (Harris, 1993). Those who had the means to fight for the normalcy of their children with dis/abilities were white and middle- to upper-class families, as they had the social, economic, and cultural capital to do so to the further marginalization of Black and Brown families of children with dis/abilities (Groce, 1999; Ong-Dean, 2009; Skrtic & Knackstedt, 2019). Scholars also described how researchers and white parents advocates pushed toward the creation of elite special education categories such as learning disability (LD), which Ong-Dean referred to as the "high road" from dis/ability to move away from the more stigmatizing categories of "mental retardation." Other categories have since been created, such as Attention Deficit Hyperactivity Disorder (ASHD) and Autism Spectrum Disorder (ASD), which rely on a clinician for the diagnosis and for whom children of Color have been under-identified and historically excluded (Gillborn et al., 2016; Ong-Dean, 2009; Pearson & Meadan, 2017; Sleeter, 1987).

In summary, the creation of the "low" and stigmatized categories of dis/abilities are reflected in their *label without love* and hence, in the racism, classism, and implicit biases through which children of Color have been so readily placed in. In many ways, parents, especially Black, Indigenous, and Latinx, Native, and other parents of color may find themselves unable to resist against this categorization, as the process of identification places these parents and caregivers in the role of "passive recipients" rather than objective observers of their children's needs (Harry, 1992).

Someone Else's Determination

As evidenced in the three cases, Martin, Isaiah, and Amira are all recipients of someone else's determination of their potential and capabilities. Whether or not these labels are accurate, static, or should be so deterministic are questions that are irrelevant to what takes place in practice. Though parents, caregivers, and advocates are present in the meetings to determine eligibility and outline the goals, whether or not they will be executed and how is at the discretion of school personnel. Quite often, as Voulgarides (2018) noted, schools will find ways to be compliant in order to evade the legal consequences of not following the letter of the law.

Parents and caregivers who also recognize that there are intrinsic differences in their children are at the mercy of systems that are presumed to be neutral, when they are rooted in the same eugenic and deficit-framed practices. In my doctoral dissertation, focused on the advocacy experiences of nine families of children with Down syndrome, mothers reported being subjected to intense pressures to confirm their children's suspected diagnosis of Down syndrome in order to terminate. As aligned with prior studies on mothers of children with Down syndrome, the children and mothers were stigmatized and robbed of the joy of a pregnancy and birth experience (Gabel & Kotel, 2015; Lalvani, 2011). However, Black mothers were even further marginalized, their concerns dismissed by professionals and receiving a diagnosis much later than any of the other parents (Ocasio-Stoutenburg, 2020). Children who are at the mercy of multiple systems, relying on external advocates, are at an even greater disadvantage without a consistent voice that is *strewn in love*.

The Disability Studies in Education Contribution

During the deinstitutionalization movement which continued into the early 1980s, Wolf Wolfensberger, who had coined the previous term "normalization" reconceptualized this into a new theory which he called "social role valorization." This proposed defining social roles for people with dis/abilities in society that others value, which in turn help them to become valued by society. Such utilitarian views of children with dis/abilities coupled with the determinism of special education left little room for exploring the intrinsic value of children with dis/abilities.

A new field, Disability Studies in Education (DSE) emerged which described how processes in the educational and social setting serve to disable children rather than there being intrinsic "deficits" (Artiles, 2013). This field aligned with a social vs. a medical-psychological model of disability. Rather than pathologizing children and operating from a "'diagnose' and 'treat' the 'problem'" framework, DSE highlighted the negative and deficit-laden assumptions that turn human variation into a disempowering condition, which can be constructed and reconstructed over time (Collins et al., 2015, p. 11).

Researchers also challenged the parameters for determining normalcy in intelligence and behaviors. These standards, based upon the average of white middle-class standard mean of errors, could not explain human beings. Dudley-Marling and Gurn (2010) in the *Myth of the Normal Curve* noted how the normal curve was never intended to be explanatory of phenomena so complex as the human experience, let alone measure intelligence. Davis and Sumara (2010), for example, proposed complexity theory as a way of understanding human difference, rejecting the concept of "normal" which is a foundational assumption upon which special education is based, adding: "Teachers can understand the learning of individual children, for example, but predicting future performance based on a test score or educational label, which in turn is based on normative assumptions—is foolhearty and destructive" (p. 4). In addition to the issues of identification, DSE problematizes the power placed within professionals as making the determination about children based on their dis/ability, family socioeconomic experience, race, and ethnicity. It assumes that the clinician can make these determinations objectively and that their judgment is the correct one.

An additional contribution to the understanding of DSE is to highlight the social, ecological, and environmental barriers that disempower people, rather than to define their traits and attributes as lacking. Black and Brown children are surveilled in body and in mind by schools, children are policed by school personnel, and labeling is the mechanism by which students can be pushed out of the classrooms. Artiles (2013) reported how Black children are "three times more likely to be diagnosed as intellectually disabled and over 200% more likely to be diagnosed with emotional behavioral disorders" (p. 330). The means by which these children are identified are through testing, which research has also found to be inconsistent in methods across the nation as well as subject to a great degree of subjectivity (Donovan & Cross, 2002; Hosp & Rechly, 2002).

Life Without Labels

The contributions of DSE place value in the child and their unique and intrinsic qualities rather than the societally based and determined values, while also uncovering the racist, ableist, and eugenic roots of special education. This has certainly pushed back on the medicalized model of dis/ability which has in turn generalized differences, while further stigmatizing children. Critics of the DSE model discuss several concerns about this field, that it might shift worldviews so much that it could over-promote positive dis/ability identities, encourage the advocacy for inclusive placements, or compromise the field of special education (Anastasiou & Kauffman, 2011; Anastasiou et al., 2016; Connor, 2019). Though few could argue the necessity for the field of special education, which has educated children who had been excluded from public schools, it is challenging to see how the preceding concepts could be negative when they support the value of children with dis/abilities. Connor (2019) noted one very concerning critique of the DSE model specifically focused on DSE's disruption of normalcy, quoting the authors, "we find denial of disability, the idea of celebrating disability, or trying in some way to disparage the idea of 'normal' to be regressive and cruel to those with disabilities" (Kauffman & Badar, p. 59, as cited in Connor, 2019).

Special education, though supportive in its intent, operates through an extremely bureaucratic system, dense with educational and legal jargon which puts families advocating for their children at a disadvantage (Bacon & Causton-Theoharis, 2013; Ong-Dean, 2009). However stringent, this process is a gatekeeper for services for children who need them, determining therapies within and outside of the school to support the academic, emotional, physical, and social needs of children and youth with dis/abilities. In the case of all three children, Martin, Isaiah, and Amira, it determined what their classrooms and schools looked like, the kinds of supports and accommodations they needed, and where they would play, as determined by the practitioners.

Secondly, there are the "dangerous assumptions" that still prevail, once again the consequence of still being educated in an inequitable educational system. Professionals still rely on a system of labels, documents to describe, define, and plan. In a study of secondary special education teachers by Cavendish et al. (2019), one described her preference for the labels in understanding the behaviors of students, "personally, I always want to know [the disability label] because I'm like, 'Oh, that explains *that*'" (p. 22). All the while, there is the within dis/ability hierarchy to contend with, the fact that ID and EBD are labels that carry greater stigma and that these categories have disproportionate numbers of Black and Brown students who are subjected to disproportionate suspensions and expulsions from schools (Artiles, 2013; Losen et al., 2015; Ong-Dean, 2009). Dis/ability Critical Race Studies (DisCrit), a framework conceptualized by Annamma et al. (2016) to interrogate white and ability supremacy in education, is useful for exploring how this experience is even more magnified for children at these intersections, more than race or dis/ability alone.

TOWARD A VALUE-BASED COUNTERNARRATIVE

Circling back to the experiences of Martin, Isaiah, and Amira, we can understand the dilemma that parents, caregivers, and children may collectively experience. Children and families are caught in systems that provide mixed messages about their value and worth. This phenomenon has been described by Martha Minow (1990) as the "dilemma of difference" whereby understanding the unique needs of the children with dis/abilities forces one to be simultaneously thrust into a never-ending battle for the child to be valued in society. It begins with the fundamental question: "What determines children's value?" This is the question that seems to be answered for children with Intellectual Disability (ID) and Emotional Behavioral Disorder (EBD). Carlson and Kittay (2010) apply this question toward children with ID framed in justice:

> Are those with cognitive disabilities due the same respect and justice due to those who have no significant cognitive impairments? Are the grounds of our moral obligation different when a human being may lack certain cognitive faculties that are often understood as the basis for moral personhood? Are those with significant cognitive impairment moral persons? . . . Are the people with cognitive disabilities, especially those labelled as "mentally retarded," distinct, morally speaking, from nonhuman animals? (pp. 1–2)

In their work, *Why Are So Many Students of Color in Special Education*, Harry and Klingner (2022) eloquently described how special education is a result of the set of social dynamics by which disempowerment is created, constructed, and accepted as reality. In their description of Matthew, a boy labeled under EBD, these scholars illustrated the dilemma that causes the very contention between special education and DSE:

> This is not to say that Matthew had no problems. Rather, it is to say that, once the discourse of disability was set in motion, Matthews' problems came to be defined as a dis/ability, and that dis/ability as a fact. The concept of dis/ability become reified—made into a "thing" that belonged to Matthew, a thing that would be very difficult to discard. (2022, p. 42)

Harry and Klingner (2022) went further to address the potential counterarguments:

> A common objection to this interpretation of events might be the question, "But are you saying Matthew did not have a disability? Or is there no such thing as a dis/ability?" We would answer that there is an infinite range of abilities among individuals, and that, while there are certainly individuals whose capacities are much more limited than the average, it is society's decisions related to such individuals that determine whether they will be called *disabled*. (p. 12, emphasis mine)

It is important to note that the preceding excerpts posit Matthew's dis/ability as a deficit. Problematizing this framing is essential from both a Disability Justice and Critical Disability Studies framework, as these approaches would not position dis/ability as a deficit or something we would need to "fix," "cure," or "avoid," but rather as a reality of the full human expression. Given that from a biological and anthropological point of view, as human beings, we will all, at some point in our human trajectory, experience dis/ability, it is not something to avoid. In proposing that scholars begin to use a DSE framework in addressing the issues of disproportionality, Collins et al. (2016) noted the importance for researchers to "doing no harm" when students of Color are constantly in jeopardy in school contexts, subjected to continual surveillance and being funneled into categories and segregated classrooms. I would take this one step further to add the intentionality and application of a love ethic.

DSE AND SPECIAL EDUCATION: INTENTIONALITY OF A LOVE ETHIC

Because children and youth with ID and EBD carry a more stigmatized label, there is a need to be more intentional about teaching practices that are rooted in a practice of care and love. Gay (2018) described the importance of providing nurturing environments for children of color. It is also of even greater relevance to apply Thorius and Tan's (2016) extension of Ladson-Billings' (2006) educational debt toward Black, Brown, Native, and Indigenous students carrying stigmatized dis/ability labels of ID and EBD. Subjected to decades of mistreatment, misidentification, and inequitable opportunities that may have begun so early on, we can understand how intentional we need to be in order to repay what we owe.

I borrow the work of scholar and activist bell hooks (2000) who spoke extensively about love as an intentional, political, and transformational practice. Rooted in African American traditions and addressing issues of oppression, hook's conceptualization of love as an emancipatory action is particularly applicable to Black, Brown, Native, and Indigenous students with ID and EBD, whose experiences in schools have denied them of the care, love, and value by the systems and persons entrusted to provide for them. Countering the dominant narrative on Black children with EBD and ID, who are given devaluing messages, hooks' words, "everyone has the right to be free, to live fully, and well," are particularly radical and juxtaposed against traditions and a climate that dictates otherwise (2000, p. 87). Most central to this ethic is the recapturing of the dignity, value, and worth of students who are among the marginalized of the marginalized, not just through discourse but through intentional actions.

Incorporating this love ethic into the *collective contributions of both DSE and Special Education*, fields that have been traditionally diametrically opposed, may seem daunting, but it is promising. Special education has contributed to the construct of what normal is and how that conceptualization manifests in schools. DSE, on the other hand, has challenged that construction by providing powerful counternarratives to the deficit-driven definitions of "normal" by reframing dis/ability as an expression of humanness while reimagining schools as inclusive spaces. Both fields have also demonstrated the power to redress systems of inequity for children with dis/abilities, though in different ways. I apply the love ethic to the contributions from each field in order to develop a series of questions:

(1) Do we accept that all children have value? Are we presuming a color-evasiveness stance (Annamma et al., 2018; Bonilla-Silva, 2006)? Are we taking a color-evasive stance to dis/ability (Annamma et al., 2018)? Do we acknowledge that there are stigmas attached to dis/abilities? Do we love the children we support, unconditionally?

(2) How are we giving our labels to children and their families? Are we telling them with love and care in mind? Are we congratulating them on the birth of a child who may need supports that others might not? How do we deliver that diagnosis, that label? Do we frame that in love?

(3) How do we evaluate? Do we emphasize that it is one test, one snapshot but not inclusive of that child's potential? Do we note the limitations, and acknowledge the standards upon which they were created? Are we relying on this as our data to understand children? Is it informed by love, by care?
(4) How have we come to understand why there are labeling, identification, and referral processes in the first place? Do we accept this as determination? Do we explore the historical and underlying issues of racism, ableism, classism, and implicit bias in these processes? In reporting data? How do we redress these issues at the microlevel and the systemic level?
(5) Do we remind ourselves that families of children with dis/abilities are engaged in discourses with professionals that reflect power differentials? Can we understand how these engagements may have an impact on the services their children receive? Are we simply complying with the law or are we incorporating their input? Do we address families with respect and garner their input?
(6) Do we acknowledge that all children do not receive services equitably and appropriately? How can we address this issue?
(7) Are we willing to share power with stakeholders, including teachers, parents and caregivers, community workers, administrators, and other support persons? Even if that means giving up some of our own?

This is by no means an exhaustive list. Godden (2019), in her adaptation of a love ethic for social work practice, reiterates an important caveat for understanding hooks' work, "Glass (2010) accentuated hook's standpoint that love alone cannot resolve difficulties, but is a vital starting point for transformative action" (p. 409). These questions are the beginning toward the intentional love we need to have for Black children with ID and EBD.

CONCLUSION

They say normal is constructed
But it's hatred deconstructed
Joy of motherhood disrupted
Through that label they're inducted
Without us being consulted
Black childhood interrupted
They say they need it to be instructed
Their walk, their speech adjusted
It's a system still corrupted
Children overlooked and mistrusted.

The fight continues until you see them:
None of it matters when love is your lens.

I am grateful to be able to share parts of Martin's story, Amira's, through the eyes of Rhonda, and Isaiah's story through my own eyes. Though these stories recount systemic failure and testimonies that are painful, they are also telling a story of resistance, people of value who are recognizing that something is wrong in the school environment. Though each of these children has a need for support, the weight of issues they experience falls on the barriers imposed upon them. These stories are our collective responses to Kübler-Ross' (1960) grief model, a model of death and mourning that professionals have so inappropriately imposed upon parents of children with dis/abilities for years, that I find particularly unmatched to Black dis/ability families. They believe we are in denial; they believe we are all grieving the loss of normalcy, normalcy by the established, generated standards. These are societal standards, not ours, and in many ways we were already out of alignment by virtue of our Blackness in a world that maintains white race, ability and middle to high socioeconomic wealth as supreme. By our own assessments, our children are "normal" in every way. This is not undone by our participation in a system that unfortunately labels and socially stigmatizes children in order to get their needed supports and services, as noted in my dissertation:

> We must subscribe to the very system we hate in order to get what he needs. And until we have that, very sadly, we are conceding to the framing of systems in education, health and communities that use the term "special" to describe the very basic things that any child would need. This is our painful dilemma. (Ocasio-Stoutenburg, 2020, p. 88)

Today the ice cream truck drove by in our neighborhood and my daughter Olivia flagged down the driver in order to buy an ice cream cone for Isaiah. When she paid for his cone, the driver said to her,

> "Listen, even if you don't have money, always wave me down. I'll always give him ice cream for free."
> "Oh no, you don't have to do that," Olivia said. "We'll pay for it."
> He touched his heart and said, "For him, no charge. If he's happy, I'm happy."

A critical step in my own emergence as an advocate is the ability to recognize love as a radical yet quintessential factor in all things. When Olivia shared this with me, I paused for a moment and thought about the joy my son brings people without uttering a word, without having to merit their approval by passing a test or displaying some sort of special talent. What a different world we might have for our children with dis/abilities if everyone—from practitioners to community members to law enforcement to policymakers—saw children this way. A little light, a little joy, a little love.

REFERENCES

Aldrich, C. A. (1947). Preventive medicine and mongolism. *American Journal of Mental Deficiency, 69*, 391–401.

Anastasiou, D., & Kauffman, J. M. (2011). A social constructionist approach to dis-ability: Implications for special education. *Exceptional Children, 77*(3), 367–384.

Anastasiou, D., Kauffman, J. M., & Michail, D. (2016). Disability in multicultural theory: Conceptual and social justice issues. *Journal of Disability Policy Studies, 27*(1), 3–12.

Annamma, S. A., Boelé, A. L., Moore, B. A., & Klingner, J. (2013). Challenging the ideology of normal in schools. *International Journal of Inclusive Education, 17*(12), 1278–1294.

Annamma, S. A., Connor, D. J., & Ferri, B. (2016). *DisCrit: Disability studies and critical race theory in education*. Teachers College Press.

Annamma, S. A., Jackson, D., & Morrison, D. (2016). Conceptualizing color-evasiveness: Using dis/ability critical race theory to expand a color-blind racial ideology in education and beyond. *Race, Ethnicity and Education, 20*(2), 147–162.

Artiles, A. J. (2011). Toward an interdisciplinary understanding of educational equity and difference: The case of the racialization of ability. *Educational Researcher, 40*(9), 431–445.

Artiles, A. J. (2013). Untangling the racialization of disabilities. *Du Bois Review, 10*(2), 329–347.

Artiles, A. J., Trent, S. C., & Palmer, J. (2004). Culturally diverse students in special education: Legacies and prospects. In J. A. Banks & C. M. Banks (Eds.), *Handbook of research on multicultural education* (2nd ed., pp. 716–735). Jossey-Bass.

Bacon, J. K., & Causton-Theoharis, J. (2013). "It should be teamwork": A critical investigation of school practices and parent advocacy in special education. *International Journal of Inclusive Education, 17*(7), 682–699.

Baldwin, J. (1993). *The fire next time* (First Vintage International ed.). Vintage International.

Binet, A. (1903). *L'étude expérimentale de l'intelligence*. Schleicher frères & cie.

Blanchett, W. J., Mumford, V., & Beachum, F. (2005). Urban school failure and disproportionality in a post-brown era: Benign neglect of the constitutional rights of students of color. *Remedial and Special Education, 26*(2), 70–81.

Bochner, A., & Ellis, C. (2016). *Evocative autoethnography : Writing lives and telling stories*. Routledge.

Bonilla-Silva, E. (2003). *Racism without racists: Color-blind racism and the persistence of racism in the United States*. Rowman & Littlefield.

Bourdieu, P. (1998). *Practical reason: On the theory of action*. Stanford University Press.

Boylorn, R. M., & Orbe, M. P. (Eds.). (2020). *Critical autoethnography: Intersecting cultural identities in everyday life*. Routledge.

Carey, A. C. (2009). *On the margins of citizenship: Intellectual disability and civil rights in twentieth-century America*. Temple University Press.

Carlson, L., & Kittay, E. F. (2010). Introduction: Rethinking philosophical presumptions in light of cognitive disability. In E. F. Kittay & L. Carlson (Eds.), *Cognitive disability and its challenge to moral philosophy* (pp. 1–26). Wiley-Blackwell.

Castles, K. (2004). "Nice, average Americans": Postwar parents' groups and the defense of the normal family. In S. Noll & J. W. Trent Jr. (Eds.), *Mental retardation in America: A historical reader* (pp. 351–370). New York University Press.

Cavendish, W., Morris, C. T., Chapman, L. A., Ocasio-Stoutenburg, L., & Kibler, K. (2020). Teacher perceptions of implementation practices to support secondary students in special education. *Preventing School Failure: Alternative Education for Children and Youth, 64*(1), 19–27.

Charlton, J. I. (1998). *Nothing about us without us* (1st ed.). University of California Press.

Connor, D. J. (2019). Why is special education so afraid of disability studies? Analyzing attacks of disdain and distortion from leaders in the field. *Journal of Curriculum Theorizing, 34*(1), 10–23.

Denzin, N. K. (1994). Romancing the text: The qualitative researcher-writer-as-bricoleur. *Bulletin of the Council for Research in Music Education, 122*, 15–30.

Donovan, S., & Cross, C. (2002). *Minority students in special and gifted education*. National Academy Press.

DuBois, W. E. B. (1994). *The souls of Black folk*. Dover.

Dudley-Marling, C., & Gurn, A. (Eds.). (2010). *The myth of the normal curve* (Vol. 11). Peter Lang.

Eitle, T. M. (2002). Special education or racial segregation: Understanding variation in the representation of Black students in educable mentally handicapped programs. *The Sociological Quarterly, 43*(4), 575–605.

Gabel, S., & Kotel, K. (2015). Motherhood in the context of normative discourse: Birth stories of mothers of children with Down syndrome. *Journal of Medical Humanities, 39*(2), 179–193.

Gay, G. (2010). *Culturally responsive teaching* (2nd ed.). Teachers College Press.

Gillborn, D., Rollock, N., Vincent, C., & Ball, S. (2016). The black middle classes, education, racism, and dis/ability. In D. Connor, B. Ferri, & S. Annamma (Eds.), *DisCrit: Disability studies and critical race theory in education*. Teachers College Press.

Godden, N. J. (2017). The love ethic: A radical theory for social work practice. *Australian Social Work, 70*(4), 405–416.

Gould, S. J. (1996). *The mismeasure of man*. W.W. Norton and Company.

Groce, N. (1999). Disability in cross-cultural perspective: Rethinking disability. *The Lancet, 354*(9180), 756–757.

Harris, C. I. (1993). Whiteness as property. *Harvard Law Review, 106*(8), 1707–1791.

Harry, B. (1992). An ethnographic study of cross-cultural communication with Puerto Rican-American families in the special education system. *American Educational Research Journal, 29*(3), 471–494.

Harry, B., & Klingner, J. K. (2022). *Why are so many students of color in special education? Understanding race & disability in schools*. Teachers College Press.

Harry, B., & Ocasio-Stoutenburg, L. (2020). *Meeting families where they are: Building equity through advocacy with diverse schools and communities*. Teachers College Press

Hernández-Saca, D. I. (2019). Re-framing master narratives of dis/ability through an affective lens: Sophia Cruz's LD story at her intersections. *Anthropology & Education Quarterly, 50*(4), 424–447.

hooks, bell. (2000). *All about love: New visions* (1st ed.). William Morrow.

Hudak, G., & Kihn, P. (2001). *Labeling: Pedagogy and politics*. Routledge Falmer.

Iqtadar, S., Hernández-Saca, D. I., & Ellison, S. (2020). "If it wasn't my race, it was other things like being a woman, or my disability": A qualitative research synthesis of disability research. *Disability Studies Quarterly, 40*(2).

Kauffman, J. M., & Badar, J. (2018). Extremism and disability chic. *Exceptionality, 26*(1), 46–61.

Kittay, E. (2019). *Learning from my daughter: The value and care of disabled minds*. Oxford University Press.

Kübler-Ross, E. (1969). *On Death and Dying*. Routledge.

Lalvani, P. (2011). Constructing the (m)other: Dominant and contested narratives on mothering a child with Down syndrome. *Narrative Inquiry, 21*(2), 276–293.

Losen, D. J., Ee, J., Hodson, C., & Martinez, T. (2015). Disturbing inequities: Exploring the relationship between racial disparities in special education identification and discipline. In D. Losen (Ed.), *Closing the school discipline gap: Equitable remedies for excessive exclusion* (pp. 89–117). Teachers College Press.

Losen, D. J., & Orfield, G. (2002). *Racial inequity in special education*. Harvard Education Publishing Group.

Mercer, J. R. (1973). *Labeling the mentally retarded* (pp. 197–221). University of California Press.

Minow, M. (1990). *Making all the difference: Inclusion, exclusion, and American law*. Cornell University Press.

Ocasio-Stoutenburg, L. L. (2020). *Voices of diversity in parent advocacy for children with down syndrome: Intersectional and contextual considerations for special education and health care practitioners* (Doctoral dissertation), University of Miami.

Ong-Dean, C. (2009). *Distinguishing disability: Parents, privilege, and special education*. University of Chicago Press.

Sleeter, C. (1986). Learning dis/abilities: The social construction of a special education category. *Exceptional Children, 53*(1), 46–54.

Thorius, K. A. K., & Tan, P. (2015). Expanding analysis of educational debt: Considering intersections of race and ability. In S. A. Annamma, D. J. Connor, &

B. Ferri (Eds.), *DisCrit: Disability studies and critical race theory in education* (pp. 87–970). Teachers College Press.

Turnbull, A. P., Turnbull, R., Erwin, E. J., Soodak, L. C., & Shogren, K. A. (2011). *Families, professionals, and exceptionality: Positive outcomes through partnerships and trust*. Pearson.

Voulgarides, C. (2018). *Does compliance matter in special education? IDEA and the hidden inequities of practice*. Teachers College Press.

Chapter 6

Boundaries of Disability Studies and Special Education

Radical Pedagogy and Relatedness

Jane Strauss

E. O. Wilson was a biologist in the middle of the last century when he developed the concept of consilience, the integration of knowledge from a variety of perspectives and fields of study, for the physical and natural sciences. Physics, chemistry, and biology do integrate well, as all address matter, individuals, and communities at a variety of levels of complexity. Wilson acknowledged that social sciences can generally be integrated into the model; his view was very broad, but he did not include educational policy, research, or theory.

Disability Justice (DJ) takes the perspective that all forms of bias and discrimination including ableism intersect and magnify each other. This is seen in the school setting, in which males of color are often labeled as deviant and set on the school to prison pipeline in the early grades, (Flynn, 2009.) and in which, when I was a child, in the 1960s, girls were not given extra help to succeed academically just because of their gender (Lived Experience, 1958–1971). These patterns continue to the present day, even with changes in legal requirements for "Special Education," and analyzing *how* the process functions/dysfunctions through a DJ lens and across disciplines may help to reorient gals and provide new directions toward improvement.

I have chosen to integrate educational theory, philosophy, literature, social psychology, and the pragmatic application of law and regulation in analysis of the intersection of Special Education (SpEd) and Disability Studies in Education (DSE). The texts chosen for analysis have all informed my own thinking over the course of five decades, and have helped develop my praxis—the analytical thought that leads to my modes of action as a radical advocate. A radical advocate goes to the root of issues rather than just acting on surface perceptions. These works interact with each other and with law and systems as they currently exist—and, viewed through their lenses, law and systems are found wanting. Input of a critical friend (Schuck & Russell, 2005) was crucial to the process of final analysis, writing, and editing.

I have approached this material as a participant-observer (wearing the hats of dis/Abled[1] person, student, parent, advocate, and teacher over time) with an interdisciplinary academic background.[2] Using as a framework the history and current status of modern special education policy, limited as it is by Law and Precedents attempts to define everything precisely (in the process losing humanity), this work will apply concepts raised in Freire's (1970), Buber's (1970 trans.), de Saint-Exupéry's (2000 trans.), and Goffman's (1963) work.[3] The need for relatedness, human-to-human, as a larger part of teacher-student interactions is borne out by these works, a reality too often left out in legal policies and decisions. DJ (Berne et al., 2018), however, requires relatedness from its beginnings: intersectionality (Tenet 1), cross-movement (Tenet 4), cross-disability (Tenet 7), and solidarity and interdependence (Tenet 8) all require relationships. Special education law must be radically reshaped through DJ and the works cited above and below in order to gain humanity. The special education system exists, and all these disciplines are related to its application, either in its functionality or potential for improvement in the twenty-first century.

This work was initially conceived in 2017, more than two years before the COVID-19 pandemic turned educational services as previously known on their heads, closing schools and largely transforming education into a distance learning proposition. As my focus in this work is on the crucial nature of relationship and humanizing SpEd, and remote learning mediates this task through electronic communication, a potential barrier to relatedness, the means of accomplishing it may be more challenging than before.

Students may need or benefit from application of SpEd techniques; however, this discipline is currently wandering (Alvarez, 2016; Levenson, 2011): Modifications in the system to improve its effectiveness and render it more humane will, in the long term, result in greater comfort for students and improved learning and academic progress (Sparks, 2013). A critical part of comfort in the school environment results from relatedness and the students' ability to relate to instructional personnel (Egalite & Kisida, 2018). From Martin Buber (1970), Antoine de Saint-Exupéry (1942), Paulo Freire (2014), and subsequent authors, we learn that relatedness and relationships are imperative. From Erving Goffman (1963) we learn that stigma breeds in alienation and lack of relatedness, and results in a spiral of failure. DJ mandates cross-disability and intersectional considerations in education. This is at the boundary of traditional SpEd and DSE.

HISTORY OF MODERN SPECIAL EDUCATION POLICY

SpEd is a creature of Federal and State public policy, law, and regulation. Those working within the realm of public policy are familiar with the cycle of public policy development in a democratic Republic. Briefly, it encompasses, as I depict it for instructional purposes:

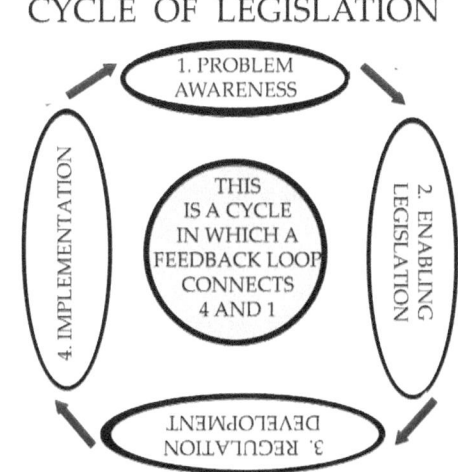

Figure 6.1   Cycle of Legislation. *Source*: Jane Strauss.

Educational policy is no different from any other. In the case of special education policies, the legislative cycle really began in the middle of the twentieth century as detailed below.

Governmental awareness of an issue is generally brought to the fore through financial relevance, lobbying by interest groups, legal action or court decisions. These sources of interest *may* be informed by changes in demographics, research, professional practice, or case law. Special education was no different. In the 1950s, improvements in medical practice resulted in children who might not previously have survived birth or birth defects, surviving, often with lifelong disabilities. In the 1950s and 1960s, disabled students began being counted for purposes of federal school funding, making them relevant to school finances, and largely white upper and middle-class disabled children's parents formed associations which lobbied and brought suit on behalf of their children. Rulings such as *PARC v. Commonwealth of Pennsylvania* (1971) in Pennsylvania and *Mills v. Board of Education* in the same year in the District of Columbia gave disabled children the right to attend public schools and public school districts the responsibility to serve them, bringing awareness of the issue to the public's, school administrators' and lawmakers' attention.

P.L. 94-142, the *Education for All Handicapped Children Act* (EAHCA), the original enabling legislation for special education services as we now know them, was passed in 1975. Its primary purposes were:

> To assure that all children with disabilities have available to them . . . a free appropriate public education which emphasizes special education and related services designed to meet their unique needs, to assure that the rights of children with disabilities and their parents . . . are protected, to assist States and localities to provide for the education of all children with disabilities to assess and assure the effectiveness of efforts to educate all children with disabilities. (PL 94-142, 1975) (20 USC 1401 Sec 3(c) as Amended)

These lofty goals presumed that parents would have equal access to due process with schools and that schools would deal fairly with parents and students. Due process is the procedure outlined in the law that defines roles, actions, and timelines in an effort to provide fairness. That parents are considered equal partners on the Individual Education Program (IEP) team was clearly stated in the Individuals with Disabilities Education Improvement Act (IDEIA), the 2004 revision of the EAHCA. Despite this clarification, schools today rarely pay attention to parents' wishes or opinions, regardless of their areas of expertise, and most parents cannot afford the legal representation required to prevail in a conflict with a school district over identification or service provision. Parents with dis/Abilities are significantly discounted and *not* included as equals in the IEP team: which is against the law (Strauss & Rydeen, 2019). Looking at this from a DJ framework, it is clear that parental dis/Ability plays a role along with race and class in the actual functioning of special education systems. When SpEd systems do not include the student's advocate, their parent, in co-equal relationship with other members of the IEP team, how can the school staff truly be in relationship with the student? DJ requires that regardless of legal mandate, relationship with both students and parents is critical at their intersections of race, class, and other markers of differences (see Artiles, 1998). Existing structural inequality has complicated the course of development of the SpEd system, including identification, planning services, and providing instruction and related services for students with disabilities up to age 21 (Cavendish & Connor, 2018a; Strauss & Rydeen, 2019). Regulations and implementation of EAHCA followed, though even at full implementation it only provided 140% of the average amount allotted per unlabeled student for each dis/Abled child, regardless of the mandates placed upon School Districts (P.L. 94-142, sec 611 (a) (5)).[4] Districts have not always complied with the spirit of the law, if cost was involved.

In case of disagreements about diagnosis or services to (not) be provided, the original law offered a number of resolution methods, including a school-paid Independent (External) Evaluation upon parent's written request, complaints to the state education agency, an "impartial due process hearing," and a private lawsuit. The parent/child and the school administration oppose each other, as each provides legal argument and documentation that their respective wishes should prevail. The solutions provided do not lend themselves to true collaboration (working together); the system of individual implementation has become adversarial. Due to insufficient Federal funding, services continue to be unevenly allocated, based in part on local school revenues. By 2015, "The federal government only provides about one-third of the funds for special education that it had committed to in the original legislation—placing a greater financial burden on state and local governments" (Griffiths, 2015, p. 1). The original amount was 40% more than the average amount provided per unlabeled student, and the actual amount was less than 15% more. Historically, education law has not provided guidelines for what a "successful" education is. Recent applications of such guidelines have had a major impact across the educational spectrum—not always positive.

The Accountability Movement and the Current Situation

In the past 30 years, U.S. Public Education has been pushed by the neoliberal political stream to demand "accountability," as defined by standardized test scores, without concomitant increases in attendance days, teacher staffing, or funding (Fontaine, 2016; Jorgenson & Hoffmann, 2003; Ravitch, 2002). The relatively short school year originally implemented for student availability to help on the family farm has not gone the way of the family farm. Since initial passage of PL 94-142, the Law and Regulations have been modified and re-implemented several times, with some modification of its initial implementation.

In an attempt to improve national educational outcomes with the passage of *No Child Left Behind* (PL 107–110, 2002) policy-makers relied upon standardized examinations to render documentation of "success" objective and consistent. For Freire (2014) this creates a dilemma. Objectivity and subjectivity, to Freire, are two sides of the same coin, inescapably linked. Neither can truly exist without consideration of the other.

The separation of objectivity from subjectivity, the denial of the latter when analyzing reality or acting upon it, is objectivism. . . . Neither objectivism nor subjectivism, nor yet psychologism is propounded here, but rather subjectivity and objectivity in *constant dialectical relationship* . . . World and human beings do not exist apart from each other (Freire, 2014, pp. 632–638).

This dialectic raises the question of whether it is even possible for a system of education focusing on only the subjective or objective to function at all. As the two viewpoints are Yin and Yang, complementing and in a sense completing each other, both are needed to construct reality.

Both anecdotal and research findings show that disabled students in SpEd programs are often not getting a "free and appropriate public education"[5] preparing them for integrated life in the community (Mulligan, 2011; Peters, 2014; Raj, 2016). Many are not learning adequately to graduate from high school with diplomas in a climate in which undergraduate college education is (for purposes of employment) the baseline to acquire steady income in U.S. society (Butrymowicz & Mader, 2017; Grindal & Schifter, 2017; Kineavy, 2016; Samuels, 2015). The system, were it a student, would get at best a D minus grade based on its results. Drawing from my participant-observer experience in the system as a parent, a teacher, and advocate, and sources in educational theory, social psychology, literature, and philosophy, I suggest a rationale for this failure and propose a different path forward.

Humanization and Dehumanization in Learning

Paulo Freire, in his *Pedagogy of the Oppressed*, references dehumanization as a historical reality, the source of violence, and the basis for alienation and participation in an unjust order by the oppressed and oppressors. His analysis of humanization and dehumanization parallels Martin Buber's discussion in his classic *I and Thou*. The I-it relationship dehumanizes and makes the Other an inanimate subject, possessed by the actor. I-it defines a student as their disability, their deficits, and without including student or parent input. It is a traditional viewpoint, lacking DJ concepts. The I-thou relationship requires communication between human beings; relationship, resulting in full realization of humanity. I-thou sees the whole person, presuming competence, requesting, accepting, and including feedback. Freire's goal for education is dialectical, and both parties to the dialectic teach each other, creating the epitome of Buber's I-thou relationship. Freire (2014) writes "this pedagogy makes oppression and its causes objects of reflection by the oppressed, and from that reflection will come their necessary engagement in the struggle for their liberation" (p. 48). Pedagogy as Freire defines it incorporates the I-thou relationship at the boundary of DSE and SpEd, encouraging students to examine ways in which they have been oppressed and use this examination as a stepping-stone to learning and growth.

Historic, Philosophical, and Literary Issues

Much literature of the twentieth century addressed themes of dehumanization, viewing people as numbers resulting in stigmatization. Among those popular publications are *I and Thou*, by Martin Buber, first published in 1923 in German and translated into English in 1937, even as the Nazi regime dehumanized a broad swath of the European population, and *The Little Prince*, by Antoine de Saint-Exupéry, first published in 1943 during World War II (WWII) and translated into English in that same year. *Stigma: The Management of Spoiled Identity*, by Erving Goffman, a work of social psychology first published in 1963, and Freire's signature work, *Pedagogy of the Oppressed*, first published in 1968, and in English in 1970, as the U.S. legal system had recently addressed issues of school integration in *Brown vs. Board of Education* and subsequent cases, had addressed broader Civil Rights issues such as voting and was beginning to come to terms with the exclusion of disabled students from public schools.

P.L. 94-142 was a product of its time. During WWII, several combatant nations dehumanized segments of their populations, with horrifying results. The Soviet government did this after the war and displayed policies antithetical to the manner in which the United States wished the democratic republic enshrined in the Constitution and Laws to be seen. The 1950s were a time of great economic and population growth for working-class and middle-class whites and those who could pass in this country. The Civil Rights movement of the 1950s and 1960s resulted in the theoretical constructs of school, housing, and workplace integrations.

The new generation of parents, having seen the world and some of its horrors, were sensitized to the treatment of individuals by governmental bureaucracies; the Civil Rights movement, disabled rights movement, and parental advocacy within the schools all grew from this experience. Parents appalled that their children were not served by local schools supported by their taxes brought lawsuits against governmental entities (*PARC v. Commonwealth of Pennsylvania* (1971); *Mills v. Board of Education* (1971)). When Congress saw the clear directive from the Courts and their constituents that schools did need to provide services to these students too, development of P.L.94-142 became imperative.

Stigma in School

Including students with obvious disabilities in public schools rendered them, often for the first time, visible to peers outside their own families and to school staff. This visibility increased the likelihood of stigmatization within the school setting. Goffman, writing in the early 1960s, defined stigma as the situation of the individual who is disqualified from full social acceptance, and further defined its parameters as "an attribute that is deeply discrediting, but it should be seen that a language of relationships, not attributes, is really needed" (Goffman, 1963, p. 2).

Goffman references three kinds of stigma:

- Physical, based on appearance or physical disability
- Character/psychological
- Racial, religious, or ethnic

All are relevant to the school setting, and impact on students and teachers alike. Some are more acknowledged than others; most are addressed in law and regulation. Today, it is affirmed that these may be intersectional and as such are far more complex than a single attribute may indicate (McColl, 2005). The "School to Prison Pipeline," commonly referred to at the intersection of race, disability, and ethnicity (in addition to gender and low-income social class), is one current example of the result of multiple stigmatization in the school setting (Annamma, 2014; Disability Rights Education & Defense Fund, 2017). While such stigmatization is often declared to be illegal by statutes or ordinances, denial of its existence to avoid prosecution is both common and a fool's errand.

The law recognizes disparate impact (having the effect of discrimination) as equally culpable to intentional discrimination. The Supreme Court originally applied this doctrine to employment discrimination law but broadened it to include Titles VI, VII, and IX and other Titles of the Civil Rights Act of 1964 (Flynn et al., 2015). Disability, race, and gender-based claims relating to schools and other entities receiving Federal funds have been litigated. As development of EAHCA and its successors was historically linked to racial and religious rights, other Civil Rights law developed in parallel tracks. Lawsuits can only be brought under statutes, regulations, or other written laws, not under case law or precedent in the absence of a specific law. The statutes as currently written do not support intersectional causes of action (lawsuits). Although at present no intersectional causes of action exist in the U.S. Courts, as such causes are defined by statute and case law rooted in societal bias and a positivistic base, it is critical that future developments include intersectional justice, not only in disability claims but in all Civil Rights actions. Moving into a future in which intersectional causes of action can be litigated on a regular basis, it is important that theories of intersectionality be clearly communicated to the populace and their government representatives so that a case can be made of the NEED for new statutes supporting such causes of action. (For information about recent documentation on the impact of intersectionality, see Powers et al., 2018.)

Having addressed social science and law applicability to the conundrum of special education, next it is time to examine some sources in the humanities, namely Buber and de Saint-Exupéry.

I-Thou and I-It

The major theme of Buber's short work is relationship and relatedness. He posits two contrasting types of relations, termed I-Thou (You) and I-it. The first is subjective and personal, the second objective. In the original German, the term later translated as "Thou" or "You" was the familiar "Du," used when speaking with family members, intimate acquaintances, children, and animals. In formal relationships, the term "Sie" is used instead. I-you humanizes the one with whom "I" interacts, I-it objectifies, dehumanizes. I-you can only be spoken with the whole being, as by nature, communication among humans as spiritual beings is, and must be, reciprocal. I-it can never be spoken with the entire being; one is experiencing an object. The I-world of such experience is not reciprocal. Even so, "I" does not truly exist except in a relationship, and that requires a relationship with You. A You interaction is in relation, and It interaction is in possession. Objectification is possession.

The summation of Buber's thesis is:

> Exclusiveness comes into being miraculously again and again—and now one can act, help, heal, educate, raise, redeem. Love is responsibility of an I for a You: . . . Relation is reciprocity. My You acts on me as I act on it. Our students teach us, our works form us. (Buber, 1970, pp. 66–67)

This definition parallels that of Freire when he discusses "Banking" versus true, dialectical education. Dialectical education is by its nature interactive; it exists in relation to the Other. It is conducted by an I with a You. Banking education pours a defined topic in defined amounts into the objectified Other, the It. Banking possesses rather than relating to the Other, and it loses any spiritual or related aspect it could have had. "Dehumanization, which marks not only those whose humanity has been stolen, but also (though in a different way) those who have stolen it, is a distortion of the vocation of becoming more fully human" (Freire, 2014, pp. 530–531). As Freire's work emphasizes the description of dialogue and its role in education, he specifies its critical elements in relatedness, defining radical love.

> Love is at the same time the foundation of dialogue and dialogue itself. . . . Because love is an act of courage, not of fear, love is commitment to others. No matter where the oppressed are found, the act of love is commitment to their cause—the cause of liberation. And this commitment, because it is loving, is dialogical. As an act of bravery, love cannot be sentimental; as an act of freedom, it must not serve as a pretext for manipulation. (Freire, 2014, pp. 1271–1275)

Friendship, Numbers, and Responsibility

The Little Prince is a deceptively simple, yet deep "fairytale" about a planet-hopping alien boy whom the author has encountered in the midst of the

Sahara Desert. Its themes include friendship, responsibility, and attitudinal differences between children and adults, and has much to teach us about education, the nature of relationships, and the difference between myth and reality in those realms.

The text begins with the narrator telling about being discouraged in artistic endeavors, at the age of six, by adults who did not recognize his illustration of a boa constrictor who had swallowed an elephant. This tale sets the stage for an ongoing critique of "grown-ups" beliefs and norms. Through engaging in dialogue with the Prince, he rethinks truisms about relationships and what is important in life.

Early in the book, the author, explaining why he is using figures rather than descriptive terms to discuss a planet, tells how he has observed grownups' responses to actual verbal descriptions. He foreshadows the later observations the Little Prince makes of various adults and the "adult" manner of response and evaluation.

> If you tell grown-ups: "I saw a beautiful red brick house, with geraniums at the windows and doves on the roof," they won't be able to imagine such a house. You have to tell them: "I saw a house worth a hundred thousand francs." Then they exclaim: "What a pretty house!" (de Saint-Exupéry, 2000, p. 21).

Later in the book, the bases for relatedness are discussed. The Little Prince's interaction with the fox introduces Taming, developing a particular I-Thou relationship. Within the mythos of Special Education, this concept of taming is often, with others, negatively applied to the relationship of Anne Sullivan with her pupil, Helen Keller (Carlson, 2016). Typically, autistic children are also depicted as feral, and in need of taming (Albury, 2011). The fox defines taming as establishing ties, a specific relationship, with another, not in a negative sense.

> "The only things you learn are the things you tame," said the fox. "People haven't time to learn anything. They buy things ready-made in stores. But since there are no stores where you can buy friends, people no longer have friends. If you want a friend, tame me!" (de Saint-Exupéry, 2000, p. 71)

Taming is a time-consuming process; it occurs over time, with repetition and ritual. It occurs through developing trust in the other. The fox and the Little Prince develop a friendship, and eventually, the time comes when the Little Prince must move on. The fox then leaves him with one final teaching: "One sees clearly only with the heart. Anything essential is invisible to the eyes ... You become responsible forever for what you've tamed" (de Saint-Exupéry, 2000, pp. 74–75). Taming does not happen in the limited space-time for relatedness left by rigid schedules defined by regulation, assessment, and protocols. It is unlikely to occur when schools emphasize numbers and achievement instead of relationships.

The Little Prince is, at its base, an examination of the roots of adult dysfunction, from the point of view of an alien participant-observer (Konnikova, 2012). The author's greatest fear is that: "I might become like the grown-ups who are no longer interested in anything but numbers" (de Saint-Exupéry, 2000, p. 23). Adults are in charge of developing and administering schools; it is no surprise that schools are subject to adult dysfunction.

Grown-ups like numbers. They base grading, rating, and assignments on numbers. They ignore the "invisible to the eye" (de Saint-Exupéry, 2000, p. 74) essentials of relatedness, favoring instead defined and counted assessments—the craze of Positivism, "scientifically based" educational analysis, which has mushroomed since the middle twentieth century. In taking a positivist viewpoint, they are trying to teach children from grownups' perspectives and miss important nuances. Positivism is rooted in the theory that the only real method of documenting the existence of anything or any concept is mathematical, experimental, and logical. Positivism is the basis for judging educational outcomes by standardized testing alone. Positivism eliminates (or severely limits) subjective analysis and so limits the scope of education and, ultimately, limits progress. Many aspects of teaching and learning, key among them, those aspects based upon relationships, cannot be measured by paper and pencil exams (Amrein-Beardsley, 2008; Douglas et al., 2012; Popham, 1999).

Reform and Repression

Just as the leaders of a revolution can become oppressors when not leading through dialectical communication, educational "reform" becomes repressive when it succumbs to the lure of positivism, judging everything by numbers. Nowhere is this more obvious than in the SpEd system, a creature of legislative intent developed in a communicative vacuum. It's rooted in what education was in the 1970s, funded at less than half the stated level, and hogtied by recent reliance on numbers acquired through standardized testing (McCann, 2014). While new technologies for accommodation may be available, funding for implementation is often lacking. While new attitudes about disability blossom in academe, staff often stagnate at the philosophies and attitudes which first led them to the field, learned in their initial training. The SpEd system, like that on the Lamplighter's planet in *The Little Prince*, is caught in a morass of the past.

> "It's a terrible job I have. It used to be reasonable enough. I put the lamp out mornings, and lit it after dark. . . ."

"And since then orders have been changed?"

"Orders haven't changed," the lamplighter said. "That's just the trouble! Year by year the planet is turning faster and faster, and orders haven't changed!" (emphasis added)

"Which means?"

"Which means that now that the planet revolves once a minute, I don't have an instant's rest. I light my lamp and turn it out once every minute." (de Saint-Exupéry, 2000, p. 53)

And so in SpEd, the situation has changed, yet the orders are the same. Testing in addition to that required for *child find*[6] and ongoing assessment takes time away from actual teaching and learning (personal communication, Patricia Rydeen, 2019). As an advocate and parent for over thirty years, I have personally seen that society has changed, yet school *IEP*[7] goals remain the same. Resources have changed, and new options are available, yet computers, *Augmentative and Alternative Communication (AAC)*,[8] and similar options fall victim to ignorance, Information Technology (IT) challenges, lack of funding, or inertia.

Redefinition and Relatedness

SpEd terminology has changed over time, from "crippled" to "handicapped" to "person first language," all in the name of humanizing and somehow making those students who are still objectified as the degree of deficit qualifying them for "services" feel better about themselves, be more included, and be less stigmatized. However, Gernsbacher (2017) has published research indicating that mandated, enforced use of Person First Language in scholarly research emphasizes the differences between disabled and unlabeled children and may increase stigmatization rather than lessening it. Will praxis take note of this effect and change?

Discovering himself to be an oppressor may cause considerable anguish, but it does not necessarily lead to solidarity with the oppressed. Rationalizing his guilt through paternalistic treatment of the oppressed, all the while holding them fast in a position of dependence, will not do (Freire, 2014, pp. 617–619).

Even when staff realize their complicity in the system as it oppresses students, they err on the side of familiarity, standardized programming, and objectification. Some do so because they know no different, others to protect their place in the hierarchy (and maybe their jobs). The reason makes no difference to the student for whom appropriate programming has not been provided. If the system is to become humanized and students more than cogs in a machine, this is not acceptable.

The routines and protocols set up for developing and implementing IEPs are based on standardized measurements, regardless of whether those reflect the realities of the student for whom the program is developed. All guidelines, in an effort to be "fair and consistent," are numerically based—they were set up by grown-ups. While there are broad guidelines in Federal law, notably in sections 300.301, 304 and 306 and 303.303 of the Regulations (IDEA (2004) Regulations Part B), much of the detail on assessments and service provision is left to the individual states. Requirements are broadly stated as (IDEA (2004) Regulations Part B Sec. 300.304).[9]

Each state has more specific oversight of the special education realm than the Federal Regulations provide, and the Department of Education issues periodic Advice documents to explain specific applications and issues (see https://sites.ed.gov/idea/policy-letters-policy-support-documents/).

Because placement, programming, and retention in SpEd are based on standardized testing, the entire program is based upon numbers. Eligibility for assistance and services is also based not upon the student's potential but upon deficits in academic work. This results in students not getting the help they need to actually learn or progress within accepted norms, but only not to fail as badly as they might otherwise. In order to continue receiving assistance, students cannot improve beyond a set numerical limit (often as much as 1.5 standard deviations (SD) below the norm) regardless of their potential to learn with proper accommodations. This number is set state by state, and the system for its determination and for appeals is nothing if not bureaucratic (IDEA, Part C, 2015). Freire's observation of bureaucracy is:

> the moment the new regime hardens into a dominating "bureaucracy" the humanist dimension of the struggle is lost and it is no longer possible to speak of liberation ... the authentic solution of the oppressor-oppressed contradiction does not lie in a mere reversal of position, in moving from one pole to the other. Nor does it lie in the replacement of the former oppressors with new ones who continue to subjugate the oppressed—all in the name of their liberation. (Freire, 2014, p. 35)

The oppressors in the school system are those instructors who in their praxis ignore their students' humanity and that of the students' parents. They are the administrators who are *The Little Prince's* prototypical adults, requiring that at all levels those participating in school programs must be judged numerically. The oppressors either rarely interact with actual students, or view students as compilations of their assessment numbers.

Those between administration/rigid instructors and students, the teachers and aides who do their jobs as best they can become dehumanized as well. They are the means of production. They lose their humanity in being held to the rigid format of implementation and assessment.

In order to regain freedom and humanity, one must develop the ability and take the opportunity to think outside the proverbial box, applying a broad range of thought to issues and daring to be in a relationship. This is consilience at its best—a unity of knowledge applied to the problem at hand.

> What is essential is *lived* in the present, *objects* in the past (emphasis added). The I of the basic word I-It, the I that is not bodily confronted by a You but surrounded by a multitude of "contents," has only a past and no present. In other words: insofar as a human being makes do with the things that he experiences and uses, he lives in the past, and his moment has no presence. He has nothing but objects; but objects consist in having been. (Buber, 1970, p. 64)

The challenge for those working within the SpEd system is complex. They must, while conforming to the requirements of bureaucracy, law, and regulation and navigating the goals of inter-, intra-, and hierarchical-school and departmental politics, be human. They must see beyond the numerical-descriptive-analytical labels placed upon their students to their full personalities. They must maintain human interaction even as the guidelines, programs, curricula, timelines, and goals by which they are bound to minimize the possibility of such interaction because it "simply takes too much time" or the student's label gets in the way. They must also, despite its potential inconvenience, make time to dialogue with parents and craft the IEP as though parental knowledge about their child mattered (Strauss & Rydeen, 2019).

Treating the student and the parent as objects without inherent value renders the IEP irrelevant. Goals presume existence of a present looking toward a future when they will be attained. Depersonalization leaves the entire entity wallowing in the past defined by the teachers' and experts' observations of a student engaged in defined tasks at a particular point in time, at which time their performance might well have been adversely impacted by socially mediated stressors. The student has become a static object, defined as a series of numbers. Objects cannot learn. Objects will never reach goals. Students treated as objects comprehend their lack of importance to the system and perform accordingly. Students who have real relationships with their instructors perform accordingly (Gallagher, 2013).

Teaching that Matters

I had a math teacher in high school whose goal was teaching us HOW math worked, and WHY math worked, decrying "Gorge and regurgitate" instruction. Her method was unusual for the time, contemporaneous with Freire's comparison of revolutionary and banking modes of education. Hers was more dialectical than depository. She related to her students as individuals, and we knew she cared whether we understood her communication or not. I learned math from her, despite subsequent failures and a (much) later diagnosis of dyscalculia, and I remember those concepts to this day.

Students, both in SpEd and in the mainstream, need and deserve more teachers like Mrs. Merrifield. Ironically, she was not a product of any advanced professional program, but the old Normal School in Keene, New Hampshire. Communication is relational, and excellent teaching is, as imparted by communication, built upon relationship as well. Relationships are developed between human beings, and not with objects; they are an I-Thou proposition. Relationships last, as deposited information may not—more than 50 years after learning from this teacher, I am teaching what I learned to my own son. The reason for teaching him at home is that our local school district consistently declined to collaborate or to acknowledge his potential to learn over the course of a decade.

Newer theories of effective teaching have emphasized social support and other relationship-based aspects of the skillset. Racial and gender similarities have shown some positive impact on students' impressions of their teacher. Studies have also shown small gains in academics for students who are similar in race or gender to their teachers (Egalite & Kisida, 2018). Similarity, as Goffman noted in *Stigma*, *decreases* objectification and stigma, *increasing* relatedness and communication. Learning is more effective when it takes place in an emotionally comfortable environment. These studies are not performed, it appears, within the special education environment, generally labels and objectification, along with deficit-based models, trump comfort, and relationship. This is still so even with *person-first language (PFL) (also known as "People-first language")* being mandated within the reauthorization of IDEA of 2004 (P.L. 108-446) and in some localities. There is some debate about the propriety of requiring *PFL*, and some disability communities prefer *Identity-first language*.[10] I freely admit to using identity-first language, both in my personal and professional lives. If others need to use *PFL* to remember that I am a person, they may lack empathy, social skills, or both (see Kapitan (2017) for a good summary of "person-centered" respectful terminology vs. "person-first," rote terminology).

In my experience as a teacher, parent, advocate, and learner, schools encourage dependency, pity dominates, and strong emphasis is placed upon compliance in response to all interactions. In my experience, the very people insisting on the use of PFL do so by rote, not because they respect dis/Abled people. Their attitudes and actions show otherwise. In the special education worldview, students are not to question. To question is to be difficult. To challenge authority is to be "bad." Behaviors other than complete, "easy" docility are included in the behavioral plan, to be eliminated. Students with IEPs are rarely viewed as having agency, and may, as I saw in the

Minneapolis Public Schools, be slotted into a school-to-institution pipeline. *Agency* can be defined as the capacity to exert control and to transform social relations (Berger, 2008). For students to develop and increase their agency, it is crucial that they be exposed to disability studies as part of their education. Only with such exposure can they maximally increase emotional and practical independence.

The Role of Disability Studies and Disability Justice

Identity politics as epitomized in disability studies can reinforce positive self-concept in students, both providing context for their lives and models for growth, owning their futures (Gill, 2004; Johnstone, 2004). Teaching disability studies within the context of SpEd has value for both staff and students (Cosier & Pearson, 2016). It reminds staff of their students' essential humanity and brings students' new information and historic context for making sense of their lives. Disability studies within special education programs can counteract some staff persons' denying students' agency by demonstrating to the students that it has been and is valuable to plan a future, work for it, and be an agent of one's own dreams. It can serve as a reminder that the "I" in "I.E.P." means individualized, and the student is the basis for that individualization. Acknowledging that the disability aspect of identity is neither shameful nor defective, but another aspect of humanity, represents the core of intersectionality as expressed in DJ.

The junction of DSE and SpEd is where student agency and plans for a future meets institutional inertia and standardization. It exists where the student sees life in community and staff members see only barriers to that dream. It exists where funding only provides side stream or segregated programs, so staff ignores that dream rather than engaging in creative dialogue about alternatives. Staff who wish to work with students in relationship and to help them gain skills for independent living must bring in DSE to overcome those challenges at the margin.

To do otherwise is to continue being an oppressor. Those who work for liberation must not take advantage of the emotional dependence of the oppressed—dependence that is the fruit of the concrete situation of domination which surrounds them and which engendered their unauthentic view of the world. Using their dependence to create still greater dependence is an oppressor tactic (Freire, 2014, pp. 882–884).

Partnership between the school, parent, and student is usually noticed more in the breach than in the reality. Parents are at best tolerated as members of the "team," and often their input is entirely left out of the finished plan (Strauss & Rydeen, 2019). Students fare no better; in the interest of standardized paperwork unique wishes, goals, or outcomes are forgotten. Two means of facilitating real student-centered planning and genuinely successful educational outcomes are truly viewing the parent as a collaborator and continuing, as the student reaches transition age, to increase student responsibility and communication of their personal goals (Cavendish & Connor 2018b; Valle, 2018).

If students are partners in devising their programs, they can take ownership. I have seen "autistic," "Disabled," "EBD" students[11] who, when the program is based on something they value and they have ownership, engage actively with the program. Youth are like adults that way—they are more likely to actively work at something they see as useful or leading to their own goal rather than another's. Staff who ignore this basic aspect of humanity view students as a charitable enterprise, objectifying rather than being in relationship with them. This is what Freire calls false generosity or false charity. It condescends, rather than lifting up. At the juncture of SpEd and DSE is a ramp—a ramp that is uplifting, meeting the student where they are, and helping them gain skills and strength to achieve self-initiated goals and direct their future.

NOTES

1. Throughout the chapter, I use "dis/Ability" to underscore the social, emotional, political, historical, and economic construction of both disability and ability. "Disability" without the / relates primarily to actual impairment or challenges. The latter term is also used in quotations from the Law or literature in which that was the original term used (Hernandez Saca et al., 2018).

2. My academic arc since high school began with literature, traversed the social sciences to the natural sciences, and then took detours through the professions of theology, education/developmental psychology/special education, and medicine to law.

3. I first encountered Buber and Saint-Exupéry while a High School student, studied Goffman in my Undergraduate years, Freire and Buber (again) in my year and one half of Seminary, Freire (again) as a post-Baccalaureate Undergraduate in Education at the University of Minnesota, and have revisited them all at intervals since. Various aspects of Special Education Law have been part of my life at the College of Education, as a student at Hamline University in the Law and Public Policy programs and during my parenting, advocacy, and research roles since.

4. For each "disabled student" the Federal government was to start by providing 105 percent of the average per pupil grant in 1978, and increase that to 140 percent by 1982 and every year thereafter.

5. *free appropriate public education* (FAPE) means special education and related services that:

> are provided to children and youth with disabilities at public expense, under public supervision and direction, and without charge;

meet the standards of the State educational agency (SEA), including the requirements of IDEA;

include preschool, elementary school, or secondary school education in the State involved; and

are provided in keeping with an individualized education program (IEP) that meets the requirements of IDEA. 34 CFR §300.17.

6. *Child Find* is defined in Statute as "(1) . . . policies and procedures to ensure that—(i) All children with disabilities residing in the State are identified, located, and evaluated; and (ii) A practical method is developed and implemented to determine which children are currently receiving needed special education and related services" (34 CFR 300.111).

7. *Individual Education Programs (IEPs)* is defined as "a written statement . . . developed, reviewed, and revised in a meeting . . . that must include . . . child's present levels of academic achievement and functional performance . . . measurable annual . . . academic and functional goals . . . how and when . . . progress will be measured . . . special education . . . and supplementary aids and services . . . the extent, if any, to which the child will not participate with nondisabled children in the regular class," along with definitions of accommodations, alternative assessment methods, and the projected date for services to begin (34 CFR 300.320).

8. *Augmentative and Alternative Communication* is defined by the American Speech and Hearing Association as "all the ways we share our ideas and feelings without talking" including variations on sign language, pen and paper, letter boards, and speech generating devices.

9. *(a)* Notice. The public agency must provide notice to the parents of a child with a disability . . . that describes any evaluation procedures the agency proposes to conduct.

(b) ... In conducting the evaluation, the public agency must—

(1) Use a variety of assessment tools . . . Including information provided by the parent, that may assist in determining—

(i) Whether the child is a child with a disability . . .

(ii) The content of the child's IEP, . . .;

(2) Not use any single measure or assessment as the sole criterion for determining...disability and . . . an appropriate educational program . . .

(3) Use technically sound instruments that may assess . . . cognitive and behavioral . . . physical or developmental factors.

10. Person-first language is not without its detractors. Some disabled activists prefer reclamation of "older" terms and "identity-first language." This is particularly seen in the Deaf, Blind, and parts of the Autistic and Mad communities. Research at the University of Wisconsin has also shown a dark, stigmatizing aspect to use of PFL in scholarly journals (Brown, 2011; Gernsbacher, 2017; Haller, Dorries, & Rahn, 2006; Kapitan, 2017; Ladau, 2015; Liebowitz, 2015; N.C.D.J., 2018; Sequenzia, 2016).

11. Quotation marks are used here to specify that these are the labels provided by schools, which often resulted in presuming incompetence on the part of educators and others.

REFERENCES

Albury, W. R. (2011). From changelings to extraterrestrials: Depictions of autism in popular culture. *University of New England.* http://hekint.org/2017/01/30/from-changelings-to-extraterrestrials-depictions-of-autism-in-popular-culture/

Alvarez, B. (2016). Promising changes for special education under ESSA. *Nea Today.* http://neatoday.org/2016/06/30/special-education-essa/

Artiles, A. J. (1998). The dilemma of difference: Enriching the disproportionality discourse with theory and context. *The Journal of Special Education, 32*(1), 32–36.

Berger, R. J. (2008). Agency, structure, and the transition to disability: A case study with implications for life history research. *The Sociology Quarterly, 49*(2), 309–333.

Berne, P., Morales, A. L., Langstaff, D., & Invalid, S. (2018). Ten principles of disability justice. *WSQ: Women's Studies Quarterly, 46*(1), 227–230.

Brown, L. (2011). The significance of semantics: Person-first language: Why it matters. *Autistic Hoya.* http://www.autistichoya.com/2011/08/significance-of-semantics-person-first.html

Buber, M. (1970). *I and thou.* (Trans. W. A. Kaufmann). Kindle edition: Charles Scribner's Sons.

Carlson, L. A. (2016). "You only need three senses for this": The disruptive potentiality of cyborg. In C. Foss, J. Gray, & Z. Whalen (Eds.), *Disability in comic books and graphic narratives* (pp. 140–154). Palgrave MacMillan.

Cavendish, W., & Connor, D. J. (2018a). Introduction to special series: Parent voice in educational decision making for students with learning disabilities. *Learning Disability Quarterly, 41*(1), 4–6.

Cavendish, W., & Connor, D. J. (2018b). Toward authentic IEPs and transition plans: Student, parent, and teacher perspectives. *Learning Disability Quarterly, 41*(1), 32–43.

Cosier, M., & Pearson, H. (2016). Can we talk? The underdeveloped dialogue between teacher education and disability studies. *Sage Open, 6*(1), 1–14.

de Saint-Exupéry, A. (2000). *The Little Prince* (Trans. R. Howard). Kindle edition: Mariner Books, Houghton Mifflin Harcourt Publishing.

Egalite, A. J., & Kisida, B. (2018). The effects of teacher match on students' academic perceptions and attitudes, *Educational Evaluation and Policy Analysis, 40*(1), 59–81.

Flynn, R., Hirji, R., Morris, E. S., & Brown, A. (2009). Disparate impact under Title VI and the school-to-prison pipeline. *American Bar Association Children's Rights Litigation Committee.* https://www.njjn.org/uploads/digital-library/disparate-impact-memo-2015.authcheckdam.pdf

Fontaine, C. (2016). The myth of accountability: How data (Mis)use is reinforcing the problems of public education. *Data & Society Research Institute.* https://datasociety.net/pubs/ecl/Accountability_primer_2016.pdf

Freire, P. (2014). *Pedagogy of the oppressed* (30th Anniversary ed.). Bloomsbury Publishing. Kindle Edition.

Gallagher, E. (2013). The effects of teacher-student relationships: Social and academic outcomes of low-income middle and high school students. *Applied Psychology OPUS.* https://wp.nyu.edu/steinhardt-appsych_opus/the-effects-of-teacher-student-relationships-social-and-academic-outcomes-of-low-income-middle-and-high-school-students/

Gernsbacher, M. A. (2017). Editorial perspective: The use of person-first language in scholarly writing may accentuate stigma, *The Journal of Child Psychology and Psychiatry, 58*(7), 859–861.

Gill, M. (2004). Disability counter-narrative: Transforming ideas among high school students. *Disability Studies Quarterly, 24*(4).

Goffman, E. (1986). *Stigma: Notes on the management of spoiled identity.* Kindle Edition: Touchstone books.

Griffith, M. (2015). The progress of education reform: A look at funding for students with disabilities. *Education Commission of the States, 16*(1), 1–6.

Haley, K., Allsopp, D., & Hoppey, D. (2018). When a parent of a student with a learning disability is also an educator in the same school district: A heuristic case study. *Learning Disability Quarterly, 41*(1), 19–31.

Haller, B., Dorries, B., & Rahn, J. (2006). Media labeling versus the US disability community identity: A study of shifting cultural language. *Disability & Society, 21*(1), 61–75.

Hernández-Saca, D. I., Gutmann Kahn, L., & Cannon, M. A. (2018). Intersectionality dis/ability research: How dis/ability research in education engages intersectionality to uncover the multidimensional construction of dis/abled experiences. *Review of Research in Education, 42*(1), 286–311.

IDEA, Part C. *States' and Territories Definitions of Criteria IDEA Part C Eligibility.* http://ectacenter.org/~pdfs/topics/earlyid/partc_elig_table.pdf

Johnstone, C. J. (2004). Disability and identity: Personal constructions and formalized supports. *Disability Studies Quarterly, 24*(4).

Kapitan, A. (2017). On "person-first language": It's time to actually put the person first. *Radical copyediting.* https://radicalcopyeditor.com/2017/07/03/person-centered-language/

Konnikova, M. (2012). The big lesson of a Little Prince: (Re)capture the creativity of childhood. *Scientific American.* https://blogs.scientificamerican.com/literally-psyched/the-big-lesson-of-a-little-prince-recapture-the-creativity-of-childhood/

Ladau, E. (2015). Why person-first language doesn't always put the person first. *Think Inclusive.* https://www.thinkinclusive.us/why-person-first-language-doesnt-always-put-the-person-first/

Levenson, N. (2011). Something has got to change: Rethinking special education. *AEI.* http://www.aei.org/wp-content/uploads/2011/06/AEI-Working-Paper-Rethinking-Special-Education.pdf

Liebowitz, C. (2015). I am disabled: On identity-first versus people-first language. *The Body is Not an Apology.* https://thebodyisnotanapology.com/magazine/i-am-disabled-on-identity-first-versus-people-first-language/

McCall, L. (2005). The complexity of intersectionality. *Signs: Journal of women in culture and society, 30*(3), 1771–1800.

McCann, M. (2014). IDEA funding. *New America.* http://www.edcentral.org/edcyclopedia/individuals-with-disabilities-education-act-funding-distribution/

Mehan, H. (1993). Beneath the skin and between the ears: A case study in the politics of representation. In S. Chaiklin & J. Lave (Eds.), *Understanding practice: Perspectives on activity and context* (pp. 241–268). Cambridge University Press.

Mehan, H., Hertweck, A., & Meihls, J. L. (1986). *Handicapping the handicapped: Decision making in students' educational careers.* Stanford University Press.

Mehan, H., Villanueva, I., Hubbard, L., & Lintz, A. (1996). *Constructing school success: The consequences of placing low achieving students in high track classes.* Cambridge University Press.

National Center on Disability and Journalism (N.C.D.J.). (2018). *Disability language styleguide.* http://ncdj.org/style-guide

Olmstead v. L.C., 527 U.S. 581 (1999).

Peters, D. B. (2014). Gifted+learning disabled = No desk for you, says new study. *Huffington Post.* https://www.huffingtonpost.com/daniel-b-peters-phd/ gifted-learning-disabled-_b_5052115.html

Powers, J., Fischman, G., & Tefera, A. (2018). The challenges and possibilities of intersectionality in educational research. *Review of Research in Education, 42*(1). American Educational Research Association.

Raj, C. (2016). The misidentification of children with disabilities: A harm with no foul. *Arizona State Law Journal, 48*(373), 373–437.

Ravitch, D. (2002). Testing and accountability, historically considered. https://www.hoover.org/sites/default/files/uploads/documents/0817938826_9.pdf

Sequenzia, A. (2016). Person first language and ableism. *Ollibean.* https://ollibean.com/person-first-language-and-ableism

Sparks, S. D. (2013). Social-emotional needs entwined with students learning, security. *Education Week, 32*(16), 16–21.

Strauss, J., & Rydeen, P. (2019, April). Lived experience of dis/abled parents advocating for their children within the IEP process. Paper presented at the annual meeting of the American Educational Research Association, Toronto, Canada.

Valle, J. W. (2018). Across the conference table: Private and public mothering of children with Learning Disabilities, *Learning Disability Quarterly, 41*(1), 7–18.

Chapter 7

Critical Coalition with/in the Boundaries

A Radical Love Response to Neoliberal Debilitation in Special Education

M. Nickie Coomer, Ashley Cartell Johnson, Ganiva Reyes, and Brittany Aronson

Special education services and professional learning related to special education are largely based on positivist research (Kroesbergen & Van Luit, 2003; Thorius, 2019) and atheoretical approaches to considering what disability is and how it is treated in schools (Artiles, 1998). Similarly, *atheoretical* teacher education programs that do not teach from a critical disability studies lens perpetuate cycles of disenfranchisement by continuing to produce teachers whose deficit thinking leads to reductionist teaching. Thorius (2019) describes atheoretical approaches to special education that serve to promote a presumed beneficence of special education as its "cloak of benevolence" (p. 324).

Although scholars have been problematizing the cultural disconnects that occur in a teaching field that has maintained the status quo of white and female for decades (Ladson-Billings, 1999; Loewus, 2017; Sleeter, 2001; Villegas & Lucas, 2002), limited attention has been paid to the role of disability. Boveda and Aronson (2019) found that special education has focused on limited definitions of disability variance, without regard for multiply oppressed social identities (Boveda & Aronson, 2019). Importantly, much of the literature around white women teachers tends to expose problematic ways that deficit thinking manifests in their actions, for example, through a savior mentality (Matias, 2016) as well as by silencing students' expression of difference in the classroom (Castagno, 2014, 2019). Other critiques focus on how white femininity gives in to and upholds patriarchy. Leonardo and Boas (2013) refer to this as the "white racial army":

> Just as every army is composed of different tactical positions in order to secure or conquer a territory, so does whiteness consist of its own foot soldiers, officers, and generals who perform different functions but whose allegiance to whiteness is not the question. With respect to white women, although they may not call the shots, they often pull the trigger. (p. 315)

Accordingly, at the nexus of disability and whiteness, special education has served to exclude students through disciplinary action (Sullivan et al., 2014), criminalization (Annamma, 2017), and pathologization (Ware, 2005), and has, ultimately, served to segregate and marginalize students at the intersections of disability, race, gender, class, and other social markers (Ferri & Connor, 2005; Reid & Knight, 2006),

To further complicate matters, while whiteness manifests itself through the teaching profession in ways that are damaging for multiply marginalized students, neoliberal approaches to education limit the agency of both students *and* teachers. Drawing upon Jasbir Puar's notion of "debility" (2013), an institutional logic that rests on deficit narratives of condition and treatment dehumanizes students and their teachers by positioning teachers as technicist deliverers of curriculum and behavior management, and students as the object to be managed. According to Puar (2013), "debility" takes into account how capitalist interests, high-stakes testing, and the overall neoliberal reform of education exclude the day-to-day lives and particular needs of students so that disability is actually constructed and produced systematically within schools, and more specifically within and by special education. Students who do not fit the norm or standards dictated by neoliberal, white supremacist, ableist, patriarchal, Eurocentric, and capitalist structures (Reyes et al., 2018) are thus "disabled" by an unjust school system. Structural debility, mechanized through a system of "general" and "special education," limits the possibilities for teachers to teach against the grain and work outside the boundaries of teacher-scripted and teacher-proof curriculum within a high-stakes accountability regime (Reyes et al., 2018).

Thus, we theorize the ways in which teachers are positioned in schools, and how shifting teacher positionality can open possibilities for coalition building across differences (e.g., Thorius & Waitoller, 2017) among teachers and students to resist structures of debilitation.

In this chapter, we respond to atheoretical approaches to special education that silo general and special education and serve to exclude students who embody an array of intersectional identities and differences (Reid & Knight, 2006), as well as the overall oppressiveness of schooling structures for teacher and students. We offer a framework rooted in justice, coalition, and bridge-building across the boundaries of critical disability studies, special education, and general education. In this way, we align with the overall purpose of this book in applying *a disability justice, radical love, meta-critical emotionality,* and *consiliencatory boundary work* praxis to unsilo longstanding divisions between disability studies, special education, and general education. Through a theoretical prism of critical and feminist theories, we piece together a *consiliencatory framework* (Wilson, 1999) in which we connect critical approaches in disability and feminist studies to humanize the interconnected lives of teachers and students across multiple intersecting identities. In doing so, we not only reveal singular experiences of privilege and oppression among teachers and students but also make visible larger interlocking systems of domination that seek to categorize, divide, and dehumanize teachers and students. More specifically, this theoretical and *consiliencatory* prism pushes educators to engage in critical reflection of their everyday experiences and interactions with students, across differences, to carve out knowledges and pedagogical approaches that break down binary modes of thinking and transgress the boundaries between disability studies, special education, and general education.

This chapter is a conceptual and critical introspective piece in which we define and explain our theoretical, *consiliencatory* prism, then offer our own situated positionalities and curriculum fragments (Poetter & Googins, 2015), or brief narratives, of our own teaching. We discuss how we border-cross (Akkerman & Bakker, 2011; Anzaldúa, 2015) disciplinary and practitioner divides as educators to construct our own nepantlan pedagogical orientations (Abraham, 2014; Anzaldúa, 2015; Cashman, 2016). To offer a roadmap for the organization of this chapter, first, we position ourselves as education scholars, past teachers, and teacher educators to show who we are and what brought us together for this book chapter. We then discuss the gendered and neoliberal context of the teaching profession to identify roadblocks that keep teacher education from being rooted in the transformative legacy and underpinnings of critical disability studies (CDS) and feminist thought. We then unpack CDS and feminist disability theory as a springboard to offer a theoretical framing for preparing critically engaged educators. Finally, we provide our own curriculum narratives as examples of our theoretical, *consiliencatory* prism that bridges disability and feminist orientations in teaching.

WHO WE ARE AND HOW WE CAME TOGETHER

We come together as education scholars and current teacher educators from different disciplines and different levels within the hierarchy in academia as a first step toward understanding the silos and divisions that we must bridge to overcome the problems of atheoretical teacher training and preparation, as well as the isolation of disability studies from justice-oriented pedagogies and curriculum studies and theories. Before we situate our theoretical grounding and the context of teachers and teaching, below we provide our positionalities and how we came together for this book chapter. We do this to situate our identities in relation to one another and show how our experiences and perspectives inform this work.

Nickie

Ashley and I became close friends during our undergraduate study in special education at Miami University. In 2004, as juniors, we worked with our favorite faculty members, Dr. Kathy McMahon-Klosterman, Dr. Kathy Hulgin, and Dr. Frank Fitch, to form a student group called "Social Agents for Justice Education (SAJE)." Ashley and I, along with one other student, were the organization's only members. As we both moved into our teaching careers, and later graduate and doctoral study, it became clear to me that we had been oriented to special education in a very specific way: and this orientation as *disruptors* became important to our professional relationship, but also deepened our bond and our friendship. I understand, now, that Dr. McMahon-Klosterman and Dr. Hulgin are both academic legacies of Disability Studies, and that Ashley and I, in our classrooms at our university in rural Ohio, became the academic grandchildren of this discipline: ready to approach special education with a critical eye on how disability was constructed, and used, in schools.

As an Asian American, special education teacher, and self-identified advocate in rural Ohio, I was on the receiving end of racialized, gendered objectifications by my administration and some of my colleagues. Nothing about my being was without critique: from the way I wrote Individualized Education Programs to how I spoke and dressed. My maiden name, Negrelli, was often mispronounced in such a way that it sounded like a racial slur, sometimes over the school's loudspeaker. As a special education teacher, for preschool ages through sixth grade, I, even in subordinated positions to my peers, made decisions that were harmful to my students. Thus, I came to this project to make sense of my positioning as a cisgendered, feminized, infantilized, de-intellectualized, and racialized teacher, and to make clear the political positionings of teachers and the roles teachers play—even if unwittingly—in upholding systems of oppression through the subordination of students. I want to provide a theoretical grounding for upending neoliberal, productivity-based classifications of people in schools in order to move schooling toward a place of radical relationship.

Ashley

As undergraduates, Nickie and I always sat together in class. Early in our special education program, we took several classes from adjunct professors who were practicing teachers who proudly spent the semester sharing the "realities" of the field—I clearly recall furiously taking notes, wanting to remember every piece of advice from these educators who had rushed to McGuffey Hall after a full day of teaching. What we learned, though, from Dr. Kathy McMahon-Klosterman, Professor Molly Kelly, and Dr. Kathy Hulgin, was something very different. Our SAJE meetings gave Nickie and I a space where our professors taught us about disability studies and encouraged us to seek out different critical perspectives, particularly from members of the disability community, and challenged us to reimagine what could be in socially just education—a wildly different experience from the "here's how it is" experiences in our methods courses. As a first-year middle school teacher working with students labeled with intellectual disabilities, I got a very full dose of "how it is" with students who were continually excluded from our school community. While we taught in different school districts, Nickie and my stories as early career teachers ran many parallels in segregation and frustration. In our daily morning commute phone conversations, we often came back to our professors' call to reimagine what could be in education and to seek to disrupt the lack of access for our students in our own classrooms. Our shared purpose of reimagined teacher education that continually seeks out critical theory and perspectives has been our driving force in our teaching and scholarship.

As colleagues across three education departments at Miami University, Ganiva and Brittany have played a significant role in shaping my understanding and application of critical theory in teacher education. In 2016 we received an interdisciplinary grant to bring colleagues in teacher education, inclusive special education, and educational leadership together to revise curricula and co-teach lessons in our core teacher preparation programs to be grounded in critical pedagogy and social justice. In this process, Ganiva and Brittany have greatly deepened my understanding of feminist theory, Critical Race Theory, and Critical Whiteness Studies. As a white, middle-class, cisgender woman, their stories and perspectives in critical theory have been crucial in the way I make connections with CDS and other fields of critical theory, while also strengthening my ability to teach from intersecting critical theories, such as DisCrit and feminist disability theory. Through our interdisciplinary curriculum development and co-teaching, we have experienced how coming together around a theoretical prism of critical and feminist theories (Wilson, 1999) can strengthen coalition building across teacher educators where we can together reimagine teacher education centered in critical pedagogy.

Seeking new critical perspectives with my friends, professors, and colleagues has been my most important influence as an educator—the catalyst for my reckoning from a former special education teacher who advocated *for* my students, who fought for inclusion *for* my students to a teacher educator, and who challenges my teacher candidates *to learn with and from* their future students, to *learn from* members of marginalized communities, and *to support* their future students in *their fight* for access and justice.

Ganiva

I am Chicana/Tejana, cisgender, working-class woman who grew up along the U.S./Mexico border, so code-switching between Mexican and white ways of knowing, being, and speaking is second nature to me. I was also a high school Biology teacher. Border-crossing is integral to who I am as a person and as an educator. I like to connect with people despite disciplinary boundaries and institutional silos. It is no wonder that when I came across this opportunity to work with Nickie, Ashley, and Brittany on an interdisciplinary piece, I was ready to jump in. My goal was to think through my experiences working as a Pre-school Program for Children with Disabilities (PPCD) Teacher Assistant when I was a graduate student in order to think of new ways to connect my feminist ways of knowing with Disability Studies. I also sought to help break down barriers between special education and general education in how we prepare future teachers.

Brittany

I identify as a racially white, ethnically Latina, cis-hetero female who is middle-class and able-bodied. I was previously an elementary school general education teacher and am now a teacher educator preparing preservice teachers. My work has mainly focused on race and whiteness using Critical Race Theory (CRT) and Critical Whiteness Studies (CWS). I have depended upon my ability to connect with preservice teachers whom I share many experiences with, including the denial and eventual acceptance of my light-skinned privilege (the proximity to whiteness). Despite my Latin American heritage, I grew up most of my life steeped in whiteness, and so have grappled with much of the same resistance the literature reports about preservice white female teachers. As of recently, I have worked to more intentionally engage with intersectional ways of knowing and being. CDS was introduced to me during my appointment as a professor and I began to see the parallels throughout our fields. It was at this point I realized the profound impact we could have on the field of teacher education if we worked collaboratively across our critical disciplines.

EDUCATION SILOS: FRAMING CONTEMPORARY CONTEXTS OF K-12 TEACHING THROUGH RACE, GENDER, AND MARKET REFORM

In order to consider the ways in which Pre-K-16 teachers can employ a transdisciplinary, Disability Studies perspective in their pedagogical and/or curricular approaches to education, we have to consider the ways in which the institutional and cultural organizing of teaching and learning serve to dehumanize both teacher and student.

Primary education has been historically considered "women's work" as teaching became a way for white women to move from the working to the middle class (Hilda & Oram, 2007). Though teaching as semi-professionalized work emerged as an option for white women, for Black women, teaching remained outside the purview of publicly administered education, and more firmly rooted in the emancipation and liberation of Black people (Perkins, 1993; Taylor, 2005). As a historical legacy of the feminization and white racialization of teaching as white women's work, assumptions and stereotypes about women teachers have served as justification for the underpayment of women as compared to men in similar roles within education (Wong, 2019). These stereotypes have exploited the "sentimentality of teaching" (Grumet-Hobart & Colleges, 1981, p. 182) to justify the underpayment of both Black and white teachers.

Galvanized by neoliberal reform principles in education, legislation such as No Child Left Behind (Bush, 2001) produced an embedded over-reliance on test scores to measure learner output, and had profound impacts on curriculum development, teaching, and learning (Chapman, 2010). These impacts include a curricular emphasis on "high-stakes test-taking skills . . . memorization and conformity, and reductionistic, decontextualized, and fragmented curriculum" (Giroux, 2010; Salazar, 2013, p. 124; Nichols & Berliner, 2007). Importantly, since the passage of No Child Left Behind (2001), market education reformers have mobilized bias against teachers and teacher unions through pop culture and social media that largely depict teachers' labor interests as selfish and harmful to kids (Strauss, 2014). These characterizations are pointedly aimed at women teachers, specifically, through the tacit assumption that women should enjoy working with children by nature of their sex. Generally, women teachers are left open not only to the labor risks of market education reforms that value efficiency over equity but also to glass ceilings due to the gendered expectation of how women should be compensated and the manners in which they should act in their roles (National Women's Law Center, 2013). Importantly, NCLB also does the cultural work of maintaining whiteness by upholding the logics of white privilege through "objectifying" curriculum, scoring, and achievement.

To make matters worse, the market-based approaches to labor in educational contexts rely on hyper-specialization and isolation of teachers in ways that reduce opportunities for collaborative work, as well as discourage collective bargaining and disempower professional labor organizations, resulting in the de-professionalization of teaching (Laitsch, 2013). In neoliberal organizations of teaching, teachers are isolated in increasingly taylorized approaches to delivering instruction (Laitsch, 2013), distilling teaching to "a checklist of behaviors, dispositions, measures, and standards" (Rodgers & Raider-Roth, 2006, p. 265).

Importantly, NCLB also does the cultural work of maintaining whiteness by upholding the logics of white privilege through "objectifying" curriculum, scoring, and achievement (Leonardo, 2007). In this way, NCLB compels teachers to focus on standardized achievement measures, positioning teachers in such a way that they are subject to the dehumanization of standardized tests as they enact the curricular impact of a hyper-focus on achievement. In this way, teachers are positioned to enact not only their own whiteness but the silent logic of white supremacy in otherwise "neutral"—seeming policy (e.g., Leonardo, 2007).

Moving toward Humanizing Teaching and Learning through Critical Theory

Thus, while a teacher and her students are differentially impacted by high-stakes accountability at their school (teachers train students for the standardized test, while students take the test), they are both nonetheless measured up against a one-size-fits-all standard. Teachers and students critiquing such a system from their own situated experiences can foster solidarity to speak back against an oppressive schooling system. In connecting to the theme of consilience, or *the joining and co-creation of knowledge and movement*, this opens up the possibilities for teaching practices that not only address the needs of students but also invite coalition building in which the teacher and students can work together to critically question their social conditions and circumstances in ways that can drive action and social change. However, in order for this consilience-*ing* to happen, teachers must be equipped with theoretical tools from which they can develop and practice "critical consciousness" (Freire, 1974) to unravel how neoliberal, patriarchal systems of classism, sexism, racism, and ableism serve to disadvantage both teacher and student. In the following section we discuss CDS and feminist disability theories as a point of departure to assemble our own theoretical and *consiliencatory* prism that teacher educators can use to prepare critically engaged and reflexive teachers.

CRITICAL DISABILITY STUDIES, FEMINIST DISABILITY THEORY, AND DISABILITY STUDIES IN (SPECIAL) EDUCATION

Critical Disability Studies

CDS challenges the portrayals, perceptions, and practices of oppressive discourses regarding disability status (Garland-Thompson, 2018; Linton, 1998) through a critical theoretical framework that co-constitutively frames and is framed by ongoing disability justice movements. CDS, as a theoretical frame, actively disrupts oppressive and unjust social systems, practices, and policies that seek to enforce segregation, prejudice, and discrimination for the Disabled[1] community (Linton, 1998) and serves to reimagine disability as a "civil and human rights issue, a minority identity, a sociological formation, a historic community, a diversity group, and a category of critical analysis in culture and the arts" (Garland-Thompson, 2018, p. 12). CDS complicates the theoretical relationship between deficit models of disability that rely on placing disability solely "beneath the skin and between the ears" (Mehan, 1993) of an individual and social models of disability that define disability by intersecting systems of discrimination (Meekosha & Shuttleworth, 2009). Deficit-based models of disability locate the source of disability within individuals and frame disability as an individual condition to be fixed, remediated, or otherwise treated through medical, psychological, or educational intervention, while broad definitions of social models of disability contend that disability is related to disabling conditions of society (Haegele & Hodge, 2016). CDS theorizing, however, complicates disability beyond discursive binaries of "impairment" or "social construction," and instead focuses analyses on the relationships between disability, capitalism, and class to examine oppression and to work toward "social, political, and economic change" (Meekosha & Shuttleworth, 2009, p. 49). Importantly, CDS engages critical theory, including feminist, queer, and critical race theories, to consider disability through the multidimensional, lived experiences and sociohistorical, sociocultural, and sociopolitical identities of Disabled people (Goodley, 2013). Accordingly, CDS offers a lens through which to consider the physical, cognitive, and emotional attributes of disability in interaction with broader systems, including education (e.g., Brantlinger, 2006; Hernández-Saca & Cannon, 2019; Erevelles, 2000; Gabel & Peters, 2004; Ware, 2001). Importantly, scholars, activists, and artists who engage CDS advocate for policies and practices that facilitate inclusive communities and educational spaces beyond retro-fitted accommodation by focusing on accessibility through design.

What CDS offers, then, is a framework to ground teacher education programs for preservice teachers in developing a "critical consciousness" (Freire, 1974) around how the general education curriculum marginalizes students, often *through* special education (Boveda et al., 2019), employing disability as a rationale for the exclusion of students who embody an array of intersectional identities and differences (Reid & Knight, 2006). CDS provides an opportunity for educators to surface and disrupt the taken-for-granted assumptions around what a normalized educational experience is, and who is availing of its benefits. Furthermore, CDS provides a critical framework through which to examine how the identities of white teachers interact with the policies, processes, and tools of special education to exclude, surveil, and incarcerate students who exist along intersectional axes of race, gender, class, and disability (Annamma, 2018; Dumas & Nelson, 2016). This framework compels an interrogation, and disruption, of the ways teachers uphold their own places of authority and oppression while disadvantaging those students who are disenfranchised along intersecting axes of oppression (Brantlinger, 2006) through the processes of assigning "normal" and "abnormal," "belonging" and "excludable," and the apportioning of the disparate benefits and disadvantages of special education services (e.g., Annamma, 2018). Through CDS, teachers can examine their own experiences to cultivate self-knowledge and develop a "deepened understanding of history and systemic oppression" (Reyes et al., 2018, p. 821). This enables teachers to connect to their students' personal experiences and to better understand their role in how bodyminds (Price, 2014) are systematically afforded or refused value in their future classrooms.

Feminist Disability Theory

Mainstream, second-wave, white feminism has long had a history of rein-scribing structural social inequities based on race, class, and able-bodiedness. Intersectional and Black feminist perspectives offer strong critiques of the ways in which feminist theory can better examine the intersectional aspects of identity and multiple forms of oppression women of Color experience (Crenshaw, 1991). Disability and gender permeate all facets of culture, including social identities, social institutions, and the shared human condition (Garland-Thomson, 2002). Thus, Garland-Thomson (2002) advocates for a feminist disability theory as a way to "amplify" (p. 1) feminist theory through "representation, the body, identity, and activism" (p. 1). As CDS asserts that disability cannot be defined as a unidimensional attribute and is rather a condition imposed by a social order that separates normal from Other through a variety of marked difference (Goodley, 2013), Feminist Disability Theory (e.g., Garland-Thomson, 2002) centers the body as a site for critical inquiry of the social order. Building on feminist disability theory, queer, feminist scholars of disability extend embodiment to include the reflexive relationship between bodily experience and neurological experience, using the term "bodymind" to denote the relationship (Carter, 2015; Price, 2014;

Schalk, 2013). Sami Schalk, in particular, mobilizes her embodied, sociopolitical identity as a "fat, black, queer woman" (Schalk, 2013) to both add a racialized identity into Disabled spaces and a Disabled identity into already racialized spaces, and in doing so materializes the tensions with and between whiteness, disability studies, and otherwise "intersectional analyses in race and ethnic studies, queer and sexuality studies, and women's and gender studies" (Schalk, 2013). Taken together, CDS and feminist disability theory provide a means by which to conceptualize how "embodiment" (Niedenthal et al., 2005) is physically, metaphysically, and socially constructed through mutable social value systems that, though changing, depend on value assumptions that favor specific bodies as "normal" (Garland-Thomson, 2002).

As a theoretical framework, feminist disability theory offers a complicated "matrix" of theory, methodology, and pedagogy (Garland-Thomson, 2002, p. 3). This complicated theoretical matrix, in conjunction with CDS, can form the foundation of a robust pedagogical orientation that can enable teachers to connect with their students across variations of difference. This connection is a critical step for radical love-*ing* (e.g., Freire, 2005; Reyes et al., 2018; Stern & Brown, 2016) in which teachers develop relationships with students that can lead to transformative change for everyone involved. In this way, we conceptualize *Radical* love-ing as going beyond a one-side, provision of applied affection from teacher to student, and instead as an engaging, together, in resistance against the bounded activities of schooling: activity bounded by state and federal mandates related to achievement, activity bounded by merely legal adherence or "compliance" with federal and state law (see Voulgarides, 2018). In other words, we extend Reyes, Radina, and Aronson's conceptualization of radical love in teaching to include "vulnerability, collective support, and healing" (2018, p. 818) as well as collective resistance to the organizational structures of teaching that position teachers to enact, embody, and uphold oppressive practices within their positions.

In order to further unfold our theoretical and *consiliencatory* prism, we build upon CDS and feminist disability theory by sharing our own brief stories of consilience-*ing* and radical love-ing as educators. In the following section we provide the methodological orientation we employed to reflect upon our experiences, engage in reflexive dialogue, and produce bits of narrative.

METHODOLOGY: CURRICULUM FRAGMENTS

For this chapter, we used curriculum "fragments" or "regressive bits" (Poetter & Googins, 2015) to construct short pedagogical narratives that bring our conceptual reimagining to life. Curriculum fragments are short narratives of teaching experiences told through currere-oriented stories to shape the participants' understanding and futures as scholars and teacher educators. Our process in sharing our curriculum fragments occurred through conversation and dialogue during two separate Zoom call meetings. For the first Zoom call meeting, we discussed our pedagogical approaches as past classroom teachers and current teacher educators/scholars. Through our conversation, we found that a critical and feminist current united our teaching orientations. We also realized that for us, there are no clear-cut boundaries between special education and general education. Our conversation led to note-taking and the organic development of identifying key threads in our teaching approaches (i.e., radical love, nepantla, and engaged pedagogy), which make up our overall theoretical, *consiliencatory* prism that bridges disability and feminist orientations.

For our second Zoom meeting, we decided to share more specific stories of our teaching experiences in PK-12 classrooms. As we shared bits of our narratives, we collectively wrote notes in a Google document to identify key stories that show our proposed theoretical, *consiliencatory* framework. These notes culminated in the telling of our positionalities for this chapter, and curriculum fragments of how we engage in our *consiliencatory* framing that brings together radical love, engaged pedagogy, nepantla, and "access is love" (as is discussed below). Our storytelling also led to lessons learned about disrupting binary ways of thinking and oppressive norms for youth labeled with disabilities and the educators who work with them, including ourselves. We also engaged in critical introspection by thinking about our own positionalities in relation to our students.

Curriculum Fragments

Through these stories we offer important lessons learned by working with historically marginalized and multiply oppressed students. These experiences reveal the workings of everyday school life and why it is important to work from multiple lenses to disrupt boundaries that marginalize and silo bodyminds in educational spaces.

Nickie

I watched Miguel as he walked, hand-in-hand with two other preschoolers, down the sidewalk. I snapped a quick photo for his mom on my new phone. His mom had rightly chastised me earlier in the week because I had left Miguel, in his own wheeled chair, velcroed in to support his posture, facing the whiteboard while the other four students in our preschool "resource room" sat around a table for snack. In my fragility, I remember feeling embarrassed and also quick to defend myself: it was just a moment, did it really matter? More deeply, I wondered how much school participation for

Miguel, and others, was more symbolic than materially productive; especially at 3, 4, and 5 years old, segregated from the rest of the preschoolers in a resource room.

I was used to "pushing in," even with students with histories of aggressive behavior, against the wishes of my general education teaching friends. I am naturally extroverted, if not people-pleasing, but I often had to use my years of waitressing to diplomatically address the displeasure of some of my colleagues when I suggested the classroom milieu for "my" students be normed with their peers. Administrators and colleagues openly questioned my intelligence and effectiveness. In front of parents, teachers, and district administrators, one principal sardonically called an IEP I had written "Nickie's grand experiment," noting the level of frustration and work I was causing both teachers and administration, to nobody's actual benefit. My own desperate need to be liked aside, these types of characterizations made me question my competence and my commitment to my own pedagogical values.

But, after having taught in three states and overseas, it seemed to me that the same patterns were only repeated time and again: a teacher makes a vague comment about a student "needing more," spurring the referral processes of special education, ending with a child in a segregated resource room.

I can remember now that it had been suggested to me that it was unsafe for Miguel to be on the playground with forty other preschoolers during recess. But that day, as I watched Miguel walk with his friends and begin, with their help, to climb the play structure on the playground, I solidified my own affective inklings toward realizing that no child exists in isolation: and the inclusion of a child does not have to be justified in a transactional exchange of "benefit."

It seems to me that the children I was watching that day already knew something I did not yet: that we are simply because we *are*.

Their understanding stood in stark contrast to those of the adults on the playground: wondering if Miguel should be on the swing, or running with the other children. Now, I find myself wondering what we mean when we start to question who deserves to be in certain spaces: to be honest, I'm not sure the spaces we have created are deserving of us.

But there I was, and here I am today, still thinking about Miguel and the futility in measuring "inclusion" in IEP minutes and support services, convinced that no document, no law, can truly govern the immeasurable relational ecologies of the spaces we inhabit when we cross the boundaries to be together.

Ashley

In five years of teaching middle school-aged students labeled intellectual disabilities, it's impossible to remember how many times my students were denied access to the general education curriculum and their same-age peers. Even on rare occasions when a colleague would agree to partner with me and include any of my students in their class, my students were never given full access. During my first year of teaching, after significant resistance, our choir teacher agreed to let four of my students participate in her choir class. I remember the excitement that I could barely contain on the night of their first choir concert—excitement that turned to embarrassment and furry when my students were the only four students removed from the risers at the end of the first song. The anger I communicated was quickly lost in the accolades our choir teacher received for including "those kids" and giving them a chance. Exhausted by the fight to give my students any sliver of access as a first-year teacher, I made the decision to start a sign language program and have our students try out to perform a song in sign language for the talent show on the last day of school. I chose a song I knew would make an impact on our school community—*You Raise Me Up* by Josh Groban. They practiced, they were selected, and they performed. Every person in the auditorium jumped to their feet and cheered for my students. I vividly remember the glowing smiles on each of my students' faces as they watched 300 members of their school community scream and cheer for them when the music stopped. This, I thought, would change everything.

That August, when I knocked on doors asking our guidance counselors and teachers to sign my students up for their classes—I was given the same answer as before, though the responses were sugar coated with accolades of how inspirational, amazing, and beautiful my students were.[2] The only thing that changed was that I further exceptionalized my students. I made them an inspiration to our school community. I failed my students in my early teaching career. I objectified them to try to create opportunities for them. My school community failed them—we failed to recognize their humanity and basic right to be given access to an equitable school experience.

These experiences brought me to a call with my professor and mentor Dr. Kathy McMahon-Klosterman where she brought me right back to conversations shared with Nickie in our SAGE meetings—she asked me hard questions and I reexamined everything.

Ten years later I began a summer program for college-age students labeled with intellectual disabilities at Miami University. My reckoning continued. I coordinated a program for nine of my former middle school students to live in a dorm for a week and take a disability studies class with current Miami students. I reimagined my teaching with the same group of students and guided my curriculum by critical theory. We examined the differences between inclusion and access and explored how disability justice is another word for love, specifically that "Access is Love" (Mingus et al., 2019). The students named our program Access Miami. As a culminating project, we attended a conference with our local city council and my students made recommendations for how to make our community more accessible. My student Joe told our city council members, "I don't need to change, the city needs to change." I still reflect on the questions Nickie and I grappled with many years ago and continually ask myself the question grounded in radical love, "How can I reconfigure my education spaces to be a place of shared power?" (Coomer & Cartell Johnson, 2018).

Ganiva

Yet again Tyrell was sent to the back of the room for jumping up in place and calling out answers to the music teacher's questions. Or at least, I think that is what he was being called out for? It looked like most of the other students were doing the same thing, but like always, Tyrell was singled out. As Tyrell, a vibrant Black boy, got up to walk over to the usual time-out spot at the back of the room, the white male teacher, Mr. Thorn, reminded him to keep quiet and not speak to anyone. There I was at the back with Julián, listening and witnessing the event unfolding. Tyrell joined us and sat next to Julián. At the time I was working as a Teacher Assistant for the *PPCD* and Julián was one of my bilingual students with autism. Julián was a bright and loving Brown boy who was eager to interact with Tyrell. As usual, Julián and I were both at the back of the room for "inclusion time," yet we were rarely included. So, this time I rebelled. I decided to include Tyrell with us. I ripped out pages from a notebook and gave Tyrell and Julián each a sheet of paper to draw on. With great excitement and not a moment to lose, Tyrell picked up a pen and drew himself and Julián holding hands with a heart in the center. He wrote "I love school" and "I love Julián." Tyrell showed the picture to me and Julián. Julián laughed with joy, which caused some students to turn around to see what was happening on the sidelines. Mr. Thorn did not look pleased. Tyrell then began drawing music notes in his picture. I was thrilled to see his knowledge of music. Using my own experience with music passed down from my own family, I decided to engage in a mini lesson with Tyrell and Julián. All this activity meant that we were talking when Tyrell was supposed to be silent. I didn't care, we talked right on, but soon Mr. Thorn interrupted us reminding Tyrell that he is not supposed to talk during time out. He then asked Tyrell to move to another seat across the room. Even from a distance, Julián and Tyrell smiled at one another, and I smiled along with them. I thought to myself, "this isn't the last time that we'll push up against the margins of the classroom."

Brittany

Ryan has been with most of the same peers since kindergarten, so by the time he was in 4th grade, him being autistic wasn't anything unusual to most of the kids. I had already been teaching for four years so I was familiar with working with students with differences—now I know this is neurodiversity—but I didn't know that then, nor was I prepared well in my teacher preparation program to be the best teacher I could be. Fortunately, we had one of the best special education teachers (that is still the title the school used) that I had ever worked with. Kim was a wonderful resource and taught me so much. My class was fully inclusive, so instead of Ryan leaving my class to go to the "resource room," Kim would come and co-teach with me weekly. It was awesome. She didn't just hang around Ryan the whole time—rather we truly integrated our teaching practices during our time together. Yet despite how *normalized* I thought everyone was in our classroom, the students seemed to think of Kim as my "helper teacher." Therefore, Ryan was signaled out again in ways that alienated him from the class. Despite us as co-teachers trying to disrupt this, the culture of the binary between gen ed and special ed was too strong. The students were socialized in this difference.

CRITICAL COALITION WITH/IN THE BOUNDARIES: CRITICAL DISABILITY STUDIES, FEMINIST WAYS OF KNOWING, AND RADICAL LOVE

In this section we draw upon our curriculum fragments to assemble our theoretical and *consiliencatory* prism that bridges CDS and feminist disability studies with three specific pedagogical concepts from feminist of Color onto-epistemologies and Disability communities: (1) engaged pedagogy (Berry, 2010; hooks, 1994), (2) the concept of nepantla (Anzaldúa, 2015), (3) radical love (Freire, 2005; Reyes et al., 2018; Stern & Brown, 2016), and (4) "access is love" (Mingus et al., 2019). We unpack important lessons learned from our narratives as we discuss each concept below. We do this to "flesh out" (Moraga & Anzaldua, 1983) our theoretical framework and point out how this foundation can equip educators with the tools to develop "a disability justice radical love meta-critical emotionality consiliencatory boundary work praxis" (as articulated in the framing of this book). That said, we also engage with the critical introspective work of our own positionalities in relation to our students, contexts, and situations.

Engaged Pedagogy

According to bell hooks (1994), engaged pedagogy takes the experiences of students of Color into account in order to charge educators with the responsibility of challenging white, Eurocentric ways of knowing. Stemming from a critical feminist lens, engaged pedagogy "incorporates passions, dialogue, and interaction through the entrance of lived experiences" (Berry, 2010,

p. 22) of students of Color in the classroom. It also encompasses mutual vulnerability in which the teacher and students reveal personal stories in connection with oppression and privilege. Berry (2010) states that "life experiences, when permitted into the classroom and given voice, can call to task the established" (p. 21) curriculum. White, female, non-Disabled teachers may see themselves as completely different from their students. But how can an engaged pedagogy open up dialogue about their lived experiences in ways that enable teachers to see the full humanity of their students?

Nepantla

Incorporating a dialogic relationship that is focused on students' experience, critiques, and subjugated knowledge (e.g., Bacon & Lalvani, 2019; Blevins & Talbert, 2016) opens up a space in which Disabled students are welcomed and encouraged to share their understandings and sense-making of their experiences with oppression, and teachers are able to do the same if they are indeed practicing engaged pedagogy. However, this can invoke discomfort for teachers who are not familiar with learning from student experiences with oppression. Nepantla (Anzaldúa, 2015) is a useful concept that can help teachers navigate this discomfort. Nepantla is a "Nahuatl word/concept for that ambiguous, tentative, ever-changing space we all inhabit" (Pérez, 2005, p. 1). It is the in-between space where permeable identities overlap to break down fixed categories of identity. This is the space where the subaltern resides, a "decolonial imaginary—that space between colonial and postcolonial . . . where [one] makes sense of [one's] agency" (Pérez, 2005, p. 4). Nepantla is a useful theoretical tool that opens up possibilities for teachers to tap into vulnerability as an opportunity to open up and conncct with Disabled students in ways that can build common ground across differences.

Importantly, then, breaking the barriers of assigned values in neoliberal schooling contexts provides the opportunity to redefine "difference" away from a fixed conception, and rather as mutable. In nepantlan space, a classroom community that values difference is not rooted in binary objectivities of same vs. different, normal vs. abnormal, deserving vs. undeserving, but is rather rooted in authentic relationships built on both care and coalition, intentionally disruptive of the hegemonic, institutional practices of schooling that dehumanize students and teachers.

Radical Love

It is crucial to make these connections in order to understand the context of disability in schools as intertwined with the contexts of teaching. This stands in sharp contrast to adopting the deficit and medical models of special education, and considers resistance to these models of normative schooling as an act of love (Freire, 2005; Reyes et al., 2018; Stern & Brown, 2016), favoring the spirit of disruption from the disability justice movement over dogmatic application of assigned curriculum, adherence to exclusionary discipline, and the invocation and implementation of special education law and policy as it is used to label and exclude students.

Thus, we consider radical love as the binding that compels teachers to understand their students not as entirely separate from them and their positions as teachers, but as part of themselves and constitutive of the potentialities of education. Teachers are more than allies to and advocates for their students: radical love compels teachers to understand their own emotions and embodied experiences of their role as teacher as inextricably linked to their students' embodied experiences of the structures of schooling. Radical love pushes teachers beyond simply educating through a prescribed curriculum, and into the space of collective and authentic care; and as students' partners in developing creative ways to promote change. As critical pedagogues, theorists, and activists have declared, teachers must see their own liberation from dehumanizing education policy as intimately tied with the liberation of their students, even though their experiences may seem to be completely separate (e.g., Lorde, 1977; Watson, n.d.). Radical love forces the acknowledgment that teachers' and students' experiences in school and subjugated knowledges are bound together.

"Access Is Love"

Technical, roboticized approaches to teaching and the sorting mechanisms of atheoretical applications of special education harm both teachers and students, especially in neoliberal contexts where teachers' and students' worth and deservedness of belonging is determined by their productivity, output, and ability to assimilate to the practices of schooling. Shifting teaching practices away from teacher education rooted in atheoretical technicist deliveries where "white women, although they may not call the shots, they often pull the trigger" (Leonardo & Boas, 2013, p. 315) toward a reimagined paradigm where teaching is an act of love—of radical love—where we enact "Access is Love" (Mingus et al., 2019) can empower educators to create classroom communities where power and leadership are shared. "Access commands the creation of classroom spaces for students, disabled and non-disabled, that is theirs as much as it is ours" (Cartell Johnson & Hineman, 2019, p. 71).

Accordingly, teaching as an act of resistance rooted in social justice alliance building cannot define inclusion as the end goal, but rather establish a space and praxis where collective work with Disabled students should begin.

This paradigm shift in teacher education will happen when we step back from teaching practices centered in atheoretical technicist deliveries to practices rooted in our entangled embodiments, working toward our collective and enmeshed interests. More, centering the subjugated knowledges in Disability communities moves from addressing a social environment to be more inclusive toward shifting the fundamental assumptions about ability that underlie schooling, and society more broadly. In her work toward disability justice, Patty Berne (2018) states, "we know to truly have liberation we must be led by those who know the most about these systems and how they work" (p. 1).

This is work toward teaching as an act of resistance rooted in social justice access and alliance building must be a collective effort. Teaching through radical love enacts disability justice as love (Mingus, 2018) and materializes the call to action in Mia Mingus', Alice Wong's, and Sandy Ho's project, #accessislove (https://disabilityvisibilityproject.com/2019/02/01/access-is-love/, 2019). Access as an act of love in schools calls on educators to "incorporate access in their everyday practices and lives" (https://disabilityvisibilityproject.com/2019/02/01/access-is-love/, 2019) and thus disrupt the everyday interactions that use special education to separate, rather than authentically value and create authentic access.

CONCLUSION

A reimagined teacher education centered in feminist disability theory and CDS challenges preservice teachers to examine their own identities and positionalities, particularly in race, gender, and disability, and the ways in which their own identity and agency serve to uphold and maintain the social contexts of schooling that both privilege and disempower them. This examination allows for possibilities where teacher candidates can understand how systems of schooling focused on classifying students rely on their complicity, and how this complicity maintains their position in "women's work" that has historically relied on their own exploitation. Examining the spaces where teachers' labor intersects with students' school experiences can empower teachers to ground their praxis in engaged pedagogies as an act of radical love that disrupts their positions of power in order to center the interests of their students who have been historically marginalized and disenfranchised by formal education. In this space of possibility, preservice teachers can reconfigure conceptualizations of general and special education away from sorting mechanisms, and instead as places of shared power. This reframes special education as a means for intersectional revolutionary access that is situated in the lives of students in authentic relationships that account for contextual, critical, and technical praxis, and invokes the spirit of activism and resistance to position teaching as a commitment to social justice through pedagogically enacted radical love in school.

NOTES

1. In accordance with social and relational models of disability, as applied in this chapter, we follow leaders in disability justice advocacy movements to use Identity-First language. For discussion, see Liebowitz, C. (2015, March 20) I am Disabled: On Identity-First versus people-first language. The Body is Not an Apology. Retrieved from https://thebodyisnotanapology.com/magazine/i-am-disabled-on-identity-first-versus-people-first-language/.

2. "Inspiration porn," made popular by Stella Young's Ted Talk "I am Not Your Inspiration" (2014), has been characterized as "the representation of disability as a desirable but undesired characteristic, usually by showing impairment as a visually or symbolically distinct biophysical deficit in one person, a deficit that can and must be overcome through the display of physical prowess" (Grue, 2016).

REFERENCES

Abraham, S. (2014). A nepantla pedagogy comparing Anzaldúa's and Bhaktin's ideas for pedagogical and social change. *Critical Education, 5*(5), 1–20.
Access is love. (2019, February 1). Disability Visibility Project. https://disabilityvisibilityproject.com/2019/02/01/access-is-love/
Akkerman, S. F., & Bakker, A. (2011). Boundary crossing and boundary objects. *Review of Educational Research, 81*(2), 132–169.
Annamma, S. A. (2017). *The pedagogy of pathologization: Dis/abled girls of color in the school-to-prison nexus*. Routledge.
Annamma, S. A. (2018). Mapping consequential geographies in the carceral state: Education journey mapping as a qualitative method with girls of color with dis/abilities. *Qualitative Inquiry, 24*(1), 1–15.
Anzaldúa, G. E. (2015). *Light in the dark/luz en los oscuro: Rewriting identity, spirituality, reality*. Duke University Press.
Artiles, A. (1998). The dilemma of difference: Enriching the disproportionality discourse with theory and context. *The Journal of Special Education, 32*(1), 32–36.
Bacon, J. K., & Lalvani, P. (2019). Dominant narratives, subjugated knowledges, and the righting of the story of disability in K-12 curricula. *Curriculum Inquiry, 49*(4), 387–404.
Berne, P., Morales, A. L., Langstaff, D., & Invalid, S. (2018). Ten principles of disability justice. *WSQ: Women's Studies Quarterly, 46*(1), 227–230.
Berry, B. (2010). Engaged pedagogy and critical race feminism. *Educational Foundations, 24*(3–4), 19–26.
Blevins, B., & Talbert, T. L. (2016). Challenging the neo-liberal social studies perspective. In A. R. Crowe (Ed.), *Rethinking social studies teacher education for twenty-first century* citizenship (pp. 23–39). Springer.

Brantlinger, E. (2006). Conclusion: Whose labels/ Whose norms? Whose needs? Whose benefits? In E. Brantlinger (Ed.), *Who benefits from special education?: Remediating (fixing) other people's children* (pp. 233–248). Lawrence Erlbaum Associates.

Boveda, M., & Aronson, B. (2019). Special education preservice teachers intersectional diversity, and the privileging of emerging professional identities. *Remedial and Special Education, 40*(4), 248–260.

Boveda, M., Reyes, G., & Aronson, B. (2019). Discipline to access the general education curriculum: Girls of color, disabilities, and specialized education programming. *Curriculum Inquiry, 49*(4), 405–425.

Bush, G. W. (2001). No Child Left Behind. U.S. Department of Education, Office of the Secretary.

Cartell Johnson, A., & Hineman, C. (2019). A duoethnographic journey of inclusion to access. *Currere Exchange Journal, 3*(1), 65–73.

Carter, A. M. (2015). Teaching with trauma: Disability pedagogy, feminism, and the trigger warnings debate. *Disability Studies Quarterly, 35*(2).

Cashman, T. G. (2016). Navigating the intersection of place-based pedagogy and border pedagogy: Resituating our positions through border dialogism. *International Journal of Critical Pedagogy, 7*(1), 29–50.

Chapman, L. H. (2010). An update on No Child Left Behind and national trends in education. *Arts and Education Policy Review, 109*(1), 25–40.

Coomer, M. N., & Cartell Johnson, A. (2018, April). *Accomplices not advocates: A feminist disability accompliceship proposal for teachers of students with disabilities*. Presentation at the 17th Annual Multiple Perspectives Conference, Columbus, OH.

Crenshaw, K. (1991). Mapping the margins: Intersectionality, identity politics, and violence against women. *Stanford Law Review, 43*(6), 1241–1299.

Dumas, M., & Nelson, J. D. (2016). (Re)Imagining Black boyhood: Toward a critical framework for educational research. *Harvard Educational Review, 86*(1), 27–47.

Erevelles, N. (2000). Educating unruly bodiese: Critical pedagogy, disability studies, and the politics of schooling. *Educational Theory, 50*(1), 25–47.

Ferri, B. A., & Connor, D. J. (2005). Tools of exclusion: Race, disability, and (re)segregated education. *Teachers College Record, 107*(3), 453–474.

Freire, P. (1974). Conscientisation. *Cross Currents, 24*(1), 23–31.

Freire, P. (2005). *Teachers as cultural workers: Letters to those who dare to teach.* Westview Press.

Gabel, S., & Danforth, S. (2008). *Vital questions facing disability studies in education.* Peter Lang.

Garland-Thomson, R. (2002). Integrating disability, transforming feminist theory. *NWSA Journal, 14*(3), 1–32.

Garland-Thomson, R. (2018). Critical disability studies: A knowledge manifesto. In K. Ellis, R. Garland-Thomson, M. Kent, & R. Robertson (Eds.), *Manifestos for the future of critical disability studies* (pp. 11–19). Routledge.

Giroux, H. A. (2010, November 23). Lessons to be learned from Paulo Freire as education is being taken over by the mega rich. http://archive.thruthout.org/lessons-be-learned-from-paulo-freire-education-is-being-taken-over-mega-rich65363

Goodley, D. (2013). Dis/entangling critical disability studies. *Disability & Society, 28*(5), 631–644.

Grue, J. (2016). The problem with inspiration porn: A tentative definition and a provisional critique. *Disability & Society, 31*(6), 838–849.

Grumet-Hobart, M., & Colleges, W. S. (1981). Pedagogy for patriarchy: The feminization of teaching. *Interchanging, 12*(2–3), 165–184.

Haegele, J. A., & Hodge, S. (2016). Disability discourse: Overview and critiques of the medical and social models. *Quest, 68*(2), 193–206.

Hilda, K., & Oram, A. (2007). Men must be educated and women must do it: The National Federation (later Union) of Women Teachers and contemporary feminism. *Gender and Education, 19*(6), 663–667.

hooks, B. (1994). *Teaching to transgress*. Routledge.

Kroesbergen, E. H., & Van Luit, J. E. (2003). Mathematics interventions for children with special educational needs: A meta-analysis. *Remedial and Special Education, 24*(2), 970–114.

Ladson-Billings, G. (1999). Preparing teachers for diverse student populations: A critical race theory perspective. *Review of Research in Education, 24*(1999), 211–247.

Ladson-Billings, G. (2014). Culturally relevant pedagogy 2.0: AKA the remix. *Harvard Educational Review, 84*(1), 74–135.

Laitsch, D. (2013). Smacked by the invisible hand: The wrong debate at the wrong time with the wrong people. *Journal of Curriculum Studies, 45*(1), 16–27.

Leonardo, Z. (2007). The war on schools: NCLB, nation creation and the educational construction of whiteness. *Race Ethnicity and Education, 10*(3), 261–278.

Leonardo, Z., & Boas, E. (2013). Other kids' teachers: What children of color learn from white women and what this says about race, whiteness, and gender. In M. Lynn & A. Dixson (Eds.), *The handbook of critical race theory in education* (pp. 313–324). Routledge.

Linton, S. (1998). *Claiming disability: Knowledge and identity*. New York University Press.

Lorde, A. (1977). *Poetry is not a luxury*. Druck & Verlags Cooperative.

Matias, C. E. (2016). "Why do you make me hate myself?": Re-teaching Whiteness, abuse, and love in urban teacher education. *Teaching Education, 27*(2), 194–211.

Meekosha, H., & Shuttleworth, R. (2009). What's so "critical" about critical disability studies? *Australian Journal of Human Rights, 15*(1), 47–75.

Mehan, H. (1993). Beneath the skin and between the ears: A case study in the politics of representation. In B. A. U. Levinson (Ed.), *Schooling the symbolic animal: Social and cultural dimensions of education* (pp. 259–279). Rowan & Littlefield Publishers.

Mingus, M. (2018, October). "Disability justice" is simply another term for love. Presentation at the 2018 Disability Intersectionality Summit, Cambridge, MA.

Mingus, M., Wong, A., & Ho, S. (2019). Access is love. https://disabilityvisibilityproject.com/2019/02/01/access-is-love/

Moraga, C., & Anzaldúa, G. (Eds.). (1983). *This bridge called my back: Writings by radical women of color* (2nd ed.). Kitchen Table/Women of Color Press.

National Women's Law Center. (2013). Sex stereotypes: How they hurt women in the workplace and in the wallet [Fact sheet]. http://www.nwlc.org/sites/default/files/pdfs/suits_fact_sheet_-_sex_stereotypes_01.30.2013.pdf

Nichols, S. L., & Berliner, D. C. (2007). *Collateral damage: How high-stakes testing corrupts America's schools.* Harvard Education Press.

Niedenthal, P. M., Barsalou, L. W., Winkielman, P., Krauth-Grubeer, S., & Ric, F. (2005). Embodiment in attitudes, social perception, and emotions. *Personality and Social Psychology Review, 9*(3), 184–211.

Pérez, E. (2005). Gloria Anzaldúa: La gran nueva Mestiza theorist, writer, activist-scholar. *NWSA, 17*(2), 1–10.

Perkins, L. M. (1993). The role of education in the development of Black feminist thought, 1860–1920. *History of Education, 22*(3), 265–275.

Poetter, T. S., & Googins, J. (Eds.). (2015). *Was someone mean to you today? The impact of standardization, corporatization, and high stakes testing on students, teachers, communities, schools, and democracy.* Van Griner Publishing.

Price, M. (2014). The Bodymind problem and the possibilities of pain. *Hypatia, 30*(1), 268–284.

Puar, J. (2013). *The right to maim.* Duke University Press.

Reyes, G., Radina, R., & Aronson, B. (2018). Teaching against the grain as an act of love: Disrupting white Eurocentric masculinist frameworks within teacher education. *The Urban Review, 50,* 818–835.

Rodgers, C., & Raider-Roth, M. (2006). Presence in teaching. *Teachers and Teaching: Theory and Practice, 12*(3), 265–287.

Salazar, M. D. C. (2013). A humanizing pedagogy: Reinventing the principles and practice of education as a journey toward liberation. *Review of Research in Education, 37*(1), 121–148.

Schalk, S. (2013). Coming to claim crip: Disidentification with/in disability studies. *Disability Studies Quarterly, 33*(2).

Sleeter, C. E. (2001). Preparing teachers for culturally diverse schools: Research and the overwhelming presence of whiteness. *Journal of Teacher Education, 52*(2), 94–106.

Stern, M., & Brown, A. (2016). "It's 5:30. I'm exhausted. And I have to go all the way to f*%#ing Fishtown.": Educator depression, activism, and finding (armed) love in a hopeless (neoliberal) place. *The Urban Review, 48*(2), 333–354.

Strauss, V. (2014, October 25). A Time magazine cover enrages teachers again. *The Washington Post.* https://www.washingtonpost.com/news/answer-sheet/wp/2014/10/25/a-time-magazine-cover-enrages-teachers-again/

Sullivan, A. L., Van Norman, E. R., & Klingbeil, D. A. (2014). Exclusionary discipline of students with disabilities: Student and school characteristics predicting suspension. *Remedial and Special Education, 35*(4), 199–210.

Taylor, K. A. (2005). Mary S. Peake and Charlotte L. Forten: Black teachers during the Civil War and Reconstruction. *The Journal of Negro Education, 74*(2), 124–137.

Thorius, K. K. (2019). Facilitating en/counters with legacies of white supremacy and ableism through professional learning to eliminate special education disproportionality. *International Journal of Qualitative Studies in Education, 32*(3), 323–340.

Thorius, K. K., & Waitoller, F. R. (2017). Strategic coalitions against exclusion at the intersection of race and disability—a rejoinder. *Harvard Educational Review, 87*(2), 251–257.

Villegas, A. M., & Lucas, T. (2002). Preparing culturally responsive teachers: Rethinking the curriculum. *Journal of Teacher Education, 53*(1), 20–32.

Ware, L. (2005). Many possible futures, many different directions: Merging critical special education and disability studies. In S. Gabel (Ed.), *Disability studies in education: Readings in theory and method* (pp. 13–124). Peter Lang Publishing.

Watson, L. (n.d.) The origin of "Our liberty is bound together." https://invisiblechildren.com/blog/2012/04/04/the-origin-of-our-liberty-is-bound-together/

Wilson, E. O. (1999). *Consilience: The unity of knowledge* (Vol. 31). Vintage.

Wong, A. (2019). The U.S. teaching population is getting bigger, and more female. *The Atlantic*. https://www.theatlantic.com/education/archive/2019/02/the-explosion-of-women-teachers/582622/

Chapter 8

Introspecting the Radical Love Boundaries between Deaf Studies and Special Education in an African Setting

Martin Musengi

SEKA HUREMA WAFA [LAUGH AT DISABILITY WHEN YOU ARE DEAD]—AFRICAN PROVERB

This chapter analyzes the love-fear dynamics underlying boundary crossings in the education of deaf learners with the aim of unmasking the oppressive context of their education and laying the foundation for countering oppression through liberating pedagogy. The chapter uses an empirical study in the form of an autoethnographic case study in which, as a hearing adult I searched for the meaning of teaching deaf children in residential institutions for the deaf in Zimbabwe. I thought it necessary to explore my own knowledge and beliefs in light of a growing dissonance with traditional special education which was grounded on their deficits. To this end, the chapter analyzes my understanding of disability, deafness, and also outlines the procedures around the lesson observations that provided data for the autoethnographic episodes in order to provide context.

CONTEXT

No education which is meant to be liberating can remain distant from the oppressed by treating them as unfortunates and by presenting for their emulation, models from among the oppressors (Freire, 1970). This critical pedagogy dictum holds particularly true for D/deaf[1] learners about whom contemporary African tradition based on the disabled versus nondisabled binary has shown ambivalence as either nondisabled[2] equals or disabled unfortunates. D/deaf people are viewed as "unfortunates" in medical model thinking that only sees their inherent deficiencies or shortcomings about which society should be charitable. They are viewed as equals worthy of respect in sociocultural model thinking which, as in the proverb, recognizes and does not undervalue their Deaf culture. In this light, ambivalent boundary crossings in the special education of D/deaf children are intriguing as most of their teachers are hearing and do not necessarily share their Deaf culture. Whether operating within medical or sociocultural models, the teachers do generally profess radical love (Agnello, 2016) for their students. Radical love refers to being dedicated to, wanting the best for, concerned about, caring for, encouraging, supporting, connecting with, recognizing, praising, guiding, inspiring, humanizing interrelations with, going beyond the call of duty for, sticking up for, protecting, mentoring, and working with for world transformation (Agnello, 2016, p. 68).

From a sociocultural perspective "disability" is a social construct (Armstrong & Barton, 1999) and therefore attempts to universalize the term disability and related constructs such as "deafness" run into conceptual problems. Devlieger (1998) observes that the practice of grouping people together into a recognizable category as "disabled" is traceable to the histories and cultural contexts of specific Western societies. He explains that many contemporary African languages do not have generic vocabulary related to disability as they have not "benefited" from language exchange resulting from contact with colonial languages. The process of importing disability-related terminology from the colonial official languages has mostly involved the local term for "physical disability" acquiring broader meanings that incorporate people with a variety of impairments (Devlieger, 1998). In this chapter, I follow through on this line of thinking by exploring how my beliefs about physical disability and disability in general may have influenced the meaning that I attached to praxis with deaf learners. By praxis I mean the manner in which I integrated theory and beliefs with reflection and practice to either domesticate or liberate the learners. Proverbs, which include many that are related to disability, are a primary means of reflecting on beliefs in Southern Africa where I write from. In the example of the proverb above, the implications of laughing at a person with a disability illuminate what Devlieger (1999) calls the existential insecurity of life.

I reflect in this chapter on how my primary beliefs about disability and deafness in African culture may serve as a mirror of my own existential insecurity as a non-deaf[3] teacher. I tentatively explore how this may have played a role in liberating or domesticating praxis in the residential schools for the deaf where I spent a significant proportion of my teaching career as someone firmly grounded in African indigenous culture. I was born into African culture of Zimbabwe, and growing up I acquired norms and values related to this culture. In this culture, the extended family system is strong (Chiswanda,

1997). Members of the extended family were traditionally expected to eat communally from the same plate, support each other in every way, and learn the values of cooperation, sharing, and respect (Gelfand, 1959). Communality and uniformity therefore came naturally to me, and it was not difficult for me to excel in teacher-training which taught me to strive to achieve teaching objectives for a mythical "average" student. It is only after I underwent further training, this time specializing in Special Education, when I began to appreciate the importance of individual differences in teaching and learning situations.

Misgivings about my competencies as a non-deaf teacher who underwent lengthy specialist training in Special Education to teach children whom we called "hearing-impaired" and the apparent perennial failure of these learners are contradictory facts which inspired the empirical study on which this chapter is grounded. Specifically, the study sought to construct the meaning that I and probably many other specialist teachers of deaf learners attach to the everyday lived experience of teaching in special residential schools for the deaf. The intention was to analyze my story in light of boundary work between the system and canon of, on the one hand, Disability Studies in Education and, on the other hand, traditional Special Education (Danforth & Gabel, 2006; Ware, 2005). Akkerman and Bakker (2011) describe boundary work as sites for sociocultural differences involving sameness and continuity within their discontinuity in participation and collaboration at boundaries that cross a diversity of sites. My principal aims after Van Manen (1984) were to uncover how I accounted for the academic outcomes of the deaf students I taught and how I explained and managed my lived experience. I interpret my experiences within the broader sociocultural context as suggested by Sparkes (2000) and Holt (2003).

By placing myself as the main actor within the "play" of autoethnography (Butler, 1997) I hope to stimulate other non-deaf teachers of deaf learners and readers in general to reflect upon their own lives in relation to mine. Like Humphreys (2005), my intention is to provide the reader access to some of my natural and spontaneous reactions and dispel any notion that I am an independent, objective researcher. As in the work of Ellis and Bochner (1992) I emphasize participating with you rather than describing for you. In this way I hope to better understand some of the assumptions that underlie my own praxis and possibly that of other teachers of the deaf. At the time of writing this, most teachers of the deaf in Zimbabwe are non-deaf adults who also come from African culture that appears to be undecided about deafness (Musengi, 2014) which is why I think this narrative might resonate with many of them. The following section outlines the methodology used to carry out the empirical study.

METHODOLOGY

For my PhD thesis, I had initially planned focus group discussions and individual interviews for teachers of deaf learners at three special schools for the deaf in Zimbabwe, but these interviews invariably turned into interviews *by* these participants. Toward the end of each interview in the schools for the deaf, I was always asked about my own experiences as a teacher of the deaf. I learned a lot about myself in these "impromptu" interviews and was surprised at the extent to which the other teachers' narratives intertwined with my own. In this regard I realized that I was inadvertently engaging in what is variously called interactive introspection (Ellis, 1991), personal history (Bullough, 1994), and personal history self-study (Samaras, Hicks & Berger, 2004). I was emboldened to continue on this track because, as Ellis (2001) explains, it is important to understand self in order to understand others. I therefore decided to carry out a formal autoethnography, which in this case was a form of personal history self-study informed by the widely shared belief that teaching is a fundamentally autobiographical act (Samaras et al., 2004; Finley, 1998; Knowles, 1998).

Self-study is supported by the notion that who we are as people affects who we are as teachers and consequently our students' learning (Samaras et al., 2004). Rushing (2006) says that autoethnography has been perceived as "feminine" or "soft," while Sparkes (2000) explains that criticism has largely been based on misapprehensions since autoethnography is located at the boundaries of disciplinary practices. For this method at the boundary, I facilitated recollection of data from personal memory following Chang (2008) who advises the employment of inventorying techniques. I did an inventory of work artifacts in the form of principals' and schools-inspectors' critique reports on lessons that they had observed me teaching in the residential schools for the deaf. As part of this self-study methodology (Bullough, 1994; Samaras et al., 2004), I was able to reconstruct significant life events to inform the way I made meaning of pedagogy for deaf students. It is on the basis of self-study that I add a personal voice to my writing.

To facilitate recollection of data from my personal memory and therefore operationalize self-study, I followed advice by Chang (2008) to employ interactive introspection, inventorying techniques as well as creating an autobiographical timeline. Interaction in individual and focus group interviews with other teachers was the main activity which triggered recollection and introspection of my own story as a teacher of the deaf. Samaras et al. (2004) explain that one of the hallmarks of personal history self-study is its collaborative nature which gives the opportunity to disrobe, unveil, and engage in a soul-searching truth about the self while also engaging in critical conversations and continuing to discover the alternative viewpoints of others. Chang

(2008) explained that collecting the stories of others through conversations and interviews with them in order to respond to their self-narratives is an important autoethnographic data collection technique.

To operationalize this technique in my data collection, immediately after each focus group discussion and individual interview for my PhD thesis, I would make notes in a field journal highlighting similarities and differences between the teachers' experiences and my own. Ellis (1991) called this "interactive introspection" and said it could be taken further and become a situation where the researcher and other participants can interview one another, helping to recreate and describe their recollection of experiences. My being interviewed by the teachers in the schools for the deaf initially happened spontaneously rather than by design. In the focus group discussions and individual interviews, several teachers asked me about my experiences in a special school from the mid-1980s to late 1990s. I used this as an opportunity to take up the interactive introspection suggested by Ellis (1991). I made notes in my field journal on what I was experiencing during these interactions with the teachers in both focus group discussions and individual interviews and how it is related to the past. I was careful to defer answering the teachers' questions until the end of the discussions or individual interviews in order to remain nondirective and avoid being over-involved. In this way I tried to avoid getting results that reflected my personal interests rather than those of the teachers, as advised by Knodel and Pramualratana (1987).

In addition to this autoethnographic data collection technique I also chronicled an autobiographical timeline into my field journal. This timeline included the following: my educational history, typical day, week, favorite and disliked activities as well as life cycle during my teaching career in two special schools for the deaf. In coming up with this timeline I was guided by, but not restricted to items on my autoethnography guide, in what Bullough (1994) called an "education-related life-history." As articulated by Knowles and Holt-Reynolds (1991), the purpose of the life history is to get one to consider how and what one was thinking about teaching and themselves as teachers. Personal history self-study is about self-knowing toward personal and professional growth that is necessarily enriched through conversation and critique within a self-study community of scholars (Samaras et al., 2004). This self-reflective process which collected data on the past from personal memory was triangulated as suggested by Chang (2008). To triangulate, I inventoried six of my supervisors' critique reports on lessons they had observed me teaching. I retained the original reports and analyzed their content as work artifacts in order to re-create conversations with my principals and inspectors who wrote them. These conversations are highlighted as part of the autoethnography presented in the following sections.

The next section presents a reconstructed dialogue between myself and one of my assessors based on an observed lesson. The reconstruction utilizes data from lesson-critiques and like Rushing (2006) before me, I have shaped some of what the principals and school-inspectors told me into the voice of a composite character, meaning that I condense two or more people's stories into one in order to protect the identities of the participants and reduce the number of people I am asking you to know. For the purposes of context some information on the lesson observation process in the Zimbabwe education system may be necessary. It is a requirement that every teacher in the schools be assessed while teaching their class. Early in one's teaching career, the purpose of the initial assessment is to formally confirm a teacher after the mandatory two years of probation so that they become an "established" or tenured teacher. For this probationary purpose, the assessor as in the dialogue below is a school-inspector. The assessor would typically walk in unannounced, ask for lesson plans and other record books, and take a seat at the back. From that position they would observe and write detailed comments and evaluations on whatever lesson was being presented at the time. At the end of the 30-minute lesson the assessor would discuss with the teacher the strengths and weaknesses of the just observed lesson. A written critique of the lesson would also be handed over in order to be constantly referred to in order to improve practice. I had been teaching in the school for nearly three years and was now up for probationary review when the following dialogue takes place.

The Probationary Lesson Review

Inspector: *It is good that there is communication between you and the learners. You also make deliberate efforts to infuse speech-training exercises in your lessons which results in more voicing from your hearing impaired pupils.*

Teacher: *Thank you, but now my lessons take longer and I can hardly achieve stated lesson objectives. My class performs poorly.*

Inspector: *That is normal. It is their nature. You will get used to them with time. That is Special Education. It is good that you have rapport with this class – you just need more confidence in order to do very well.*

Teacher: Thinking—something is not quite right here but saying aloud: *Thank you for the feedback.*

The setting is the school office at a special school for the deaf in Zimbabwe. The inspector has just observed my lesson and is giving feedback. It is on the basis of the above complimentary comments arising from an early career probationary assessment that I feel uneasy. It does not feel right to be applauded for simply communicating with one's class—it should be taken for granted that anyone who purports to teach someone can communicate with them.

Something is also amiss when emphasis is placed on teaching speech and voicing at the expense of mastering subject content. The inspector's comments value the use of aural-oral activities such as speech-training (articulation) which apparently has aided the class to produce more voice than before. He associates the increased voicing of the deaf learners with improved rapport between the class and the teacher. All that is needed now is increased confidence on the part of the teacher as all apparently is well, the weak delivery of subject content notwithstanding. An aural-oral inclination toward teaching is probably premised on the well-documented speech-language gains achieved by deaf children who receive intense auditory-based intervention as early as two or three months since technology now makes early detection through neonatal screening possible in the Western world (Nicholas & Geers, 2006; White et al., 2010). Some studies found that under these conditions, education through an auditory/oral approach can lead to age-appropriate literacy attainments for deaf children, for example, in the United States (Geers & Moog, 1989) and in the United Kingdom (Lewis, 1996).

However, Musengi (1999) cited in Musengi (2014) found that detection in a developing country such as Zimbabwe is considered to be early at three or four years of age and that amplification and other auditory-based intervention measures are generally only possible upon entry into school at the age of six or seven years. Insisting on beginning aural-oral interventions at this stage is unlikely to result in the same well-documented speech-language gains as recorded elsewhere. The focus on deaf learners' increased voicing, while probably commendable in the mindset of a hearing-speaking public, should however not be the sole measure of success and should definitely not be at the expense of learning academic subject content. Early in my career there was a growing realization that even though I was passing the standards set by schools inspectors, I did not seem to be making much headway with the deaf learners. It began to feel as if the local culture accepted lower standards for Special Education, standards that would have been unacceptable for hearing children in the mainstream. The difference of opinion between observers of my lessons and me can be explained in Conle's (1999) terms when she observes that certain classroom events are interpreted differently by different experiencers of these events based on personal and cultural biographies that shape those interpretations.

This, therefore, also implies that the deaf learners I was teaching are likely to have had different interpretations of the classroom events they were undergoing as a result of their different personal and cultural biographies. The vast majority of deaf learners in my classes had severe to profound congenital deafness and were children born to mostly hearing parents. Deafness was usually diagnosed just before entry into school at five or six years of age. It is at this time of confirmation of the deafness and entry into school that donated school-owned second-hand hearing aids would then be worn in class and left for safe-keeping in the classrooms overnight, over the weekends, and during school-holidays (Musengi, 1999). Many of the mostly poor parents of deaf children could not afford to buy personal hearing aids for their children, let alone getting cochlear implants which were just coming onto the horizon in the distant developed world at that time. The next section outlines the sociocultural context in which I taught and is intended to analyze the cultural baggage that may have a bearing on my experience of teaching these deaf learners.

Disability and Deafness in Zimbabwe

My realization that there was a cultural and linguistic element to perceptions and beliefs about deafness was triggered by a bachelor's degree course I undertook which included a topic on the political correctness of using "person-first" language. For example, rather than writing "hearing impaired person" we were encouraged to write "person with hearing impairment." It was argued in the course that language is a primary means of communicating attitudes, thoughts, and feelings (Froschl et al., 1984) and so using person-first language demonstrates respect for people with disabilities by referring to them first as individuals and then referring to their disability when it is needed (Blaska, 1993). I was however rather uneasy about the inadequacy of just transplanting this person-first philosophy from Western culture to the local Shona language where deaf people are referred to as *mbeveve* or *chimumumu* both of which mean "mute" (Nyota, 2013) and have concordial agreement with the pronoun "it" suggesting that deaf people have a thing-like quality setting them beneath human beings. I was also uncertain about the historical inclusion of deafness in the group "disabled" about which many traditional-indigenous Zimbabweans experience shame (Mpofu et al., 2007).

This latter uncertainty follows the finding by Devlieger (1998) about "physical disability" generalizing to incorporate other impairments in the process of importing disability-related terminology from colonial languages. Similarly, precolonial harmony is recognized in the disability justice tenet number eight that highlights interdependence as integral to meeting each other's needs and therefore liberating whole communities (Berne et al., 2018). Interdependence in precolonial Africa is espoused in the African view of personhood articulated by Mbiti (2008:108) as, "I am because we are: and since we are, therefore I am." By implication, community was central to the African conception of personhood and this was usually based on family, focusing on humanness, caring, sharing, respect, and compassion. This harmony is at the heart of the precolonial African worldview or philosophy of *Ubuntu* which is in tandem with the disability justice tenet of being interdependent for the good of the whole community. The worldview is based on the primary values of intense humanness and associated values that ensure a happy and quality community.

I propose in this chapter that in precolonial times deaf people may not have been considered as disabled. I argue that since the morpheme *rema* from the Shona word for disability *chirema* means being heavy, failing, or lacking competence (Devlieger, 1998), then deaf people are unlikely to have been viewed as a burden in precolonial hunter-gatherer or agrarian communities as they are physically able to fend for themselves. They could therefore have been held to the same standards as the rest of the largely hunter-gatherer and agricultural communities. This line of thinking supports Nielsen (2014) who found that the historical formation of disability in the West resulted in the loss of indigenous ways of knowing and viewing disability. Unfortunately as a result of the colonial project obscuring deafness and disability in *Ubuntu* contexts, the harmony that must have existed in precolonial communities only has rather tenuous and tentative evidence based on local sociocultural explanations of disability.

The sociocultural perspective's explanation of disability as a social construct (Armstrong & Barton, 1999) does lend credence to the possibility that in precolonial Zimbabwean society the ability of deaf people to contribute to the well-being of the hunter-gatherer communities had not yet necessitated their being classified together with other disabled people. With the advent of colonialism many indigenous people came under pressure from Western disability service organizations to find terms equivalent to disability and so just provided the term locally used for physical disability to subsume all other conditions (Devlieger, 1998). This might explain why a deaf person would concurrently be classified as *chirema* in modern-day Shona while someone without arms may have no other label except *chirema*. In addition a precolonial term for deafness, *matsi*, has concordial agreement with pronouns for humans which supports the idea that deaf people were accepted into personhood.

In this light there is a strong possibility that in precolonial times, Zimbabwean culture did not perceive deafness as a disability. This would mean that even though teachers come from a culture which may be perceived as viewing disability generally negatively as a burden, deafness in the collective unconscious may not be thought of as a burden and may therefore not be perceived as a disability. However, the current Shona terms *mbeveve* or *chimumumu* have generalized to mean deafness therefore suggesting that this precolonial, romantic view of deafness was disrupted. Teachers, therefore, come into the teaching of deaf learners with cultural baggage whose precolonial and present stance toward deafness can only be described as opaque. To compound this uncertainty the position of the Western scientific teacher-education that teachers undergo is similarly ambivalent toward deafness (Livingston, 1997) reflecting the competing perspectives in deaf education that Paul (2001) calls clinical and sociocultural.

Deafness in Teacher-education

I was trained at my university, in in-service workshops as well as through role modeling to look at deaf learners as having inherent limitations related to impaired hearing, which discourse Paul (2001) refers to as the clinical perspective. Paul (2001) explains that within this perspective, deaf children's learning is typically approached as a problem in which deaf teenagers are performing at the level of eight- or nine-year-old hearing children as in literacy studies (Karchmer & Mitchell, 2003; Wauters et al., 2006) or in numeracy studies which find delay of about three years between deaf and hearing learners (Bull et al., 2005; Nunes & Moreno, 2002). In this perspective, a teacher is limited in what they can do for them especially if they are identified to have a hearing loss late and only begin to receive intervention services when they start school. This exclusion from teacher-education of positive information about deafness is what Knight and Miller (2021) call, from a disability justice perspective, an epistemic injustice. Epistemic injustice is the silencing or misrepresentation of undervalued groups (Knight & Miller, 2021).

Teacher training in deaf education tends to focus on deaf learners' "deficits" in order to remedy them. I spent a large part of specialist training focusing on how to teach deaf learners to speak and to listen for meaningful sounds using appropriate technology such as hearing aids. This Western scientific approach of deficiency is congruent with contemporary indigenous perceptions of deaf people as having a thing-like quality as that would justify attempts to remedy the situation by teaching them to speak and to listen. Chiswanda (1997) says that deafness is highly connected to lack of speech by many Zimbabweans who then begin to try to correct the organs of speech by cutting the frenulum. The preoccupation with the correction of speech may be because the Shona, like many other cultures, put emphasis on orally socializing their young whom they expect to learn, for example, from proverbs. This social construction which perceives speech as the most fully human form of language is disparaged by Baumann (2004) who argues that there is nothing intrinsically less human about nonphonetic forms of communication such as sign or writing.

SPEECH AND SIGN LANGUAGE

The following dialogue reflects principals' comments which may show their position on Speech and Sign Language. In recreating the discourse in the excerpt below, some of the comments provided by assessors of lessons after nearly two decades of teaching in a residential school for the deaf are used as data. These more routine assessments were done at least once a year in order to give continuous guidance. For this purpose an assessor could be a teacher-in-charge, deputy principal, or principal. In the following dialogue the principal is a composite character of various assessors' comments. Analysis of the dialogue shows that it reflects the beliefs that my superiors had about the deaf learners I was teaching.

Beliefs About Speech, Sign, and Academic Learning Outcomes

Principal: *I must congratulate you on a noticeable improvement in your signing. It is clear that you are in control in this class.*

Teacher: *Thank you, but I still cannot sign beyond basic greetings and issuing instructions. As I speak to my class, I skip rather a lot of signs which I do not know.*

Principal: *That is normal. You will get better with practice. Practice makes perfect. Learn from them and develop more confidence in yourself.*

Teacher: *But my class is still performing as poorly as before.*

Principal: *That is natural, remember they are language-handicapped. It is in their nature. You will get used to them with time. You should however use more concrete media in order to allow them to see. They are visualizers and will benefit from seeing real things. The important thing now is that you have developed a positive attitude towards these learners as is evident in the rapport between you. Keep it up.*

In analyzing these comments, emergent patterns in the content of the lesson critiques are noticeable. There were some comments which showed that an observer was "impressed" by whatever communication appeared to be successfully taking place between myself as a non-deaf teacher and my class of what were called "language-handicapped" learners. Other comments suggested that it was "normal" and "natural" for deaf learners to perform poorly and that what would happen is that I would eventually get used to this poor performance, although the use of concrete media would enhance outcomes for these visually oriented learners. These comments are reminiscent of similar ones during the probationary assessments nearly twenty years earlier, suggesting that there had been no substantive change in beliefs over time, even though the focus had shifted to manual communication.

Teaching orally had initially come naturally because it was the way in which I communicate most proficiently. I had also been specially trained and mentored in oral teaching while the superiors commended any effort in the oral direction. I continued to teach orally because that is what put bread on the table: performance-related pay meant that I literally had to sing for my supper. Performance-related pay is a neoliberal tenet derived from the market logic and principles of self-interest and competition. It is paradoxical that such radical marketization actually undermines related market principles of efficiency and outcomes in deaf education. This is because in the neoliberal system, unconditional love for deaf learners is paradoxically subverted by the ideology of normal (Annamma et al., 2013; Horejes, 2009) guided by an unnecessary disabled versus nondisabled binary. Teaching efforts that were commended were those misdirected toward continued oralism in order to "normalize" these profoundly deaf children from generally low socioeconomic status backgrounds. The intersection of these children's low socioeconomic statuses with delayed and inadequate audiometric interventions may well have resulted in low expectations of the deaf children.

According to Berne et al.'s (2018) disability justice tenet of intersectionality, the intersection of such factors in the lives of disabled people results in the differential experiencing of disability. The foundation of intersectionality is that two separate categories of identification, when combined, can create a third new category of identification that has its own set of experiences that differ from the original two categories (Crenshaw, 1989). Intersectionality, therefore, captures the multidimensionality of disabled people's experiences. As a result of intersectionality the concept of love that is not based on merit or competition had inadvertently become part of a pathologizing discourse which undervalued deaf learners as the label "deaf" compounded by their low socioeconomic status, as well as delayed and inadequate audiometric interventions were used to exonerate them of the responsibility of high academic standards. Graham (2008) called the use of labels for children with disabilities in this way an "exonerating construct." Deafness was used to exonerate the pupils from striving for high academic standards on the grounds that their learning was deficient. These low expectations were personally frustrating even though they also exonerated me as their teacher from striving for higher goals.

The implied low expectations for deaf learners become apparent through comments which value apparently improved communication between the learners and me even though my signing is rudimentary. It is thought to be "normal" and "natural" for deaf children to perform poorly and even though the principal expects me to improve with practice he also expects me to, in time, get used to their poor performance. Possibly subtly revealing of the principal's ableist mindset is his idea of concrete media for the deaf learners to visualize as it may also imply that he thinks deaf learners are unable to go beyond the concrete to the abstract. Gabel (2009) explains ableism as social biases against people whose bodies function differently than what is considered normal, which takes us back to Annamma et al.'s (2013) ideology of normal.

An inclination toward simultaneous communication seems to be reasonable in its recognition of deaf learners as visualizers who need to access a Sign Language which they can see. However, this inclination toward simultaneous communication would also appear to have flaws that are similar to those in an aural-oral inclination. Johnson et al. (1989) point out that because Sign Language is so different in structure from spoken language, it would be impossible to speak full sentences and sign complete Sign Language sentences simultaneously. Reliance on simultaneous communication might therefore be indicative of lack of acceptance of Sign Language as a proper language. Kiyaga and Moores (2009) observe that many teachers of deaf learners in sub-Saharan Africa do not believe that Sign Language is a language. The principal's belief that the learners are "language-handicapped" could be an ableist symptom of not believing Sign Language to be a language. This is because it is contradictory to expect the same "language-handicapped" deaf learners to teach the teacher a language, that is, Sign Language. As reported by Nziramasanga (1999) specialist teachers in Zimbabwe had to be taught Sign Language by their deaf pupils. In this light it would appear that only spoken languages are considered as languages when the principal talks of language-handicap. This kind of ableism is referred to as "audism." Audism is the deficit notion that one is superior based on one's ability to use sound-based, spoken language (Baumann & Murray, 2010). Audism negates the lived reality of many d/Deaf learners who may find the visual-gestural nature of Sign Language more accessible than the auditory nature of spoken language. It would appear, therefore, that even simultaneous communication has not moved away from a deficit perspective of deafness as it maintains ableist views.

In addition to the focus on deficits the principal's comments commended traditional approaches of class control and spoon-feeding. Advocating slow, step by careful step teaching focuses on order and control in lessons, which from the point of view of management, determine the teacher's success and survival in the classroom. However, this is the antithesis of Freire's critical pedagogy which according to Allen (2012) poses that such educational processes are not neutral as they can domesticate rather than liberate learners. Critical pedagogy argues for practices in which the lived experiences of empowerment for the vast majority of students become the defining feature of schooling (Giroux, 2010; Beacon & Golder, 2015). Therefore, critical pedagogy attempts to give a voice to D/deaf learners in schools and advocate for their liberation and the promotion of critical thinking and consciousness. In this way D/deaf learners would move from what Aliakbari and Faraji (2011) call being objects of education to subjects of their own autonomy and emancipation.

Traditional methods of class control are inconsistent with the development of critical thinking and consciousness espoused in critical pedagogy but rather with what Hargreaves (2000) called pre-professional teaching. Pre-professional teaching is not concerned with the learning experiences of the individual learner but with the overall instructional flow of the lesson. Observers of my lessons were probably just satisfied with how well my lessons proceeded to their intended conclusion, maintaining order as I went. Nystrand and Gamoran (1991) identify practices in which teachers implicitly agree not to demand too much of learners and learners acquiesce to the standards of conduct required by teachers as a form of bargaining. These bargains are done in order to avoid emotionally or intellectually upsetting challenges that could result in conflicts between teachers and learners. When teachers are willing participants in the establishment of orderly but lifeless classrooms for D/deaf children like this, they negate radical love (Agnello, 2016) since critical consciousness which questions and challenges domination is not achieved.

The foregoing recreated discourses appear to indicate that it is possible for managers who are supposed to hold teachers to account to encourage a traditional rather than critical pedagogy approach, most probably based on a false sense of radical love (Agnello, 2016) for the d/Deaf learners. This is given credence by the managers' advice to be more confident as all apparently is well, ignoring the teacher's rudimentary signing and therefore poor delivery of subject content. Moores and Martin (2006) explain that the field of deaf education is marred by a cycle of low expectations. According to Johnson et al. (1989), the system has come to expect that deaf children cannot perform as well as hearing children and has structured itself in ways that guarantee that result. This is consistent with Connor (2014) who found that special education practices tend to further actively disable children who are already struggling to succeed in schools.

Managers' expectation that their subordinates will eventually get used to deaf children's "natural" poor academic performance appears to be one way in which the system has structured itself in such a way as to guarantee weak results. Another way in which the system structures itself in such a way as to guarantee poor results is the supervisors' implied belief that deaf learners are unable to learn abstract ideas and may need to be constrained to concrete ideas with concrete media that they can visualize.

I cannot really pinpoint the exact stage at which I became most uncomfortable about the easy satisfaction we all had with the rudimentary communication we managed to have with deaf learners. It must have been a gradual process of questioning and setting aside the set of beliefs, assumptions, and practices that constituted my internalized ableism. There was however a critical incident in my teaching which brought me face to face with the realization that deaf learners were not necessarily "learning disabled."

The critical incident which disabused me of my notion that deaf pupils were "learning disabled" occurred while I was teaching a science lesson in which I could see from the faces of the pupils that they were more blank than usual. They really could not understand what I was trying to put across. I was using all kinds of concrete objects and repeatedly explained in a very animated way, but still they did not seem to understand. I became very frustrated. In my frustration, I looked out through the large windows and saw a Deaf sports coach who was following my lesson from outside. He must have been closely watching my struggle all this time. When my eyes met his, he left his position outside the window and came into the classroom where he abruptly took over my science lesson. He did not utter a single word throughout as he was signing silently and pointing to key words I had already put up on the chalkboard as well as the materials on my desk. In a very short time the entire class understood. The learners signed that they now understood. When I eventually asked them to do the written exercise on this lesson most of them did very well.

This incident shocked me into realizing that it was not so much the pupils who were deficient, but me—their teacher. The belief that it was normal and natural for deaf learners to perform poorly, and that I should just get used to this poor performance was crushed in a few minutes. Realizing these things took a heavy toll on me emotionally. All along I had been convinced that I was performing heroic acts in the name of radical love (Agnello, 2016) only to be rudely awakened into the realization that I was actually part of the problem! My use of deficiency-focused special education techniques had only served to delay learning for many of them. After the shock had worn off, instead of feeling embarrassed I was relieved. It was as if a weight had been lifted from my shoulders. Now I had more than just a strong suspicion of what was wrong. I had observed the Deaf coach quickly and successfully deliver key scientific concepts using only signs, and I now knew without any doubt that the problem was my deficiency in signing. I set about learning as many of these signs as I could in order to use them in my teaching. I would still utter the appropriate spoken words, but this was now more to guide my own thoughts. I reached the point where I would learn the signs for key concepts beforehand and emphasize these in the lesson. Having made this adjustment I was rather surprised that I was not as successful as the Deaf coach had been. If there were an improvement in my class's performance, it was not all that remarkable. I concluded that the learners needed someone like the Deaf coach, someone with native-like competency in Sign Language.

I had by now realized that many deaf learners may not require special education after all. For them, it now appeared to be a matter of recognizing and utilizing the language that was most accessible to them—Sign Language. The most competent teachers in this language were also readily apparent—people like the Deaf coach. What deaf learners clearly required were fluent Sign Language users who would teach them using this language and not necessarily having to resort to Special Education techniques. In this way, the wholeness of deaf learners would be recognized and valued in line with disability justice. The use of Sign Language would enhance the deaf learners' ability to generate and disseminate knowledge. Insisting on the use of inaccessible languages as languages of instruction imposes what Walker and Martinez-Vargaz (2020) call epistemic limitations or injustices. However, ordinary deaf education needs to be supported by special education in areas where specific learners need support in what becomes a consilience (Wilson, 1999) of the two disciplines. Otherwise, many deaf learners can and should be taught using Sign Language as they have a right to the language and the attainment of epistemic justice within the wider ambit of disability justice. Rather than disciplinary tensions between special education and deaf education, the ideal appears to be interdisciplinarity in which the two support each other.

CONCLUSION

This chapter set out to examine what could be learned from the work of a career teacher of deaf learners by analyzing the discrepancy between lengthy Special Education experience and the perennial underachievement of deaf learners. My role and identity throughout my early teaching career had been premised on the notion that I was doing a work of "charity," that I was a "benevolent" benefactor impeded in the extent I could help them by their circumstances. When I became more experienced the outcomes of deaf learners still resulted in frustration while the *laissez faire* attitudes of management disillusioned me.

The academic underachievement of deaf learners could be accounted for by the disproportionate focus on Special Education expertise inclined toward speaking and listening—areas in which the learners are deficient. This focus resulted in grossly inadequate education which disabled the learners and in Erevelles' (2009) words, permitted only a few of them to be later employed in jobs located at the lowest rungs of the social division of labor while the rest of them swelled the ranks of the permanently unemployed. Teachers need to reflect on their practice, theory, and research to ensure that deafness has not become so firmly entrenched in the deficit thinking associated with the narrow, rigid understanding of human differences in Special Education. Focus in theory and practice should not be so firmly on the disability to the point that it symbolizes the whole child. Self-study after my experience with the Deaf coach's success pointed toward an alternative, conciliatory framework for conceptualizing education for deaf learners.

A conciliatory framework would locate disability as the central ordering force of social relations of schooling and allow focus on the location of disabled people in the social division of labor. It is clear that if education for deaf learners is to be liberating, there is need for more Deaf role models who are native users of Sign Language to be employed as teachers. The education of deaf children has to be conceptualized from a sociocultural perspective which views such learners as different but not necessarily deficient. In this perspective, the learners need to be supported in their weaknesses and strengths by teachers who share or at least respect their Deaf culture. Without unconditional acceptance of the Deaf culture, hearing teachers of deaf learners would continue to be representative of the oppressive class thereby making schools for the deaf oppressive places that overwhelm the learners. It has to be understood that love for deaf children need not be predicated on the condition that they have to aspire to a speaking/listening culture which is irrelevant to many deaf learners anyway. Deaf learners are not deficient aspirants of hearing society. Conditional love for them may actually be masking the fear that many hearing teachers have of these learners. Unconditional acceptance of deaf learners as a part of human diversity would lay the foundation for a truly liberating pedagogy for this group of learners. Boundary crossing in which the education of deaf learners goes from an enterprise strictly under the aegis of special education to Deaf Studies has an in-between space that can be exploited for the benefit of the learners. That in-between space should not carry with it uniform rigid learning standards that mandate all to be educated in virtually the same way. The activity systems of the canon of traditional individualized Special Education on the one hand and multilingual Deaf Studies on the other hand can cross boundaries to flexibly take full advantage of the in-between space so as to enrich Deaf Education.

NOTES

1. In this chapter Deaf with a capital letter "d" refers to those who belong to a cultural grouping whose main defining feature is membership of Deaf culture and the use of Sign Language, while deaf with a small letter "d" denotes all those who have the audiological status of hearing loss but do not necessarily subscribe to Deaf culture. Wherever this distinction is unclear or unnecessary, D/deaf is used.

2. The term "non-disabled" is preferred in this chapter because it centers disability as normal and whole in line with the disability justice principle number five as propounded by Berne et al. (2018). In this light, terms such as "able-bodied," "normal," and so on are not used in the chapter as they are demeaning through their failure to recognize the wholeness of disabled people.

3. In this chapter I use the term "non-deaf" to highlight not just my audiological status as a hearing person but also to respect possible cultural differences between my

hearing-speaking cultural background and the Deaf cultural heritage to which the deaf pupils I taught have a right.

REFERENCES

Agnello, M. F. (2016). Enacting radical love: Joe L. Kincheloe's 10 precepts of teachers as researchers. *International Journal of Critical Pedagogy*, 7(3), 67–78.

Akkerman, S. F., & Bakker, A. (2011). Boundary crossing and boundary objects. *Review of Educational Research*, 81(2), 132–169.

Aliakbari, M., & Faraji, E. (2011). *Basic principles of critical pedagogy*. IACSIT Press.

Allen, B. (2012). *Critical communication pedagogy as a framework for teaching difference and organizing*. University of St. Marks.

Annamma, S. A., Boele, A. L., Moore, B. A., & Klinger, J. (2013). Challenging the ideology of normal in schools. *International Journal of Inclusive Education*, 17(12), 1278–1294.

Armstrong, F., & Barton, L. (Eds.). (1999). *Disability, human rights and education: Cross-cultural perspectives*. Open University Press.

Baumann, H. D. L. (2004). Audism: Exploring the metaphysics of oppression. *Journal of Deaf Studies and Deaf Education*, 9(2), 239–246.

Baumann, H. D. L., & Murray, J. J. (2010). Deaf Studies in the 21st century: Deaf gain and the future of human diversity. In M. Marschark & P. Spencer (Eds.), *The Oxford handbook of Deaf Studies, language and education* (Vol. 2, pp. 210–225). Oxford University Press.

Beacon, A., & Golder, G. (2015). Developing disability sport: The case for a critical pedagogy. *Journal of Sport for Development*, 3(5), 71–88.

Berne, P., Morales, A. L., Langstaff, D., & Sins, I. (2018). Ten principles of Disability Justice. *WSQ: Women's Studies Quarterly*, 46(1/2), 227–230.

Blaska, J. (1993). The power of language: Speak and write using person first. In M. Nagler (Ed.), *Perspectives on disability* (pp. 25–32). Health Markets Research.

Bull, R., Marschark, M., & Blatto-Vallee, G. (2005). Examining number representation in deaf students. *Learning and Individual Differences*, 15(3), 223–236.

Bullough, R. V. (1994). Personal history and teaching metaphors: A self-study of teaching as conversation. *Teacher Education Quarterly*, 21(1), 107–120.

Butler, R. (1997). Stories and experiments in social inquiry. *Organisation Studies*, 18(6), 927–948.

Chang, H. (2008). *Autoethnography as method*. Left Coast Press.

Chiswanda, M. V. (1997). *Hearing mothers and their deaf children in Zimbabwe: Mediated learning experiences*. PhD University of Oslo.

Conle, C. (1999). Moments of interpretation in the perception and evaluation of teaching. *Teaching and Teacher Education*, 15(7), 801–814.

Connor, D. J. (2014). The disability studies in education annual conference: Explorations of working within, and against Special Education. *Disability Studies Quarterly*, 34(2), 57–70.

Crenshaw, K. (1989). Demarginalizing the intersection of race and sex: A black feminist critique of antidiscrimination doctrine, feminist theory and antiracist politics. *University of Chicago Legal Forum, 1989*(1), Article 8.

Danforth, S., & Gabel, S. L. (Eds.). (2006). *Vital questions facing Disability Studies in Education.* Peter Lang.

Devlieger, P. J. (1998). Physical "disability" in Bantu languages: Understanding the relativity of classification and meaning. *International Journal of Rehabilitation Research, 21*(1), 63–70.

Devlieger, P. J. (1999). Frames of reference in African proverbs on disability. *International Journal Disability, Development and Education, 46*(4), 439–451.

Ellis, C. (1991). Sociological introspection and emotional experience. *Symbolic interaction, 14*(1), 23–50.

Ellis, C. (2001). What counts as scholarship in communication? An autoethnographic response. *American Communication Journal, 1*(2), 1–8.

Ellis, C., & Bochner, A. P. (1992). Telling and performing personal stories: The constraints of choice in abortion. In C. Ellis & M. Flaherty (Eds.), *Investigating subjectivity* (pp. 79, 70, 101). Sage.

Erevelles, N. (2009). Rewriting critical pedagogy from the periphery: Materiality, disability and the politics of schooling. In S. L. Gabel (Ed.), *Disability Studies in Education: Readings in theory and method* (pp. 65–84). Peter Lang.

Finley, S. (1998). Professional lives in context: Becoming teacher-educators. In A. L. Cole, R. Elijah, & J. G. Knowles (Eds.), *The heart of the matter: Teacher educators and teacher education reform* (pp. 329–351). Caddo Gap Press.

Freire, P. (1970). *Pedagogy of the oppressed.* Herder and Herder.

Froschl, M., Colon, L., Rubin, E., & Sprung, B. (1984). *Including all of us: An early childhood curriculum on disability.* Educational Equity Concepts.

Gabel, S. (2009). Introduction: Disability Studies in Education. In S. L. Gabel (Ed.), *Disability Studies in Education: Readings in theory and method* (pp. 1–20). Peter Lang.

Geers, A. E., & Moog, J. (1989). Factors predictive of the development of literacy in profoundly hearing impaired adolescents. *Volta Review, 91*(2), 69–86.

Gelfand, M. (1959). *Shona ritual.* Juta & Company.

Giroux, H. (2010). *Rethinking education as the practice of freedom: Paulo Freire and the promise of critical pedagogy.* Continuum.

Graham, L. J. (2008). From ABCs to ADHD: The role of schooling in the construction of behaviour disorder and production of disorderly objects. *International Journal of Inclusive Education, 12*(1), 7–33.

Hargreaves, A. (2000). Mixed emotions: Teachers' perceptions of their interactions with students. *Teaching and Teacher Education, 16*(8), 811–826.

Holt, N. L. (2003). Representation, legitimation and autoethnography: An autoethnographic writing story. *International Journal of Qualitative Methods, 2*(1). http://www.ualberta.ca/~iiqm/backissues/2_1/html/holt.html

Horejes, T. P. (2009). *Constructions of deafness and deaf education: Exploring normalcy and deviance.* ProQuest LLC.

Humphreys, M. (2005). Getting personal: Reflexivity and autoethnographic vignettes. *Qualitative Inquiry, 11*(6), 840–860.

Johnson, R., Liddell, S., & Erting, C. (1989). *Unlocking the curriculum: Principles for achieving access in Deaf Education*. Gallaudet University Press.

Karchmer, M. A., & Mitchell, R. E. (2003). Demographic and achievement characteristics of deaf and hard of hearing students. In M. Marschark & P. Spencer (Eds.), *The Oxford handbook of Deaf Studies, language and education* (pp. 21–37). Oxford University Press.

Kiyaga, N. B., & Moores, D. F. (2009). Deafness in Sub-Saharan Africa. In D. F. Moores & M. S. Millers (Eds.), *Deaf people around the world*. Gallaudet University Press.

Knight, A., & Miller, J. (2021). Prenatal genetic screening, epistemic justice, and reproductive autonomy. *Hypatia, 36*(1), 1–21.

Knodel, J., & Pramualratana, A. (1987). Focus group research as a means of demographic inquiry. *Research Report, 87*(106), 1–7.

Knowles, J. G. (1998). The power of personal experience: Place, perspective and pedagogy. In A. L. Cole & S. Finley (Eds.), *Conversations in community*. Proceedings of the Second International Conference on the Self-Study of Teacher Education Practices. Herstmmonceux Castle, East Sussex, England (pp. 21–25). Kingston, Ontario: Queen's University.

Knowles, J. G., & Holt-Reynolds, D. (1991). An introduction: Personal histories as medium, method and milieu for gaining insights into teacher development. *Teacher Education Quarterly, 21*(1), 5–12.

Lewis, S. (1996). The reading achievement of a group of severely and profoundly hearing impaired school leavers educated within a natural aural approach. *Journal of the British Association of Teachers of the Deaf, 20*(1), 1–7.

Livingston, S. (1997). *Rethinking the education of deaf students: Theory and practice for a teacher's perspective*. Heinemann.

Mbiti, J. S. (2008). *African religions and philosophy*. Heinnemann.

Moores, D. F., & Martin, D. S. (2006). *Deaf learners: Developments in curriculum and instruction*. Gallaudet University Press.

Mpofu, E., Kasayira, J. M., Mhaka, M. M., Chireshe, R., & Maunganidze, L. (2007). Inclusive education in Zimbabwe. In P. Engelbrecht & L. Green (Eds.), *Responding to challenges of inclusive education in southern Africa* (pp. 66–79). Van Schaik.

Musengi, M. (1999). *The impact of hearing aid fitting practices on ways of teaching hearing impaired pupils in Zimbabwe's special schools*. Bachelor of Education Research Project, University of Zimbabwe, Harare.

Musengi, M. (2014). *The experience of teaching deaf learners in residential institutions for the deaf in Zimbabwe*. PhD Thesis, University of the Witwatersrand, Johannesburg.

Nicholas, J. G., & Geers, A. E. (2006). Effects of early auditory experience on the spoken language of deaf children at 3 years of age. *Ear and Hearing, 27*(3), 286–298.

Nielsen, K. E. (2014). *A disability history of the US*. Beacon Publishing.

Nunes, T., & Moreno, C. (2002). An intervention program for promoting Deaf pupils' achievement in mathematics. *Journal of Deaf Studies and Deaf Education, 7*(2), 120–133.

Nyota, S. (2013, April 06). Pre-colonial meanings of some Shona terms. Personal Communication.

Nystrand, M., & Gamoran, A. (1991). Student engagement: When recitation becomes conversation. In H. C. Waxman & H. J. Walberg (Eds.), *Effective teaching: Current research* (pp. 1–28). McCutchan Publishing.

Nziramasanga, C. T. (1999). *Report on the Presidential enquiry into education and training*. Harare.

Paul, P. V. (2001). *Language and deafness* (3rd ed.). Singular Thompson Learning.

Rushing, H. J. (2006). *Erotic mentoring: Women's transformations in the university*: Left Coast Press.

Samaras, A. P., Hicks, M. A., & Berger, J. G. (2004). Self-study through personal history. In J. J. Loughran, M. L. Hamilton, V. K. LaBoskey, & T. Russell (Eds.), *International Handbook of Self-Study of Teaching and Teacher Education Practices* (pp. 905–942). Dordrecht Kluwer Academic Publishers.

Sparkes, A. C. (2000). Autoethnography and narratives of self: Reflections on criteria in action. *Sociology of Sport Journal, 17*(1), 21–43.

Van Manen, M. (1984). Practicing phenomenological writing. *Phenomenology and Pedagogy, 2*(1), 36–69.

Walker, M., & Martinez-Vargaz, C. (2020). Epistemic governance and the colonial epistemic structure: towards epistemic humility and transformed South-North relations. *Critical Studies in Education*. doi:10.1080/17508487.2020.1778052

Ware, L. (2005). Many possible futures, many different directions: Finding the links to critical special education. In S. L. Gabel (Ed.), *Disability studies in education: Readings in theory and method* (pp. 103–129). Peter Lang.

Wauters, L. N., van Bon, W. H. J., & Tellings, A. E. J. M. (2006). Reading comprehension of Dutch deaf children. *Reading and Writing: An Interdisciplinary Journal, 19*(1), 49–76.

White, K., Forsman, I., Eichwald, J., & Munoz, K. (2010). The evolution of early hearing detection and intervention programs in the United States. *Seminars in Perinatalogy, 34*(2), 170–179.

Wilson, E. O. (1999). *Consilience: The unity of knowledge* (vol. 31). Vintage.

Chapter 9

Ethics of Care/ing Work/ers at the Boundary of Critical Dis/ability Studies and Special Education

Christina A. Bosch

> With the Disability Visibility Project I feel a keen urgency to publish as many pieces about the pandemic because our perspectives and warnings are not heeded. And here we are today with eugenics and systemic ableism displayed nakedly upon the altar of capitalism and white supremacy. I resent the implication that we have to prove our value and reveal our traumas in order to be seen as human and worthy of 'care.' – *Alice Wong, introduction to High Risk Pandemic Stories: A Syllabus, 2022*

Wong's two resentments are special education cornerstones that limit the system's potential/promise to provide care as justice for youth with disabilities. Referral, eligibility, and compliance processes often require traumas to be revealed inequitably, or themselves create trauma (Hernandez-Saca, 2017; Voulgarides, 2018). Ethical implications of the concomitant roles carried out by special education teams, whose jobs entail proving the value of their own instruction as well as youths' academic and social capabilities through progress monitoring, IEP meetings, etc., are the focus of this chapter. This does not mean that the human inclination to care, love, and serve does not appear within such a system; it is often the core driving critical special educators, and should be treasured, especially before the context deforms it into codependent, controlling, patronizing care (Connor & Ferri, 2021). Whatever opportunity special education offers exists in paradoxical tension with the systematic limitation of worthiness as well as capabilities for receiving and giving care among disabled youth along with those predominantly female, working-class adults providing them "special" education.

Care is tricky to define, particularly within a patriarchal racial-capitalism paradigm that hierarchically divides public from private labor (Glenn, 2010); this chapter attempts to unravel relevant conceptualizations. But to begin, I argue that a political precedent for care as justice exists in the U.S. Individuals with Disabilities Education Act (IDEA, 2004). For all its manifested shortcomings, it is unique for establishing education as a right, and, in tandem with other hard-fought civil rights like the Americans with Disabilities Act, for legally encoding proxies for care (accessibility, appropriateness, accommodations). True democracy and inter/personal freedom become possible when care and justice are congruent in value and application(Gilligan, 2013). To be clear, these ideals have never been reality, as President Ford bluntly acknowledged when signing the original bill that would become IDEA (Moody & Dougherty, 2012). As Jill Lepore (2022) summarizes, public education tethers capitalism and democracy, ameliorating the class divisions inherent to the former to fulfill the promise of equality under the latter.

As leaders of color at the intersection of law, criminality, justice, and education put it, "special education, created as an opportunity for disabled youth to be educated in their communities, has become another way to criminalize Black youth" (Annamma & Stovall, 2020). Despite the law's framing of "disability" as "a natural part of the human experience" (IDEA, 2004), professional judgments about dis/ability and how to "treat" various impairments in education have functioned to (further) oppress and marginalize youth based on impairments and/or psychological processes that are constructed as deviant (Annamma et al., 2020; Coles, 1987; Fish, 2017, 2019; Gilligan, 2013; Harry & Klinger, 2014; Waitoller et al., 2010). By now, narrative/qualitative inquiries, disability studies in education (DSE) scholarship, as well as critiques (namely, DisCrit—discussed shortly) have revealed special education's rootedness in a paradigm premised on positivist objectivity, race-colorblindness, and tenets incompatible or in tension with holism, interdependence, anti-racism, and subjectivity (Brantlinger et al., 2005; Campbell, 2012; Connor, 2019; Connor & Ferri, 2007, 2021; Goodley, 2018; Erevelles & Minear, 2010; Gallagher, 1998; Gallagher et al., 2014; Heshusius, 1989). The "chronic" special (and general) education "teacher shortage" is a symptom, not a cause, of taking a step for civil rights but failing to sustain the marathon toward democracy.

I work in (critical) special education and study disability activism/advocacy because marginalized perspectives often reveal not only the heart of the matter but also throw into relief the matter/dark matter/antimatter of which the whole universe is composed. After steeping in disability justice, DSE, or the company of critical special educators, that which I perceive is revealed differently; that which I cannot perceive is revealed; and the vast mystery usually humming along in the background of daily submission to/resistance of globalized neoliberal affect economies (Richard & Rudnyckyj, 2009), the medical and nonprofit industrial complexes (Smith, 2007), U.S. democracy, and white supremacy becomes omnipresent and omnipotent, however fleetingly. As a tiny, privileged human, those moments offer me a renewed connection, solidarity with the collective (un)consciousness that supports me in the discipline of hope (Kaba, 2021). I hope for new ways of being in love with/in our world, including disrupting the nineteenth-century template of public schooling to birth free, dignified, lifelong, networked learning systems (Illich, 1970). As a teacher, I was shaped by the Universal Design for Learning (Meyer et al., 2014) mantra that "what's necessary for the few is good for everyone." Now as a researcher and teacher educator, I use that logic to tug on the thread of special education with the hope that it will unravel oppressive educational structures for everyone, most urgently those wounded by school. Yet again, the gifts of disability culture and history teach me to ask: *How to do radical work at the boundaries of special education and DSE without replicating histories of experimentation on the vulnerable? How to center the most affected, without abdicating my responsibility to create?*

I turn to ethics, a field that receives scant critical attention in special education teacher preparation, seeking professional ethics that might guide the aids, teachers, academics, administrators, and bureaucrats employed in this field. If there is to be guidance for ethically sound work in this context, it likely lives at the edges of the field where the noblest human impetus to care (Dass & Gorman, 1985) comes under the loving scrutiny of critical perceptivity and radical praxis. Because special education comes from activism and self-advocacy rooted in care for self/others, this field presents a unique potential for rethinking the model of public schooling inherited from Horace Mann (Goldstein, 2015). In this chapter, *boundary work* describes all human efforts toward dignity for self/others that occur in the gaps between special education and DSE, which I also associate with efforts to achieve radical, intersectional inclusion (Waitoller, 2020) inside or outside traditional brick-and-mortar-based schooling. By boundary *workers*, I mean the aides, paraeducators, general and special educators, administrators, and even bureaucrats who channel their contractual labor toward goals that subvert problematic special education traditions: honoring the lived experiences and knowledge in DSE critiques; reducing, or eliminating, the harms of a functionalist special education approach (Skrtic, 1991); and imagining or creating ethical, just, loving ways of learning and teaching. Boundary work is a shifting, messy, vulnerable, and risky venture (Starr-Glass, 2019).

In this chapter, I share my inquiry into the potentials of an ethic of care as a mode of *consilience*—understood here as synthesis and harmony in individual/collective ethical approaches to the work that occurs in schools under the guise of caring for students with disabilities. This chapter seeks guidance from the feminist lineages within *ethic of care* scholarship to explore an ethic of care as a guide for the boundary work/ers thinking, resisting and laboring between critical special education and DSE. My goal is to offer and ask for collaborative theorizing on an ethic of care, as a praxis of consilience.

CARING FOR DAVID ALMOND

I tell a tragedy though it is not mine; I hope that by sharing it here, I invite a widened circle to honor a valuable lost life, and move readers to care more about care. Rather than reduce a life lost into a touch point in a chapter's argument, I hope it invokes all the power stories hold to shift minds, change worlds (Niles, 1999).

During the wintery Northeast U.S. lockdowns of the COVID-19 pandemic, I was writing my dissertation on inclusion; I was safe, a privilege that should be a natural right. But less than an hour away, a 14-year-old named David Almond died of starvation/neglect/abuse while living with five other family members—three generations—in a one-bedroom apartment permeated by pharmaceutical opioid abuse. David was survived by a disabled sibling who was also found emaciated; their white bodies were marked with indications of physical use, all hidden during remote learning. Disability identification, special education enrollment, and "inclusion" at his local high school put David at the intersection of numerous policies ostensibly enacted to serve justice and care for him; recognizing failure, administrative leaders vowed to essentially, do more (Fiandaca, 2021). Despite being made the locus of various mechanisms of surveillance and social "service," David's life became invisibilized.

The response from officials involved accountability and more policies. I was baffled. I wondered if their professional positionalities have ever exposed them to Disability Justice or complexities of care. With over a decade of teaching and learning in the field of special education, my own has been sparse at best. David Almond's life story illustrates how "the complexity of a term that seems so simple—*care*" (Irvine, 2001) can be a matter of life and death for youth classified in terms of "what we so imprecisely call disability" (Stiker, 2009, p. 1).

CARE AS AN UNDER-EXAMINED ETHIC IN EXPANSIVE JUSTICE

While the litigious compliance characteristic of special education might arguably be a form of care, the loss of David Almond illustrates the inadequacy of care rendered through or subsidiary to rights-based approaches to justice. Instead of relying on bureaucratized care/justice, "expansive notions of justice" (Annamma, 2017) like Disability Justice (Berne, 2017; Berne et al., 2018) help me imagine a feminist, resplendent care congruent with genuine justice. But the transition from the current dysfunctional special education into an emergent strategy (brown, 2017) for something altogether more human, just, and caring necessitates ethical guidance for decision-making. In this section, I address gaps and possibilities for an ethic of care within approaches to expansive justice to map out what I have learned up until now.

Movements for justice in education may neglect special education or disability issues (Harriet Tubman Collective, 2016). Calls for justice from critical special education scholarship may not mention ethics or care. Yet justice without care and education without disability reinscribe paternalistic ableism in schooling, prolonging a false democracy whereby feminized, diverse, and disabled bodyminds are disposable capital. In schools, special education students' marginalization occurs along multiple interlocking axes (Collins, 2019; Crenshaw, 1991), such as race and immigration status, giving way to outright exclusion and criminalization through "ableist and racist practices that [force] students to fit within the normative disciplinary and academic parameters, while offering limited and poor supports for students with disabilities" (Waitoller, 2020, p. 10; Annamma et al., 2013; Harriet Tubman Collective, 2020; Matus et al., 2019; Naraian & Natarajan, 2013). In other words, injustices are systemic in special education. Less interrogated are the role of care in pursuit of justice, and workers' ethics of care.

An expansive notion of care as justice would be rooted in Disability Justice, centering vulnerable young multiply marginalized lives at the intersections of interlocking systems of oppression to prevent potentially lethal exposure to injustice (Annamma, 2017). Because of its paradigmatic scope, Disability Justice elides cooptation into succinct definitions, bridging, binding, and rebuilding social justice and rights-based approaches (Piepzna-Samarasinha, 2018). Most relevant to the question of what an ethic of care might look like as special education becomes saturated by Disability Justice approaches are DisCrit analyses of justice because of how DisCrit accounts for the legacies and logics of anti-Black intersecting oppressions in schooling (Annamma & Handy, 2020). Yet—to the best of my decidedly outsider knowledge—ethics and ethics of care, specifically, remain under-explored in DisCrit scholarship. I mention this loving critique to strengthen the expansive notions of justice DisCrit puts forward, to fine-tune imagined structural and interpersonal transformations in education that would come with broad application of DisCrit classroom ecologies and praxis (Annamma & Morrison, 2018).

DisCrit is all about ethics, love, and care: these are empirically obvious in the purpose, claims, intellectual lineages, and references throughout this intersectional theory of oppression and liberation that centers Black and Brown youth with disabilities. In elucidating a "DisCrit Classroom Ecology," for example, Annamma and Morrison "root our work in scholars who have deeply considered the importance of care (Valenzuela, 2010), hope (Duncan-Andrade, 2009; hooks, 2003), and love (Freire & Freire, 1998; Morrell, 2014) in the classroom" (2018, p. 76). My intention here is to delve into that nook where care is referenced in passing in a deeper way. Care is a component of, not a replacement for, love (hooks, 2002). In schooling systems premised on medicalized control of care, where disability and diversity are pathologized, a critique focused on ethics of care contributes to inclusion and striving for radical love in education. Cornel West's phrase that "justice is what love looks like in public" saw wide uptake in the wake of Breonna Taylor, Ahmaud Arbery, and George Floyd's murders in 2020; bell hooks frequently instructed that there can be no justice without love. Elucidating an ethic of care at the boundary of DSE and special education might illuminate the path toward a broadened love of disabled lives, love in and for lifelong learning.

As disabled activists, artists, scholars, and people have already shown, the care current "democratic" systems offer can be imposed, hostile, morbid, dehumanizing, and negligent to the point of being lethal (Irwin, 2020; Piepzna-Samarasinha, 2018; Robinson, 2017; Torres, 2020). This is the first problem in the unexamined ethos of justice in (special) education: care is presumed integral to praxis without the concomitant recognition of how broken care is imbricated in neoliberal public schooling (Hochschild, 2012; Waitoller & Thorius, 2016). Workers/professionals entangled in education offer their care as an integral if unconscious part of their work. When special education replicates un-interrogated assumptions of caring, the history of what Leah Lakshmi Piepzna-Samarasinha calls "fucked up care" (2018, n. p.) is carried forward. Teju Cole is quoted as saying, "The White Savior Complex is not about justice. It is about having a big emotional experience that validates privilege" (cited in Safir & Dugan, 2021, p. 35). Within such a system, how can practitioners conscious of white savior/care complexes avoid having their genuine heart work hijacked—or hijacking another being's dignity? Caring in ways that liberate rather than dominate is a knife's-edge form of labor in this field. Students and deprofessionalized educators are on the spectrum of oppression. An ethic of care moves the shrinking segment of the U.S. population that still enters into teaching away from pathology-oriented perception. Ethical decisions that advance care as justice could also ripple outward into the policies and contexts that keep care work devalued (Nawaz, 2021).

Examining care as an *ethical* issue supports navigating toward the intersectional justice of collective liberation within systems premised upon remediating deficits. Boundary workers seeking an ethic of care might begin by privileging the many knowledges of multiply marginalized communities, including youth (Gonzalez et al., 2017). Although this initial "ethical leap of community fueled by 'a sense of, 'I can't accept this'" (hooks & powell, 2015) is critical, an ethic of care reveals it insufficient for moving beyond the special education paradigm. As hooks would go on to clarify in the 2015 talk with john a. powell, ethics allow for a better aim toward justice. Care shaped through an ethical system based on collective liberation might extend the benefits of de-pathologization, rather than bestow "normalcy" upon one favored group identity at a time (Powell et al., 2019).

Caring in special education is not straightforward, even when guided by social justice aims refined through critiques of the white-washed emotionality in education (Coomer, 2019; Hulgin et al., 2020; Slaten et al., 2015). I contend that special education qualifies as part the "broken care system" (Hochschild, 2009, as cited in Hochschild, 2012). Teaching involves Hochschild's conceptualization of emotional labor: teachers are hired and monitored according to their management and production of feelings aligned with prevailing moral models of care work (Brady & Tajalli, 2018). Special educators perform emotional labor specific to their roles, in addition to the emotional labor required of non-white, queer, and even masculine workers in this white-cisgender-woman-dominated field (Kerr & Brown, 2016). Care work, morally valued as feminine and socioeconomically devalued as unskilled or unproductive, is closely related to issues of disability, with important consequences for youth identified with disabilities, given the legacy of the moral model of disability (Nario-Redmond, 2019). Multiple dialectics link professional ethics, teachers' emotional labor, special education as care work and impairment/disability in the political-economic project of schooling. Yet within the pseudo-medical euphemisms that typify "special" education discourse—and mark its boundaries with critical pedagogy and DSE—care is either omitted or, like *disability*, often assumed rather than operationalized. A prime example is the Council for Exceptional Children's "Special Education Professional Ethical Principles," which mention neither.[1]

CONTOURING AN ETHIC OF CARE IN BOUNDARY WORK/ER PRAXIS

Ethics of care are not exclusively theoretical. Ethics of care can be practiced. Rather than an isolated practice of self-care (which may indeed be ethical in some sense), practicing care is a relational transmogrification, from abstracted ethical quandary to metaphysical intervention in space, necessitating networked interdependence/connectedness between subjects, or at least a meeting of equals. An ethic of care is not compatible with a subjective being caring for an objectified being. Hence, here I review seminal theorizing on care in education.

That a dialectic characterizes ethical care is evident in the fractal field of geography, which encompasses everything from investigation of the features of the earth to the lives dispersed across it. Describing "geographies of care" in ethical terms, Conradson (Conradson, 2003)p. 451) defines care as an "ethic of encounter, or a set of practices which shape human geographies beyond the familiar sites of care provision." This research produced "landscapes of care" (Milligan & Wiles, 2010), where care is a *practice* that occurs in museums, examples of public spaces charged with caring through strategic collaborations with other sectors in society—Similar to public schools, whose resources vary based in part on the partnerships school leaders forge. Practicing care ethically might prove a "connective tissue" within various public enterprises. Given that Western social systems and governance are steeped in neoliberal white heteropatriarchal settler colonial capitalist white supremacy,[2] such connective tissue might also be—*unless* the local ethical care practices distributed across geographies of care could be anti-racist, anti-sexist, anti-colonial, anti-capitalistic, and culturally responsive and sustaining of Black, Indigenous, Latina/ao/x, and other people of color with disabilities. Morse and Munro (2018) write that

> One potential danger with such an understanding of care, however, is that care could be seen as "everywhere," effectively masking the complex social, political and cultural forces that shape geographies of care, and closing down critique of the gendered and, increasingly, racialised nature of care. (p. 360)

These same authors also tie their conceptualization of care as a practice emerging from museum labor to prevailing economic contexts of austerity, particularly in the United Kingdom, situating care as a politicized form of resistance to such policies (Morse & Munro, 2018). Public spaces such as museums have been studied as sites of "social care" and "care thinking," with care being defined as community engagement work carried out by workers who engage in "practices of care" (Morse, 2020). Dowling's book on the contemporary crisis of care work uses feminism to analyze the neoliberal socioeconomic context that shapes caregiving today (Dowling, 2021).

In education there is increasing guidance on caring praxis: from reframings of socio-emotional learning that de-normalize whiteness (Higheagle Strong & McMain, 2020) to reconceptualizations of trauma-informed care as a widespread experience under neoliberal education (Hulgin et al., 2020); from anti-racist, culturally responsive/sustaining, honor-based UDL (Fritzgerald, 2020) to transformative teaching involving love for students (Whitaker,

2019). Yet even "good" teachers may not care all the time or for all students, or they may care about pushing students toward values or goals using means that are cruel or problematic. Furthermore, much of the historical writing on pedagogy and caring in education, feminism, psychology, and disability studies has assumed and centered whiteness, perpetuating colorblindness and racism in the guise of care (Annamma, 2015).

In the 1980s and 1990s, Noddings explicated ethics in education, drawing on the feminist psychologist Carol Gilligan's elevation of care and relationships into the realms of ethics and justice. Gilligan began her work on care through *In a Different Voice*, published in the 1960s. More recently, Gilligan (2013) described the ethic of care this way:

> When care is described as a feminine ethic, subsidiary to justice, a matter of special obligations or interpersonal relationships, the framework is patriarchal. Care is being interpreted in terms of a gender binary and hierarchy, where justice is masculine, care is feminine, and justice is privileged over care. . . . Care, aligned with equal voice and relationships, with core democratic values, becomes a feminist ethic, guiding the historic struggle to free democracy from patriarchy. It is an ethic of resistance to injustice.

However, Gilligan's perspective hinges on equality and may elide identity politics as originally defined by the Combahee River Collective in 1977.

Noddings expanded Gilligan's earlier concepts into teaching and learning, significantly shaping feminist philosophies of education (Eken, 2017). Noddings' seminal work established relational care in education (1984) as a specific occurrence whereby the teacher aims to establish a caring, trustworthy dynamic with a student. The claim to a caring relationship hinges not only on the teacher's perspective but also on the students' experience of the teacher's care. In contrast to this kind of morally oriented care for relationships (Valenzuela, 1999/2010), schools are structured around *aesthetic care*, which values ideas and things as instruments (Noddings, 1984; Valenzuela, 1999/2010). In a seminal ethnography on subtractive education (the experiences of Mexican American students in a white-dominated school), Valenzuela explains what aesthetic care looks like in practice:

> the privileging of the *technical* over the *expressive* . . . technical discourse refers to impersonal and objective language, including such terms as goals, strategies, and standardized curricula, that is used in decisions made by one group for another . . . (1999, p. 22)

In light of Valenzuela's work, the cliche that 'some' students need to 'care' more about school is revealed as an unjust 'demand that multiply marginalized students embrace their teachers' view of caring . . . tantamount to requiring their active participation in a process of cultural and linguistic eradication' (Bartolomé 1994, as cited in Valenzuela 1999, p. 62).

A precursor for this unjust application of care in the teaching-learning dynamic in schools comes from the deleterious effects on Black student and teacher well-being in the United States after the *Brown v. Board of Education* decision that catalyzed racial integration in schools. In *Teaching to Transgress*, bell hooks showed readers all the ways in which Black women teachers in segregated schools deeply knew and cared for Black students. She also described the instrumentalism of education in a white-dominated learning environment:

> Gone was the messianic zeal to transform our minds and beings that had characterized teachers and their pedagogical practices in our all-black schools. Knowledge was suddenly about information only. It had no relation to how one lived, behaved. (hooks, 1994, n.p.)

Citing this same phenomenon widely in the scholarly literature, Critical Race Theory (CRT) in education, and an original study of Black teachers' voices, Roberts (2010) offers culturally relevant critical teacher care. Roberts (2010) found that Black teachers enact a pedagogy of care with Black students in at least two unique ways: expertly rendered sociopolitical critiques and communicating concern for their futures. Sociopolitical critique is congruent with what prior scholarship from Beauboeuf-Lafontant (2002) had termed "political clarity." Along with an "embrace of the maternal" and "an ethic of risk," these three features characterize "womanist caring" among exceptional Black women teachers (Beauboeuf-Lafontant, 2002). Citing researchers like Noddings and Valenzuela among others who sounded the alarm at inept or lacking caring practices in schools, Beauboeuf-Lafontant claimed that the "womanist tradition" in African-American culture was essentially what care theories in education had sought to name.

A critical node in the lineage of critical Latina/o/x scholarship, Sonia Nieto has also dedicated significant attention to questions of care in urban Latina/o/x communities over the course of her career. She too draws on bell hooks (see, for example, Nieto on "Teaching, Caring, and Transformation" in 2012). Nieto's work informed Rolón-Dow's (2005) ethnography of Puerto Rican girls' experiences with care in schools, which extended care theory through CRT applied with LatCrit. Rolón-Dow showed that teachers used "stock stories perpetuating the ideology of meritocracy, individualism, objectivity, and equal opportunity . . . to explain how caring influenced the success of students" (2005, p. 93), "mask" white privilege, and entrench racism through the praxes of "well-intentioned teachers" (p. 98). Through this study, Rolón-Dow contributed a theorization of care as "color(full)" critical praxis:

> A critical care praxis begins by acknowledging that, to care for students of color in the United States, we must seek to understand the role that race/ ethnicity has played in shaping and defining the sociocultural and political conditions of their community . . . A color(full) critical care praxis also calls on teachers to unpack their ideologies of progress, opportunity, and success within our society. (2005, p. 104)

In other words, the relational ethic of care—rather than aesthetic care—at both individual and institutional levels aligns with critical approaches to antiracist education.

While addressing disproportionality in school-based metrics of well-being and achievement, none of the previously described scholarship refers to dis/ability or special education. Relational ethics of care in education must next account for gender, race, and disability justice framings as well as critical disability scholarship. Consider the following recollection from Piepzna-Samarasinha (2018):

> For many of us, care had been something that was forced on us—something abusive family members or teachers or health care workers did, whether we liked it or not. . . . Maybe as disabled people, if we wanted to have any kind of independence, we had to deny that we needed any help at all—in order to stay in mainstream classes, go to college, or date, we had to say that we didn't have any needs. I can remember my mother clearly telling me in high school, when I first thought I might be neurodivergent . . . that it was unsafe for me to say that I might need a tutor—tutors and accommodations, newly allowed under the brand new ADA, were for rich which boys; I just had to be twice as smart and keep up if I wanted to get a scholarship. I couldn't afford to look 'stupid.' (2018, n.p.)

As the only teachers systematically engaged in advancing collective access, at least in formal/legal terms, special educators might be inflection points for change. Certainly a critical consciousness widespread amongst practitioners might wield the paradigmatic influence necessary to "shift in our ideas of access and care . . . from an individual chore, and unfortunate cost of having an unfortunate body, to a collective responsibility that's maybe even deeply joyful" (Piepzna-Samarasinha 2018, n.p.) In writing about care work within healing and disability justice paradigms, Piepzna-Samarasinha (2018) points toward this next dimension of care theory.

THE POSSIBILITIES AND LIMITS
OF SCHOOL-BASED CARE

> Because this is the system we live within, this imperialist white supremacist capitalist patriarchy, and to be able to say, where do I enter into that, as a person with potential power to harm others? And what keeps me from engaging in those violent acts of estrangement? As we talk about our revisionary struggles for liberation, we have to include ethics more, and ethical sensibility, because how do we know what is right, what is just, if we don't have an ethical sensibility?—*bell hooks (2015 talk with john a powell)*

As the U.S. social welfare system and public education expanded after World War II, disability became an important "'boundaries' category" for those bodies and minds that could not be made to function like machines within a bureaucratic system that distributed "benefits" (according to needs dictated primarily by medical and social welfare technocrats, rather than the recipients or "clients" with disabilities) (Rosenthal, 2019). Parallels to special education are discernable in segregation catalyzed by eligibility for services (determined by the positionality and resources of caregivers in conjunction with those of the IEP team members, and often without the student) as well as in the co-occurring pressure to perform in factory-like settings with standardized academic achievement metrics requiring retrofitting and/or accommodations/modifications. Both versions of technocratic paternalism conflict with self-determination, leaving advocates for progressive, life-affirming disability social policy in the difficult position of, as Mladenov (2015) succinctly puts it, "defend[ing] self-determination while criticising market-based individualism, and [defending] the welfare state while criticising expert-based paternalism" (p. 445).

Under neoliberalism in the United States there has been a persistent narrative of failing public schools and "bad teachers" since *A Nation at Risk* (1984) that undergirds deteriorating conditions for education workers. The narrative facilitates unwarranted or misguided forms of scrutiny, narrow conceptions of accountability, and attacks on public and teacher education, culminating in reduced socioeconomic support for education while the state increases funding for incarceration (Cochran-Smith et al., 2018; Kumashiro, 2010). U.S. public education is "the state's most massive apparatus, with a labor force larger than the combined military branches" (Vaught, 2019, p. 3). Nevertheless, around half of the federal discretionary spending budget typically goes to the military, while around 5% funds dwindling national education priorities like special education. The effects are suggested in trends such as the Boston Public School system's gradual consolidation of multiple roles into a single, triple-certified teacher (e.g., English Language Learner, special education, and content-instruction licenses): normalizing the overtaxation of teachers without corresponding increases in compensation.. The only limits have come from what could be described as ethical care work at the boundaries of special education: teachers organizing within the Inclusion Committee of the Boston Teachers Union, guided by principles of racial and disability justice (Fialka-Feldman, 2021).

These conditions suggest teachers are at once replaceable and essential. Their socioeconomic positioning is usually in the middle class, which tends to align politically with the capitalist rather than the working class (Katch, 2015); however, about one in six teachers are now decidedly more representative of the latter, working a second (non-summer) job and, according to a 2019 Pew survey, about three times as likely as U.S. workers overall to balance multiple jobs. In this landscape of income scarcity, teachers may seek to maximize their value (as perceived externally) in ways that reproduce social inequities incompatible with an ethic of care—for example, as solo competitors buying and selling their labor on emerging digital marketplaces, such as the popular *teacherspayteachers.com*, or through a focus on standards-based student outcomes that sacrifices holism and pedagogy (Shelton et al., 2021).

In sum, working conditions are untenable for many teachers in socioeconomic terms, but also in spiritual terms. To conform into systems predicated on segregation and fragmentation, we tender our subjectivity for self-objectification. Objectification appears at the individual level concretely, as stress, trauma, and other forms of psychological distress (Gilligan, 2013). Broadly speaking, special education teachers in U.S. public schools face numerous kinds of stress, registering burnout rates as high as 50% (Brunsting et al., 2014). Brantlinger, discussing the colonization techniques operant in special education, pointed out that "for there to be care providers, Others must be identified as having 'special needs'" (2001, p. 2). In this way, a core function of special education is to erase commonalities between groups through Us/Them distinctions (Brantlinger, 2001) that cause objectification of self and others, concomitant stress, and limits on capabilities (Robeyns et al., 2021) for ethical care.

The revolutionary Black militant queen, Assata Shakur, who resisted one of the most concerted campaigns of dehumanization waged by the United States against its own citizen, described the practice of division and objectification, a kind of atomization, in her reflection on the elementary education provided publicly in New York City in the 1950s:

> The usual way that people are taught to think in amerika is that each subject is in a little compartment and has no relation to any other subject. For the most part we were see fragments of unrelated knowledge and our education follows no logical format or pattern. It is exactly this kind of education that produces people who don't have the ability to think for themselves and who are easily manipulated. (Shakur, 1999, p. 34)

Shakur positioned curriculum and instruction within the U.S. education system as an imposition that partitions off pieces of a whole, implying that education artificially fragments that which is essentially boundless, borderless, and inclined toward the opposite: synthesis and connection. Gilligan similarly invoked the ethic of care to disrupt gendered framings of concepts like justice that reproduced hierarchical binaries.

Atomization normalizes domination in education. Domination is premised upon Othering those who are deviating from the standards reflective of the "Us" in power (Brantlinger, 2001). In writing about love and race (2012), hooks describes how domination produces an abandonment of the self. Reflecting Freire's influence, hooks explains that self-abandonment is a betrayal of self. Betrayal of self is experienced by both the dominated (special education students, in this case) and the dominators (special education aides, teachers, related service providers, administrators, and general education teachers, in this case) as dehumanization, internal disassociation, and the denial of access to love and empathy (hooks, 2012). Poignantly, some research suggests that the higher educated among us have less empathy (Kauffman, 2020). For hooks, the cultivation of empathy, a form of responsiveness to others, is tied up in the development of our own self-awareness. Loving ourselves through a deepening of that awareness is what allows us to love our shared humanity beyond categories that confine spirits (hooks, 2000). Contexts that enable oppressor/oppressed dehumanization through self-betrayal and abandonment also negate our shared human needs.

Shared human needs are the basis of critically compassionate service (Dass & Goreman, 1985). Without it, teacher education easily perpetuates dysconscious ableism (Broderick & Lalvani, 2017) among those who wish to serve (Darling-Hammond, 2010) by not systematically exploring the socioeconomics of the "broken care system," whereby obscured emotional labor nonetheless requires educators to draw on what remains of their subjectivity while practicing "transmutation," or the act of self-regulation according to guidelines imposed through "large organizations, social engineering, and the profit motive" (Hochschild, 2012, pp. 122, 19, 21). Given the primacy of emotions as embodied drivers of cognition (Immordino-Yang, 2011) along with teachers' metacognitive appraisals of self, other, and environment (Rodriguez, 2013; Rodriguez & Solis, 2013), the costs of neoliberalism on educational environments and labor may limit teachers' skills to detect and disrupt (their own roles in) nested intersectional oppression (Lyiscott, 2019). There may be a cycle at work wherein people may comply with absurd, racialized external indicators of their "goodness"—satisfying their needs for self-esteem and social acceptance—because they lose their self-appraisal through the transmutation normalized in a broken care system (Hochschild, 2012), whereby emotion is negated and regulated by agents other than the Self-in-equitable-relationships. Perhaps this loss of connection with the emotions that constitute a thinking, feeling subject also plays a role in the savior mentality that situates broken (care) systems solely outside the self. Perhaps this loss of connection with the emotions that constitute . . . outside the self, a reinforcement of denial that limits our agency . . . (Kaba, 2021).

In a scathing disability studies critique of U.S. special education, Baglieri et al. (2011) associate "an ethic of care, equity, social justice, reform, and the need for change" with "Commitment to, and collaboration with, those who share concerns about marginalization, segregation, and exclusion of diverse peoples who 'do not fit' the norm" (p. 2146). Yet such commitment is precisely why many people pursue credentials and advanced degrees in special education (Connor & Ferri, 2021). The commitment is not enough. (White) teachers may be prone to (white) salvation complexes, and/or to orient their actions toward the more immediate gratification and satisfaction of their own psychological needs in their work with students (Whitaker, 2019). In a study of the education services offered to incarcerated Black girls through educators working in residential juvenile justice facilities, for example, Annamma observed that the mostly white "Teachers cared very much for students as evidenced in interviews and observations. However, care did not mean that students get services they were legally required to receive" (2015, n.p.). Naraian and Schlessinger (2021) found that among a small group of urban special educators completing a teaching residency at a top institution oriented toward inclusion and critical DSE, exposure to critical ideas through coursework was insufficient to shift paradigms and support sustainable orientations toward praxis at the boundary of inclusion and traditional special education; these candidates, who were already inclined toward social justice, needed a caring community where their emotional life could be processed in a supportive collective.

In order to advance an ethic of care, boundary workers enmired in special education processes may need to strategically love. Love is "a force that has historically empowered people to resist domination and create new ways of living and being in the world" (hooks, 2000, p. 195). A contribution to care theory arising out of the boundary of special education and disability studies is poised to bridge with bell hooks' work on education as well as a love ethic, which drew on Paulo Freire's work, and defined love as the combination of care, commitment, knowledge, responsibility, and trust. bell hooks warned against the common error of equating care with love. Without love, there is no justice; love cannot coexist with abuse and neglect (hooks, 2000). Whitaker (2019) writes that "It is that multilayered ethic of care that engenders a pedagogy of love that traverses social groups" (n.p.). adrienne maree brown describes love as a key, a prerequisite practice, and a goal that guides us toward imagining futures of collective liberation (brown, 2019, p. 10). Like the relational ethic of care, brown's articulation of emergent strategy hinges on deep relationships between people that practice vulnerability and empathy in their engagement with each other (brown, 2017, p. 10).

Unjust structures can be better resisted if, as Piepzna-Samarasinha and Midnight shared in a 2018 talk at Smith College, "I see you in me and me in you." To be sure, *not caring* is *not* an option; caring is essential to life, foundational to transformation in feminine mysticism (Starr, 2019), and a spiritual as well as secular or material component of love—which means that care can seed a revolution in special education, or at least consilience along its boundaries with critical disability studies.

NOTES

1. The CEC attempts to at least name an ethical orientation for special education, but because of their language choices, their current code of ethics cannot support an ethic of care nor consilience with DSE.
2. Thanks to the late bell hooks for reminding us to say the whole thing, even when word counts are tight.

REFERENCES

Annamma, S. (2017). Not enough: Critiques of Devos and expansive notions of justice. *International Journal of Qualitative Studies in Education, 30*(10), 1047–1052.

Annamma, S., & Morrison, D. (2018). DisCrit Classroom Ecology: Using praxis to dismantle dysfunctional education ecologies. *Teaching and Teacher Education, 73*(2018), 70–80.

Annamma, S. A. (2015). Whiteness as property: Innocence and ability in teacher education. *The Urban Review, 47*(2), 293–316.

Annamma, S. A., & Handy, T. (2020). Sharpening justice through DisCrit: A contrapuntal analysis of education. *Educational Researcher, 20*(10), 1–10.

Annamma, S. A., & Stovall, D. (2020). Do #BlackLivesMatter in schools? Why the answer is "no." *The Washington Post*.

Annamma, S. A., Boelé, A. L., Moore, B. A., & Klingner, J. (2013). Challenging the ideology of normal in schools. *International Journal of Inclusive Education, 17*(12), 1278–1294.

Annamma, S., Handy, T., Miller, A. L., & Jackson, E. (2020). Animating discipline disparities through debilitating practices: Girls of color and inequitable classroom interactions. *Teachers College Record, 122*(5), 1–30.

Beauboeuf-Lafontant, T. (2002). A womanist experience of caring: Understanding the pedagogy of exemplary Black women teachers. *The Urban Review, 34*(1), 71–86.

Berne, P. (2017). Skin, tooth, and bone—The basis of our movement is people: A Disability Justice primer. *Reproductive Health Matters, 25*(50), 149–150.

Berne, P., Morales, A. L., Langstaff, D., & Invalid, S. (2018). Ten principles of disability justice. *WSQ: Women's Studies Quarterly, 46*(1), 227–230.

Brady, G., & Tajalli, H. (2018). An analysis of educators sanctioned for misconduct. *Research in Education, 102*(1), 62–80.

Brantlinger, E. (2001). Poverty, class, and disability: A historical, social, and political perspective. *Focus on Exceptional Children, 33*(7), 1–19.

Brantlinger, E., Jimenez, R., Klingner, J., Pugach, M., & Richardson, V. (2005). Qualitative studies in special education. *Exceptional Children, 71* (2), 195–207.

Broderick, A., & Lalvani, P. (2017). Dysconscious ableism: Toward a liberatory praxis in teacher education. *International Journal of Inclusive Education, 21*(9), 894–905.

brown, adrienne maree. (2017). *Emergent strategy: Shaping change, changing worlds*. AK Press.

Brunsting, N. C., Sreckovic, M. A., & Lane, K. L. (2014). Special education teacher burnout: A synthesis of research from 1979 to 2013. *Education and Treatment of Children, 37*(4), 681–712.

Campbell, F. K. (2012). Stalking ableism: Using disability to expose 'abled' narcissism. In D. Goodley, B. Hughes, & L. Davis (Eds.), *Disability and social theory* (pp. 212–230). Palgrave Macmillan.

Cochran-Smith, M., Carney, M. C., Keefe, E. S., Burton, S., Chang, W. C., Fernandez, M. B., Miller, A. F., Sanchez, J. G., & Baker, M. (2018). *Reclaiming accountability in teacher education*. Teachers College Press.

Coles, G. (1987). *The learning mystique: A critical look at "learning disabilities"*. Pantheon Books.

Collins, P. H. (2019). *Intersectionality as critical social theory*. Duke University Press.

Connor, D. J. (2019). Why is special education so afraid of disability studies? *Journal of Curriculum Theorizing, 34*(1), 10–23.

Connor, D. J., & Ferri, B. A. (2007). The conflict within: Resistance to inclusion and other paradoxes in special education. *Disability & Society, 22*(1), 63–77.

Connor, D. J., & Ferri, B. A. (2021). *How teaching shapes our thinking about dis/abilities: Stories from the field*. Peter Lang.

Conradson, D. (2003). Geographies of care: Spaces, practices, experiences. *Social & Cultural Geography, 4*(4), 451–454.

Coomer, M. N. (2019). *Centering equity in social emotional learning*. Midwest & Plains Equity Assistance Center.

Crenshaw, K. (1991). Mapping the margins: Intersectionality, identity politics, and violence against women of color. *Stanford Law Review, 43*(6), 1241–1299.

Darling-Hammond, L. (2010). Teacher education and the American future. *Journal of Teacher Education, 61*(1–2), 35–47.

Dass, R., & Gorman, P. (1985). *How can I help? Stories and reflections on service*. Knopf.

Dowling, E. (2021). *The care crisis: What caused it and how can we end it?* Verso Books.

Duncan-Andrade, J. (2009). Note to educators: Hope required when growing roses in concrete. *Harvard Educational Review*, 79(2), 181e194.

Eken, G. (2017). *Documenting the influence of noddings's theory of care in moral education and philosophy of education: 2003–2013* [Doctoral Dissertation.].

Erevelles, N., & Minear, A. (2010). Unspeakable offenses: Untangling race and disability in discourses of intersectionality. *Journal of Literary & Cultural Disability Studies, 4*(2), 127–145.

Fialka-Feldman, E. (2021). *The story of one union's journey toward disability justice*. Rethinking schools. https://rethinkingschools.org/articles/the-story-of-one-unions-journey-toward-disability-justice/

Fiandaca, C. (2021, March 30). Report: Fall River schools, DCF could have done more to prevent teen's death. *CBS Boston WBZ4*. https://boston.cbslocal.com/2021/03/30/i-team-david-almond-death-fall-river-state-report-neglect-abuse/

Fish, R. E. (2017). The racialized construction of exceptionality: Experimental evidence of race/ethnicity effects on teachers' interventions. *Social Science Research*, 62(2017), 317–334.

Fish, R. E. (2019). Standing out and sorting in: Exploring the role of racial composition in racial disparities in Special Education. *American Educational Research Journal*, 56(6), 2573–2608.

Freire, P., & Freire, A. M. A. (1998). *Pedagogy of the heart*. New York: Bloomsbury Publishing USA.

Fritzgerald, A. (2020). *Antiracism and universal design for learning: Building expressways to success*. CAST Professional Publishing.

Gallagher, D. J. (1998). The scientific knowledge base of Special Education: Do we know what we think we know? *Exceptional Children*, 64(4), 493–502.

Gallagher, D. J., Connor, D. J., & Ferri, B. A. (2014). Beyond the far too incessant schism: Special education and the social model of disability. *International Journal of Inclusive Education*, 18(11), 1120–1142.

Gilligan, C. (2013, May). *Resisting injustice a feminist ethics of care* [Video]. Fundació Grifols. https://youtu.be/rfGT7PhAqlw

Glenn, E. N. (2010). *Forced to care: Coercion and caregiving in America*. Harvard University Press.

Goldstein, D. (2015). *The teacher wars: A history of America's most embattled profession*. Anchor.

Gonzalez, T. E., Hernandez-Saca, D. I., & Artiles, A. J. (2017). In search of voice: Theory and methods in K-12 student voice research in the US, 1990–2010. *Educational Review*, 69(4), 451–473.

Goodley, D. (2018). The Dis/ability complex. *DiGeSt. Journal of Diversity and Gender Studies*, 5(1), 5–22.

Harriet Tubman Collective. (2016). Disability solidarity: Completing the "vision for Black lives." In D. M. Purnell (Ed.), *Harvard Kennedy School Journal of African American Public Policy* (pp. 69–72). President and fellows of Harvard College.

Harriet Tubman Collective. (2020). *In defense of no new jails: An open letter on disability justice to Darren Walker, President of the Ford Foundation*. The Harriet Tubman Collective. https://harriettubmancollective.tumblr.com/post/188063892118/in-defense-of-no-new-jails-an-open-letter-on

Harry, B., & Klinger, J. (2014). *Why are so many minority students in special education? Understanding race and disability in schools*. Teachers College Press.

Hernandez-Saca, D. (2017). Reframing the master narratives of dis/ability at my intersections: An outline of an educational equity research agenda. *Critical Disability Discourses*, 8, 1–30.

Heshusius, L. (1989). The Newtonian mechanistic paradigm, Special Education, and contours of alternatives: An overview. *Journal of Learning Disabilities*, *22*(7), 403–415.

Higheagle Strong, Z., & McMain, E. (2020). Social emotional learning for social emotional justice: A conceptual framework for education in the midst of pandemics. *Northwest Journal of Teacher Education*, *15*(2), 1–11.

Hochschild, A. R. (2012). *The managed heart: Commercialization of human feeling*. University of California Press.

hooks, bell. (1994). *Teaching to transgress: Education as the practice of freedom*. Routledge.

hooks, bell. (2000). *All about love: New visions*. William Morrow.

hooks, bell. (2002). *Communion: The female search for love*. William Morrow Paperbacks.

hooks, bell. (2003). *Teaching community: A pedagogy of hope* (Vol. 36). New York: Routledge.

hooks, bell. (2012). *Writing beyond race: Living theory and practice*. Routledge.

Hulgin, K., Fitch, E. F., & Coomer, M. N. (2020). Optimizing a critical juncture: Trauma, neoliberal education and children's agency. *Journal of Curriculum and Pedagogy*, *17*(2), 158–185.

Illich, I. (1970). *Deschooling society*. KKIEN Publishing International.

Immordino-Yang, M. H. (2011). Implications of affective and social neuroscience for educational theory. *Educational Philosophy and Theory*, *43*(1), 98–103.

Individuals with Disabilities Education Act, Pub. L. No. 20 U.S.C. § 1400 (2004).

Irvine, J. J. (2001). *Caring, competent teachers in complex classrooms*. 53rd annual meeting of the American Association of Colleges of Teacher Preparation, Washington, DC.

Irwin, C. E. (2020). Catching a break: Accessibility, empathy, and COVID-19. *Qualitative Inquiry*, *27*(7), 798–805.

Kaba, M. (2021). *We do this' til we free us: Abolitionist organizing and transforming justice*. Haymarket Books.

Katch, D. (2015). *Socialism...Seriously*. Haymarket Books.

Kauffman, S. B. (2020). *Transcend: The new science of self-actualization*. TarcherPerigee.

Kerr, M. M., & Brown, E. L. (2016). Preventing school failure for teachers, revisited: Special Educators explore their emotional labor. *Preventing School Failure*, *60*(2), 143–150.

Kumashiro, K. K. (2010). Seeing the bigger picture: Troubling movements to end Teacher Education. *Journal of Teacher Education*, *61*(1–2), 56–65.

Lepore, J. (2022, March 21). Why the school wars still rage. *New Yorker*. https://www.newyorker.com/magazine/2022/03/21/why-the-school-wars-still-rage

Lyiscott, J. (2019). *Black appetite. White food.: Issues of race, voice, and justice within and beyond the classroom*. Routledge.

Matus, C., Rojas-Lasch, C., Guerrero-Morales, P., Herraz-Mardones, P. C., & Sanyal-Tudela, A. (2019). Diferencia y normalidad: Producción etnográfica e intervención en escuelas. *Magis, Revista Internacional de Investigación en Educación, 11*(23), 23–38.

Meyer, A., Rose, D. H., & Gordon, D. (2014). *Universal design for learning: Theory and practice*. CAST Professional Publishing.

Milligan, C., & Wiles, J. (2010). Landscapes of care. *Progress in Human Geography, 34*(6), 736–754.

Mladenov, T. (2015). Neoliberalism, postsocialism, disability. *Disability & Society, 30*(3), 445–459.

Moody, A., & Dougherty, J. (2012). The Education for All Handicapped Children Act: A faltering step towards integration [Research Essay]. *Trinity College EDUC 300*. https://commons.trincoll.edu/edreform/2012/05/the-education-for-all-handicapped-children-act-a-faltering-step-towards-integration/

Morse, N. (2020). *The museum as a space of social care*. Routledge.

Morse, N., & Munro, E. (2018). Museums' community engagement schemes, austerity and practices of care in two local museum services. *Social & Cultural Geography, 19*(3), 357–378.

Morrell, E. (2014). Toward a critical model of teacher learning: Lessons from the South Carolina Reading Initiative. *Reading & Writing Quarterly*, 30(3), 207e210.

Naraian, S., & Natarajan, P. (2013). Negotiating normalcy with peers in contexts of inclusion: Perceptions of youth with disabilities in India. *International Journal of Disability, Development and Education, 60*(2), 146–166.

Naraian, S., & Schlessinger, S. (2021). When theory meets the "reality of reality": *Teacher Education Quarterly, 44*(1), 81–100.

Nario-Redmond, M. R. (2019). *Ableism: The causes and consequences of disability prejudice*. John Wiley & Sons.

Nawaz, A. (2021, October 12). Raising the future: The child care crisis – A PBS NewsHour Special. *PBS Newshour*. https://www.pbs.org/newshour/nation/raising-the-future-the-child-care-crisis-a-pbs-newshour-special

Niles, J. D. (1999). *Homo narrans*. University of Pennsylvania Press.

Piepzna-Samarasinha, L. L. (2018). *Care work: Dreaming Disability Justice*. Arsenal Pulp Press.

Powell, J. A., Menendian, S., & Ake, W. (2019). Targeted universalism: Policy & practice. *Haas Institute for a Fair and Inclusive Society, University of California, Berkeley*. haasinstitute.berkeley.edu/targeteduniversalism.

Richard, A., & Rudnyckyj, D. (2009). Economies of affect. *Journal of the Royal Anthropological Institute, 15*(1), 57–77.

Roberts, M. A. (2010). Toward a theory of culturally relevant critical teacher care: African American teachers' definitions and perceptions of care for African American students. *Journal of Moral Education, 39*(4), 449–467.

Robeyns, I. and Morten F. B., "The Capability Approach", *The Stanford Encyclopedia of Philosophy* (Winter 2021 Edition), Edward N. Zalta (ed.), URL = <https://plato.stanford.edu/archives/win2021/entries/capability-approach/>.

Robinson, S. A. (2017). Phoenix rising: An autoethnographic account of a gifted Black male with dyslexia. *Journal for the Education of the Gifted, 40*(2), 135–151.

Rodriguez, V. (2013). The human nervous system: A framework for teaching and the teaching Brain. *Mind, Brain, and Education, 7*(1), 2–12.

Rodriguez, V., & Solis, S. L. (2013). Teachers' awareness of the learner–teacher interaction: Preliminary communication of a study investigating the teaching brain. *Mind, Brain, and Education, 7*(3), 161–169.

Rolón-Dow, R. (2005). Critical care: A color(full) analysis of care narratives in the schooling experiences of Puerto Rican girls. *American Educational Research Journal, 42*(1), 77–111.

Rosenthal, K. (Ed.). (2019). *Capitalism and disability: Selected writings.* Haymarket Books.

Shakur, A. (1999). *Assata: An autobiography.* Chicago Review Press.

Shelton, C. C., Koehler, M. J., Greenhalgh, S. P., & Carpenter, J. P. (2021). Lifting the veil on TeachersPayTeachers.com: An investigation of educational marketplace offerings and downloads. *Learning, Media and Technology, 47*(2), 1–20.

Skrtic, T. (1991). The Special Education paradox: Equity as the way to excellence. *Harvard Educational Review, 61*(2), 148–207.

Slaten, C. D., Irby, D. J., Tate, K., & Rivera, R. (2015). Towards a critically conscious approach to social and emotional learning in urban alternative education: School staff members' perspectives. *Journal for Social Action in Counseling & Psychology, 7*(1), 41–62.

Smith, A. (2007). *The revolution will not be funded: Beyond the non-profit industrial complex.* INCITE!

Starr, M. (2019). *Wild mercy: Living the fierce and tender wisdom of the women mystics.* SoundsTrue.

Starr-Glass, D. (2019). Engagement, publishing, and the scholarship of teaching and learning: Reconsidering the reconsidered. In V. Wang (Ed.), *Scholarly publishing and research methods across disciplines* (pp. 234–256). IGI Global.

Stiker, H. J. (2009). *A history of disability.* University of Michigan Press.

Torres, L. E. (2020). Straddling death and (re)birth: A disabled latina's meditation on collective care and mending in pandemic times. *Qualitative Inquiry, 27*(7), 895–904.

Valenzuela, A. (2010). *Subtractive schooling: US-Mexican youth and the politics of caring.* Suny Press.

Vaught, S. E. (2019). Vanishment: Girls, punishment, and the education state. *Teachers College Record, 121*(7), 1–36.

Voulgarides, C. (2018). *Does compliance matter in special education?: IDEA and the hidden inequities of practice.* Teachers College Press.

Waitoller, F. R. (2020). *Excluded by choice: Urban students with disabilities in the education marketplace.* Teachers College Press.

Waitoller, F. R., & Thorius, K. A. (2016). Cross-pollinating culturally sustaining pedagogy and universal design for learning: Toward an inclusive pedagogy that accounts for dis/ability. *Harvard Educational Review, 86*(3), 366–389.

Waitoller, F. R., Artiles, A. J., & Cheney, D. A. (2010). The miner's canary: A review of overrepresentation research and explanations. *The Journal of Special Education, 44*(1), 29–49.

Whitaker, M. C. (2019). Us and them: Using social identity theory to explain and re-envision teacher–student relationships in urban schools. *The Urban Review, 52*(1), 691–707.

Chapter 10

Daring to Speak/Teach from Our Hearts

A Self-study of Critical Disability Studies Teacher Education at the Boundaries of Ableism, Racism, and Sexism as Faculty of Color

Shehreen Iqtadar and David I. Hernández-Saca[1]

This chapter interrogates the traditional hegemonic structures of special education from a Critical Disability Studies (CDS) lens (Connor, 2009) within higher education (Cosier & Pearson, 2016). CDS is an "emancipatory and developing discourse" as well as a critical reevaluation of traditional hegemonic special education. Traditional special education teacher preparation programs prepare preservice teachers within the paradigm of traditional special education. Special education upholds deficit and medicalized ableist, racist, and capitalist views about students who receive services under the Individuals with Disabilities Education Act of 2004 (Thorius, 2019; Voulgarides, 2018). In contrast, Disability Justice (Berne et al., 2018) values individuals as whole and "understand(s) that people have inherent worth outside of capitalist notions of productivity" (p. 228). Through a CDS paradigm and Disability Justice *consiliencatory* approach (Berne et al., 2018; Wilson, 1999), we conceptualize teaching and teacher education through critical[1] emotion praxis—critical thinking, feeling, and reflection before acting in educational systems (Artiles & Kozleski, 2007; Zembylas, 2015). We define our theoretical, methodological, and pedagogical approach as *critical consiliencatory critical emotion praxis counter-narrating generativity* (Miller et al., 2020) for personal, professional, and program renewal for liberation and justice in higher education (Kosnik et al., 2006) at the boundaries of special education and DSE. By *critical consiliencatory critical emotion praxis*

---

[1] Both are co-lead authors given that we worked collaboratively and democratically in our division of labor on the writing. We are listed in alphabetical order by last name.

counter-narrating generativity we mean engaging in critical and courageous dialogues within ourselves and with others to generate a third space of centering individual voices (See Nelson & Castelló, 2012) that are historically wounded by the systemic oppression (Gutiérrez, 2008). It is not simply to "give voice" or to "center voice" but to really challenge the status quo in our day-to-day interactions and experiences in schools and in society to change the systems of thought (Foucault, 1980) and master narratives about who we are as historically and systematically minoritized individuals of Color with and without dis/abilities. This generativity and third space, within the context of this chapter, is situated at the boundary work between traditional special education and disability studies in education.

In this chapter, we see learning through a cultural-historical activity (CHAT) approach, which theorizes agency as collective (Stetesenko, 2020). Stetesenko (2020) writes:

> *Transformative ethico-ontoepistemology* . . . suggests that it is directly through and in the process, and moreover, precisely as the process of people constantly transforming and co-creating their social world and thus moving beyond the status quo (rather than as an addition to it) that people simultaneously create and constantly transform their very life, therefore also changing themselves in fundamental ways while, also in and as this very process, becoming individually unique and gaining knowledge about themselves and the world. (pp. 11–12)

Such improved learning allowed us to be agents of collaborative and transformational change. In doing so, we were theoretically and methodologically (Kosnik et al., 2006; Samaras, 2011) transparent, critical, and systematic toward knowledge generation and dissemination (Miller et al., 2020) within general and special education preservice teacher preparation.

CDS is an emancipatory and developing discourse that critically reevaluates systems of hegemonic traditional special education (Hall, 2019). Scholars using a CDS approach explore the lived experiences of dis/Abled[2] people and students by engaging in transformative, coalitional, and global intersectional analyses (Hall, 2019, para. 6). In this self-study (Samaras, 2011) and analytical autoethnography (Anderson, 2006) as *critical consiliencatory critical emotion praxis counter-narrative generativity* (Miller et al., 2020) chapter, we discuss how we—as co-teachers—operationalize intersectionality within critical special education by engaging with a CDS approach (Bell, 2010). Intersectionality refers to an individual's multiple minoritized identities in society (such as gender, race, and disability) and the process of subordination through compounding vulnerabilities and discrimination (Crenshaw, 1990). In the spirit of DSE's intersectionality and interdisciplinarity, we have an open inquiry of radical love (Fromm, 1956). As scholars of Color, we disrupt the hegemony of white and ability supremacy by critically teaching about special education law, assistive technology, advocacy, and transition programming and planning while we train general and special education teachers at a predominantly white institution (PWI) in the Midwest.

We ask: *(1) How does being teacher educators of Color with and without traditional and subjective special education disability labels impact the co-teaching experiences within an upper- and middle-class Midwestern PWI? (2) How do we, with our multiple and intersectional identities, feel vulnerable within this institution, as we disrupt white, patriarchal, and ableist hegemonic power structures? (3) How do we operationalize critical emotion praxis within our special education preservice teacher program, which is at the boundaries of traditional special education and Critical Disability Studies, through a self-study teacher education methodology?*

First, we situate our critical consiliencatory critical emotion praxis counter-narrative (Miller et al., 2020) framework within scholarship on: (a) the teaching experiences of postsecondary educators of Color, (b) co-teaching experiences of adjuncts and doctoral candidates of Color and faculty of Color, and (c) preservice teacher preparation for general and special education programs. We specifically emphasize the operationalization of inclusive education within teaching preparation programs, specifically for immigrant and refugee students of Color. Second, we present our conceptual framework, which includes the theoretical frames of CDS and Disability Justice. Third, we outline our research design and methods and contextualize our self-study in order to be transparent of our analytic tools and reflective positionalities within the U.S. education system. Finally we present our *critical consiliencatory critical emotion praxis counter-narratives* (Miller et al., 2020) as theoretical, methodological, and pedagogical generativity at the boundaries of special education and CDS.

LITERATURE REVIEW

Teaching Experiences of Educators of Color in Higher Education

Historically, whiteness—embodying the superiority of the English language and white ways of doing and being—has served as a white property in the U.S. public education (Bell, 1980, 1992; Harris, 1993). Teachers of Color within higher education are subject to racialization through assumed or real racial, linguistic, ability, behavioral, and immigrant/refugee identity markers and differences (Endo, 2019). Faculty of Color (including adjuncts) and doctoral candidates of Color experience gendered, racialized, linguistic, and ability oppression and discrimination in many forms. In particular, female educators of Color are often subjected to gendered and racial discrimination (Anderson, 2015). Similarly, those from Global South backgrounds are further stereotyped for their linguistic differences (Hernández-Saca et al., 2020). Female faculty of Color are often juxtaposed to their white counterparts to reaffirm historically accepted feminine roles and accepted-unaccepted actions through the perceived norm of whiteness (Hernández-Saca et al., 2020). Similarly, male faculty of Color are often perceived as intellectually inferior to white male professors (Price, 1999), and yet are privileged over female faculty of Color in ways that reinforce racial and gender hierarchies in the academy and in society (Moore, 2017, para. 9).

Within higher education, these deficit assumptions about the identities of faculty and emerging scholars of Color, and the discrimination they experience, have negative effects on their personal and professional selves. It is increasingly important to *listen to their voice* and to document their narratives and experiences to (a) counter-narrate the hegemony of whiteness and ableism in educational institutions, (b) prepare ALL preservice and in-service teachers for diverse classrooms and society, and (c) help current and future preservice educators of Color at their intersections of power and identities navigate the academy (Cioè-Peña et al., 2016).

Co-teaching Experiences of Graduate Assistants of Color and Faculty of Color

Co-teaching is a proven effective pedagogy within K-12 education (Chandler-Olcott et al., 2012), and specifically, an effective teaching strategy for creating inclusive classrooms for ALL students (Hang & Rabren, 2009). Research on co-teaching reports benefits such as (a) built-in support from co-teachers in the classroom, (b) exploring and learning new teaching methods from co-teachers, (c) greater opportunities for reflexivity, and (d) modeling co-teaching for students (Chanmugam & Gerlach, 2013). Some reported challenges include (a) extra time needed for co-planning (Chanmugam & Gerlach, 2013), (b) diverse teaching styles between the co-teachers (Crow & Smith, 2005), (c) less classroom autonomy, (d) more work-load (Dugan & Letterman, 2008), (e) competition to gain student approval (Burns & Mintzberg, 2019), and (f) potential power dynamics between co-teachers (Letterman & Dugan, 2004).

Morelock et al. (2017) argued that research on co-teaching in higher education is limited, mainly focuses on the advantages and disadvantages of co-teaching, and omits the important power dynamics and factors affecting relationships between co-teachers. Their study demonstrated that co-teachers' unique positions (e.g., senior faculty and newly hired/tenure track faculty) influenced the power relations between co-instructors and affected their teaching relationships. Further, minimal documentation of co-teaching experiences of doctoral students/candidates serving as adjunct faculty (Burns & Mintzberg, 2019) exists.

Preservice teacher preparation at the boundaries. According to Van den Berg (2017) preservice teacher preparation should foreground the following elements to maximize inclusive education for all, grounded in culturally relevant and sustaining pedagogy (Ladson-Billings, 2009; Paris, 2012): (1) previous experience with diversity, (2) connecting theory and practice, (3) modeling, (4) learning through a community of learners, and (5) critical reflection. Within the U.S. context, teacher preparation programs and the teaching profession have more white women, while the majority of the urban public school population comes from historically multiply marginalized communities, such as Black, Indigenous, and Youth of Color (BIYOC; Gutstein, 2003). This disproportionality often leads to the existence of dysconscious racism (King, 2015; Van den Berg, 2017) or prejudice toward BIYOC children. Van den Berg (2017) explores "how preservice teachers can improve their culturally relevant pedagogy to facilitate equal treatment and opportunities in education for [ALL] learners" (p. 7). Culturally responsive pedagogy is at the heart of our co-teaching of courses on special education law, assistive technology and advocacy, and transition planning and programming.

The sixty-year-old problem of disproportionality of students of Color in special education began more than 400 years ago and relates to the legacy of U.S. systems of slavery and settler colonialism and global imperialism (Patton, 1998). Historically, traditional special education has been resistant to critiques, and this is a characteristic of the boundary work (Akkerman & Bakker, 2011) that traditional special education has firmly constructed against alternative perspectives regarding disability, intersectionally (Connor, 2019). Nevertheless, for faculty of Color with diverse identities based on dis/Ability, ethnicity, race, gender, and sexual orientation, it is paramount to center our *transformative ethico-ontoepistemology* (Stetesenko, 2020) that culls from Critical Disability Studies in Education (CDSE) from an interdisciplinary and intersectional approach. This is so given the paradigm within traditional special education that does not take into account issues of power, privilege, and culture but only reproduces the medical-psychological model of disability (Baglieri et al., 2011). We engaged special education teacher preparation topics to anchor our humanity and that of our preservice teachers and their future BIYOC youth. The onto-epistemological turn of CDSE helps us stand united against hegemonic epistemologies of dis/Ability at the intersections of power and identity. We employ CDSE for social and educational change and liberation from institutionalized ableism and racism that hurt our souls and the souls BIYOC youth and communities due to the deficit labels within master narratives of policy (Hernández-Saca, 2016). For example, how can we (re)imagine the master narratives of intersectional dis/Abilities in and outside of special and general education systems for BIYOC with and without dis/abilities for transformative change and (un)learning? DSE scholars have been asking such questions and critically analyzing the traditional structures of special education such as the Individuals with Disabilities Education Act (IDEA) (Hernández-Saca & Cannon, 2019; Valle et al., 2005).

The erasure of culture, power, and emotionality also inherent to IDEA is exacerbated by a culture of compliance (Voulgarides, 2018) to the technicalities of policies and practices, without accounting for the contextual and critical components of praxis. While the contextual aspects are people, backgrounds, and local, national, and global histories and contexts, the critical aspects that come with human interaction include emotionality, power, privilege, difference, identities, and social justice. In turn, the work of inclusion is not only related to discourses of inclusion such as "tolerance," or "acceptance," but has to do with radical love. We define radical love as care, respect, knowledge, and responsibility for self and others within systems of support for individual and societal transformation about ethical practice. In this case, these issues of practice are the ones that teacher candidates will encounter in schools and classrooms with their BIYOC with and without dis/abilities and their families at their intersections of power and identities.

CONCEPTUAL FRAMEWORK

Critical Disability Studies. CDS is a transformative emancipatory framework which allows us to reevaluate and problematize the social, emotional, political, material, and historical understandings of intersectional dis/Ability identity (Erevelles, 2000; Hall, 2019; Meekosha, 2006). We use CDS to (counter) narrate and reanalyze our personal experiences in relation to systemic discrimination and oppression (Endo, 2019; Meekosha & Shuttleworth, 2009). We argue that within higher education, such a lens allows us to: (a) interrogate and examine the intersectional experiences of faculty of Color and doctoral candidates of Color teaching as adjunct faculties, and (b) humanize their teaching experiences within a predominantly and historically white majority public institution. In addition, we also employed CDS as a co-teaching lens to prepare our preservice general and special education teachers for their diverse future classrooms.

Disability Justice. We also use the grassroots concept of Disability Justice, which seeks to understand the lived experiences of those marginalized in society by emphasizing intersectionality, leadership by those most impacted, anti-capitalist politics, interdependence, mixed ability organizing, and cross-disability solidarity (Invalid, 2017). We reexamine the white "able-bodied" institutional spaces and challenge the prevalent heteropatriarchal practices, as well as the invisibility of disabled people of Color, female immigrants—specifically from the Global South, disabled people who practice marginalized religions, in particular, those experiencing the violence of anti-Islamic beliefs and actions, queer with dis/Abilities, and trans and gender nonconforming people with dis/Abilities. Anti-immigrant, anti-Islamic rhetorics subjectify people to medical scrutiny through the pathologizing lens of race, dis/Ability, nationality, and immigration (Dolmage, 2018). Our commitment to CDS and Disability Justice within our department of special education also shapes our classroom teaching from dis/Ability, race, immigration status, culture, emotionality, and religious background at the boundaries.

RESEARCH DESIGN

Using self-study in teacher education (Kosnik et al., 2006; Samaras, 2011) and critical analytic autoethnography (Anderson, 2006), we reflect on and analyze our teacher education practices in an attempt to learn about ourselves and our pedagogies in relation to the institutional practices and policies that (dis)empower us in multiple ways. Self-studies of teacher education in higher education research "refer to teacher educators researching their practices with the purpose of improving it, making explicit and validating their professional expertise and, at the same time, contributing to the knowledge base of teacher education" (Vanassche & Kelchtermans, 2015, p. 508). The goal of self-studies of teacher education is to make *tacit knowledge from their practices cognizant* and vice versa. These self-studies also advance the public knowledge about teacher education, for the public good and critical public debate (Vanassche & Kelchtermans, 2015). Self-studies provide critical incidents, which lead to intensive self-reflection. These self-reflections are important for understanding how one's "normative beliefs and aspirations" remain hidden if not reflected upon for a more socially and emotionally just pedagogy (Vanassche & Kelchtermans, 2015).

For the purpose of this chapter, we used critical analytic autoethnographic data as texts from our co-taught classes from Spring 2020 to Spring 2021. According to Anderson (2006) critical analytic autoethnography includes five key features: (1) complete member researcher status, (2) analytic reflexivity, (3) narrative visibility of the researcher's self, (4) dialogue with informants beyond the self, and (5) commitment to theoretical analysis. Within this chapter we explore these key features, including dialogue with informants beyond the self, since we co-taught and co-planned and also included student-check-in questionnaires to reflect on our teaching. We taught two undergraduate and graduate level introductory bloc courses for special education teacher candidates. The courses are SPED 4150/SPED 5150 Introduction to

Special Education: Legal, Advocacy, and Assistive Technology Practices and Issues, and SPED 4151/SPED 5151 Educational and Post-School Transition Programming for Individuals with Disabilities. We co-taught SPED 4150/SPED 5150 in Spring 2020 and 2021, and taught the two sections of this course individually in Fall 2020. We both taught, SPED 4151/SPED 5151 individually in Spring 2020 and Fall 2020, and then together in Spring 2021. However, in Fall 2020, we co-planned the course while Shehreen individually taught the course as adjunct faculty at the University of Northern Iowa. Since David previously taught the class, this co-planning and co-mentoring provided space to self-reflect and engage our pedagogies critically. We understand *co-teaching as co-mentoring* for which co-teachers do not necessarily have to be together within time and space. Our students were white, upper-, middle-, and working-class cisgender females and white males who also embodied other intersectional identities such as belonging to the LGBTQIA community.

We used analytic reflexivity (Anderson, 2006) as a tool for critical analytic autoethnography, while also engaging in dialogue about our teaching philosophies and methodologies. As co-teachers and co-constructors of knowledge—we engaged in critical friendship (Kosnik et al., 2006; Samaras, 2011; Schuck & Russel, 2005) through acting as a sounding board for each other (after teaching every class and beyond), asking challenging questions (from our own positionalities), joining professional learning experiences through conferences together, co-publishing peer-reviewed articles, and co-creating podcasts about educational experiences of students and educators of Color in higher education (Schuck & Russell, 2005).

Context and background. In the Fall of 2019, Shehreen reviewed and evaluated (after our mutual agreement) the course syllabus for SPED 4150/5150. At this point, David was teaching both sections of this class and the evaluation was conducted as a final project of Shehreen's doctoral course ELEMECML 7354 Curriculum Implementation and Evaluation. She also reviewed literature related to her analysis and the identified gaps. One of the identified gaps in the syllabus was related to the topic of intersectionality within past and current critical educational issues and advocacy bloc. The topic of intersectionality was introduced in the following terms:

> In addition, consider critical theory and pedagogy theories of justice as it relates to issues of class, gender, sexual orientation, language, immigration, and other categories of difference at their intersections. (CEC/ICC 9S1; 9S2; Iowa Teaching Standards 1, 7, 8; INTASC 1, 6, 9, 10; UNIEPPCF 1, 3, 4, 5. (Hernández-Saca, 2019, p. 3)

We discussed how there was room to expand on the intersectional resources in the course readings and assignments. As the course was designed from a DSE and CDS lens, this was specifically important, as intersectionality and disproportionate representation of students of Color are critical scholarly issues. Further, expanding our consideration of literature on immigrant and/or refugee students with/without disabilities, we concluded that it was timely to include their educational experiences within the advocacy and educational issues bloc of the course. Hence, we began our co-teaching and collaboration in Spring 2020. We incorporated lecture and table discussions in our law bloc and carefully introduced assignments and readings, while also inviting local ELL teachers as our guest speakers to better help our students learn about their diverse future student populations.

Data Collection and Analysis

The data for this self-study stemmed from an eighteen-month co-teaching collaboration in different contexts before and during the COVID-19 crisis. After every class, we stayed behind for approximately two hours to discuss our teaching, share our feelings/thoughts, and co-plan for the next class. We audio recorded those meetings, which became our live journaling sessions. We used a range of communication mediums such as emails, Zoom meeting recordings, telephone conversations, text messages, and Google Documents for data collection (Vanassche & Kelchtermans, 2015). We also individually journaled and memoed about our co-teaching experiences. Further, we administered two student check-in questionnaires each semester—one after the first section of the course during week 7 and one after the second section of the course during week 14—to understand students' needs and reflect on our teaching and students' learning. Due to COVID-19, we used a hybrid model, teaching classes both face-to-face and online for all semesters. During the online teaching week, we continued to meet after every class and recorded those meetings on Zoom. Throughout, we engaged in critical friendship to make sense of our experiences with each other and with our students.

This rigorous process of continued data collection and self-reflexivity is helpful in our own teaching, co-teaching, and growing as educators and persons of Color within the academy. In the next section, we share our findings as counter-narratives to help the reader reimagine the nature of *self-study as counter-narrative* to hegemonic structures in teacher education. In our case, we engage with the education system to foreground our personal and professional experiences as faculty of Color at our intersections of power and identities.

OUR ANALYTIC REFLECTIVE POSITIONALITIES

David's analytic reflexivity of the education system in the U.S. I am a fairly recent naturalized citizen of the United States from El Salvador. I am bilingual in Spanish and English. My family and I immigrated to the United States when I was two years old from El Salvador due to the civil war there in 1985. I am a Latino of mixed ethnicity—El Salvadorean and Palestinian. It was during my immigration to the United States that I became introduced to the world of intersectional dis/Ability. While crossing the Rio Grande with my oldest brother, I developed a high fever of 105 degrees, which eventually caused childhood seizures and convulsions (Hernández-Saca, 2019). These early childhood dis/Ability experiences also led to my eventual placement in special education. However, the abuse, microaggressions, and unequal treatment, due to my status as a child of Color, English Language learner and Latino ethnicity, and dis/Ability experiences in segregated special education settings and speech and language communication issues that accompanied my seizures and convulsions, shaped my Post-Traumatic Stress Disorder experiences that later in life I had to unlearn and undo to recover my spirit (Hernández-Saca, 2020, 2021).

Shehreen's Analytic Reflexivity of the Education System in the United States. Within the U.S. education system, I am a South Asian female student and instructor of Color. Living as an international student and a recent immigrant woman of Color from the Global South has shaped and informed my identity in multiple ways. I first moved to the United States from Pakistan in 2014 to complete master's in Special Education. My previous education and work experience was in the field of Speech and Language "Pathology" in Pakistan. While I now critically engage with the underlying deficit ideologies of the medical model that stereotypes people with dis/abilities, I must acknowledge that my work is interdisciplinary at the critical boundaries of communication sciences and special education. This means that I critically engage with both systems of education within higher education. I am "able-bodied," and while I approach my research and praxis from a CDS lens, I acknowledge the privilege inherent in my research and practice. Through this self-study, I engaged and continue to engage with the system of higher education as a student and educator of Color who has experienced multiple global cultures academically and socially, and has lived as "majority" and "minority" in many contexts throughout life.

TOWARD A CRITICAL CONSILIENCATORY CRITICAL EMOTION PRAXIS COUNTER-NARRATING GENERATIVITY AND BEING AS PEDAGOGY AT THE BOUNDARIES

According to Miller et al. (2020) critical reflection for transformative learning includes: (1) assumption analysis (e.g., ideology of ability, I don't see Color, race doesn't matter), (2) contextual awareness (such as resisting decontextualized educational policies), (3) imaginative speculation, (4) reflective skepticism, (5) reflection-based actions, (6) reflection on the effect of reflection-based actions, and (7) coming full circle with new praxis or assumption analysis once again. In reanalysis, we have been enveloped in such a hermeneutic cycle of critical reflection for our own transformative learning.

It is important to counter-narrate our experiences at our personal and professional positionalities and relationalities since such felt theory (Million, 2008) is largely absent from K-12 policy. It is through this safe, and we argue, brave space for risk-taking, or what Miller et al. (2020) call a model of generative change through a Vygotskian Zone of Proximal Development that the following occur: (1) The dialect between awakening and reflection leads to narrativization of personal literacy, in which one can speak and challenge the past experiences and long-held beliefs or perspectives. This is a meta-cognitive process and awareness. (2) Agency and introspection at the personal level involves a desire and motivation for new perspectives that can be embraced or rejected. This can empower a (3) critique and advocacy stance leading to action research that comes from a perceived need for change. Lastly, this leads to (4) efficacy and voice in the construction of new knowledge applied continuously to problem-solving and ongoing learning, which cumulatively results in generativity. Miller et al. (2020) do not stop there; they outline a critical reflection and generativity critical counter-narrative praxis model for educational contexts that we adopted to our self-study and collaboration. We postulate and find grace and breathe in the following statements that summarize Miller et al.'s (2020) model of praxis for critical counter-narrativizing: (1) we are in this situation due to structural problems, (2) we can change this situation, (3) here's how we might change this situation, (4) this is how we changed the situation, and (5) this is what we learned from action and what comes next.

Since spring 2020, we thematized both classes from the perspectives of immigrant and/or refugee students. Inspired by Shehreen's dissertation research on the educational experiences of immigrant and/or refugee students labeled disabled, we co-designed the syllabi with this particular sub-theme. Our pedagogy reflects the importance of critical reflections, on listening to students' and our feelings about our affective personal and professional experiences, and on K-12 special education laws and practices. Specifically, we focused on this student population because in recent years, the Midwest—which was historically celebrated as "preserving authentic America"—has seen an increase in international and secondary migration (Fennelly, 2008). Knowing this, we prepared lectures, shared personal narratives and experiences, hands-on activities and class discussions (such as reading the law from a critical stance and/or critically exploring organizations working with immigrant/refugee student populations), carefully designed legal assignments and case studies, invited guest speakers in our classes (such as CDS Guest Speakers from other countries who work with immigrant and refugee student population globally, ELL teachers, and parents of students of Color with dis/abilities), and conducted interviews with immigrant and/or refugee students with dis/abilities about their educational experiences. This pedagogy has proven to help our preservice teachers critically engage (a) with the special education laws and (b) in self-study to reflect on their own ideological narratives about diverse student backgrounds and cultures from a CDS lens.

For me, David, I am realizing that since I became aware of being labeled with an auditory learning disability (ALD), my mind and psychology has been robbed from my own self and spirit (Hernández-Saca, 2021). Teaching has become a practice of freedom from intersectional dominant discourses that have attempted to spirit murder (Williams, 1987) me, allowing transcendence to some extent from the psychological damage that the Big Discourse (Gee, 2015) has had on my personal and professional life. I cannot be afraid to write that anymore, and also bring it to my teaching in ways that can be transformative. This transformation has begun to free me from the binaries constructed at different levels of the educational system, especially for others like me at the intersection of dis/Abled, cisgender, Latinx, gay, immigrant, and refugee at the hands of hegemonic special and general education teachers and personnel.

For me, Shehreen, my past experiences of group projects with white female students, when I often felt othered, surfaced during our first semester of co-teaching. During the first student survey for the Spring 2020 SPED 4150/SPED 5150 course, David and I realized the gender bias in students' responses. It was actually David who suggested that we bring this up with our students in a way that allowed an opportunity to grow and engage in self-reflection about our own biases. Events such as students waiting for David after class so that they can ask him a question or directing their emails to him alone often made me feel othered during the Spring 2020 semester. However, David and my constant vulnerable and deliberate attempts—such as discussions with students after student surveys—to engage our intersecting positionalities and create a welcoming and radically loving atmosphere within our classrooms have been a part of our co-teaching pedagogy. This has helped our students and ourselves to be more radical in valuing diversity within and between us all. I recognize that as a female instructor of Color and with my own multiple affective intersectional identities, I ideologically and structurally counter-narrate the systems of education while creating a safe and brave third space for radical love and belonging for our future generations of students and teachers with my lived and experienced realities (Gutiérrez, 2008).

We are in this situation due to structural problems aligns with assumption analysis and awakening as meta-cognitive awareness. However, we add to this by centering meta-emotive, meta-affective, and meta-feeling processes, in order to further decenter Eurocentric and the coloniality of power embedded within the academy and Global North contexts where we are physically situated. We do this because as scholars from the Global South, our roots to our individual life histories connect us to the epistemologies of the South (de Sousa Santos, 2018).

For me, Shehreen, whenever I talk about my multiple identities, I struggle as I understand that I am a Muslim, a South Asian, multilingual female, and a recent immigrant to a country where all these identities are politically and culturally viewed from deficit and ableist thinking and language (Patton Davis & Museus, 2019). Alluding to the above-mentioned incident, I often felt othered in many of my on-campus classes. My first recollection of feeling "othered" is as a master's student in 2014 when I worked on a group project with four white female students. Contrary to my repeated requests to discuss the project and collaborate, my group decided to not respond to my emails while still collaborating with each other. In the end, I asked the professor to change my group. I have experienced that moment multiple times ever since, and while I did not fully comprehend why these students were reluctant to work with me then, looking back, I am certain racism, linguicism, and xenophobia were often at play in these instances, even if unintentional. Their actions related to the system that privileges U.S.-centered white middle-class ways of being and doing in the society and often "others" any ways of being and dispositions that do not align with mainstream white culture and values.

For me, David, I find grace in knowing that all of my negative affective intersectional discourses, emotions, and historically and materially embodied experiences (Siebers, 2008) in special education and the master narratives of learning disabilities are socially and emotionally constructed in ways that did not originate in me. The practices of the traditional canon and system of special education, embedded in having children and students achieve "automaticity" (Fletcher et al., 2019) in their speech and language performance and actions in schools, is couched in a positivist scientism that has shaped my life (Gallagher, 2010). This is not something that I and others like me who have been labeled had a choice about. The rules of learning and teaching and human development are written through a technical and technician model (Gallagher, 2004). In turn, how dis/ability is constructed in traditional special education is through the cultural-historical, policy, and professional master narratives and its discursive, emotive, and material practices (Hernández-Saca, 2017).

We can change this situation Ideological becoming. This is an important one. For me, David, I have lived for a very long time feeling that I cannot change the hegemony of special education and its systems of labeling, classifying, and identifying that result in intersectional disablism (Iqtadar et al., 2020). However, I realize that I have been pushing back all along and trying to free myself from the deficit thinking and language of special education that has restricted the life chances of students, especially Black, Indigenous, and People of Color. This process is connected to the contextual awareness and agency that both Shehreen and I experience within our processes of personal, professional, and program renewal, made possible through co-mentoring and co-teaching in educational spaces.

Co-Teaching as Co-Mentorship for Personal, Professional, and Program Renewal. We conceptualize our co-teaching and co-planning relationship as co-mentorship for personal, professional, and program renewal at our intersections of identity and power at the boundaries of traditional special education and Critical Disability Studies in Education (CDSE). In the spirit of Paulo Freire (1996), we center our co-teaching and co-planning relationship as co-mentorship, which is bidirectional and dialogical within our teacher preparation programming. According to Redmond (1990), "mentoring, the act of providing wise and friendly counsel, has been practiced throughout the ages" (p. 188). Within the context of a historically white institution and White Disability Studies (Bell, 2010), we cull from the literature on culturally diverse mentorship in higher education (Redmond, 1990) to construct new knowledge at the boundaries of traditional special education and CDSE and white and ability supremacy with self, each other, and our teacher candidates. We do so in order to conceptualize and practice an intersectional CDSE that accounts for our critical analytic autoethnography experiences and texts (Anderson, 2005). According to Redmond (1990), "effective mentoring requires that people listen to each other, care about each other, engage in cooperatively and mutually satisfying ventures, and manipulate systems to meet individual and group needs" (p. 202). Such mentor-mentee relationship characteristics in co-teacher education practices are critical, not only for the personal, interpersonal, and professional well-being and development of mentor and mentee, but for teacher candidates and their education and orientation to the boundaries of traditional special education and DSE. It is also critical for systemic change at the programmatic levels of special and general teacher education through self-study teacher education methodology in higher education.

Here's how we might change this situation. Internalization. This is done through reflective skepticism and advocacy. This is important because of the hegemony of special education and the field and ideologies of learning disabilities have been internalized in me, David, from which I have been working to free myself: the never-ending dilemma of the stigma of learning disabilities and special education systems that structure what counts dis/Abilities from the hegemony of traditional psychological science (Dirth & Adams, 2019). To express my skepticism and advocacy for the power that the system of special education has had on my spirit, psychology, and body, I wrote the following poem:

LD
Special Education
Damage
Let me go
No more LD

The ideology of LD
Has tramped me
To my Core
How can I engage in a consilience praxis given the constant trauma and LD emotions?
Radically loving self and other
Radically advocating for self and social and emotional justice
Co-creating a more humane inclusive educational system for all at our intersections of power and identities

For me, Shehreen, my lived experiences as a female of Color from Global South as well as my critical scholarly engagement and pedagogical approaches and collaboration with David and other critical scholars have been helpful in critically understanding systems of power, including the education system. My journey, which I call the journey of liberation, has helped me unpack and underscore how the ableism, linguicism, and other types of *isms* that I have experienced in the last seven years of my education and teaching is something that did not originate in me. Rather, I understand that these are systems of oppression that systematically and ideologically (through us humans) suppress those who are not represented as "normed members" of society yet are vulnerable and strong to counter-narrate the systems of power and oppression in their personal and professional lives. I also understand that this phenomenon is quite true for most immigrant and refugee students. Oftentimes, they are not aware of the prevailing deficit narratives surrounding their multiple identities until months or years after they arrive in the United States (Barajas-López, 2014). In my ongoing learning and teaching I counter-narrate these deficit views through the operationalization of critical emotion praxis within our special education preservice teacher program to encourage our preservice students to disrupt white, patriarchal, and ableist hegemonic power structures.

This work is personal, professional, and programmatic for the life chances of historically multiply marginalized youth and their families within K-12 educational systems and their future teachers at their intersections of power and identities. This work has conceptual, theoretical, and methodological implications for our persons, our profession, and our programs, as well as for others who might be experiencing such systems of power and identities within the boundaries of traditional special education and disability studies in education. Given such systems of power, privilege, and identities, our mental health is on the line. This work is personal, and since it is personal, it is political.

Revisiting our definition of *critical consiliencatory critical emotion praxis counter-narrating generativity* we welcome educators and practitioners in the fields of DSE and traditional Special education to employ emotive pedagogies (e.g., valuing emotions in our spaces as sources of knowledge about systems; critical emotion praxis that we embedded in our generativity framework) within our sacred spaces we call classrooms and come forward to create such third and brave spaces within the structures by sharing our personal and political narratives. As educators, such courageous acts of speaking from our experiences would not only help us as humans who are wounded by the systems but would also be a cultural model (Freire et al., 2018) for our future educators' critical consciousness (Freire, 2005) within K-12. We would like to leave our readers with the following self-probing questions.

We would like to leave our readers with the following self-probing questions: 1) How would you practice emotive pedagogies in your classroom at the boundaries between traditional special education and Disability Studies in Education? 2) What are different assumptions that you may have regarding Black, Indigenous and Youth of Color with or without disabilities? And women faculty members with intersectional identities in higher education? How do you disrupt these assumptions in your day-to-day practice with your students and/or colleagues? 3) In what ways would you practice co-mentorship for personal, professional and program renewal on campus or in your department?

NOTES

1. We define "critical" as "a condition of criticality, when it is encountered in a context that allows for translations or communication across differences; when it is taken seriously, and not distanced as exotic or quaint; and when one does not use the excuse of 'incommensurability' as a reason to abandon dialogue" (Burbules & Berk, 1999, para. 53). This distinction is important because we are living within a historical moment when dominant institutions are having a racial reckoning with the non-ways in which race and other social markers of difference are integrated into their institutional cultures. However, from a *critical consiliencatory critical emotion praxis counter-narrating generativity* (Miller et al., 2020) we account for the micro and macro levels of educational systems at the boundaries of traditional hegemonic special education and DSE within our courses that envision an interdisciplinary collaborative approach to technical, contextual, and critical problems of practice that our future in-service teachers would undertake in an increasingly and highly polarized world within and across differences.

2. By dis/Ability we mean the social and emotional construction of both dis-abilities and abilities at the personal, interpersonal, structural, and political levels of society (Crenshaw, 1990) along gender, race, and other markers of difference in educational contexts. We purposefully capitalize the A in dis/Ability to recognize the assets of students and people with disabilities at their intersections of power and identities and their capabilities to counter-narrate overwhelming deficit thinking and language about Black, Indigenous, and Youth and Faculty of Color in elementary,

secondary, and postsecondary settings. Furthermore, within Disability Studies (DS), the "A" with dis/Ability is typically capitalized to draw attention to "ability" rather than "disability" and takes issue with wording that suggests those labeled have an inability to learn, such as with the case of learning disabilities (e.g., learning disabilities versus learning dis/Abilities).

REFERENCES

Akkerman, S. F., & Bakker, A. (2011). Boundary crossing and boundary objects. *Review of Educational Research, 81*(2), 132–169.

Anderson, L. (2006). Analytic autoethnography. *Journal of Contemporary Ethnography, 35*(4), 373–395.

Anderson, E. (2015). The white space. *Sociology of Race and Ethnicity, 1*(1), 10–21.

Barajas-López, F. (2014). Mexican immigrant students' schooling experiences and the construction of disengagement in mathematics learning contexts. *Journal of Latinos and Education, 13*(1), 14–32.

Bal, A. (2009). *Becoming learners in US schools: A sociocultural study of refugee students' evolving identities.* Arizona State University.

Baglieri, S., Valle, J. W., Connor, D. J., & Gallagher, D. J. (2011). Disability studies in education: The need for a plurality of perspectives on disability. *Remedial and special education, 32*(4), 267–278.

Bell, C. (2010). Is disability studies actually white disability studies. In L. J. Davis (Ed.), *The Disability Studies reader* (pp. 374–382). Taylor & Francis.

Bell, D. (1992). *Faces at the bottom of the well: The permanence of racism.* Basic Books.

Bell Jr, D. A. (1980). Brown v. Board of Education and the interest-convergence dilemma. *Harvard Law Review, 93*(3), 518–533.

Berne, P., Morales, A. L., Langstaff, D., & Invalid, S. (2018). Ten principles of disability justice. *WSQ: Women's Studies Quarterly, 46*(1), 227–230.

Berry, M., & Russell, T. (2014). Critical friends, collaborators and community in self-study. *Studying Teacher Education, 10*(3), 195–196.

Boser, U. (2011). *Teacher diversity matters: A state-by-state analysis of teachers of color.* Americans for Progress.

Burbules, N. C., & Burke, R. (1999). Critical thinking and critical pedagogy: Relations, differences and limits. In T. S. Popkewitz & L. Fendler (Eds.), *Critical theories in education: Changing terrains of knowledge and politics*, (pp. 45–65). Routledge.

Burns, V. F., & Mintzberg, S. (2019). Co-teaching as teacher training: Experiential accounts of two doctoral students. *College Teaching, 67*(2), 94–99.

Chandler-Olcott, K., Burnash, J., Donahue, D., DeChick, M., Gendron, M., Smith, J., Taylor, M., & Zeleznik, J. (2012). Grouping lessons we learned from co-teaching in a summer writing institute. *Voices from the Middle, 20*(2), 10.

Chanmugam, A., & Gerlach, B. (2013). A co-teaching model for developing future educators' teaching effectiveness. *International Journal of Teaching and Learning in Higher Education*, *25*(1), 110–117.

Cioè-Peña, M., Moore, E., & Rojo, L. M. (2016). The burden of 'nativeness': Four plurilingual student-teachers' stories. *Bellaterra Journal of Teaching & Learning Language & Literature*, *9*(2), 32–52.

Connor, D. J., Gabel, S. L., Gallagher, D. J., & Morton, M. (2008). Disability studies and inclusive education—implications for theory, research, and practice. *International Journal of Inclusive Education*, *12*(5–6), 441–457.

Crenshaw, K. (1990). Mapping the margins: Intersectionality, identity politics, and violence against women of color. *Stanford Law Review*, *43*(6), 1241.

Crow, J., & Smith, L. (2005). Co-teaching in higher education: Reflective conversation on shared experience as continued professional development for lecturers and health and social care students. *Reflective Practice*, *6*(4), 491–506.

de Sousa Santos, B. (2018). *The end of the cognitive empire: The coming of age of epistemologies of the South*. Duke University Press.

Dirth, T. P., & Adams, G. A. (2019). Decolonial theory and disability studies: On the modernity/coloniality of ability. *Journal of Social and Political Psychology*, *7*(1), 260–289.

Dugan, K., & Letterman, M. (2008). Student appraisals of collaborative teaching. *College Teaching*, *56*(1), 11–15.

Endo, R. (2019). Male of color refugee teachers on being un/desirable bodies of difference in education. *Equity & Excellence in Education*, *52*(4), 448–464.

Fennelly, K (2008). Prejudice toward immigrants in the Midwest. In Massey, D. (Ed). *New faces in new places: The changing geography of American immigration* (pp. 151–178). Russell Sage Foundation.

Freire, P. (1996). *Pedagogy of the oppressed* (revised). Continuum.

Freire, P. (2005). *Education for critical consciousness*. Bloomsbury Publishing.

Freire, P., Macedo, D., Koike, D., Oliveira, A., & Freire, A. M. A. (2018). *Teachers as cultural workers: Letters to those who dare teach*. Routledge.

Fletcher, J. M., Lyon, G. R., Fuchs, L. S., & Barnes, M. A. (2018). *Learning disabilities: From identification to intervention*. Guilford Publications.

Gallagher, D. (2010). Hiding in Plain Sight: The Nature and Role of Theory in Learning Disability Labeling. *Disability Studies Quarterly*, *30*(2).

Gallagher, D. J. (2004). Educational research, philosophical ortho- doxy and unfulfilled promises: The quandary of traditional research in U.S. special education. In G. Thomas & R. Pring (Eds.), *Evidence-based practice in education* (pp. 119–130). Berkshire, UK: Open University Press.

Gannon, S. (2006). The (im)possibilities of writing the self-writing: French poststructural theory and autoethnography. *Cultural Studies/Critical Methodologies*, *6*(4), 474–495.

Gee, J. P. (2015). Discourse, small d, big D. The international encyclopedia of language and social interaction, 3, 1–5.

Gutiérrez, K. D. (2008). Developing a sociocritical literacy in the third space. *Reading research quarterly*, *43*(2), 148–164.

Gutstein, E. (2003). Teaching and learning mathematics for social justice in an urban, Latino school. *Journal for Research in Mathematics Education, 34*(1), 37–73.

Hall, M. C. (2019). Critical disability theory.

Hang, Q., & Rabren, K. (2009). An examination of co-teaching: Perspectives and efficacy indicators. *Remedial and Special Education, 30*(5), 259–268.

Harris, C. I. (1993). Whiteness as property. *Harvard Law Review, 106*(8), 1707–1791.

Hernández-Saca, D. I. (2016). *Re-framing the master narratives of dis/ability through an emotion lens: Voices of Latina/o students with learning disabilities*. Arizona State University.

Hernández-Saca, D. I. (2017). Reframing the master narratives of dis/ability at my intersections: An outline of an educational equity research agenda. *Critical Disability Discourses*, 8, 1–30.

Hernández-Saca, D. I. (2019). [Invited]. Transitioning through an inclusive model of dis/ability at the intersections: It takes an inclusive village and spirit. In J. W. Valle & D. J. Connor (Eds.), *Rethinking disability: A disability studies approach to inclusive practices* (pp. 265–266). Routledge.

Hernández-Saca, D. I. (2021). Recovering the spirit. In D. J. Connor & B. Ferri (Eds.), *How teaching shapes our thinking about disabilities: Stories from the field* (pp. 263–276). Peter Lang.

Hernández-Saca, D., & Cannon, M. A. (2019). Interrogating disability epistemologies: Towards collective dis/ability intersectional emotional, affective and spiritual autoethnographies for healing. *International Journal of Qualitative Studies in Education, 32*(3), 243–262.

Invalid, S. (2017). Skin, tooth, and bone-The basis of movement is our people: A Disability Justice primer. *Reproductive Health Matters, 25*(50), 149.

King, J. E. (2015). *Dysconscious racism, Afrocentric praxis, and education for human freedom*. New York: Routledge.

Kosnik, C., Beck, C., Freese, A. R., & Samaras, A. P. (Eds.). (2006). *Making a difference in teacher education through self-study: Studies of personal, professional and program renewal* (Vol. 2). Springer Science & Business Media.

Ladson-Billings, G. (2009). *The dreamkeepers: Successful teachers of African American children*. John Wiley & Sons.

Letterman, M. R., & Dugan, K. B. (2004). Team teaching a cross-disciplinary honors course: Preparation and development. *College teaching*, 52(2), 76–9.

Meekosha, H., & Shuttleworth, R. (2009). What's so "critical" about critical disability studies? *Australian Journal of Human Rights, 15*(1), 47.

Miller, R., Liu, K., & Ball, A. F. (2020). Critical counter-narrative as transformative methodology for educational equity. *Review of Research in Education*, 44(1), 269–300.

Moore, M. R. (2017). Women of color in the academy. *Social Problems, 64*(2), 200–205.

Million, D. (2009). Felt theory: An Indigenous feminist approach to affect and history. *Wicazo Sa Review*, 24(2), 53–76.

Morelock, J. R., Lester, M. M., Klopfer, M. D., Jardon, A. M., Mullins, R. D., Nicholas, E. L., & Alfaydi, A. S. (2017). Power, perceptions, and relationships: A model of co-teaching in higher education. *College Teaching, 65*(4), 182–191.

Nelson, N., & Castelló, M. (2012). Academic writing and authorial voice. In M. Castelló & C. Donahue (Eds.), *University writing: Selves and texts in academic societies* (pp. 33–51). Brill.

Paris, D. (2012). Culturally sustaining pedagogy: A needed change in stance, terminology, and practice. *Educational Researcher, 41*(3), 93–97.

Patton, J. M. (1998). The disproportionate representation of African Americans in special education: Looking behind the curtain for understanding and solutions. *The Journal of Special Education, 32*(1), 25–31.

Patton Davis, L., & Museus, S. (2019). What is deficit thinking? An analysis of conceptualizations of deficit thinking and implications for scholarly research. *Currents, 1*(1), 117–130.

Price, J. (1999). Racialized masculinities: The diploma, teachers, and peers in the lives of young African American men. *Youth and Society, 31*(2), 224–263.

Redmond, S. P. (1990). Mentoring and cultural diversity in academic settings. *American Behavioral Scientist, 34*(2), 188–200.

de Sousa Santos, B. (2018). *The end of the cognitive empire: The coming of age of epistemologies of the South.* Duke University Press.

Samaras, A. P. (2011). *Self-study teacher research: Improving your practice through collaborative inquiry.* SAGE Publications.

Schuck, S., & Russell, T. (2005). Self-study, critical friendship, and the complexities of teacher education. *Studying Teacher Education, 1*(2), 107–121.

Siebers, T. (2008). *Disability theory.* University of Michigan Press.

Stetsenko, A. P. (2020). Critical challenges in cultural-historical activity theory: the urgency of agency. Cultural-Historical Psychology, 16(2), 5–18.

Thorius, K. A. (2019). The construction, expression, and consequences of difference in education practice, policy, and research. *International Journal of Qualitative Studies in Education, 32*(3), 211–216.

Valle, J. W., Connor, D. J., & Reid, D. K. (2006). [Editors' Introduction]. IDEA at 30: Looking back, facing forward—A Disability Studies perspective. *Disability Studies Quarterly, 26*(2).

Vanassche, E., & Kelchtermans, G. (2015). The state of the art in self-study of teacher education practices: A systematic literature review. *Journal of Curriculum Studies, 47*(4), 508–528.

Van den Berg, F. M. (2017). Promoting culturally relevant pedagogy amongst pre-service teachers: A systematic literature review on how pre-service teachers in teacher education programs can develop culturally relevant pedagogy that enables them to establish a classroom environment that suits the needs of all learners. *School of Education and Communication (HLK)*. Masters Thesis. Jönköping University.

Williams, P. (1987). Spirit-murdering the messenger: The discourse of fingerpointing as the law's response to racism. *U. Miami L. Rev.*, 42, 127.

Chapter 11

Grappling with the Tensions

Cultivating Justice-Oriented Praxis through Collaborative Autoethnographic Poetry

Amanda L. Miller, Chelsea Stinson, and Maria T. Timberlake

The interdisciplinary relationship between the fields of Disability Studies in Education (DSE) and special education is typically conceptualized as oppositional by education scholars, especially in discourses of inclusive education (e.g., Connor, 2019). This is evident in the tensions experienced by educators working in teacher preparation programs, which tend to sustain rigid special education frameworks which emphasize the spatialization of student learning (Naraian, 2016), regulatory compliance, and procedural approaches to schooling under the guise of commitments to inclusive education (Slee, 2013). Teacher preparation programs frequently fail to transform teachers' thinking regarding disability and instead affirm prevailing ableist beliefs which support that children do not notice disability (Baglieri & Lalvani, 2020). Moreover, teacher preparation programs often maintain the general and special education distinctions (Skrtic, 1995), even while wrestling with similar frustrations and limitations imposed by neoliberal policies that both parties consider detrimental to children's well-being (Clift & Liaupson, 2019). As teacher educators in a dual certification program at a small state university in the Northeastern United States that maintains a "general education only" major, we find ourselves practicing within this systemic paradox.

As Connor (2019) affirmed, DSE emerged from the work of critical special education scholars such as Brantlinger (1997) and Skrtic (1991) to (a) contextualize disability within political and social spheres; (b) privilege the interest, agendas, and voices of people labeled with disability/disabled[1] people; (c) promote social justice, equitable and inclusive educational opportunities, and full and meaningful access to all aspects of society for people labeled with disability/disabled people; and (d) assume competence and reject deficit models of disability.

These tenets urge stakeholders (e.g., scholars, practitioners, community members, students) in the field of DSE to action and engagement beyond the philosophical boundaries of DSE. That is, bringing the work of DSE into other intellectual, discursive, emotive, material, and practical spaces—interrogating this work from myriad perspectives—to place "current ideas of disability within their broadest possible context," where they might not implicitly emerge (Society for Disability Studies, 2016, n.p.). However, the requirement to meet special education standards and state certification requirements results in our *performing boundary maintenance* (Waitoller et al., 2016) thus upholding hegemonic notions of normalcy, whiteness, and power in education. While committed to DSE tenets (Connor et al., 2018) and disability justice principles (Berne et al., 2018), we also inadvertently reinforce determinations of "expertise" and "benevolence" which securely position education professionals as helpers (Coomer, 2019; Timberlake, 2019). Aspiring special education teachers, therefore, are taught to implement evidence-based practices (i.e., praise for desired behavior and the provision of direct instruction; Schles & Robertson, 2019; Sweigart et al., 2016). Thus, while traditional special education scholars continue to endlessly affirm and uphold the status of positivism, objectivity, and the need for "scientific evidence" to remediate individually intrinsic deficits (e.g., Odom et al., 2020), DSE scholarship emphasizes, "the interest, agendas, and voices of people labeled with disability/disabled people" (Disability Studies in Education Special Interest Group 143, 2019, para. 1).

Despite commitments to interdisciplinary theory, praxis, and anti-oppressive approaches to inclusive education (Buffington-Adams & Vaughan, 2019), DSE stakeholders acknowledge how they both experience and are complicit in interlocking systems of oppression (e.g., ableism, racism, linguicism). For example, if teacher preparation programs do not problematize "disability awareness day" and activities that patronize youth labeled with disability, then such programs do not raise awareness about the systematic nature of ableism at the intersections of power and privilege (Baglieri & Lalvani, 2020) before teacher candidates become indoctrinated into school systems as professionals. Furthermore, if teacher preparation programs do not engage with the Black Lives Matter movement (Cioè-Peña, 2017) and the overrepresentation of Black youth in harsh disciplinary practices (Annamma et al., 2016) and special education (Blanchett et al., 2009), then they fail to condone racism and ableism and transform schooling mechanisms that (re)produce marginalization for Black youth labeled with disability. That said, the desire to respect students' histories and aspirations (e.g., Ashby, 2012) is held in delicate contention with the uncomfortable awareness that schools reproduce societal oppressions and reinforce conflicting theorizations of identity and justice, unequally among historically multiply marginalized youth and their families, especially girls, Black youth, Indigenous youth, and youth of color with and without disabilities (Petersen et al., 2018).

Simultaneously, the principles of disability justice (Sins Invalid, 2016) and the work of disabled community scholars and activists of color are often excluded from the academy (Nusbaum & Steinborn, 2019). This exclusion lives on through how community knowledge is positioned and ignored by faculty (e.g., course material selection, guest speaker invitation). In addition, when disabled people are seen as knowledgeable by academics, it is often the perspectives of white disabled scholars and community members (Bell, 2006) that are honored rather than the perspectives of historically multiply marginalized individuals, families, and communities. Such practices reflect the ideology of normal wherein disabled community scholars and activists of color are constructed as deficient and less than (Annamma et al., 2013). That said, traditional special education scholarship and pedagogy is anchored in this ideology (Brantlinger, 2006).

Extant literature focused on the contention between DSE and special education partially reflects our experiences teaching in a comprehensive state university system. Simultaneously, this context presents unique challenges and tensions given our individual life experiences or historicities, the longstanding presence of special education in state licensure requirements, and our collective desires for more critical, humanizing, and justice-oriented approaches. As such, we were particularly interested in investigating how our prior historicities influenced our beliefs and actions across personal and professional trajectories. Moreover, we were also concerned with how we engaged in contextualized consilience (Wilson, 1999)—boundary work within interacting yet independent contexts at our state university. Thus, we drew on Akkerman and Bakker (2011a, 2011b) to conceptualize our boundary work within a systemic paradox which compels us to endlessly teach "against the grain" (Danforth, 2017, p. 7). Two research questions guided this process:

1. How does our historicity impact how we address hegemonic values in our boundary work?
2. How and where does contextualized consilience emerge in our separate and shared experiences?

CONCEPTUAL FRAMEWORK

We drew on a blended conceptual framework encompassing cultural historical activity theory (CHAT; Cole & Engeström, 1993) and critical pedagogy (Freire, 1993; hooks, 1994). CHAT afforded an examination of learning and teaching as cultural systems and practices situated within local, social, emotional, and historical contexts (Cole, 1998; Roth, 2007) that evolve over time with varying degrees of accessibility and meaningfulness (Rogoff, 2003). Because we were concerned with educational change and social transformation (Shor & Freire, 1987), we blended CHAT with critical pedagogy. Critical pedagogy strengthened CHAT with an explicit discussion on how *power* is (re)produced and maintained (Esmonde & Booker, 2016) within university activity systems (e.g., classrooms) as practices, rules, and artifacts and who is most impacted, including historically multiply marginalized students, families, and communities. This blended framework afforded an exploration of the tensions between the medical model alive within special education and teacher preparation and how we are/were generating (or not) more critical, humanizing, and justice-oriented approaches to teacher development (Pearson et al., 2016).

In this way, our individual and collective experiences are transposed onto an adapted three-dimensional version of Vygotsky's basic mediational triangle (Engeström, 1987; Hancock & Miller, 2017). Figure 11.1 illuminates the multiple players, artifacts, objects, and outcomes within our coursework. Moreover, the activity system on the left delineates the components inherent, yet fluid, in the other two activity systems. The three activity systems, each representing one of the authors, converge at shared objects and outcomes.

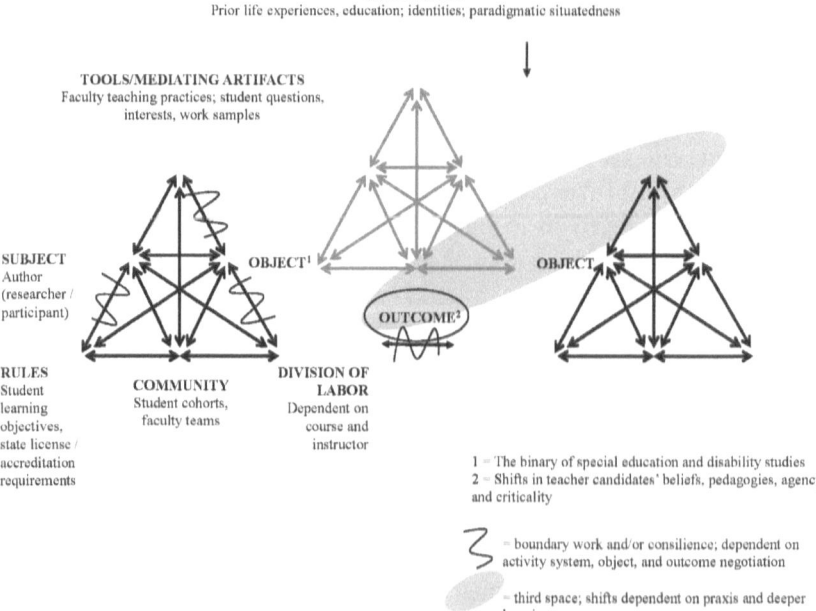

Figure 11.1   Three Interacting and Discrete Activity Systems.

Roles and identities develop and transform over time like activity systems. Therefore, we focused on historicity—our prior life experiences—to question "our ideological beliefs and (pedagogical) intentions" as university faculty, among other identities (e.g., pre-service and in-service teachers, helpers, care workers), and took note of our own "adherence to the status quo" (Darder, 2011, p. 182). Yet, historicity, the multiple components of the activity system, and the activity system itself are inherently informed by and inform one another. As such, we use the activity system and CHAT to operationalize and guide our self-study (Samaras et al., 2004) as a collaborative autoethnography (Chang et al., 2012; discussed next). In sum, because we wanted to interrogate our complicity and resistance, our reflections on past and present self were imperative to the study.

In addition, we considered how, as university faculty seeking to unravel the binary between special education and DSE, our work exemplified boundary crossing (Akkerman & Bakker, 2011a). We looked for the types of learning that were occurring (or not) at the boundary (Akkerman & Bakker, 2011b). Boundary work (Giroux, 1992) or consilience (Wilson, 1999) may exist in multiple spheres (e.g., between subject and artifact, between artifact and object) where there are opportunities for shifts in thought and feelings and when participants are open to ideas from the outside. By *contextualized consilience* we mean boundary work within separate yet shared contexts at this state university. Both are moveable and dependent on the activity system. In sum, we used third-generation CHAT (Engeström, 2001) and critical pedagogy to identify how and why we cultivate *contextualized consilience* within teacher development.

METHOD

We used collaborative autoethnography (Chang et al., 2012) to focus on how our historicity impacted our boundary work and how and where consilience was cultivated in our teaching context. Collaborative autoethnography was an appropriate strategy of inquiry because our work was concurrently collaborative in data collection and analysis (Ellis et al., 2011). In addition, our project was autoethnographic as we not only journaled (individually and collaboratively) about and reflected on our experiences, but our stories were situated in the university's sociocultural and political contexts (Chang et al., 2012). As such, we occupied dual roles as researchers and participants (Lapadat, 2017).

Contexts, Participants, and Positionalities

The setting was a state college campus within a large (sixty-four institutions) state system. As of fall 2019, Enrollment Facts showed undergraduate enrollment just over 6000 and racial/ethnic demographics reveal a predominately white institution in faculty, staff, and student makeup. Teacher preparation enrollment data showed three of the top six majors were education-related: physical education, early childhood education, and grades 1–6 dual certification major (Inclusive Childhood Education), in which the co-authors taught. The dual certification major is housed in an intradisciplinary department with educational foundations and educational leadership. The teacher candidates study educational foundations in their first semester, focused on educational inequities and systems of oppression, and a critical focus is maintained throughout their teacher preparation. The first inclusive education course is offered sophomore year and focuses on educational inequities with a particular focus on ableism (and other intersecting oppressions depending on instructor). All co-authors taught courses for juniors and seniors where pedagogy as well as traditional (e.g., assessment, IEP writing, positive behavioral supports) and critical education (e.g., overrepresentation of students of color in special education and harsh disciplinary practices) topics were covered.

Three university faculty, the chapter's co-authors, participated in the inquiry. At the time of the study, one participant was a tenured faculty who identified as a white female navigating a chronic illness. She has experience as a family member in the special education process. Another was a nondisabled white female who was a doctoral candidate working as an adjunct lecturer. Finally, the third was a junior faculty who identified as a white female with non-visible disabilities. These positionalities informed and complicated aspects of our work through the project's self- and group-study.

Data Sources and Collection

Data collection sources and methods included personal journals, group discussions, and collaborative writings. Each author journaled individually for at least six weeks in response to a variety of prompts focused on the current (and then as time lapsed, previous) semester. Prompts were generated during group discussions and included: *How did you get here? When did you feel you were compromising your justice-oriented praxis? Give pedagogical or praxical examples of struggling with special education and DSE conflicts.* Group discussions were informed by one another's reflexivity and unrecorded, yet the group took notes. As such, meeting notes were included as data sources as one author regularly reflected in writing within the notes afterward. Moreover, these reflexive notes would often inform the personal journaling and/or next group discussion. Lastly, the team used collaborative writing to gain a deeper understanding of a topic (e.g., time and space, boundary crossing) through self-other study (Chang et al., 2012). We chose collaborative autoethnography rather than duoethnography to honor two disability justice principles:

recognizing wholeness and interdependence (Piepzna-Samarasinha, 2018). Like the collaborative and contextualized nature of personal history self-study (Samaras et al., 2004), collaborative autoethnography allowed us to explore self in the presence of others (Belkhir et al., 2018) while generating collective understandings of shared experiences (Ngunjiri et al., 2010).

Data Analysis and Poetry

The team used narrative analysis (Merriam & Tisdell, 2015) of journals, discussions, and collaborative writings. Data analysis was iterative (Bhattacharya, 2017) as preliminary analysis of personal journaling informed the next phase of questions for the autoethnographic conversations. The research team repeatedly read and reviewed the data to look for patterns (Saldaña, 2013). We confirmed the patterns through discussions and when disagreement emerged, we reached a consensus through additional dialogue. Then, the team returned to the data for additional cycles of analysis, adjusting emerging patterns as needed. We ensured trustworthiness through multiple rounds of coding and meaning-making as well as triangulation across data sources and team members (Lincoln & Guba, 1985).

Following narrative analysis, we co-created a praxical and theoretical knowledge production written as three-voice poems with the most salient patterns (Saldaña, 2013). Poetry enabled us to temporarily step out of our academic discourse and "make sense of swirling ideas" through language (Suskin, 2020, p. 19). In addition, three-voice poetry (Deckman & Ohito, 2019) operated as a "dialogical learning mechanism" (Akkerman & Bakker, 2011a, p. 150) illuminating our multiple points of views and positions. Once the team confirmed patterns (as described above), each author composed three-voice poems using quotes from our data. Each poem was presented to the team and dialogically negotiated and reworked. Additional meaning-making of the data through poetry ensured trustworthiness of our interpretations and conclusions (Ohito & Nyachae, 2019).

COLLABORATIVE AUTOETHNOGRAPHIC POETRY

Our findings are organized into three themes and visually displayed as three-voice poems, each voice representing one of the authors. Each poem is read left to right, top to bottom. While each column represents the voice of one of the authors, the authors' positions change from poem to poem. In other words, the same author does not maintain the same position (e.g., first) across poems. First, we discuss how our historicity impacted our boundary work. Then, we describe how consilience was enacted through our pedagogy and praxis. Finally, we discuss how joy lived on through our work inside and outside classroom activity systems.

Historicity: How We Got Here

Guided by the disability justice principles of recognizing wholeness and sustainability (Sins Invalid, 2016), historicity emerged as an essential element of boundary work. In addressing our individual historicity within the context of our work as DSE scholars and educators, we chose different entry points which gave rise to an intergenerational, intertemporal conversation. In a three-voice poem, which addressed our journey to and through the field of DSE, each participant began by engaging her historicity at a different moment in her career: undergraduate student, graduate student, and professional teacher. This drew the voices into a conversation as educators remembering together along a memory reel of professional convalescence typical for many in education, including the teacher candidates at the university.

> Many years ago, I was a teacher in a self-contained classroom that was actually a portable classroom attached to the back of the school building by a wooden ramp. My first students were labeled as "severe" and "multiple disabilities" and I loved that classroom, that job and those students.

> [B]y way of a small liberal arts college in rural MN (elementary education major, life science middle school concentration) that focused on critical pedagogy and student-centered learning, teaching without a curriculum, only one class on inclusive education though.

I knew I liked working with kids early on, and so did my father. Although he had attended private universities after attending community college, he told me to lower my aspirations. After all, teaching was not an intellectual or academic pursuit like engineering or science, so all I needed was a "teacher factory" if I was going to be a teacher (especially working with young children) ... his advice served as the only concrete guidance I was really offered during my transition.

I was excited to teach graduate students, envisioning all the theoretical and critical discussions we'd enjoy. In reality, the students were often beginning teachers taking numerous grad courses in the evenings to obtain their certification. I struggled to respect the context, adjust my expectations, and engage in meaningful ways.

Each author grappled with conflicting expectations (e.g., from educational systems, school districts, state standards) for students and teachers, including themselves, across their pre- and in-service experiences, as illustrated in the poem above. Then, these memories gave rise to an exchange which underscored the contentious relationships between the daily practice of teaching, larger institutional barriers, and justice-oriented praxis:

There was either a paraprofessional between me and my student and I relied on someone else to interpret what the students were experiencing, or I was in the gen ed class but focusing on "all students."

...but changing folks minds about disability as deficit takes time too ...

I chose a graduate program in special education because so many of my emergent bilingual students at my first teaching job had been dually identified with education labels of "English language learner" and "learning disabled" and I wanted to find out how to better support them—you see, under this fantasy of identification [Samuels, 2014], the best support for struggling students is more individualized, specially certified support.

When my teacher candidates now express a desire to work in a self-contained setting, I understand the impulse and as much as I teach inclusive practice, I know the feeling of autonomy, control, creativity, and love that I felt as a teacher of my own self-contained classroom ... Those feelings were rarely replicated in general education.

... we were *helpers* separate from those *to be helped* ...

I don't want to be self-critical for the sake of being self-critical.

[T]heory and critical frameworks of education freed my thinking from the traditional special education framework that had cultivated my professional learning and practice up to that point.

In a tense moment between the first and third voices, mediated by the second voice, we explore how even (a) well-intentioned "helping" praxis and (b) educators' yearning for professional agency within the activity system can cultivate harm and reinforce special education labels and spaces. However, the authors' voices are freed from special education frameworks when boundaries are crossed and critical theories (e.g., DSE) are introduced and embraced.

Consilience through Pedagogy and Praxis

One way in which the authors tended to the boundary of special education and DSE while cultivating consilience was through their teaching practices. Oftentimes, their pedagogical decisions were in reaction to teacher candidates' responses to the content.

I share a family member's treatment in general education and the damage done by teachers who didn't universally design or differentiate and who saw the signs of struggle as a "behavior" to eliminate through punishment.

At week 6 of the semester, disability was illegible to them as a social identity beyond a superficial level of cultural knowledge.

He said "segregation" was a harsh term right before he asked/alluded to segregation being necessary.

I slowly introduce
the idea that special
education can be hurt-
ful because I've seen
how dismissing their
"helper" legacy too
quickly just makes
them more determined.

So, what do I do? I change
it. I make sure that it's
grounded in the child's
strengths and likes. That
behavior is communica-
tion. That the assignment
is cloaked in a humanizing
approach and draped in bet-
tering each students' quality of life by changing the
way the adults around them
think and act.

I adjusted the sequence of
instruction I had mapped out
for the semester to hold space
for a class session focused on
exploring different disability-
related media and how their
elements contributed to different disability narratives. I
included media produced by
nondisabled folks (e.g., eve-
ning news segments, advertise-
ments) and disabled folks (e.g.,
Sami Kadah, Stella Young).

Someone said restorative
justice made the school feel
"crazy."

I remember telling him
that there was no need, it
is everywhere, that self-
contained hasn't been
shown to produce better
outcomes, it is simply
the default—we have
to defend why we don't
want it but never have to
explain why we do.

Grappling with the Tensions 247

The language teacher candidates used to describe their thoughts, experiences, and aspirations also impacted the authors' pedagogical decisions. That said, when teacher candidates needed more time or another angle or viewpoint, the authors provided it. Moreover, when discussions or activities went awry, needed clarification, or were openings for deeper learning, then the authors adjusted accordingly and honored what was needed in the moment.

The authors also germinated consilience through their praxis. They connected theory to practice by critically reflecting on various systems and processes (e.g., institutional, university-school partnerships, their past and present actions) to inform future teaching that would result in transformative action (hooks, 1994). Moreover, they reflected (individually and collectively) on what they needed or wanted to work on and learn more about.

We adopt a rights-based framework for discussing this process because so many children do not end up receiving the educational benefits they are entitled to.

This doesn't mean I haven't changed anything in response to DSE. I have changed what we read, the examples I use, the way I shape advocacy and helping.

How do we hold space for both types of teacher candidates—change agents and status quo goers? I don't do that well. I don't hold much space for the status quo group. Notably, there is a group that doesn't fit either category. This reality is not binary.

I think one thing we must continue to do in our teaching of future inclusive educators is question the need for labels—not that diagnoses or disabilities can provide personally or culturally affirming experiences. Rather, we must question the need for labels within a "rights-based" framework.

We talk about tangible ways teacher candidates can be a part of the change when they focus on these constructs and practices.

Am I holding them to a higher standard than other people?

I think this is such nuanced work because it requires a critical understanding and literacy that we often get from DSE scholarship that many of our teacher candidates do not arrive on campus with.

Our findings revealed how consilience was occurring through praxis. Being reflective was a strength that allowed us to see where we could move and shift within the activity system (e.g., between subject and artifact, between artifact and object) as needed based on a host of contextual factors. Such contextual factors included representations of dominant, hegemonic ideologies and practices. Shifts included leadership of and learning from those most impacted (e.g., historically multiply marginalized youth and their families, especially girls, Black youth, Indigenous youth, and youth of color with and without disabilities, disabled activists of color; Berne et al., 2018), particularly for the predominately white teacher candidates within our courses.

Cultivating Joy

Joy was another important theme that emerged from the data. We found joy in teaching when pedagogy involved challenging power and when teacher candidates shared or embraced alternatives to deficit-laden narratives. We also uncovered joy when engaging in critical inquiry, grappling with tensions, and resisting hegemonic schooling practices. Notably, we continue to find joy within these processes.

Connecting with and inviting Black, Brown, and Indigenous families, who I have known for many years, to be guest speakers brought me joy. Not only did I get to reconnect with the families with the purpose of honoring their knowledge, expertise, and experiences, but this afforded a much more meaningful learning opportunity for the teacher candidates.

Teaching UDL as revolutionary, as the act of crafting a class where all students can be who they are and feel recognized. We need expanded ideas of who students might be as well as the desire to discover who they are in that particular moment. If teacher candidates are unfamiliar with the various manifestations of grief, anxiety, or love, how will we recognize them or even hold a space for their possible presence?

A teacher candidate sends me a short email to tell me her sorority is ditching "Light It Up Blue" and is instead handing out flyers about the harm of Autism $peaks which include alternative resources and organizations which people should access to donate and show support for autistic folks.

My colleagues, in ideas and theories, in remembering that social justice work takes time.

I wanted to provide an opportunity for you to hang out with me using Video Conferencing tomorrow during our regular class time. You do not have to join the video hangout session for the entire class time. Instead, you can just pop on whenever you'd like and ask me any question you might have—or you can just say, "Hi!" At least one of my dogs will probably make an appearance as well.

. . . the focus shifted to checking in on each other and listening more intently; the pace slowed. I had to change for myself and the teacher candidates because of, due to the context of the pandemic.

Sharing how we felt (emotionally, mentally, physically); helping one another find routines, solutions to meeting vital needs; affording space to commiserate about so many aspects that were hard. I could be the teacher they needed.

I'm currently assisting on a research project involving nursing and COVID-19. Not because I possess the content expertise, but the process of inquiry brings me joy—asking people invested in their work to tell me stories about it.

... because disabled girls of color are underrepresented in educational research and thus often unheard; because we have so much to learn from them; because their solutions are doable and would impact everyone, yet radical because their solutions are not happening in schools.

"I'm going to my brother's IEP meeting. I want to be there for him and my mom,"

"You are? Tell me more." I respond as my fingers close around the stack of PowerPoints shoved into the folds of a *Democracy Now!* bag. She divulges the details of the meeting and her family's past experiences with the inflexible culture of the IEP and inflexible teachers. I can't help but recall the first week of class when the same young woman challenged the tenets of cultural reciprocity. I smile as she shares a place in our textbook she's bookmarked for inspiration in preparation for the meeting.

I do not use the language of my state's special education regulations, I refuse to acknowledge the system of numbering children into caseloads as objects. Also "potential"—as in we want to help students reach their "highest

	potential." I've always been astounded at the arrogance of assuming we could possibly identify someone else's "potential."
I really enjoy being in schools but not being confined by the rigid activity systems of schools; the rules of state standards and bell schedules, curriculums as artifacts, and the inevitable inequitable power dynamics in the division of labor.	

This poem reflects how joy was a response we shared not only as we felt the impact of our pedagogy on students and colleagues but as our roles transformed outside the activity system. Joy is found in critical inquiry and advocacy (Piepzna-Samarasinha, 2018), which in turn, influenced and enriched our use of tools (e.g., classroom discussions, culturally responsive pedagogy, UDL). Poetry can convey overwhelming awe and gratitude for the world as it is while also "remaining skeptical and critical of society . . ." (Suskin, 2020, p. 3). Such tension was present in our analysis and was the impetus to move our collaborative autoethnography from story to poem. The boundary between special education and DSE, while historically a site of struggle, also became a site of joy when creativity and resistance were enacted. This is important to note because affects and emotions can influence agency (McManus, 2011) in ways that are nonlinear and messy.

Despite our personal commitments to critical pedagogy and human rights approaches to inclusive education, our findings revealed our vigilance contrasted with our complicity. The desire to respect the teacher candidates' historicities and aspirations was delicate, as was the uncomfortable awareness that current general education environments are often problematic. Our situatedness within these systems added nuance to our exploration of maintaining critical, provocative, and loving responses while remaining grounded in our justice orientations. Moreover, the principles of disability justice (Sins Invalid, 2016) allowed us to discover the unique manifestations of one another's small acts of resistance in capitalistic structures that support ableism and reify the binary of disabled and nondisabled.

Notably, even though we occupied different, hierarchical positions within the same institution, we found that we all struggled with the layered tensions presented here. Rather than being oppositional as they are often presented, DSE and special education are intertwined, and the relationships are complex. These complexities impact our work daily and our persistent questions. We also know special education systems and processes are not going away. Moreover, because inclusive education is an ongoing action (Baglieri & Shapiro, 2017; Timberlake, 2017) and a process (Danforth & Naraian, 2015), we know we are not there, and boundary work continues.

DISCUSSION

This collaborative autoethnography revealed some of the tensions we experienced between special education and more critical, justice-oriented approaches to teacher development at the university. While only three teacher educators participated in this project, the implications for pedagogy and research are applicable to teacher preparation broadly.

Our findings showed how historicity was a critical element to our boundary work. The exclusionary mechanisms (e.g., deficit-laden ideologies, segregation) we encountered as pre- and in-service teachers within various activity systems did not push us away from education. Rather, these mechanisms fueled a deeper commitment to expansive learning (Engeström & Sannino, 2010) that carried us into our separate pursuits, eventually to teacher education. Moreover, our historicity was dialectical—we were informed by our historicity while simultaneously informing it (Glass, 2001). Constructing a poem to express our historicities was a creative act that resisted the boundaries of linear narrative—our words unconstrained by paragraphs and margins. We urge our readers to center their historicities and reflect and question with colleagues and co-conspirators to generate theoretical and praxical knowledge productions with specific action steps. We encourage myriad questions, mindful that praxis does not stop at reflection but must continue with action (Cologon et al., 2019). Some questions include: What are the valleys and peaks in my journey here? Where are the shifts and turns? Who are my (implicit and explicit) biases impacting? When am I complicit? How do I resist? What sustains me in my commitments to myself and others?

Framed by CHAT (Cole & Engeström, 1993) and critical pedagogy (Freire, 1993; hooks, 1994), we explored both pushing against and gently circumventing the deficit-based narratives and segregated practices of special education in teacher development, while doing so in harmony with a supportive community. Moreover, the microinteractional processes (e.g., teacher-student interactions, colleague-colleague collaboration) we uncovered through our blended framework were often energized, rather than burdened, by the tensions and challenges of enacting DSE within the rigidity of special education systems and processes. Extant research has shown that CHAT is a generative framework when examining praxis (Gutiérrez & Vossoughi, 2010; Hancock & Miller, 2017), boundary work (Beauchamp & Thomas, 2011; Tsui & Law, 2007), and professional inquiry (Waitoller et al., 2016). As Waitoller and Kozleski (2013) explained, CHAT "helps participants understand the current structure of interaction and activity as well as understand the gaps between what currently exists and what might be imagined outcomes" (p. 39). In this study, CHAT paired with critical theory provided a supportive framework for uncovering consilience within teacher development. Yet, more research grounded in CHAT and critical theories is needed to examine how teacher educators navigate boundary crossing (Kozleski, 2011) with a particular focus on DSE (Smagorinsky et al., 2016) and special education for true equity and justice in education.

This collaborative autoethnography reflected our struggle to enact our philosophical promises to DSE and the principles of disability justice (Berne et al., 2018) within a rigid structure designed to lead teacher candidates down a prescribed path to a certificate of "expertise" in special education. Contrasting with our self and structural criticality, we continue to find joy in crafting transformative pedagogy and scholarship. In other words, our commitments (e.g., to interdependence, education as liberation, humanizing approaches to teaching, holistic accessibility) provided us with, and continue to, inspiration and energy within and across our individual journeys toward this deeply contextualized moment in teacher preparation. That said, we look forward to learning from future research that examines how justice-oriented teacher educators and scholars maintain energy for this work through joy and love (Darder, 2002), especially in times of persistent neoliberal violence on historically multiply marginalized youth, families, and communities and girls, Black youth, Indigenous youth, and youth of color with and without disabilities.

CONCLUSION

This collaborative autoethnography drew on CHAT and critical pedagogy to explore the tensions between the medical model alive within special education and more critical, humanizing, and justice-oriented approaches to teacher development grounded in DSE. Situated in a small Northeastern state university and focused on three fluid activity systems, our findings are explicitly contextual. We prepare teacher candidates within a systemic paradox, often teaching in conflict with dominant narratives and ideologies, something others may be experiencing as well. Ultimately, we hope this study reveals some of the subtleties, tensions, and possibilities of consilience within and across the boundaries of DSE and special education.

NOTE

1. We use the term "labeled with disability" alongside "disabled" to reflect the political and social nature of disability identification and disabled identity. While "disabled" is used to denote a social identity and is empowering to many individuals and social groups, the term "labeled as disabled" emphasizes the social and structural power dynamics involved in the disability identification process in schools (Cioè-Peña, 2018).

REFERENCES

Akkerman, S. F., & Bakker, A. (2011a). Boundary crossing and boundary objects. *Review of Educational Research, 81*(2), 132–169.
Akkerman, S. F., & Bakker, A. (2011b). Learning at the boundary: An introduction. *International Journal of Educational Research, 50*(1), 1–5.
Annamma, S. A., Boelé, A. L., Moore, B. A., & Klingner, J. (2013). Challenging the ideology of normal in schools. *International Journal of Inclusive Education, 17*(12), 1278–1294.
Annamma, S. A., Anyon, Y., Joseph, N. M., Farrar, J., Greer, E., Downing, B., & Simmons, J. (2016). Black girls and school discipline: The complexities of being overrepresented and understudied. *Urban Education, 51*(2), 1–32.
Ashby, C. (2012). Disability studies and inclusive teacher preparation: A socially just path for teacher education. *Research and Practice for Persons with Severe Disabilities, 37*(2), 89–99.
Baglieri, S., & Lalvani, P. (2019). *Undoing ableism: Teaching about disability in K-12 classrooms*. Routledge.
Baglieri, S., & Shapiro, A. (2012). *Disability studies and the inclusive classroom: Critical practices for creating least restrictive attitudes*. Routledge.
Beauchamp, C., & Thomas, L. (2011). New teachers' identity shifts at the boundary of teacher education and initial practice. *International Journal of Educational Research, 50*(1), 6–13.
Belkhir, M., Brouard, M., Brunk, K. H., Dalmoro, M., Ferreira, M. C., Figueiredo, B., Huff, A. D., Scaraboto Daiane, Sibai, O., & Smith, A. N. (2019). Isolation in globalizing academic fields: A collaborative autoethnography of early career researchers. *Academy of Management Learning & Education, 18*(2), 261–285.
Bell, C. (2006). Introducing white disability studies: A modest proposal. In L. J. Davis (Ed.), *The disability studies reader* (pp. 275–282): Routledge.
Berne, P., Morales, A. L., Langstaff, D., & Sins Invalid. (2018). Ten principles of disability justice. *WSQ: Women's Studies Quarterly, 46*(1), 227–230.
Bhattacharya, K. (2017). *Fundamentals of qualitative research*. Routledge.
Blanchett, W. J., Klingner, J. K., & Harry, B. (2009). The intersection of race, culture, language, and disability: Implications for urban education. *Urban Education, 44*(4), 389–409.
Brantlinger, E. (1997). Using ideologies: Cases of non-recognition of the politics of research and practice in special education. *Review of Educational Research, 67*(4), 425–459.

Brantlinger, E. A. (Ed.). (2006). *Who benefits from special education?: Remediating (fixing) other people's children*. Routledge.
Buffington-Adams, J., & Vaughan, K. P. (2019). The curriculum of disability studies: Multiple perspectives on Dis/Ability introduction: An invitation to complicated conversations. *Journal of Curriculum Theorizing, 34*(1), 1–9.
Chang, H., Ngunjiri, F., & Hernandez, K. A. C. (2012). *Collaborative autoethnography*. Routledge.
Cioè-Peña, M. (2017). Who is excluded from inclusion? Points of union and division in bilingual and special education. *Theory, research, and action in Urban Education*. https://blmtraue.commons.gc.cuny.edu/2017/02/24/who-is-excluded-from-inclusion-points-of-union-and-division-in-bilingual-and-special-education/
Cioè-Peña, M. (2018). Gifted, talented & neurodiverse: Emergent bilinguals labeled as dis/abled. *Integration*, 7–11. https://www.researchgate.net/profile/Maria-Cioe-Pena/publication/333644060_Gifted_Talented_Neurodiverse_Emergent_Bilinguals_Labeled_as_Disabled/links/5cf9132892851c4dd02c72f9/Gifted-Talented-Neurodiverse-Emergent-Bilinguals-Labeled-As-Disabled.pdf
Clift, R. T., & Liaupsin, C. (2019). Affecting education policy through border crossing between special education and general education. *Studying Teacher Education, 15*(1), 56–66.
Cole, M. (1998). Can cultural psychology help us think about diversity? *Mind, Culture, and Activity, 5*(4), 291–304.
Cole, M., & Engeström, Y. (1993). A cultural-historical approach to distributed cognition. In G. Salomon (Ed.), *Distributed cognitions: Psychological and educational considerations* (pp. 1–46). Cambridge University Press.
Cologon, K., Cologon, T., Mevawalla, Z., & Niland, A. (2019). Generative listening: Using arts-based inquiry to investigate young children's perspectives of inclusion, exclusion and disability. *Journal of Early Childhood Research, 17*(1), 54–69.
Connor, D. J. (2019). Why is special education so afraid of disability studies? Analyzing attacks of distain and distortion from leaders in the field. *Journal of Curriculum Theorizing, 34*(1), 10–23.
Connor, D. J., Gabel, S. L., Gallagher, D. J., & Morton, M. (2008). Disability studies and inclusive education: Implications for theory, research, and practice. *International Journal of Inclusive Education, 12*(5–6), 441–457.
Coomer, M. N. (2019). Deconstructing difference and inclusion in educational research: reflections on the international journal of qualitative studies in education special edition on difference. *International Journal of Qualitative Studies in Education, 32*(3), 341–345.
Danforth, S. (Ed.) (2017). *Becoming a great inclusive educator* (2nd ed.). Peter Lang.
Danforth, S., & Naraian, S. (2015). This new field of inclusive education: Beginning a dialogue on conceptual foundations. *Intellectual and Developmental Disabilities, 53*(1), 70–85.
Darder, A. (2002). *Reinventing Paulo Freire: A pedagogy of love*. Westview Press.
Darder, A. (2011). Teaching as an act of love: Reflections on Paulo Freire and his contributions to our lives and our work. *Counterpoints, 418*, 179–194.
Deckman, S. L., & Ohito, E. O. (2019). Stirring vulnerability, (un)certainty, and (Dis)trust in humanizing research: Duoethnographically re-membering unsettling

racialized encounters in social justice teacher education. *International Journal of Qualitative Studies in Education*, Advance online publication.
Disability Studies in Education Special Interest Group 143 [DSESIG]. (2019). *SIG purpose*. http://www.aera.net/SIG143/Disability-Studies-in-Education-SIG-143
Ellis, C., Adams, T. E., & Bochner, A. P. (2011). Autoethnography: An overview. *Forum: Qualitative Social Research, 12*(1), Article 10. http://nbn-resolving.de/urn:nbn:de:0114-fqs1101108
Engeström, Y. (1987). *Learning by expanding: An activity-theoretical approach to developmental research*. Orienta-Konsultit Oy.
Engeström, Y. (2001). Expansive learning at work: Toward an activity theoretical reconceptualization. *Journal of Education and Work, 14*(1), 133–156.
Engeström, Y., & Sannino, A. (2010). Studies of expansive learning: Foundations, findings and future challenges. *Educational Research Review, 5*(1), 1–24.
Esmonde, I., & Booker, A. N. (2016). Toward critical sociocultural theories of learning. In I. Esmonde & A. N. Booker (Eds.), *Power and privilege in the learning sciences* (pp. 180–192). Routledge.
Freire, P. (1993). *Pedagogy of the oppressed*. Continuum.
Giroux, H. A. (1992). *Border crossings: Cultural workers and the politics of education*. Routledge.
Glass, R. D. (2001). On Paulo Freire's philosophy of praxis and the foundations of liberation education. *Educational Researcher, 30*(2), 15–25.
Gutiérrez, K. D., & Vossoughi, S. (2010). Lifting off the ground to return anew: Mediated praxis, transformative learning, and social design experiments. *Journal of Teacher Education, 61*(1–2), 100–117.
Hancock, C. L., & Miller, A. L. (2017). Using cultural historical activity theory to uncover praxis for inclusive education. *International Journal of Inclusive Education, 22*(9), 937–953.
hooks, b. (1994). *Teaching to transgress: Education as the practice of freedom*. Routledge.
Kauffman, J. M., & Sasso, G. M. (2006). Toward ending cultural and cognitive relativism in special education. *Exceptionality, 14*(2), 65–90.
Kozleski, E. B. (2011). Dialectical practices in education: Creating third spaces in the education of teachers. *Teacher Education and Special Education, 34*(3), 250–259.
Lapadat, J. C. (2017). Ethics in autoethnography and collaborative autoethnography. *Qualitative Inquiry, 23*(8), 589–603.
Lincoln, Y. S., & Guba, E. G. (1985). *Naturalistic inquiry*. Sage.
McManus, S. (2011). Hope, fear, and the politics of affective agency. *Theory & Event, 14*(4). https://muse.jhu.edu/article/459120
Merriam, S. B., & Tisdell, E. J. (2015). *Qualitative research: A guide to design and implementation* (4th ed.). Jossey-Bass.
Naraian, S. (2016). Spatializing student learning to reimagine the 'place' of inclusion. *Teachers College Record, 118*(12), 1–46.
Ngunjiri, F. W., Hernandez, K.-A. C., & Chang, H. (2010). Living autoethnography: Connecting life and research. *Journal of Research Practice, 6*(1), 1–7.
Nusbaum, E. A., & Steinborn, M. L. (2019). A "visibilizing" project: "Seeing" the ontological erasure of disability in teacher education and social studies curricula. *Journal of Curriculum Theorizing, 34*(1), 24–35.

Odom, S. L., Hall, L. J., & Steinbrenner, J. R. (2020). Implementation science research and special education. *Exceptional Children, 86*(2), 117–119.

Ohito, E. O., & Nyachae, T. M. (2019). Poetically poking at language and power: Using Black feminist poetry to conduct rigorous feminist critical discourse analysis. *Qualitative Inquiry, 25*(9–10), 839–850.

Orsati, F. T., & Causton-Theoharis, J. (2013). Challenging control: Inclusive teachers' and teaching assistants' discourse on students with challenging behaviour. *International Journal of Inclusive Education, 17*(5), 507–525.

Pearson, H., Cosier, M., Kim, J. J., Gomez, A. M., Hines, C., McKee, A. A., & Ruiz, L. Z. (2016). The impact of Disability Studies curriculum on education professionals' perspectives and practice: Implications for education, social justice, and social change. *Disability Studies Quarterly, 36*(2). 1–7

Petersen, A. J., Gallagher, D. J., Cowley, D. M., & Iqtadar, S. (2018, April 13). Teaching in the in-between: Opportunities for and resistance to inclusive change in boundary work. Paper presented at the [2018] annual meeting of the American Educational Research Association. https://www.aera.net/Publications/Online-Paper-Repository/AERA-Online-Paper-Repository

Piepzna-Samarasinha, L. L. (2018). *Care work: Dreaming disability justice*. Arsenal Pulp Press.

Rogoff, B. (2003). *The cultural nature of human development*. Oxford University Press.

Roth, W. M. (2007). Emotion at work: A contribution to third-generation cultural-historical activity theory. *Mind, culture, and activity, 14*(1–2), 40–63.

Saldaña, J. (2013). *The coding manual for qualitative researchers*. Sage.

Samaras, A. P., Hicks, M. A., & Berger, J. G. (2004). Self-study through personal history. In J J. Loughran, M. L. Hamilton, V. K. LaBoskey, & T. L. Russell (Eds.), *International handbook of self-study of teaching and teacher education practices* (pp. 905–942). Springer.

Samuels, E. J. (2014). *Fantasies of identification: Disability, gender, race*. New York University Press.

Schles, R. A., & Robertson, R. E. (2019). The role of performance feedback and implementation of evidence-based practices for preservice special education teachers and student outcomes: A review of the literature. *Teacher Education and Special Education, 42*(1), 36–48.

Shor, I., & Freire, P. (1987). *A pedagogy for liberation: Dialogues on transforming education*. Greenwood Publishing Group.

Sins Invalid. (2016). *Skin, tooth, and bone: The basis of movement is our people: A disability justice primer*. Sins Invalid.

Skrtic, T. M. (1991). *Behind special education: A critical analysis of professional culture and school organization*. Love Publishing.

Skrtic, T. M. (Ed.) (1995). *Disability and democracy: Reconstructing (special) education for postmodernity*. Love Publishing.

Slee, R. (2013). Meeting some challenges of inclusive education in an age of exclusion. *Asian Journal of Inclusive Education, 1*(2), 3–17.

Smagorinsky, P., Cole, M., & Willadino Braga, L. (2016). On the complementarity of cultural historical psychology and contemporary disability studies. In I. Esmonde & A. N. Booker (Eds.), *Power and privilege in the learning sciences* (pp. 88–110). Routledge.

Society for Disability Studies. (2016). *What is disability studies?* [Organizational Statement]. http://disstudies.org/index.php/about-sds/what-is-disability-studies/

Suskin, J. (2020). *Every day is a poem: Feel relief and see beauty in every moment.* Sounds True Publishing.

Sweigart, C. A., Collins, L. W., Evanovich, L. L., & Cook, S. C. (2016). An evaluation of the evidence base for performance feedback to improve teacher praise using CEC's quality indicators. *Education and Treatment of Children, 39*(4), 419–444.

Timberlake, M. T. (2017). Nice, but we can't afford it: Challenging austerity and finding abundance in inclusive education, *International Journal of Inclusive Education, 22*(9), 954–968.

Timberlake, M. T. (2019). "PAAP Season": A new rationale for segregating students with significant cognitive disabilities. In G. Q. Conchas, B. M. Hinga, M. N. Abad, & K. D. Gutierrez (Eds.), *The Complex web of inequality in North American schools: Investigating educational policies for social justice* (pp. 202–216). Routledge.

Tsui, A. B. M., & Law, D. Y. K. (2007). Learning as boundary-crossing in school–university partnership. *Teaching and Teacher Education, 23*(8), 1289–1301.

Waitoller, F. R., & Kozleski, E. B. (2013). Working in boundary practices: Identity development and learning in partnerships for inclusive education. *Teaching and Teacher Education, 31*(2013), 35–45.

Waitoller, F. R., Kozleski, E. B., & Gonzalez, T. (2016). Professional inquiry for inclusive education: Learning amidst institutional and professional boundaries. *School Effectiveness and School Improvement, 27*(1), 62–79.

Wilson, E. O. (1999). *Consilience: The unity of knowledge* (Vol. 31). Vintage.

Chapter 12

Checklists and Merit Badges

On Whiteness, Ability, and the Boundary between Special Education and Radical Love

JPB Gerald

Every time I attend an education conference, the most-popular sessions are the ones with a product to sell that purports to solve several problems at once, or a technique that attendees can easily plug into their lesson plans. A conference in which I am involved was recently planning to move away from conceptual or theoretical talks in favor of shorter, bite-size presentations and "teaching tips." It is an understandable urge, the search for the silver bullet that will fix everything, a way for educators to *satisfice* (March & Simon, 1958; Voulgarides, 2018), to do just as much as needed to be left alone, to "maximize the rewards and minimize the costs of their work" (p. 16). This phenomenon is not unique to education, but it means that teachers, even those who are supposedly well-intentioned, reach for easy solutions, those that are comfortable and without risk. Too many rush to tick off educational *checklists*, compartmentalizing and externalizing the internal work necessary for growth, and they quickly declare their task finished and apply labels to themselves, seeking public approval the way a Boy Scout might display a uniform full of *merit badges*. Let me explain what I mean.

In the past few years, and increasingly so when I began to write this in late 2020, there are a few relatively new merit badges for white teachers. Many are quick to anoint themselves *anti-racist*. Indeed, I cannot count how many teachers I have encountered whose social media profiles include the phrase "anti-racist teacher." At one point in early June of 2020, almost all of the most-popular books on Amazon centered on race, racism, and anti-racism (Andrew, 2020). People—and, to be clear, primarily white people—finally started taking an interest in racial literature, particularly Kendi's *How to Be an Antiracist* (2019). However, for a white educator to have decided that their journey has proceeded far enough to publicly apply the label to themselves after a brief period of study is to have essentially missed the point, and it is this sort of behavior, this rush toward public approval, that I am describing when I speak of the search for *merit badges*. To be clear, these are wonderful first steps and should be encouraged rather than shamed, but the reality is much more complex than can be condensed into a few bullet points. We cannot apply these labels to ourselves before the work is complete.

I suspect, if you asked many of the self-described anti-racist or decolonizing teachers whether or not they practiced *radical love* (e.g., Freire, 1970; Dotson, 2013; Douglas & Nganga, 2015), they would say that they did, or that they would be able to after completing a few items on their *checklists*, trendy concepts like *grit* (e.g., Duckworth, 2016; Duckworth et al., 2007), *resilience* (e.g., Fleming & Ledogar, 2008), or *growth mindset* (e.g., Claro et al., 2016). But radical love cannot be checked off a list or sewn onto the front of a proverbial sash. Marginalized students, particularly racialized and dis/abled[1] learners, need radical love, a love that requires risk and an authenticity that eludes far too many white teachers (and some teachers of other backgrounds as well). As Dotson (2013) explains, love becomes radical "because it results in a steadfast commitment, unwavering trust, and, in some contexts, a daring that defies current dominant reason" (p. 38), and this "current dominant reason" is the interlocking set of hierarchies that combine to oppress these racialized and dis/abled learners. This tendency toward checklists and merit badges inhibits the possibility for the cultivation of radical love and prevents students from receiving the care they deserve, and an investment in whiteness and ability supremacy ensures that these qualities will never develop authentically. The twin supremacies of whiteness and ability are inextricably linked and serve as reinforcements for one another, and there are no shortcuts to the radical love that can combat their power. In this chapter, I will share my conceptualization of radical love and how whiteness and ability supremacy preclude its emergence, how teachers have sought quick checklist solutions and self-applied merit badge labels of progress instead of engaging with difficult issues and ongoing critical conversations, and reasons why Special Education itself may be the greatest obstacle to radical love. I will conclude with an argument for how wary teachers can more effectively engage in radical love without the expectation of public recognition, and, in the process, divest from whiteness and ability supremacy entirely.

APPROACHES AND TERMINOLOGY

This chapter represents a conceptual argument aimed at uniting ideas that may otherwise seem disparate. I seek to grab hold of the common narratives about who is included within whiteness and ability and tie this directly to the type of love that many students are denied. The way I hope to achieve this is through an attempt at *consilience* (Wilson, 1999), drawing upon literature from several different disciplines—for example, Disability Studies, Education, Critical Race Theory, Critical Whiteness Studies—to generate a novel line of reasoning and a fresh set of criticism for popular education books and buzzwords as well as common trends among white educators. In a way, one could see this chapter as an example of (pop)cultural criticism intertwined with autoethnographic narrative, a methodology that can be particularly powerful for racialized scholars seeking to reclaim power and heal (Hernández-Saca & Cannon, 2019). I also expect that this approach might be valuable for any scholar who has had their story mis-told by a society divested from loving them, be they racialized, dis/abled, or harmed along any axis of power.

Speaking of power, I include a slash when I write the word "dis/ability" (aside from titles where it is spelled differently) to denote that the category is created not by mere biological happenstance but by the same cultural and political forces I plan to decry in this piece, that it is not a personal attribute but the result of a series of oppressive choices made by those in power (Davis, 1995; Goodley, 2014). In other words, I would say that the slash represents a direct acknowledgment of the harm wrought by both whiteness and ability supremacy, but, like Blackness, it is a vibrant identity around which solidarity can be built.

Additionally, throughout this chapter I refer to my own *neurodivergence* as a lens through which I have come to view these topics. Coming to terms with how not just whiteness but also the standardized conceptualization of ability affected me as a child has been a fairly recent development in my life. For now, though, I will note that I have a manner of processing stimuli and paying attention that would be classified as "disordered," which some would similarly refer to as "neuroatypical," both of which I do not accept as labels because they presume there is not only an idealized order (or typicality) but that the way I (and many others) function is "wrong." Indeed, feeling as though I was deeply flawed led to other "disorders" (mood disorders, in this case) at various times in my life, and much of my writing serves as a means through which I seek to dig myself out of the decades-old belief that I was fundamentally "dysfunctional." Accordingly, I believe that *neurodivergent* acknowledges that the way my brain works is somewhat unique, but provides a measure of agency that other terminology lacks, and, at least for now, I use this term to describe myself and the people who move through the world the way that I do. I define agency, simply yet importantly, as a feeling of power and control over oneself (Moore, 2016), and, in this case, over one's own story and identity. This does not mean, by choosing this phrasing, that I will be able to avoid the potential harm involved in the way dis/ability is defined, but that, at the least, my story will be determined by my own sense of self.

AUTHOR POSITIONALITY

I was raised Black but indoctrinated into whiteness and, by extension, anti-Blackness, by the white spaces that my family's upper-middle-class status allowed me to enter but which never fully embraced me. As a Black student with the aforementioned neurodivergence, I had trouble fitting my school's and my teachers' limited conceptualizations of Blackness, as I was not an impoverished virtuoso on a lottery ticket, an athlete or artist, or a sycophant to whiteness in the Ben Carson[2] mold, although I had my shameful moments where I sought the approval of the powerful. I went to exclusive and predominantly white institutions for most of my life, starting with an expensive private school from pre-K to 12th grade, which was both deeply invested in *color-evasiveness* (Annamma et al., 2016), and suffused with and unaware of its *liberal racism* (Zamudio & Rios, 2006), a disingenuous sort of environment where "whites continue to benefit from their unearned racial privilege while simultaneously embracing the value of equality and merit" (p. 500). I then went to an Ivy League university for my undergraduate studies that alternated between hostility and paternalism toward its racialized students, and then, after a few years working, got a Master's at an institution somewhat similar to my adolescent experience, though as an adult I was less impacted by these forces.

That degree was in Teaching English as a Second or Foreign Language (TESOL), or English Language Teaching (ELT), and I spent the first decade of my career, both in South Korea and New York, bouncing from one somewhat precarious position to another. What was far more damaging than the salary, though, was the burgeoning realization that the field was actively perpetuating white supremacy and anti-Blackness, descending as it does from colonialist violence and oppression, and that it reifies what Canagarajah (1999) calls *linguistic imperialism* in several ways, from its recruitment techniques (Ruecker & Ives, 2015), to its treatment and valuing of teachers (Ramjattan, 2019), all the way down to its instructional practices. Flores and Rosa (2015) have theorized that any racialized language user will necessarily be seen as deficient to the unseen *white listener*, and by extension, racialized teachers are, both in theory and in practice, seen as "less skilled" than white teachers, regardless of their actual skill level (Faez, 2012; Sung, 2011). I mention all of this to explain that I had gone from a series of educational institutions that isolated and devalued me when they were not showing me off as a bauble, to an entire field that managed to do the same.

For too long I assumed the problem was me and my neurodivergence, but in my doctoral studies—at a public institution that is *not* predominantly white, although the faculty and administration certainly are—I came to fully understand that the thread connecting my childhood and young adult education with the field of language teaching is that both have yet to reject the trappings of whiteness, no matter how much all would claim to prioritize "diversity," "equity," and "inclusion." Additionally, within language teaching, so much of the focus remains on numerical assessment as proof of ability; that is, ability supremacy is as rampant in ELT as in the rest of education.

I have argued elsewhere (Gerald, 2020a) that the ELT field has a moral imperative to decenter whiteness, and I write today to extend this argument to education in general, and Special Education in particular, which will remain unable to practice radical love so long as it values whiteness and a narrow conceptualization of ability more than the students it continues to marginalize and harm. My experiences and my research have fused to provide me with a specific lens through which I am able to see and feel through the inauthenticity of the checklists and merit badges many white teachers would prefer to the genuine, and legitimately difficult, work of dismantling whiteness and ability supremacy in themselves, in their institutions, and in the world around them.

RADICAL LOVE, WHITENESS, AND ABILITY SUPREMACY

As Douglas and Nganga (2015) write, "trying to establish a unified and universally accepted definition of love is an exercise in futility" (p. 63). So perhaps it would be more fruitful to establish what love is not, and particularly so in the case of radical love. Freire (1970) would tell us that the banking system of education, wherein the teacher acts as sage filling vacuous students with accumulating wisdom, cannot represent love, as it places a much higher value on the educators than on their students. Most classrooms remain structured in this way, and even the teachers who have made the supposedly bold choice to rearrange their desks still treat themselves as the primary source of knowledge. Education systems silently reify these practices and loudly protect them by codifying resistance to teacher's choices as "maladaptive behavior" (Shalaby, 2017), discarding the possibility of love for their racialized and dis/abled students in exchange for pathologization and the perpetuation of the *school-prison nexus* (Annamma, 2018). Douglas and Nganga (2015) continue, "radical love requires a commitment to dialogue and the capacity to take risks for the benefit of those we teach and ourselves. One of the risks we must take as pedagogues is to relinquish oppressive practices in the classroom" (p. 64). It is inimical to whiteness to take risks that threaten its dominance, and that includes any sort of love for students that recognizes racialized and dis/abled students as *equal* to their white (and non-dis/abled) counterparts.

It is much easier for a white teacher to color inside the lines and not challenge the practices of oppression in which they participate, a phenomenon common to those with a *white savior* ideology (Straubaar, 2015). Raised on the public pedagogy of popular culture that features white teachers saving their broken and deprived students (e.g., mainstream movies such as *Freedom Writers (2007)* and *Dangerous Minds (1995)*), and often recruited by organizations promoting the same ideals (Cann, 2015), few such teachers would agree that their patronizing behavior does not represent love. I suppose, the way an owner might think of a loyal pet, there is a form of affection in these relationships, but one that is both unequal and conditional. Because of the power differential created by these schools, fully embraced by the educators who lead and populate them, this "love," if it can be called that, is tainted and weak, and does not support the students they claim to cherish. It might also be worth noting that both of the movies used as examples in the above Cann article feature white *female* teachers (who are also cisgender, middle-class, heterosexual, and nondisabled), which is certainly representative of the majority of American educators (NCES, 2021). This does not mean that the minority of male teachers are not susceptible to white savior ideologies, but that the public pedagogy from which we all learn deliberately centers a particular gender expression as well as the assumptions associated with their identities. This is a long way of saying that it is no coincidence that these are the narratives that are promoted, that their white savior version of love is what is popularized and influential.[3]

As Gomez and Jimenez (2018) write of Freire, "he connected the notion of love, when you are giving all your love to another person without expecting anything in return, with the notion of education understood in the same way" (p. 6). To give of yourself without expectation is legitimately risky in the Western capitalistic system of domination and competition, and it is no wonder that radical love remains a rarity. In some ways, radical love should not even be necessary, or at the least should become normalized enough to no longer be a radical concept, yet it speaks volumes that in most educational systems, working against oppression is working outside of expected boundaries. Returning to Douglas and Nganga (2015) a final time, they write, "pre-service teachers and school leaders are given far too few opportunities to reflect on, inquire about, and interrogate who they are as human beings, developing pedagogues, and critical agents/facilitators of anti-oppressive 21st century classrooms and schools" (p. 61). This recalls the points made in the

Approaches and Terminology section, demonstrating the potential power for autoethnography for racialized scholars. Additionally, however, as Milner (2010) and Ragoonaden (2015) have noted, this type of deep reflection and self-study would be valuable for any teacher planning to enter the profession, and should be incorporated into any teacher education program seeking to challenge the structures that recur throughout this chapter. I argue that there is a very specific, and often unmentioned, ideology preventing the critical self-reflection necessary for the development of radical love, a system of thought and practices that envelops almost all of education and leaves its practitioners unable and unwilling to embody the support that the students need.

Whiteness is anathema to radical love. The selection of metaphors across the literature is endless (Leonardo, 2016), but whether whiteness is conceptualized as *property* (Harris, 1993), as something about which white teachers consistently demonstrate a lack of awareness (Picower, 2009), or as synonymous with "niceness" (Miller & Harris, 2018), it is clear that, as an ideology, whiteness stands in stark opposition to the values espoused by those who seek to enact radical love. Kendi (2017) takes pains to demonstrate how, from before the founding of this country, whiteness was constructed as a superior category to that of other races, and that the major debates have often been about how the inferior racialized (and dis/abled) (Artiles, 2011, 2019) groups should be "dealt with." Indeed, our modern conceptualization of races is inextricable from what we now know of as dis/ability, both of which are often positioned in opposition to that idealized whiteness (Nielsen, 2012).

Much of the power of whiteness comes from its ability to hide in plain sight. The United States espouses, for example, something as seemingly neutral as *meritocracy*, allowing us to ignore how few racialized people receive the same support as whites. In other words, if a few racialized people, the "good ones," make it through the maze, then the maze does not need to be razed. The ones who survive are proof that those who struggle are either lacking in ability, effort, or both, and deserve their lot in life. Only those with exceptional merit are to be rewarded with adequate support, encouragement, and love, and if those people happen to be white, it is a mere coincidence. Indeed, Mijs (2019) found that "long-term changes in inequality are accompanied by a stronger belief in meritocracy" (p. 2). In other words, meritocratic ideologies correlate strongly with ongoing societal inequity—including the twin supremacies of whiteness and ability—because the latter depends on the former, requiring citizens' aspirations for its subsistence. It is a circular logical argument fueled by an ideology necessary for the perpetuation of inequity based upon group membership that would rather pretend its social stratification is appropriate and just.

It is worth pointing out here that I come to these topics through the vantage point of Disability Studies in Education rather than Special Education, and you might notice that few of my citations come from the latter discipline. From what I have read in traditional Special Education research, there remains far too much emphasis on resolving the, as Collins et al. (2016) called them, *dangerous assumptions* placed upon the students in question, centering on the uncritical resolution of issues such as disproportionality rather than holistic support for students themselves (Artiles, 2019). Special Education, as historically and currently conceptualized, erects tight boundaries around the people it considers its property, and plays right into the hands of whiteness, ability supremacy, and meritocratic ideologies, thereby stigmatizing those classified as disordered, upon whose subjugation the subfield depends. In other words, I am not confident that radical love is possible within Special Education, because I suspect that Special Education, as a field, actually loves dis/abling people more than it loves those who have been dis/abled.

At its core, the ideology of meritocracy depends on the idea that some individuals are entitled to more than others, which mysteriously leaves certain groups with more power. One of the ways that whiteness has retained its dominant position in the societal hierarchy is by crafting an exclusive definition of ability and intelligence,[4] concepts defined in such a way that to exemplify them is to bring one closer to a white ideal. Within education, as Leonardo and Broderick (2011) argue, some students are classified as "smart" and some as less so, and this designation indexes who is and is entitled to more in the school systems and in society. As Leonardo and Broderick (2011) ask, "what is smartness in the absence of its stratifying privilege?" (p. 2216). The concept of smartness requires those who possess less of it, and, by extension, the concept of ability is itself dis/abling, and particularly so for the racialized.

I write this as a person who was allowed the entitlement of attending exclusive educational institutions because I was classified as "smart," but my status as both racialized and neurodivergent ensured that I was always at odds with my environs. My performance on certain types of assessment allowed me to ascend several rungs of their ladder, but the way I process information and stimuli, and my racialization, made certain I would never be allowed to the very top rung. Today, I reject the concept of the ladder altogether, and I wonder how I can protect my young son before they start calling him "smart," too. Indeed, to support the idea that some students are "smart" and some are not is a means of enforcing dis/abling hierarchies, and this perpetuates ability supremacy, meritocracy, and whiteness (e.g., Hatt, 2012).

Whiteness holds onto its power by hiding itself within our language. Consider the way even a positive term, like *students of color*, separates this group from an unmentioned norm. Consider the way that, even though white students and their parents retain most of the power in our educational systems, they are rarely named as such, and ability is chiefly mentioned in reference to those who are outside of its boundaries. Or consider the fact that white educators who challenge whiteness are accurately described as in possession of *transgressive white racial knowledge* (Crowley, 2016). I will also include here my own concept of the *altruistic shield* (Gerald, 2020b), wherein well-meaning white educators use the image of their prosocial professions as a preemptive defense against any honest critical engagement with whiteness and ability supremacy.

My article above cites DiAngelo's (2011) well-known concept of *white fragility* to help build its argument about preemptive shielding from critical engagement with racism, but in the time since I wrote that essay, I have come to understand that compartmentalizing whiteness and trying to, in a way, isolate the harmful parts is to move away from the direct issue at hand, which is that whiteness *itself* is the *problem*. Not white individuals,[5] and certainly not all individuals with light-colored skin. No, as a system, as an ideology, as an epistemology, the concept of whiteness itself is not functionally separable from white supremacy, and whiteness is a major factor obstructing the love that is needed for racialized and dis/abled students.

What many of the above descriptions of whiteness have in common is defensiveness, dishonesty, and distance from the lived experiences of their racialized students (Matias, 2016). When considering what Freire proposed as a better path forward for educators in conjunction with the examples above of the many ways in which whiteness and ability supremacy reify our hierarchical structure in education, then we can see that *radical love is both rare and necessary*. We can analyze our stratification through whichever lens with which we are most comfortable, but ultimately, to practice radical love requires deep, patient work and a rejection of the ladder we are told we ought to climb, and that we ought to help students climb as well. We cannot take a shortcut to the type of love that racialized and dis/abled students deserve, because the entire educational system has been constructed to inform them that they are not entitled to this support. Unfortunately, well-meaning though educators might be, many are swayed by the buzzwords and quick fixes that proliferate through the field, and instead of offering students radical love, we often skip the hard work and look for ways we can simply check items off a list. I do not necessarily blame people for falling into this trap—I once did myself—so I feel it is important to be clear about what precisely I mean when I refer to these sorts of checklists and the harm that they can cause.

CHECKLISTS

The current academic discourse around *grit* truly got underway after the article by Duckworth et al. (2007) in which they define the term, in both the text and the subtitle, as "perseverance and passion for long-term goals" (p. 1087). Grit, of course, is not a new term (see Ris, 2015, for a history), but its specific application to academic evaluation and assessment was seen as novel, and many educators found it compelling. The phenomenon grew into a popular TED talk and a book (Duckworth, 2016) on the same topic, and even people outside of education came to understand that grit was supposedly something to be both sought and improved upon. Like most such concepts, the original article is rather measured in tone.[6] In fact, the problem is not the idea of grit itself, nor do I mean that grit is somehow the most egregious of theorizations to come along and capture the zeitgeist, but that it is merely a prominent example of an endless string of quick fixes that well-meaning and predominantly white teachers rely on in an attempt to "help" students without recognizing the inherent deficit implied by these concepts, and the avoidance of the necessary analysis of all forms of oppression. Scholars including Bettina Love (2019) have pointed out that checklist items like grit serve only to other and blame racialized students. Simply put, grit sits comfortably inside of a perpetual discourse of checklists that are ultimately harmful to students who are already marginalized.

The keywords to the original grit article (Duckworth et al., 2007) are as follows: "achievement, success, personality, persistence, performance." Without knowing what argument the authors are advancing, one could ascertain without too much difficulty that various forms of standardized assessments will be used as "evidence," and tied, one way or another, to students' traits and effort, regardless of what terminology is used. In this way, these checklists are merely a white and ability mask for an adherence to the aforementioned ideals of meritocracy, as a student lacking "grit" can be dismissed for not having earned the care and support they will thus be denied. None of these allow for the risk and selflessness required for radical love, and they are all maintained by the centering of whiteness and ability supremacy in educational institutions and the society of the United States (e.g., Gallagher, 2010; Tefera et al., 2019).

If we focus on those keywords, then the terms used to unite them are less important. This trend is evidenced in several prominent books on education. In *How Children Succeed* (2012), Paul Tough searches for a solution to the age-old question of why some learners are "high achievers." He positions his work as a contrast to traditional espousals of test scores, but grounds his argument in the supposed ability to quantify "character." I am not here to pull apart his rhetoric so much as to point out that this is the same argument as one that relies on test scores and IQ[7]: that there is something in students that needs to be found and improved if they want the best results. Unsaid remains the implication that students whose character is flawed[8] are less likely to achieve, and, of course, he writes mostly about poor, racialized children. Everyone wants to fix the children they refuse to admit they are complicit in harming (Delpit, 1988), no matter what word they use to solve the problem that they themselves do not seem to realize they represent.

In *The Smartest Kids in the World* (2013), Amanda Ripley follows three students as they find ways to succeed academically where other students have failed, drawing heavily upon national trends and practices. She does not focus on grit per se, but the narrative does promote the idea that these students—and others similar to them—possess something special, unlike others who are unable to rise above their circumstances. It does, at least, acknowledge that external forces can hamper students' progress, but ascribes their uniqueness to another ethereal checklist concept, in this case *resilience*.

Even the ancient and celebrated "marshmallow test" centers on the idea that self-control leads to success. The recent book-length version of the experiment reportage (Mischel, 2014) explores why this is, but, like every item in this list, the idea leaves out the impact of oppression, removes any complicity from the educators, and assigns them full responsibility if they manage to "save" their students. You could throw several other hot topics into this pile of popular checklist trends in recent years, whether it is *social-emotional learning*, *noncognitive skills*, or *growth mindset*, all of which contain a kernel of insight and valuable truth but are applied in such a way that allows educators, particularly white ones, to avoid confronting these structures in which they participate, as other critical scholars have pointed out (e.g., Coomer & Skelton, 2019; Hulgin, Fitch & Coomer, 2020). Thankfully, some educators do seem to have come to this understanding, taking the first tentative steps toward critical self-reflection and a consideration of their role in perpetuating oppression, and even in maintaining whiteness and ability supremacy. But unfortunately, far too many start along this vital path, only to quickly apply labels to themselves that they most assuredly have yet to earn.

MERIT BADGES

As a Boy Scout, the requirements for earning merit badges are simple, or at least they were when I was a kid. You complete a series of tasks—some more complex than others—and you submit them to an adult certified in that particular badge, who signs off on your being deserving of it. In my youth, you then received a piece of paper[9] and the right to sew a little patch onto a sash you got to wear. You felt good about yourself and the boys with the most patches were deeply impressive. I mention all of this to say that even the white teachers who will admit to being part of the problem, who do not rely solely on checklists, will sew a shiny patch onto their metaphorical sashes and let everyone know just how different they are from other teachers, and this self-aggrandizing behavior leaves them short of what is required in cultivating radical love.

It is worth pausing here to consider the distance between intentions and impact. Though there are surely some who hold an active antipathy for students, I choose to believe that most educators are well-intentioned, and, as much as this chapter is critical of the practice, the pursuit of checklists and merit badges likely comes from a "nice" place. In other words, I am being critical of people who are nice, and even if they are occasionally misguided, there are, one might say, people far more deserving of criticism. Niceness, however, is not the same as love, let alone radical love; it is a surface attribute that can cover all manner of harm. The self-described "nice white ladies" interviewed by Miller and Harris (2018) are as deeply mired in the habits and trappings of whiteness as anyone else, and, as Aronson (2017) explains, her entering the classroom well-intentioned was irrelevant when she had yet to critically examine her own whiteness and other axes of power; in fact, she had been inspired by the aforementioned *Freedom Writers*. This is a long way of saying that checklists and merit badges may be the well-intentioned acts of nice people, but without the deep work required to combat whiteness and ability supremacy in oneself and in broader society, they are destined to fail at anything other than improving the image of those who pursue them.

Along with the rise in "anti-racist teachers" I described in the introduction, there has been a great deal of discussion around educators seeking *decolonization* and *decolonizing the curriculum*. Taken literally, it is a difficult bar to reach, as returning land and funds to exploited peoples is beyond the scope of an individual educator, especially one representing a colonial power. Looking at recent literature, though (Subedi, 2013; LeGrange, 2015; Mbembe, 2016), inside of a neoliberal academic system, the concept has become something of a lyrical way to describe moving away from the unquestioned canon, centering the perspectives of racialized and dis/abled authors, and diversifying academic epistemology overall. I will reiterate that these are necessary and valuable steps to take, and that they should be encouraged, but that the fact that the phrase contains a word as strong as decolonize makes it an attractive merit badge for teachers to quickly self-apply. Like anti-racism, the term is watered down by any teacher who equates it with merely reading the work of the oppressed; this allows the teacher to, as ever, avoid implicating themselves in the colonial curriculum, and skips over the risk and challenge necessary to give enough of themselves to their students to practice radical love.

Decolonizing one's curriculum is a complex task that is more difficult and uncomfortable than changing around a few books and articles. This process requires a substantive redistribution of power, a critical analysis of colonial thought and wisdom, and a decentering of whiteness and ability. Tuck and Yang (2012) make clear that decolonization is a concrete process that is necessarily disruptive to settler colonialism, despite its having been diluted into a mere merit badge. According to Zinga and Styres (2019), decolonization requires that educators "critically engage in their own self-reflection and examine the ways they are implicated in and informed by the very things that they are asking students to critically examine and . . . use that self-examination to effectively design opportunities to get students to critically engage with the provocative and challenging course content" (p. 31). With respect to the topics at hand in this chapter, a version of decolonization that allows educators to avoid examining their implication in whiteness and ability supremacy is not decolonization at all.

You can unfortunately find passages such as the following that exemplify the distance between decolonization and the metaphorical version many have adopted. Charles (2019) writes, "One of the themes of the UKSG 2019 Conference was 'diversity and change'; decolonizing the curriculum is exactly that if done correctly." Except that it's not. "Diversity and change" without a shift in power is mere window dressing. New literature selected by the same teachers who have yet to interrogate their role in building and perpetuating the system they claim to have disrupted is little more than a button to show off to peers, a sticker for good behavior, a merit badge for the few who have gone beyond a mere checklist. Self-applied labels are facile half-measures that will not bring more than a surface affection to the students who are in need of the radical love their teachers will barely approach.

CONCLUSION

As mentioned above, I sought to bring disparate disciplines together to answer these questions, as I feel that consilience is a powerful approach for the attempted disentanglement of thorny, interconnected issues. I expect that many readers have considered the problems with whiteness, and in an audience presumably familiar with aspects of dis/ability, some may have seen the connection between the two. My hope, however, is that my choice to tie the well-known books and buzzwords to the issues of whiteness and ability supremacy demonstrates how the pursuit of checklists and merit badges can never provide students with radical love. I say this not as someone magically immune to the allure of checklists and merit badges, but indeed as a former enthusiast.

As a matter of fact, I was one of the many educators taken with grit, and indeed the very first conference presentation I made, in 2015, centered on the concept. I was convinced that it was a novel way to reach marginalized learners—in my case, these were adult English Language students—and that if we could improve our students' grit, they might stand a better chance at closing supposed "achievement gaps." There are two main problems with that line of thought. First, any checklist that supposedly works on the marginalized will inevitably be co-opted by dominant groups, so even if it worked—or *especially* if it worked—it would not stay focused on the "neediest" for long. Second, it of course places all of the flaws upon the students who are already oppressed and blames them for their lack of so-called achievement if they happen not to respond to any novel type of intervention. In other words, I would have made an excellent cheerleader for the sort of quick fixes favored by the field of Special Education.

The Special Education sector tends to focus on improving against metrics such as disproportionality (Voulgarides, 2018) without questioning the conceptualizations that have led to the way that racialized students are viewed and treated, a disappointing failing that is somewhat understandable when one considers that to challenge this orthodoxy would require interrogating the very foundations of our century-plus of positivism in American education. Similarly, I find that many empirical studies that document an intervention against standardized assessments without considering the oppression inherent to such assessments are contributing to the general belief in these students' deficits, and that this trend has negative impacts on students' academic identities (Kozleski & Atkinson, 2014). Disability Studies, although not perfect, is far better equipped to find fault with power differentials rather than within individuals who have already been pathologized, thereby dispensing with Special Education's reliance on binaries and hierarchies. So long as new educators are trained in the latter rather than the former, I fear that the chances for dis/abled students to feel the radical love they deserve will remain low.

I do not want anyone reading this to believe I emerged fully formed as a harsh critic of checklists and merit badges. I understand that teachers who fall for these trends are mostly well-meaning, because I myself truly wanted to find a way to help the students in my classroom. Over time, however, and with considerable critical analysis to accompany my pedagogical and personal experience, I began to ask myself what success truly was in a world that refuses to love these students; indeed, a world that, in many ways, had little love for me and my own identity. Can these students "succeed" in any way other than moving themselves closer to a standard of whiteness? Can a racialized and/or dis/abled student ever be seen as successful without rejecting their identity, or discarding who they are at their core? Can pathologized students ever be supported by systems that depend upon their deficiency? I think I know the answer to this last question, at least.

I long saw myself as an example of a successful student, what with my "elite" degrees, but I eventually came to see that, had I not been comfortable speaking a standardized way, had my neurodivergence been more of an obstruction, had I not been better at performing whiteness and ability, I would have struggled to achieve what I did, even taking into account the educational trauma I actually did experience. I have since come to understand that what I experienced was what happens when a student, no more or less capable than any other, is told he is loved by his schools but is fed whiteness and a narrow ideal of ability as a standard to match, and that what I needed, what all such students need and deserve, was radical love. What worries me, especially when I think my son's possible future, is that the very best support such a student might receive will be filtered through the lens of their pathologization; the best they can hope for is whatever quick fix is trendy when they are in school.

The cycle supports itself. The version of love you are shown is distant and conditional, dependent on the meeting of identity expectations, and then, even when you become a teacher yourself, this is the love that you know, safe and inauthentic and lacking in risk. You are trained not to place yourself on students' levels, not to see students as equals, and even if you genuinely want to see them do well, your imagination has been so constrained as to not allow for the possibility that the standards you want them to meet are built only for their oppression. There are exemplary Special Education teachers in classrooms around the world, but because of the structures into which the field has placed them, there is only so far they can possibly travel. As Audre Lorde (1984) once told us, "the master's tools will never dismantle the master's house. They may allow us temporarily to beat him at his own game, but they will never enable us to bring about genuine change" (p. 111). To find a new checklist to complete or a merit badge to apply to yourself is just to play the game you have already been handed as you were trained to teach, and these students will never find their way to freedom by following the same paths we have followed.

There are examples of what teachers can do to break free from their perpetuation of oppression and show their students radical love. In one study (Roy, 2017), an elementary teacher chose not to shy away from the complexity and difficulty of discussing race with refugee students, which provided the students with a full humanity in their classroom they would otherwise have been denied. In another (Clonan-Roy et al., 2020), *safe rebellious spaces* are proposed as a way for racialized students to express the emotionality that would otherwise be stolen from them, and to counteract the oppression of their system. Notably, neither of these articles mention radical love explicitly, which is, in a way, appropriate, as radical love is not a checklist for teachers to rush through or a merit badge that can be loudly self-applied.

Authentic radical love of racialized and dis/abled students requires a rejection of and a divestment from the whiteness and ability supremacy that remain centered and standardized in our educational institutions, and there are plenty of examples of how teachers can take the risks necessary to give of themselves deeply and fully. I understand why we fall for the quick fixes; I once did myself. Nevertheless, I can see now what I was missing, I can see now what these students need and deserve, and I hope, after reading this, at least a few more people can put forth the message that checklists and merit badges are no shortcut to radical love.

NOTES

1. See *Approaches and Terminology* for explanation of this word choice.
2. An exceptionally skilled Black neurosurgeon who has nonetheless aligned himself with former President Trump, served in his cabinet, and stewarded harmful, anti-Black housing policy (see Patenaude, 2020).
3. It is possible that these patterns are shifting; A Netflix movie called *The Kindergarten Teacher (2018)* features a white woman as a would-be white savior but who, the film is clear, is centering herself and damaging the young student of color on whom she has fixated. It was, however, not very popular.
4. Intelligence and ability are not quite the same concept, but considering that a low assessment of the former can classify one as "disabled"—indeed, being told one is not smart is one powerful method of dis/abling—then the connection is clear.
5. Indeed, as DiAngelo explains in a different article (2010), individualism is part of the reason that whiteness remains in control.
6. As peer-reviewed quantitative reportage tends to be, for better or worse.
7. A brief reminder that IQ is a racist and eugenicist concept (Dudley-Marling & Gurn, 2010; Reddy, 2008).
8. In his argument, students without character are those who lack curiosity or, appropriately, grit.
9. This might be electronic by now!

REFERENCES

Andrew, S. (2020, June 3). Amazon's best sellers list is dominated almost entirely by books on race right now. *CNN*. https://www.cnn.com/2020/06/03/us/amazon-best-sellers-books-race-trnd/index.html
Annamma, S. (2018). *The pedagogy of pathologization: Dis/abled girls of color and the school-prison nexus*. Routledge.
Annamma, S., Jackson, D., & Morrison, M. (2016). Conceptualizing color-evasiveness: using dis/ability critical race theory to expand a color-blind racial ideology in education and society. *Race Ethnicity and Education, 20*(2), 147–162.
Aronson, B. (2017). The white savior industrial complex: A cultural studies analysis of a teacher educator, savior film, and future teachers. *Journal of Critical Thought and Praxis, 6*(3), 36–54.

Artiles, A. J. (2011). Toward an interdisciplinary understanding of educational equity and difference: The case of the racialization of ability. *Educational Researcher, 40*(9), 431–445.

Artiles, A. J. (2019). Fourteenth annual Brown lecture in education research: Reenvisioning equity research: Disability identification disparities as a case in point. *Educational Researcher, 48*(6), 325–335.

Canagarajah, A. (1999). *Resisting linguistic imperialism in English language teaching*. Oxford University Press.

Cann, C. (2015). What school movies and TFA teach us about who should teach urban youth: Dominant narratives as public pedagogy. *Urban Education, 50*(3), 288–315.

Charles, E. (2019). Decolonizing the curriculum. *Insights, 32*(1), 1–7.

Clonan-Roy, K., Gross, N., & Jacobs, C. (2020). Safe rebellious places: The value of informal spaces in schools to counter the emotional silencing of youth of color. *International Journal of Qualitative Studies in Education, 34*(4), 1–23.

Collins, K., Connor, D., Ferri, B., Gallagher, D., & Samson, J. (2016). Dangerous assumptions and unspoken limitations: A Disability Studies in Education response to Morgan, Farkas, Hillemeier, Mattison, Maczuga, Li, and Cook (2015). *Multiple Voices for Ethnically Diverse Exceptional Learners, 16*(1), 4–16.

Coomer, M. N., & Skelton, S. M. (2019). Centering equity in social emotional learning. Equity tool. *Midwest & Plains Equity Assistance Center (MAP EAC)*. https://greatlakesequity.org/sites/default/files/201926081967_equity_tool.pdf

Crowley, R. (2016). Transgressive and negotiated white racial knowledge. *International Journal of Qualitative Studies in Education, 29*(8), 1016–1029.

Davis, L. (1995). *Enforcing normalcy: Disability, deafness and the body*. Verso.

DiAngelo, R. (2010). Why can't we all just be individuals?: Countering the discourse of individualism in anti-racist education. *InterActions: UCLA Journal of Education and Information Studies, 6*(1). https://escholarship.org/uc/item/5fm4h8wm

DiAngelo, R. (2011). White fragility. *International Journal of Critical Pedagogy, 3*(3), 54–70.

Dotson, K. (2013). Radical love: Black philosophy as deliberate acts of inheritance. *The Black Scholar, 43*(4), 38–45.

Douglas, T., & Nganga, C. (2015). What's radical love got to do with it: Navigating identity, pedagogy, and positionality in pre-service education. *International Journal of Critical Pedagogy, 5*(1), 58–82.

Duckworth, A. (2016). *Grit: The power and passion of perseverance*. Scribner.

Duckworth, A., Peterson, C., Matthews, M., & Kelly, D. (2007). Grit: Perseverance and passion for long-term goals. *Journal of Personality and Social Psychology, 92*(6), 1087–1101.

Dudley-Marling, C., & Gurn, A. (Eds.). (2010). *The myth of the normal curve* (Vol. 11). Peter Lang.

Faez, F. (2012). Linguistic identities and experiences of generation 1.5 teacher candidates: Race matters. *TESL Canada Journal, 29*(6), 124–141.

Fleming, J., & Ledogar, R. J. (2008). Resilience, an evolving concept: A review of literature relevant to Aboriginal research. *Pimatisiwin, 6*(2), 7–23.

Flores, N., & Rosa, J. (2015). Undoing appropriateness: Raciolinguistic ideologies and language diversity in education. *Harvard Educational Review*, *85*(2), 149–172.
Freire, P. (1970). *Pedagogy of the oppressed*. Continuum.
Gallagher, D. (2010). Hiding in plain sight: The nature and role of theory in learning disability labeling. *Disability Studies Quarterly*, *30*(2). https://dsq-sds.org/index.php/dsq/article/view/1231/1278
Gerald, J. (2020a). Combatting the altruistic shield in English language teaching. *NYS TESOL Journal*, *7*(1), 22–25.
Gerald, J. (2020b). Worth the risk: Towards decentering whiteness in English language teaching. *BC TEAL Journal*, *5*(1), 44–54.
Gomez, A., & Jimenez, J. M. (2018). Radical love: Remembering Freire, Joe, and Pato. *International Review of Qualitative Research*, *11*(1), 6–10.
Goodley, D. (2014). *Dis/ability Studies. Theorising disablism and ableism*. Routledge.
Harris, C. I. (1993). Whiteness as property. *Harvard Law Review*, *106*(8), 1707–1791.
Hatt, B. (2012). Smartness as a cultural practice in schools. *American Educational Research Journal*, *49*(3), 438–460.
Hernández-Saca, D., & Cannon, M. (2019). Interrogating disability epistemologies: Towards collective dis/ability intersectional emotional, affective and spiritual autoethnographies for healing. *International Journal of Qualitative Studies in Education*, *32*(3), 243–262.
Hulgin, K., Fitch, E. F., & Coomer, M. N. (2020). Optimizing a critical juncture: Trauma, neoliberal education and children's agency. *Journal of Curriculum and Pedagogy*, *17*(2), 1–28.
Kendi, I. X. (2017). *Stamped from the beginning: The definitive history of racist ideas in America*. Bold Type Books.
Kendi, I. X. (2019). *How to be an anti-racist*. One World.
LeGrange, L. (2015). Decolonising the university curriculum. *South African Journal of Higher Education*, *30*(2), 1–12.
Leonardo, Z. (2016). Tropics of whiteness: Metaphor and the literary turn in white studies. *Whiteness and Education*, *1*(1), 3–14.
Leonardo, Z., & Broderick, A. (2011). Smartness as property: A critical exploration of intersections between whiteness and disability studies. *Teachers College Record*, *113*(10), 2206–2232.
Lorde, A. (1984). *Sister outsider: Essays and speeches*. Crossing Press.
Love, B. (2019). *We want to do more than survive: Abolitionist teaching and the pursuit of educational freedom*. Penguin Random House.
March, J. G., & Simon, H. A. (1958). *Organizations*. John Wiley & Sons.
Mbembe, A. (2016). Decolonizing the curriculum: New directions. *Arts & Humanities in Higher Education*, *15*(1), 29–45.
Mijs, J. (2014). The unfulfillable promise of meritocracy: Three lessons and their implications for justice in education. *Social Justice Research*, *29*(1), 14–34.
Miller, L. A., & Harris, V. W. (2018). I can't be racist—I teach in an urban school, and I'm a nice white lady! *World Journal of Education*, *8*(1), 1–11.

Milner, H. R. (2010). Race, narrative inquiry, and self-study in curriculum and teacher education. In H. R. Milner (Ed.), *Culture, curriculum, and identity in education* (pp. 181–206). Palgrave Macmillan.
Mischel, W. (2014). *The marshmallow test: Why self-control is the engine of success.* Little, Brown Company.
Moore, J. W. (2016). What is the sense of agency and why does it matter? *Frontiers in Psychology, 7,* 1272. https://doi.org/10.3389/fpsyg.2016.01272
NCES. (2021, May). Characteristics of public school teachers. *National Center for Education Statistics.* https://nces.ed.gov/programs/coe/indicator/clr
Nielsen, K. (2012). *A disability history of the United States.* Beacon Press.
Patenause, S. (2020, January 13). How Ben Carson's new housing rule would deepen racial segregation. *The Washington Post.* https://www.washingtonpost.com/outlook/2020/01/13/how-ben-carsons-new-housing-rule-would-deepen-racial-segregation/
Picower, B. (2009). The unexamined whiteness of teaching: How white teachers maintain and enact dominant racial ideologies. *Race Ethnicity and Education, 12*(2), 197–215.
Ramjattan, V. A. (2019). The white native speaker and inequality regimes in the private English language school. *Intercultural Education, 30*(2), 126–140.
Reddy, A. (2008). The eugenic origins of IQ testing: Implications for Post-Atkins litigation. *Depaul Law Review, 57*(3), 667–678.
Ripley, A. (2013). *The smartest kids in the world (and how they got that way).* Simon and Schuster.
Ris, E. (2015). Grit: A short history of a useful topic. *Journal of Educational Controversy, 10*(1), 1–18.
Roy, L. (2017). "So what's the difference?" Talking about race with refugee children in the English language learner classroom. *TESOL Journal, 8*(3), 540–563.
Ruecker, T., & Ives, L. (2015). White native English speakers needed: The rhetorical construction of privilege in online teacher recruitment spaces. *TESOL Quarterly, 49*(4), 733–754.
Shalaby, C. (2017). *Troublemakers: Lessons in freedom from young children at school.* The New Press.
Subedi, B. (2013). Decolonizing the curriculum for global perspectives. *Educational Theory, 63*(6), 621–638.
Sung, C. (2011). Race and native speakers in ELT: Parents' perspectives in Hong Kong. *English Today, 27*(3), 25–29.
Tefera, A. A., Hernández-Saca, D., & Lester, A. M. (2019). Troubling the master narrative of "Grit": Counterstories of Black and Latinx students with dis/abilities during an era of "high-stakes" testing. *Education Policy Analysis Archives, 27*(1), 1–38.
Tough, P. (2012). *How children succeed: Grit, curiosity, and the hidden power of character.* Mariner.
Tuck, E., & Yang, K. W. (2012). Decolonization is not a metaphor. *Decolonization: Indigeneity, Education & Society, 1*(1), 1–40.
Voulgarides, C. K. (2018). *Does compliance matter in special education? IDEA and the hidden inequities of practice.* Teachers College Press.
Wilson, E. (1999). *Consilience: The unity of knowledge.* Vintage.

Zamudio, M., & Rios, F. (2006). From traditional to liberal racism: Living racism in the everyday. *Sociological Perspectives, 49*(4), 483–501.

Zinga, D., & Styres, S. (2019). Decolonizing curriculum: Student resistances to anti-oppressive pedagogy. *Power and Education, 11*(1), 30–50.

Chapter 13

Female Inclusive Educators of Color

Challenging White Privilege and the Mechanism of Dis/ablement Through Radical Love

Sarah Schlessinger

Educators in the United States have inherited a flawed system of education premised on culturally divisive, singular notions of failure (Deschennes et al., 2001) and designed to systematically exclude "deviant bodies" (Garland-Thomson, 2017). Social justice pedagogies have been positioned as projects of hope. Among these, inclusive education has been forwarded as a reimagining of schooling that conceives of failure and difference as fundamental for learning and growth (Ferguson & Nusbaum, 2012) rather than illnesses or deficits to be "fixed" or "eradicated." Over the past 40 years, however, the project of inclusivity has remained stalled-out and misunderstood (Florian, 2012) as it is stuck in the debates between scholars in the fields of Disability Studies in Education (DSE) and traditional special education, and through continued separation of disability from other categories of historically multiply marginalized populations in school. This derailment has its roots in structural, ideological, and affective resistance to "deviant bodies." Recognizing the parallel and intersecting fields of DSE and Critical Race Theory (CRT) (Annamma et al., 2013; Leonardo & Broderick, 2011; Waitoller & King-Thorius, 2016; Watts & Erevelles, 2004), this chapter explores the counter/narratives of women of Color who are drawn to the work of inclusivity and able to navigate these theoretical tensions even as they navigate their own embodied positioning within schools.

Working with narrative inquiry methodologies (Clandinin, 2013), this chapter seeks to center the experiences of women of Color in the field of special education while drawing on DSE and CRT to frame their narrative experiences. The work is intended to disclose some of the overlaps and deviations in lived experiences that create space for an affective draw toward inclusive praxis. Building from participants' shared experience of a triple-bind of being a woman, person of Color, and special educator, I consider what contexts nurture or hinder women of Color working to teach inclusively across difference to inform how we might better prepare all teachers to teach inclusively. In exploring these overlaps, radical love emerges as a key mechanism through which female teachers of Color in special education work to ground themselves and support their multiply marginalized students.

OUR FLAWED SYSTEM

Whose knowledge counts? Whose ways of knowing count? Schooling—the structures, the curriculum, attitudes, what counts as "good" or "smart" (Broderick & Leonardo, 2016; Leonardo & Broderick, 2011), the fundamental notion of what it means to teach or to learn—these are all complex and contested contexts. In the United States, these foundational components of schooling mirror the societal discourses that they have been built within and privilege a particular understanding of "normal," "typical," or status-quo. They privilege whiteness, wealth, heteronormativity, and able-bodiedness without naming these categories or interrogating them. As these standards have been centered and left uninterrogated, we, as a society, have accepted them and internalized them within our systems and within our bodies (Kendi, 2019; Schalk, 2018). By internalizing particular markers of difference as superior, intentionally or not, we, as individuals and as a society, necessarily suggest that deviation from those particular markers of difference is in fact deviance—a negative deviance.

This history of marking, labeling, and then excluding is deep within U.S. culture and explicitly evident in the practices of schooling (Brantlinger, 2006; Sleeter, 1986; Tyack, 1974). It is possible to trace the evidence of white, able-bodied privilege within the content of curricula and the disciplinary policies of schools. Standardized curricula in the United States focuses on a Eurocentric history, so-called canonical texts, decontextualized mathematical application, and the singular value of print text literacy while ignoring histories from other places or perspectives, contemporary texts and those authored by people of Color, contextualized uses of mathematics, and the very many ways that people are literate (Sleeter & Carmona, 2017). Disciplinary policies are punitive and controlling while favoring complacency and conformity rather than restorative and community driven while supporting self-expression and student voice (Milner et al., 2018). At the center of these practices and beliefs is one overpowering notion that drives our schools: failure, and specifically the failure to conform to a "mainstream" way of being and learning (Varenne & McDermott, 2018). Deschenes et al. (2001) state: "Pupils who did not learn efficiently what educators sought to teach; who misbehaved or were truant and delinquent; or who fell behind, were not promoted, and dropped out . . . did not fit the mainstream mold" (pp. 256–257) and were understood as individually or culturally "deficient." As students with disabilities, students living in poverty, and students of Color do not meet the "mainstream mold" of affluent, white, and able-bodied (not to mention male, cisgender, straight, English speaking, Christian, and so on), they are continuously and systematically excluded, overlooked, and underserved. What is more, they and those around them are made to believe that this is somehow a "deficiency" within them and/or their communities rather than the foundational systemic design of our schooling system. These students are less likely to receive compelling, rigorous, constructivist, and culturally relevant and sustaining (Paris, 2012; Paris & Alim, 2017) curricular opportunities that develop their criticality and voice. In fact, students who are deemed as "struggling" or "special education" often experience schooling singularly as remediation (Artiles, 2002; Artiles & Kozleski, 2010). Nonconforming students are also more likely to be "pushed out," criminalized, and steered from exclusionary schooling experiences into prisons (Annamma, 2015; Morrison, 2016).

These exclusionary and oppressive realities of schooling, and their eventual ripple effects, are well explored from a variety of theoretical perspectives as aligned with multiple and diverse markers of difference. Among these social justice pedagogies, the project of inclusive education has emerged (Lingard & Mills, 2007) from two seemingly disparate schools of thought to mean two seemingly divergent pedagogical approaches. On the one hand, special education scholars have conceived of inclusive education as a service delivery model to educate students with diagnosed special education disabilities and labels alongside peers without diagnosed special education disabilities and labels (Giangreco & Suter, 2015). From this perspective, the realities of a student's disability warrant specific attention and support provided through interventions in a traditional classroom setting with "typically" (Young, 2007) developing peers and a special education service provider. On the other hand, Disability Studies in Education (DSE) scholars have conceived of disability not as a deficit located within an individual but as the constructs of society that work to disable an individual by not accounting for humanity's vast array of differences. From this perspective, inclusive education as a stance whereby barriers to all students' learning are examined and addressed as issues in the curriculum (Kozleski et al., 2013). At the heart of both pedagogies is a desire to do right by students who do not do well with traditional schooling models and increase equitable access to positive educational opportunities for all students. Yet, these fundamental theoretical differences have created a history of disagreement and disequilibrium for school systems, educators, and families (Florian, 2012).

While recent research has documented the tensions that arise for teachers as they seek to navigate divergent theoretical perspectives and pedagogical enactments of the same (Naraian & Schlessinger, 2017), this book seeks to explore the possibilities of a DSE and traditional special education consilience where these two paradigms are not at war, but are instead working together to create "alternative ways of being, doing, feeling and interacting with self and others, and maximizes agency of all participants in educational contexts" (Hernández-Saca et al., 2020, para 5). Within this larger conversation, this chapter turns to one of our greatest resources, teachers *who do*, to understand the practices that sustain teachers while pushing their critical capacity as they work at this intersection of special education and disability studies in education. Through negotiating their theoretical beliefs, lived experiences, and the structural constraints of the system and society they work within, there are educators who have to pay close attention to the material realities of difference that show up in the classroom and who are simultaneously committed to dismantling systems of oppression that exacerbate negative perceptions and experiences of difference. The narratives of these educators—their maneuverings and obstacles—provide insight into potential opportunities for disability education consilience and possible paths forward on our shared commitment to social justice and equity in education.

This chapter takes a specific look at the work and experiences of two women of Color working toward inclusive education. Collins (2002) offers that Black women's specific experiences of intersectionality provide insight into racialized and gendered systems of oppressions and the intersectional experience of being both female and Black. Collins (2002) continues to suggest that understanding the experiences of Black women can serve to illuminate oppressive structures broadly as they impact other social groups as well. Understanding the intersectional oppression that Black women navigate can help us all to name the workings of those oppressive structures and ways to act within and against them. This is not to suggest that Black women hold the responsibility for educating society about these systems of oppression, as they have often been positioned to do, but rather that by centering their experiences we can make plain the oppressive impact of taken-for-granted normative systems and beliefs while also shining a light on the pedagogical legacy of Black women teachers (Watson & Devereaux, 2020). Black women educators have long championed practices of pedagogical care (Beauboeuf-Lafontant, 2002; Siddle-Walker & Thompson, 2013) driven by their own experiences at the intersection of Black and woman and their commitment to social justice in education (Beauboeuf-Lafontant, 2005; Watson & Devereaux, 2020). "Given the historical legacy of Black women educators, as well as recent research indicating the impact Black teachers have on the expansion of educational opportunities, increased academic performance, and high expectations for Black students" (Gist et al., 2018, p. 2) multiple scholars from fields of Critical Race Feminisms, Black Feminist Pedagogies, Black Womanism, and Critical Race Womanist Pedagogies have called for the centering of and research on the practices of Black women teachers. Pizarro and Kohli (2020) and Yoon (2019) extend that call to include other teachers of Color whose experiential awareness of whiteness as property informs their social justice orientation as pedagogues. Drawing on the parallel and intersecting fields of DSE and Critical Race Theory (CRT) (Annamma et al., 2013; Waitoller & King-Thorius, 2016; Watts & Erevelles, 2004) and Broderick and Leonardo's (2016) analysis of dis/ablement as a mechanism to "accomplish" and "legitimize" racism, classism, and sexism, I extend this call to include the centering of the experiences of female teachers of Color (Pizarro & Kohli, 2020; Watson & Devereaux, 2020) who teach special and inclusive education (Kozleski, 2020). Through their counter-narratives as they navigate the theoretical tensions of DSE and traditional special education from their own embodied positioning within schools as female special education teachers of Color, they provide a necessary window into the intersecting systems of oppression of schooling and possibilities for change.

Aziza and Natali, the participants in this study, were also integral in determining this specific focus on women of Color in inclusive education, as this identification felt like one that encompassed their shared experiences as teachers. Natali and Aziza were what Creswell and Creswell (2017) would call a purposeful sample, in that through my preexisting relationship with them as their professor, their relationship with each other as friends, and our mutual knowledge of their inclusive practice in schools, I was compelled to learn more from them specifically about their experiences of navigating the complexities of being special and inclusive educators as women of Color. Fine (2016) offers that "if we are to document the human consequences of structural violence and imagine radical possibilities, there is much to learn from those who dwell on the Radical Rim" (p. 347) as Natali and Aziza did in their teaching roles. Yet, navigating our various relationships and the embedded issues of race and power within them required careful consideration in the design of the study. Although Natali and Aziza had graduated and were no longer my students, our relationship had been established under the power constructs of teacher-student relationships. More importantly, as a white woman seeking to learn from the experiences of female teachers of Color, it was essential that this work not fetishize, dehistoricize, or decontextualize (Fine, 2016) participants' narratives. With this in mind, and in keeping with the DSE and CRT traditions of privileging individual stories, this study was designed as a narrative inquiry into the lived experiences of the participants (Clandinin, 2013). I designed the study alongside the participants as a series of conversational interviews between both women and between the three of us. Through an initial conversation on the focus of the study, we collaboratively developed themes to explore, I designed guiding questions for our conversational interviews and then engaged in an iterative process of conversational interviews and descriptive coding (Saldaña, 2021), using emergent themes from previous interviews to inform the guiding questions of the following interview for a total of six conversational interviews. What follows are some initial understandings gained from Aziza and Natali's experience as female special and inclusive educators of Color.

THE LESSONS THAT STORIES TEACH US

I met Natali and Aziza toward the beginning of their master's program in adolescent special education. Their program, originally designed as a traditional special education master's program, was one that had shifted over the years in two significant ways. First, the program had been moving away from traditional special education conceptualizations and pedagogies and toward learning and teaching from a Disability Studies in Education (DSE) perspective. This meant that within the program itself there were remnants of traditional special education programming alongside elements of DSE-driven programming. For example, in one course, students were asked to engage in a traditional study and practice of functional behavioral analysis (FBA) *and* to complete a discourse analysis of school-based notions of "goodness" and "smartness" as property constituted through the mechanisms of dis/ablement and whiteness (Broderick & Leonardo, 2016). An FBA "can be defined as a collection of methods for gathering information about antecedents, behaviors, and consequences in order to determine the reason (function) of behavior" and to then "design interventions to reduce problem behaviors and to facilitate positive behaviors" (Gersham et al., 2001, p. 158). This practice, which centers particular behaviors as "good" and targets other "bad" behaviors to be fixed, is a standard and well-accepted practice of traditional special education (Gersham et al., 2001). In the same course that these teaching students were asked to conduct an FBA, they were also asked to consider the ways that "good" or "smart" are "performative, cultural, and ideological systems that operate in the service of constructing the normative center" (Broderick & Leonardo, p. 57) of their schools—a particularly progressive consideration of how schools construct disability and difference (Connor et al., 2019). As such, the program presented Aziza and Natali with two very different frameworks to bring to their own teaching, offering either an opportunity for a bridged approach to supporting their students or a problematic tension for them to resolve through their practice.

Second, the program had been adapted to serve students pursuing alternative certification. This meant that Natali and Aziza (and the majority of their peers) were working full time as teachers with temporary certification while simultaneously pursuing their master's education. Students in this program often expressed their frustration with the difficulty of "learning to ride a bike while you were building it" especially given the differences between what they were being taught in their master's program and what they were allowed to do in their schools. What, for example, was the point in learning about curriculum theory and design when as a special educator you were not allowed to design any curriculum? Learning about practices like restorative justice in graduate coursework was initially exciting for these students, but often disappointing when they realized that their schools were going to continue with zero-tolerance suspension policies. Natali and Aziza were not untouched by these frustrations. Yet, in comparison and conjunction with the other frustrations of teaching special education as women of Color in schools with predominantly students of Color and white teachers, these commonly shared frustrations of first year alternative certification teachers did not seem to impede Natali and Aziza's commitments or drive toward inclusive practice. They were the teachers who would enact restorative practices in their own classrooms, regardless of school wide policies, if that is what would best serve their students. At the heart of this unwavering commitment was a complex but honest capacity orientation toward their students driven by what Freire (1970/2000) and the editors of this book would name as radical love. Building from Freire (1970/2000) and Kincheloe (1991), Agnello (2016) has defined radical love as:

> Dedicated to, want the best for, concerned about, care for, encourage, support, connect with, recognize, praise, guide, inspire, be inspired by, humanize interrelations with, go beyond the call of duty for, stick up for, protect, mentor, and work with for world transformation. (p. 69)

Aziza and Natali's experiences as female special educators of Color illustrate for us what it is and what it might take to operationalize radical love in the education of multiply marginalized youth (Annamma et al., 2013) who deserve attention paid to the material, emotive and discursive realities of their disabilities and disruption of the ways that society positions them as "deficient" and "deviant" because of the same.

Being "for the Kids"

What Agnello (2016) has qualified as "dedicated to, want the best for, concerned about . . ." Natali and Aziza explained as (and were committed to) being "for the kids." They believed in their students and were going to fight for them regardless of any specific diagnosis or lowered expectations set by the school or society at large. Both women of Color taught as special educators across two different models of service delivery. In some instances, they were teaching in integrated co-teaching classrooms (ICT) where 40 percent of students in a classroom of approximately thirty had diagnosed special education disabilities and Individual Education Plans (IEPs).[1] In these instances, they were working with another educator who had a content area certification in the subject area of the course. In other instances, they taught in self-contained classrooms where 100 percent of approximately 12–15 students had diagnosed special education disabilities and IEPs. In these instances, they were the only teacher in the classroom. Although there is a long history of problematizing this continuum of services[2] and the Least Restrictive Environment (LRE)[3] (Taylor, 1988), in common practice, it is often understood that students with more severe disabilities are taught via a self-contained service delivery model while students whose disabilities present as less severe or less of a barrier to so-called typical learning will receive instruction via an ICT service delivery model. In all instances, the presumption was that as special education teachers Natali and Aziza were qualified to teach all content to special education students.

In both schools, from Natali and Aziza's perspectives, there seemed to be a clear issue of lowered expectations for and effort put into students in self-contained classroom settings (Kurth et al., 2014). Aziza specifically noted how her class was always overlooked, and not just academically. They were left out on picture day, in assemblies, and during school trips. It was as if because they carried these disability markers and the stigma of "self-contained" they were not full members of the school community. For her, this was unacceptable. Aziza knew that her students "want inclusion, they don't want to feel left out" and that it was up to Aziza to fight for them, for their full recognition within the school and access to all opportunities. While she could recognize the value to an educator of knowing a student's specific disability diagnosis and to the student of receiving targeted instruction for particular content outside of the larger class structures, she also saw the shame that was associated with these labels, the exclusion, and ultimately, the oppression. The same was true for Natali when her students expressed to her that they could tell that other teachers did not like them and that when a teacher "just wants to yell at them and throw information at them . . . they don't care, and students don't want to be there." Natali knew that for her students, it was enough to be "treated like garbage by the police or by the people at 7-11 throwing them out" and that they did not need more of that in a climate where they were supposed to be learning. Natali knew that "they really do just want to belong in school when their experiences have not always been pretty." Both Natali and Aziza could feel and see how their students' experiences of being treated as less capable negatively affected their desire to perform student and their conceptions of themselves as learner in the context of their schooling. Both also saw the underlying desire of their students to be treated as members of a learning community and to be learners themselves.

Being "for the kids" meant starting from a place of relationship and connection. This meant seeing their multiply marginalized students first and foremost as whole people with complex, intersectional, often difficult, lives and building relationships with students that affirmed that someone saw them, their stories, and their struggle and did not negatively judge them for who they were or what they had experienced. As Aziza shared, she "might not have personally experienced all the same situations" that her students had, but she had "witnessed or been exposed in some way" to many of their same race, disability, and class-driven oppressions and struggles. This connection to and awareness of the systems of oppression undergirding her students' experiences helped Aziza feel that she was "able to see the capacity in [her] students." Aziza shared that:

> In my own life, I have witnessed the differences amongst each child: how they learn, act, react, speak, share, live, etc. And, so, I'm very accepting of my students' differences. I know my role is to educate my students' and I feel like I'll fail them if I give up simply because others felt they couldn't learn, are too troublesome, or not worth the effort.

Aziza was unwilling to let any stigma interfere with her work or "hold any weight in her classroom" sharing that "challenging or not, we find a way to get past the negativity." This did not mean that there were no questions about how to best address specific learning needs and material, emotional, and discursive realities of individual student's disabilities. Natali shared that it was sometimes difficult for her to "see potential" when individual students were not thriving in her classroom, sharing that she "WANTS to see glimmers of hope" in student participation and performance, but that it "just doesn't always happen that way." In her analysis, however, the concern was not about the student, their disability label, or any specific and material, emotional, and discursive need. Natali saw her students as "capable. They are. I know it. I believe it," but giving them the supports that they needed to demonstrate their capacity often felt impossible when the self-contained classroom felt "like the dumping ground when other people are like 'don't bother with that kid, he's a mess'" and she was overwhelmed with "so much on your plate you can really only give 75%, and even that takes a lot." Still, with what Natali would qualify as her 75 percent effort, she did her best to understand the range of needs her students had and support them to the best of her ability. This often meant that academic needs did not end up being at the forefront. Natali shared that she would "feed and clothe kids, text them, they facetime me. So many of the lines are crossed because they need the support, and they are successful when I give it to them." Through a holistic understanding and appreciation of students' needs, Natali and Aziza were able to connect to their students and support them fundamentally as people and subsequently or simultaneously as learners.

A key component to this relational work was Natali and Aziza's own experience of how the [school] system has been set up to fail certain cohorts of people, cohorts of which they and their peers growing up were also members. Natali shared that she was particularly motivated by her reflection on "all the ways that a teacher might have failed me" and that she was actively going to do her best to not recreate that experience for any of her students, especially as related to race or perceived disability. Natali shared that:

> As an educator, I have committed to myself and to my students, that their inner reality is to be nurtured and respected. I must continue to remind myself of that as I need to continue to respect and value my inner experiences and truth.

Natalie's capacity orientation toward her students, and her commitment to nurturing and respecting their reality, was both parallel and intertwined with her own self-respect.

For Aziza, her familial experience informed a similar stance in her teaching. She shared that when she was growing up her father had never relied solely on (or trusted completely in) the school. Even when she came home with good grades or having done well on a test, he would acknowledge that there had been a "good moment in school" but also that he still had to be her teacher too, so that if school failed her, he would still be supporting her progress "in the right direction." Aziza carried this philosophy into her own relational work with her students and her pedagogy. Coming from a place of optimistic realism, she considered that even if the school or other teachers were failing her students, "just in case they were failing you somehow, I still got you. You're not going to fail." These women of Color were intent on always being the teachers who were going to stand up and fight for their students. Their understanding of how society and the school system could and would fail their students, how it had failed them, positioned them to see their students' disabilities as evidence of that system rather than evidence of a deficit within any one student. From this perspective, they were able to consider that students' academic and social/emotional needs warranted specific and direct attention while also being evidence of a disabling school system and society. Their racialized and ableized critical analysis of schooling (Pizarro & Kohli, 2020) along with their commitment to care as personal and political (Watson & Deveraux, 2020) allowed them to see student need without centering "white and middle-class knowledge systems as superior to all others" or positioning their students "as incompetent and/or troubled" (Higheagle Strong & McCain, 2020, p. 2). They were able to work from a pedagogy of radical love that could simultaneously prioritize both care *and* attention to material, emotional, and discursive needs without feeling like they had to "dumb down" curriculum or lower their expectations for their students. Prioritizing care in this way also required a clear and direct acknowledgment to their students of this experience of school as a negative and disciplining space.

Un-disciplining Bodies—Respect/Power/Control/Compliance

Within a schooling system built on normative, white supremacist, and ableist ideas of "goodness" and "smartness" (Broderick & Leonardo, 2016; Leonardo & Broderick, 2011) there has been an overemphasis on disciplining bodies into normative, white, able-bodied ways of learning and being (Annamma, 2015; Erevelles, 2000). While educational scholars forward pedagogies of inclusivity and cultural relevancy, responsivity, and sustainability, schools often continue to operate from disciplinary codes and high-stakes standardized test-driven curricula that exclude and vilify students who do not fit so-called standard, normative ways of being (Annamma, 2015; Au, 2016; Morris, 2018; Waitoller, 2020). When students do not conform, these exclusionary practices and their outcomes support a narrative that positions nonconforming students as failures or deviants in need of remediation and discipline (Adams & Erevelles, 2016; Annamma, 2015; Broderick & Leonardo, 2016; Morris, 2018). Even in well-meaning institutions with well-intentioned administration and faculty, like those where Natali and Aziza taught, there were often common assumptions about what it looked like for students to participate in the curriculum in "smart" ways and to comport themselves in "good" ways. More significantly, or perhaps just more explicitly named, there were common and problematic assumptions about what it looked like for a student to be academically "low" and/or behaviorally noncompliant or "bad." As Broderick and Leonardo (2016) suggest, the ideologies of "goodness" and "smartness" operate to center a normative white, able-bodiedness that profiles students based on race and ability in schools through the ways in which they do or do not conform to that normative center. In both schools, Natali and Aziza noticed that their students with special education labels were often in power struggles with teachers, teachers who sometimes implied or directly stated that these students were "disrespectful" or "lazy," euphemisms for people of Color and people with disabilities that have been both commonly used and commonly problematized (Osborne, 2019). Annamma (2015) points out that not only is this "criminalization" of students particularly prevalent for multiply marginalized students who are both of Color and assigned special education disability labels, but it also impedes teacher support for these students and prioritizes surveillance. Part of the problem, from both women's perspectives, was the predominantly white demographics of the faculty and administration. As Natali pointed out:

> If I take a young boy from South Jamaica where a lot of these kids are from, and go alright, your teachers for high school are all going to be white females from the Midwest, who does he have to look up to? Nobody.

Aziza added that "that's why they're 'acting out.' They feel like they don't have anyone to go to for advice, or a role model, because no one represents their reality." Aziza and Natali saw that their multiply marginalized students were constructed as deviant because so many of their teachers did not question the racialized ideologies of "smartness" and "goodness" and that this racial disparity between the teaching population and the student population worked to intensify students' feelings and experiences of isolation (Kohli & Pizarro, 2016).

Beyond this evident issue of disparity in racial representation of students and faculty, there were additional and complex taken-for-granted assumptions about power and control within the curriculum and student-teacher relationships. One concern, shared by both Aziza and Natali, was that while the schools were attempting to broaden their curriculum to be more culturally responsive in its content, their expectations for students' expression of their own knowledge and understanding remained limited and standardized in a way that perpetuated problematic notions of "smartness." One clear example that they found problematic was the use of "accountable talk" sentence stems (Ferris, 2014; Michaels, 2008). In Natali's analysis, her students could "be thoughtful without using the same sentence stems all the time" and "when they don't say answers the 'right way', maybe they want to say it a different way. Who says what they're saying is not correct? Just because it's not the way that you want to hear it." Structures and tools like this, seemingly intended to support student expression, often felt like the disciplining of students' dialectical choices and an erasure of "any type of personality" or cultural self. This instance, and others like it in Aziza's and Natali's experiences, evidenced what Broderick and Leonardo (2016) refer to as the enactment of dis/ablement as a mechanism to police and control black and brown bodies. That is to say, framing sentence starters as a necessary support tool for students because of their assigned special education disability labels, leverages dis/ablement to legitimize the oppression of cultural and linguistic diversity. Drawing on their own analysis of oppressive practices in schooling,

Natali and Aziza both understood this so-called support was also being used to limit their students' self-expression and dismiss their students' knowledge contributions.

In another example that Aziza shared, a colleague of hers was unwilling to accept a completed assignment from a student because he had used the wrong paper for his submission. The student was deeply frustrated that the teacher would not accept his work and the interaction escalated into "a whole blow up." Aziza felt that the teacher was overly concerned with her position of power rather than the student's growth and learning and couldn't understand why the teacher "caused the scene. She pried and pried, and nit and pick . . . is it her goal to get him in detention? Is that her goal so she can say, 'well now I have the power.'?" Seemingly, Aziza felt, it was more important that the teacher substantiate her position as above her student, in control of her student and his actions, than it was for the student to be allowed to advocate for himself, to feel heard within his school, receive some credit for his work, or even just avoid being penalized for either infraction. These subtle and overt pedagogical moves, driven by standardized modes of being and expressing, derived from whiteness and white supremacy, served to limit Natali and Aziza's students and disallow forms of expressing that better matched students' cultural backgrounds, abilities, and whole selves.

Aside from seeing this interaction and others like it as problematic from an anti-racist, anti-ableist, feminist perspective, Natali and Aziza were also able to highlight how ineffective it was for teaching and learning. Natali shared that:

> Try to abuse your power and then the students are like, "you're not my parent. Who the f*** do you think you're talking to?" These kids aren't walking away because they respect you. They're afraid of you. Why do you have to be the one that they fear?

It was clear to both teachers that students did not come to school unwilling to learn, but that the more school showed them that they did not belong, the less willing they were to participate in it and its systems of oppression.

In outlining a Discrit Classroom Ecology, Annamma and Morrison (2018) offer that teachers should recognize and allow students to engage with resistance to oppressive structures, suggesting that "instead of forcing students into states of acquiescence, we must look for what unique practices and knowledges multiply-marginalized Students of Color already bring to classrooms" (p. 73). Working from their own analysis of oppressive structures and observation of students' resistance, Natali and Aziza both somewhat intuitively knew that, as Natali explained it, they needed to "honor students anger and mistrust and teach to that." For them that meant that first and foremost they could be in control without having "to be this attacking presence" seeking to impose their power onto their students. Beyond that, they felt it was important that they not teach their students to be docile bodies, accepting and internalizing this oppressive disciplining of their ways of knowing and ways of being. Natali explained this, sharing that she was "not teaching (her) kids to show respect to a group of people who don't respect them. (She was) teaching (her) kids how to speak in an environment so that they remain safe." Natali felt that her responsibility was to foster her students' capacity to resist the powers working to discipline their bodies without putting themselves in the way of any potential harm inflicted by the same. This commitment to a nuanced and careful resistance came from her own paralleled experience in the world, as a student, and even in this school as a teacher. She had learned to "speak a language that (was) not native" to her in order to navigate a context that did not respect her without showing that context or those in power in that context deference or "respect" that she did not have for them. And she shared with her students that she "learned to speak this language" and wanted them to "learn how to speak this language too." Seeing student resistance to problematic structures and honoring it (Iqtadar et al., 2020), supporting students in learning how to enact their resistance in ways that would not bring them harm; this was the "protect, mentor, and work with for world transformation" practice of Natali and Aziza's radical love.

Sustaining the Self

Natali and Aziza's focus on and commitment to their multiply marginalized students is particularly impressive given the context of navigating their own positioning within their schools. Each woman felt the impact of race, gender, and ability on how they were perceived and treated by their colleagues and their students. Natali and Aziza both felt a "push and pull" from their colleagues regarding their expertise as female special educators of Color. Both women were often characterized by their students and their colleagues as "mothers" to their students and were regularly sought out by their colleagues for support to better relate to individual students or asked to step in and take care of students who were not responding well to "administration or teachers who are not the same color of skin." It felt evident to Natali and Aziza that they were sought out for their expertise in working with students of Color because they were themselves people of Color. This "other mother" surrogate positioning of women of Color by themselves and others is a historically significant pedagogical approach, a "politicized care" (Watson, 2019) that Aziza and Natali both took up and appreciated, but the subsequent dismissal of their perspectives was always frustrating. Natali shared that she would support colleagues and tell them "the ways that would work for a child like this."

Because I am a child like this, and I was this person," but then her colleagues would dismiss her saying things "like, 'Oh, well, we're not gonna do that here.'" Aziza extended this analysis to include the ways that her expertise as a special educator was sought and subsequently belittled. Aziza shared that:

> We're not supported enough in special ed because nobody really trusts us and our relationships with the students, and with recognizing what they need and what they don't need. They're just like, "Well, they've always had that service or placement, so we're just gonna keep it." There isn't a move to push them into a less restrictive environment. And no matter what I say about student A, B, and, and D, it's like, "Well they've always been here, so let's just keep it the way it is."

In the end, both women of Color felt that their colleagues wanted them "to be the expert but you don't trust me to be the expert." They characterized the experience as "so many different double binds . . . you don't trust me, but then you rely on me" as a special educator, as a female mother figure, and as a person of Color. While they were relied on to "mother" multiply marginalized students, their expertise was not taken up by their colleagues as valuable to understand or learn from, and thus they began to feel like a "dumping ground" for "those kids."

Natali and Aziza wondered whether their experience of being relied upon but not trusted was perhaps indicative of a larger competitive context. For example, while both women felt that their schools should be places where teachers shared ideas and celebrated each other's contributions, their colleagues seemed to want to "upstage each other." Not only did this general culture of the schools impede collaboration, it also meant that even when colleagues sought out advice from Aziza or Natali, they were often unwilling to act on that advice and "let go of control."

While Natali and Aziza often felt positioned as outsiders because of their race, gender, and position as special educators, while they felt frequently looked over or belittled as professionals, they also knew that the work they were doing for their multiply marginalized students was essential. They maintained their commitments to being "for the kids" and to undisciplining multiply marginalized bodies. But they also knew that in order to continue to do this work, especially in a professional context that belittled their knowledge and the complexity of their work, required some alternative, external support. Natali shared that "for as much as you're managing everybody else's trauma, everybody else's problems, you don't take that moment to step away and kind of take care of yourself," and without it, it becomes impossible to sustain. Both women were conscious of their own impending burnout from engaging in counter-hegemonic teaching in what felt like unsupportive contexts. They knew that they would need to change something if they were going to continue this work. For the time being, that something had to be drawing boundaries on how much they could really invest of themselves and their time. With administration pushing workloads and expectations to the limits, colleagues leaning on them for support without lifting them up, and students relying on them for support and advocacy, there was no one left for them to turn to for support within their school communities. This meant that they both needed to step back and create space for self-care within their own families and outside communities. They needed spaces to think and be with like-minded and similarly positioned educators (like each other) who they did not need to convince of the capacity of their students and who had comparable experiences in their own schools. They needed spaces to be lifted up and valued in ways that didn't feel performed or appropriative. These alternative spaces allowed them to go back in every week with a fresh perspective and start all over again, but neither Aziza nor Natali felt that this model would be sustainable long-term. They both expressed that, ideally, they would want to work in collaborative spaces rather than competitive spaces in order to allow for diversity of experiences and perspectives to support all students. But for so long as that was not the context of their schools, their self-care needed structure and attention. It could not be an afterthought if they were going to continue to do the work of educating multiply marginalized youth, fighting against the systems and practices of schooling that worked to exclude them and their students, and simultaneously advocating for the specific material, emotional, and discursive needs of all of their students.

OPERATIONALIZING RADICAL LOVE

Aziza and Natali's experiences provide us with examples of what it can mean to operationalize radical love for the enactment of inclusive practices so that educators can simultaneously recognize the material, emotional, and discursive needs of students and structural oppressions that work to exclude those students. Being "for the students" meant fighting for appropriate services and service delivery for students, and also maintaining a deep and authentic capacity orientation toward their students. Natali and Aziza's own sociopolitical consciousness, their awareness of whiteness as property and the mechanisms of dis/ablement (Annamma, 2015; Broderick & Leonardo, 2016), allowed them to understand their students simultaneously as individuals with real material needs without understanding those needs as individual or cultural deficits (Davis & Museus, 2019; Gorski, 2007; Harry & Klingner, 2007). To need support in a school that was not designed with you in mind was not evidence of "deviance". For Aziza and Natali needing support was "normal" whether it was because of a diagnosed special education disability, oppressive and exclusionary practices of schooling, or just a need. Centering their students' needs was a critically conscious, anti-oppressive pedagogical practice (Watson & Deveraux, 2020) of inclusivity. Aziza and Natali's intersectional analysis of race and ability in schooling allowed them to see their students' capacity, the possibility in and of their students. This enactment of radical love demonstrates how when practices of care derived from a capacity orientation extend into the realm of special education through an intersectional understanding of race and ability, they necessarily allow for a recognition of both individual need *and* systemic oppression.

Natali and Aziza's stories also shed some light on the counter-hegemonic fight and the advocacy necessary to operationalize this radical love for the enactment of inclusive practice. Advocating for students and teaching them to advocate for themselves has long been built into the practices of special education (Roberts et al., 2016). Doing this counter-hegemonically to shift understandings of "goodness" and "smartness" and to speak back to the systems of schooling that work to exclude multiply marginalized youth is an act of un-disciplining bodies. It required that Natali and Aziza allowed students the space to name the practices and interactions that they found harmful. It required that they supported students in those experiences. It required them teaching students the ways to speak up and speak back that would not bring them harm. "Protecting, mentoring, and standing up for" (Agnello, 2016) their students as an act of radical love required their own ability to name, experience, and resist these structures even while participating in them. Inclusivity as a project of social justice can draw on resistance theories from CRT and DSE (Annamma & Morrison, 2018; Iqtadar et al., 2020) to enrich and empower the tools of self-advocacy from special education and to support students in learning to be heard and to find their own agency. For so long as the project of inclusivity is a counter-hegemonic project of change, it is necessary to recognize the multiple levels of resistance within this work. It is necessary to educate teachers how to resist from within the system and how to support and hear their students' resistance with love.

Both Natali and Aziza felt that they were able to be "for the kids" and to "un-discipline" bodies at the intersections of race and ability because they could relate to the experience of being "those kids" who were overlooked, underserved, or overdisciplined. Kohli and Pizarro (2016) suggest that many teachers of Color are committed to social justice in schools because of their own experiences of marginalization within a schooling system grounded in white supremacy. For Aziza and Natali, seeing themselves in their students meant that their own self-liberation was interwoven with their enactment of radical love for their students (Watson, 2019). This offers three significant considerations for the larger project of inclusivity: (1) it matters to have female teachers of Color in inclusive education; (2) it matters to recognize and value the perspectives and practices of female teachers of Color in inclusive education; and (3) it matters for all teachers in special education to be well educated about whiteness as property and the mechanism of dis/ablement and committed to anti-oppressive pedagogies.

Practices of care and being "for the kids" that allow for a focus on individual need via a consciousness of systemic oppression require a real and deep understanding of students through real relational work. This relational work must be culturally sustaining and anti-racist in order to be real (Higheagle Strong & McCain, 2020). Female teachers of Color who bring this critical consciousness from their own multiply marginalized experiences to their pedagogy must be seen as the valuable resource that they are for enacting radical love, moving toward inclusivity, and moving away from the hyper-accountability (Oyler, 2017) and hyper-surveillance (Annamma, 2013) of a system that pushes out and criminalizes students with labeled special education disabilities and students of Color. They must be seen as a resource for understanding practices of radical love needed to change schooling experiences for multiply marginalized youth and not a "dumping ground" for "those kids." The project of inclusivity needs school communities where female inclusive educators of Color do not have to fight to advocate for their students and communities while being inequitably relied upon and simultaneously belittled (Kohli & Pizarro, 2016) but are rather supported in their professional growth and turned to for leadership.

As Aziza and Natali's experiences demonstrate, this work cannot be sustained in isolation. Recognizing women of Color who teach inclusively as resources to learn from also means building community and collaboration in our schools. First, female inclusive educators of Color must not be taken for granted as the sole resources for social justice and inclusivity. They need co-conspirators (Love, 2019) who recognize the systemic racism and ableism of schools and society, their own positions of privilege within them, and are committed to challenging white privilege and the mechanism of dis/ablement. They need other people to step up and do the work with them. Second, this work of radical love is community work. It speaks back against hierarchical and competitive individualistic systems.

Inclusive educators have inherited a flawed system, premised on success and failure grounded in white supremacy mechanized through dis/ablement, but we do not have to perpetuate that system or abide by that system. We can teach all students and see them all as contributing members of our society and classrooms while also recognizing the material, emotive, and discursive realities of their lived experiences. We cannot, however, do that without shining a bright light on the intersectional ways that schools are built to exclude or without teaching our students with radical love.

NOTES

1. An Individualized Education Plan (IEP) is a legal document developed by school personnel and families to codify specific supports for an individual student who has been diagnosed as having a special education disability.
2. The continuum of services is a hierarchical array of service delivery models intended to support the provision of special education services to students with diagnosed special education disability labels.
3. The Least Restrictive Environment (LRE) is the guiding principle of the continuum of services and refers to the concept that services should be provided to students with special education disability labels in the setting "least restrictive of the person's personal liberty" (Taylor, 1988).

REFERENCES

Adams, D. L., & Erevelles, N. (2016). Shadow play: DisCrit, dis/respectability, and carceral logics. In D. J. Connor, B. A. Ferri, & S. A. Annamma (Eds.), *DisCrit- Disability Studies and Critical Race Theory in Education* (pp. 55–67). Teachers College Press.

Agnello, M. F. (2016). Enactivating radical love. *The International Journal of Critical Pedagogy, 7*(3), 67–78.

Annamma, S. A. (2013). *Resistance and resilience: The education trajectories of young women of color with disabilities through the school to prison pipeline* (Doctoral dissertation), University of Colorado at Boulder.

Annamma, S. A. (2015). Whiteness as property: Innocence and ability in teacher education. *The Urban Review, 47*(2), 293–316.

Annamma, S. A., & Morrison, D. (2018). DisCrit classroom ecology: Using praxis to dismantle dysfunctional education ecologies. *Teaching and Teacher Education, 73*(2018), 70–80.

Annamma, S. A., Connor, D., & Ferri, B. (2013). Dis/ability critical race studies (DisCrit): Theorizing at the intersections of race and dis/ability. *Race Ethnicity and Education, 16*(1), 1–31.

Artiles, A. J. (2002). Culture in learning: The next frontier in reading difficulties research. In R. Bradley, L. Danielson, & D. P. Hallahan (Eds.), *Identification of learning disabilities: Research to policy* (pp. 693–701). Lawrence Erlbaum.

Artiles, A. J., & Kozleski, E. B. (2010). What counts as response and intervention in RTI? A sociocultural analysis. *Psicothema, 22*(4), 949–954.

Au, W. (2016). Meritocracy 2.0: High-stakes, standardized testing as a racial project of neoliberal multiculturalism. *Educational Policy, 30*(1), 39–62.

Beauboeuf-Lafontant, T. (2002). A womanist experience of caring: Understanding the pedagogy of exemplary Black women teachers. *The Urban Review, 34*(1), 71–86.

Beauboeuf-Lafontant, T. (2005). Womanist lessons for reinventing teaching. *Journal of Teacher Education, 56*(5), 436–445.

Brantlinger, E. A. (Ed.). (2006). *Who benefits from special education?: Remediating (fixing) other people's children*. Routledge.
Broderick, A. A., & Leonardo, Z. (2016). What a good boy. In D. J. Connor, B. A. Ferri, & S. A. Annamma (Eds.), *DisCrit-disability studies and critical race theory in education* (pp. 55–67). Teachers College Press.
Clandinin, J. (2013). *Engaging in narrative inquiry*. Left Coast Press.
Collins, P. H. (2002). *Black feminist thought: Knowledge, consciousness, and the politics of empowerment*. Routledge.
Creswell, J. W., & Creswell, J. D. (2017). *Research design: Qualitative, quantitative, and mixed methods approaches*. SAGE.
Davis, L. P., & Museus, S. D. (2019). What is deficit thinking? An analysis of conceptualizations of deficit thinking and implications for scholarly research. *NCID Currents, 1*(1), 117–130.
Deschenes, S., Cuban, L., & Tyack, D. (2001). Mismatch: Historical perspectives on schools and students who don't fit them. *Teacher College Record, 103*(4), 525–547.
Erevelles, N. (2000). Educating unruly bodies: Critical pedagogy, disability studies, and the politics of schooling. *Educational Theory, 50*(1), 25–47.
Ferguson, P. M., & Nusbaum E. (2012). Disability Studies: What is it and what difference does it make? *Research and Practice for Persons with Severe Disabilities, 37*(2), 70–80.
Ferris, S. J. (2014). Revoicing: A tool to engage all learners in academic conversations. *The Reading Teacher, 67*(5), 353–357.
Fine, M. (2016). Just methods in revolting times. *Qualitative Research in Psychology, 13*(4), 347–365.
Florian, L. (2012). Preparing teachers to work in inclusive classrooms: Key lessons for the professional development of teacher educators from Scotland's inclusive practice project. *Journal of Teacher Education, 63*(4), 275–285.
Freire, P. (1970/2000). *Pedagogy of the oppressed* (30th anniversary edition). Continuum.
Garland-Thomson, R. G. (2017). *Extraordinary bodies: Figuring physical disability in American culture and literature*. Columbia University Press.
Giangreco, M. F., & Suter, J. C. (2015). Precarious or purposeful? Proactively building inclusive special education service delivery on solid ground. *Inclusion, 3*(3), 112–131.
Gist, C. D., White, T., & Bianco, M. (2018). Pushed to teach: Pedagogies and policies for a Black women educator pipeline. *Education and Urban Society, 50*(1), 56–86.
Gorski, P. (2008). The myth of the "culture of poverty." *Educational Leadership, 65*(7), 32–36.
Gresham, F. M., Watson, T. S., & Skinner, C. H. (2001). Functional behavioral assessment: Principles, procedures, and future directions. *School Psychology Review, 30*(2), 156–172.
Harry, B., & Klingner, J. (2007). Discarding the deficit model. *Educational Leadership, 64*(5), 16–21.

Hernández-Saca, D. I., Pearson, H., & Voulgarides, C. V. (Eds.). (2020). Call for Chapter Proposals for New Co-Edited Book at Lexington Press. *Understanding the boundaries between Disability Studies and Special Education through consilience, self-study, and radical love*. Lexington Press.
Higheagle Strong, Z., & McMain, E. M. (2020). Social emotional learning for social emotional justice: A conceptual framework for education in the midst of pandemics. *Northwest Journal of Teacher Education, 15*(2), 1–11.
Iqtadar, S., Hernández-Saca, D. I., & Ellison, S. (2020). "If it wasn't my race, it was other things like being a woman, or my disability": A qualitative research synthesis of disability research. *Disability Studies Quarterly, 40*(2).
Kendi, I. X. (2019). *How to be an antiracist*. One world.
Kincheloe, J. L. (1991). *Teachers as researchers: Qualitative inquiry as a path to empowerment*. Falmer Press.
Kohli, R., & Pizarro, M. (2016). Fighting to educate our own: Teachers of color, relational accountability, and the struggle for racial justice. *Equity & Excellence in Education, 49*(1), 72–84.
Kozleski, E. B. (2020). Disrupting what passes as inclusive education: Predicating educational equity on schools designed for all. *The Educational Forum, 84*(4), 340–355.
Kozleski, E. B., Artiles, A., & Waitoller, F. (2013). Equity in inclusive education: A cultural historical comparative perspective. In L. Florian (Ed.), *The SAGE handbook of special education: Two volume set* (pp. 231–250). Sage Publications.
Kurth, J. A., Morningstar, M. E., & Kozleski, E. B. (2014). The persistence of highly restrictive special education placements for students with low-incidence disabilities. *Research and Practice for Persons with Severe Disabilities, 39*(3), 227–239.
Leonardo, Z., & Broderick, A. (2011). Smartness as property: A critical exploration of intersections between whiteness and disability studies. *Teachers College Record, 113*(10), 2206–2232.
Lingard, B., & Mills, M. (2007). Pedagogies making a difference: Issues of social justice and inclusion. *International Journal of Inclusive Education, 11*(3), 233–244.
Love, B. L. (2019). *We want to do more than survive: Abolitionist teaching and the pursuit of educational freedom*. Beacon Press.
Michaels, S., O'Connor, C., & Resnick, L. B. (2008). Deliberative discourse idealized and realized: Accountable talk in the classroom and in civic life. *Studies in philosophy and education, 27*(4), 283–297.
Milner IV, H. R., Cunningham, H. B., Delale-O'Connor, L., & Kestenberg, E. G. (2018). *"These kids are out of control": Why we must reimagine "classroom Management" for equity*. Corwin Press.
Morris, M. W. (2018). *Pushout: The criminalization of Black girls in schools*. The New Press.
Naraian, S., & Schlessinger, S. (2017). When theory meets the "reality of reality": Reviewing the sufficiency of the social model of disability as a foundation for teacher preparation for inclusive education. *Teacher Education Quarterly, 44*(1), 81–100.

Osborne, T. (2019). Not lazy, not faking: teaching and learning experiences of university students with disabilities. *Disability & Society, 34*(2), 228–252.

Oyler, C. J. (2017). Constructive resistance: Activist repertoires for teachers. *Language Arts, 95*(1), 30–39.

Paris, D. (2012). Culturally sustaining pedagogy: A needed change in stance, terminology, and practice. *Educational Researcher, 41*(3), 93–97.

Paris, D., & Alim, H. S. (Eds.). (2017). *Culturally sustaining pedagogies: Teaching and learning for justice in a changing world.* Teachers College Press.

Pizarro, M., & Kohli, R. (2020). "I stopped sleeping": Teachers of color and the impact of racial battle fatigue. *Urban Education, 55*(7), 967–991.

Roberts, E. L., Ju, S., & Zhang, D. (2016). Review of practices that promote self-advocacy for students with disabilities. *Journal of Disability Policy Studies, 26*(4), 209–220.

Saldaña, J. (2021). *The coding manual for qualitative researchers.* SAGE.

Siddle Walker, V. (2013). Ninth annual Brown lecture in education research: Black educators as educational advocates in the decades before Brown V. Board of Education. *Educational Researcher, 42*(4), 207–222.

Sleeter, C. E. (1986). Learning disabilities: The social construction of a special education category. *Exceptional children, 53*(1), 46–54.

Sleeter, C. E., & Carmona, J. F. (2017). *Un-standardizing curriculum: Multicultural teaching in the standards-based classroom.* Teachers College Press.

Taylor, S. J. (1988). Caught in the continuum: A critical analysis of the principle of the least restrictive environment. *Journal of the Association for Persons with Severe Handicaps, 13*(1), 41–53.

Tyack, D. B. (1974). *The one best system: A history of American urban education* (Vol. 95). Harvard University Press.

Varenne, H., & McDermott, R. (2018). *Successful failure: The school America builds.* Routledge.

Waitoller, F. R. (2020). Why are we not more inclusive? Examining neoliberal selective inclusionism. In C. Boyle, J. Anderson, A. Page, & S. Mavropoulou (Eds.), *Inclusive education: Global issues and controversies* (pp. 89–107). Brill Sense.

Waitoller, F. R., & King Thorius, K. A. (2016). Cross-pollinating culturally sustaining pedagogy and universal design for learning: Toward an inclusive pedagogy that accounts for dis/ability. *Harvard Educational Review, 86*(3), 366–389.

Watson, W. (2019). We got soul: Exploring contemporary Black women educators' praxis of politicized care. *Equity & Excellence in Education, 51*(3–4), 362–377.

Watson, W., & Devereaux, C. A. (2020). Keeping it relevant: Student-centered reflections, choices, and actions of critical race womanist pedagogues. *Urban Education, 57*(4), 571–599.

Watts, I. E., & Erevelles, N. (2004). These deadly times: Reconceptualizing school violence by using critical race theory and disability studies. *American Educational Research Journal, 41*(2), 271–299.

Yoon, I. (2019). Rising above pain: An autoethnographic study on teaching social justice as a female teacher of color. *Journal of Cultural Research in Art Education, 36*(2), 78–102.

Young, K. S. (2007). *Social constructions of disability and typicality in a combined credential program.* University of California, Berkeley.

Chapter 14

Blurring Boundaries

Dreaming/s of a Neurodivergent-Teacher-Parent-Student-Researcher

Ananí M. Vasquez

Are dreams powerful enough to surpass large-scale limitations, such as disciplinary boundaries, that are the foundation for systemic injustice in education? Dreaming, or envisioning possible futures, can open current discourses to new directions. In this chapter, I engage in methodological dreaming/s to envision possible future realities that blur the "educations" (i.e., special, general, gifted, and bilingual education) and disability studies in education (DSE) through critical self-reflection. This prelude lays the foundation for dreaming/s (Arndt & Tesar, 2019) as an autoethnographic self-study (Hamilton et al., 2008; Mena & Russell, 2017) and exploration of the tensions between seemingly disparate fields. Because emergence is a premise for this writing, disability language will alternate to reflect various points of view (e.g., person-first, identity-first).

DREAMING/S, SELF-STUDY, AND AUTOETHNOGRAPHY

Because our society has for so long polarized the "educations" and DSE, it is difficult to imagine consilience. As an educational researcher with intersectional identities relevant to the topic, I will endeavor to imagine consilience (Wilson, 1999)—the unity of knowledge—through dreaming/s, by presenting actual and virtual realities across educational spaces (Arndt & Tesar, 2019). I use dreaming/s because the idea offers "an opportunity to enter productive methodological spaces that enable the emergence of events and questionings that would otherwise remain invisible and silent in 'the real world'" (Arndt

& Tesar, 2019, p. 136). The dreaming/s presented here emerges through writing and in conversation with scholarly literature across the fields of special education, gifted education, and DSE. Drawing on the basic elements of self-study, this dreaming/s is self-initiated, improvement-oriented, and interactive and integrates multiple genres for trustworthiness (Hamilton et al., 2008; Mena & Russell, 2017). Drawing on autoethnography, this dreaming/s "brings forward shifting aspects of self and creates ways to write about experiences in a broader social context" by displaying "multiple layers of consciousness" and disrupting ableist discourses in the educational "world" (Hamilton et al., 2008, p. 22). By merging self-study and autoethnography in this way, I speak both to change within myself as well as possible change for my educational world, in which I am always already entangled with people, processes and objects.

Dreaming/s: Writing for self-study. In this chapter, dreaming/s emerge(s) as an autoethnographic self-study through writing in which I position myself in more-than-human ontology, as in-process, becoming-with others, human and nonhuman, across time, space, and realities. Arndt and Tesar (2019) perceive dreaming/s "as a challenge to our ability to respond to and engage with wider possible 'real worlds' of methodological narrative and our complex relations with/in it," or entanglements with the many aspects of our environment (p. 136). Writing is thinking, analysis, a method of discovery (Richardson & St. Pierre, 2018) as well as playful, porous, incomplete, and an articulation that puts discourses into motion (Carlson, 2020). Dreaming/s through writing generates a productive space for new thought by questioning personal perceptions and orientations and is a valuable technique for recognizing discourses in motion (Arndt & Tesar, 2019).

As a neurodivergent-teacher-parent-student-researcher and becoming-teacher educator, I explore self through dreaming/s as a starting point for transforming "the real world" of education, blurring boundaries toward multiple possible future realities. I am a self-identified neurodivergent individual, a Mexican American teacher, with experience in general, special, gifted, and bilingual education, and a parent to medically and educationally categorized children. As neurodivergent, I acknowledge personal modes of perception, communication, and interaction that are markedly different from what is considered typical in U.S. culture and that often aligns with those expressed by many late-diagnosed autistic women. I have been a student, formally, across four decades. The classroom has been my world, one with many realities. Many past experiences converge to form my current iteration of "self" as a doctoral student. It is in this space of emergence that I initiate this self-study.

Through this study, I propose to not only blur the siloed "educations" and disability studies with(in) the "educations" but also the perception of binary boundaries between teacher and student and typical and atypical individuals.

Through this process, I hope to clarify my own assumptions about disability and educational systems while aiming to improve my professional practice. This dreaming/s is interactive and includes multiple methods. My self-study occurs in conversation with the scholarly literature, through reflections with my doctoral reading group and the many individuals with whom I have shared memories and stories. Multiple genres, such as memories, dialogues, pictures, narratives, and scholarly quotes, play between the boundaries of consciousness, fiction and nonfiction, and virtual and actual. I address trustworthiness by disclosing my theoretical position and personal intersectional identities and by opening this chapter to readers for continued collaborative reflection.

Autoethnographic dreaming/s. Although personal and professional improvement is one aim of this study, I also have a broader objective. In the traditional sense of autoethnography, I will state the discourses I wish to critique in the next section and will link my experiences with these cultural issues (Wall, 2016). It is my hope that this chapter will motivate readers to engage in critical self-reflection and lead to institutional critique of disability discourses in the current educational systems.

Consilience of the "Educations" and Disability Studies in Education

Formal learning experiences usually occur through the "educations," especially general, special, and gifted, which have been siloed into distinct departments for factory-like efficiency. These silos have different priorities, discourses, and practices, which have been influenced by their historical emergence along the field of teacher education timeline (Blanton et al., 2014; Rapp & Arndt, 2012). The "educations" have only recently begun to address some of the main tenets of disability studies, such as the social construction of disability, full citizenship in the classroom, and the disability justice principle of intersectionality (Berne et al., 2018; Jung et al., 2019; Rapp & Arndt, 2012). Intersectionality "highlights the need to account for multiple grounds of identity when considering how the social world is constructed" rather than ascribing identity by one attribute, such as race or disability (Crenshaw, 1991, p. 1245). Although these issues are beginning to be foregrounded, the structural separation of the "educations" limits educational transformation.

General and special education, backed by federal funding on large scales, are the dominant silos in education. Gifted education, supported only by state laws and intermittent funding, has often been devalued due to social and ethical issues in its history, such as its entanglement with elitism and eugenics (Dai, 2020; Lemann, 2000). Both gifted and special education have roots in medical and psychological domains through the development of the IQ test and have heavily focused on evaluation and placement (Blanton et al., 2014;

Dai, 2020; Kaufman, 2013; 2018). Subsequently, these practices have led to the ongoing underrepresentation of students from minoritized groups in the first and an overrepresentation in the second (Waitoller, 2020; Yaluma & Tyner, 2020). Perhaps they remain two separate fields in order to bracket, or manage, who is included or excluded from general education (see Padia & Traxler, 2020; Siuty, 2019). Thankfully, beginning in the 1970s, both fields began to undergo shifts; gifted education toward talent development and special education toward inclusion (Dai, 2020; Kaufman, 2018; Rapp & Arndt, 2012). Only recently, though, has there been focused discussion of merging these concepts through strength-based schooling (Armstrong, 2012; Kaufman, 2013). If general, special and gifted education continues to remain siloed, prospects for meeting the needs of each whole, multidimensional child are dismal.

Although there are divides between the "educations," dominant general education discourses resulting from colonization, or white supremacy, including those of standardization and ableism, greatly influence gifted and special education as well (Padia & Traxler, 2020). For the past fifty some years, the focus of education has been on standardization, learning large amounts of information, getting good grades, scoring high on tests, and getting into a good college (Rapp & Arndt, 2012; Rose, 2016; Sawyer, 2019). Although the needs of the workforce have changed, this mindset continues to prevail, promoting conformity and "one-size-fits-all" curriculum and instruction. Rose (2016) states:

> We continue to enforce a curriculum that defines not only what students learn, but also how, when, at what pace, and in what order they learn it. In other words, whatever else we may say, traditional public education systems violate the principles of individuality. (p. 188)

Students, as sorted, quality-controlled, products are unsupported in identity and talent development. Dai (2020) eschews the sorting mindset and advocates for a rethinking of human potential so that all students have access to learning opportunities that build on strengths and supply supports in needed areas.

While this strength-based, human potential mindset offers promise of consilience, Siuty (2019) explains that the school system's ableist implicit and explicit rules supersede attempts to blur the educations in the best interest of the individual student. Special and gifted education are constrained by general education ableist expectations as "students are not seen as individuals, but as entities to be categorized and expected to perform on an often limiting and inaccurate label" (Rapp & Arndt, 2012). Special education teachers tend to be the "gatekeepers" of general education access for students with disabilities (Siuty, 2019). In the same way, access to gifted education often occurs through general education teachers and school psychologists (Ottwein, 2019). This "gatekeeping," along with other white supremacist structures and practices, contributes to the disproportionality in representation of students, especially for students at intersections of race, disability, giftedness, gender, and language (Fish, 2017). Although disproportionality is a complex issue, it has been posited that increasing the numbers of teachers of color (Fish, 2019) as well as training in cultural differences for all teachers could mitigate the problem as "educators tend to see Whiteness as the norm and consequently the academic skills, behavior, and social skills of African American and other students of color are constantly compared with those of their White peers" (Blanchett, 2006, p. 27). Beyond teacher gatekeeping, the "norm" in education is also systematically based on white standards and "abilities" (Annamma et al., 2013; Dudley-Marling & Gurn, 2010).

Once a student has passed that gatekeeper and is "accepted," individualized educational programming tends to be deficit-focused for students receiving special education services, limited by funding for students receiving gifted services and biased, either deficit-focused only or talent-focused only, for students in both gifted and special education (Baum & Novak, 2010; Jung et al., 2019; Worrell et al., 2019). Additionally, students of color tend to achieve gains more slowly and take longer to exit special education services than white peers (Blanchett, 2006) and students in schools with high poverty tend to have less funding for gifted programming than more affluent, white schools (Crabtree et al., 2019). The related identification processes and service delivery methods continue to violate student "principles of individuality" (Rose, 2016, p. 188). Rose lists the three principles of individuality as: (a) the jaggedness principle, representing a multidimensional understanding of talent rather than one-dimensional; (b) the context principle, representing a situational shifting of personality rather than fixed traits; and (c) the pathways principle, representing the idea that each person's path is unique rather than the idea that all people should follow a normative path. Identification processes are based on essentialist and normative principles. Strength-based programs, including talent development, are rare and typically are reserved for identified gifted students only (Sabatino & Wiebe, 2018).

Identification and identity take on new meanings through a DSE lens. In the educational system, access to needed supports for a student requires a label. Societal stigma around disability labels, including the belief that disability is bad, scary, and that it creates a general inability or dependence on abled people, is an ongoing lived reality for families (Brown, 2013; Davis, 2013; Longmore, 2013; Rapp & Arndt, 2012). Jung et al. (2019) state that although technology and workplace innovations have grown from the participation of intersectional individuals with and without disabilities

"... school remains a place where these intersections are systematically minimized" due to centuries of working within the medical model, focusing on impairment rather than on the understanding that disability is a "social construct that is shaped by policy, theory, and ethics" (p. 3). DSE proponents perceive disability as a social construct. Disability, along with race, culture, language, gender and economic status, influence identity, and students should not be separated based on one dimension of their intersectional identities (Jung et al., 2019). Individuals, with their unique and varied characteristics and whose identity emerges through social entanglements, can be full citizens in classrooms that are designed on the premises of DSE tenets. Importantly for educational researchers, these tenets also promote inquiry that (a) views disability as a social-political construct, (b) privileges the voices of people with disabilities, (c) promotes inclusive education, and (d) always assumes competence (Hunter, n.d.).

Possible realities of consilience can be imagined by exploring the tensions between the "educations" and DSE through self-study. The first section of dreaming/s emerges as memories, quotes, pictures, and imaginings and is followed by an interlude. In the interlude, I question how dreaming/s might move thought toward consilience of the "educations" and DSE and how this change might affect my practice as an educational researcher and teacher educator. The second dreaming/s emerges as one imagining of a classroom in 2040. Finally, the coda serves as a conclusion that does not conclude but continues to question.

DREAMING/S

To this point, the text in this chapter has been academic, expository, and didactic. Dreaming/s will now shift away from explicating, toward a thinking-feeling and a reflecting-speculating. In the original manuscript, textboxes and photographs were interspersed throughout these sections. Captions and bolded titles were inserted in various locations to assist the reader in drifting between dreaming/s, which might initially seem disconnected or surreal. Because of publishing standards, most of these visual cues have been removed. It is, therefore, left to the reader to detect the, sometimes abrupt, shifts in tone and feel of the dreaming/s that the reader is invited to dream with.

Multidisciplinary Evaluation Team Meeting (MET) 2:

I am warm, crinkled tightly in the folds of her hand, as she shivers in the frigid, air-conditioned conference room. She sits stunned. "What does that mean?" The school psychologist says, "Intellectual disability ... in the past it was called mental retardation, but we don't use that word anymore." Her eyes fill and one teardrop lands on her hand, slowly leaking in to find my tissue-paper embrace. "It doesn't mean your daughter won't be able to do the things you have dreamed she would do. She can still have a job, get married, have children, live a happy life. It just means she will need extra support along the way, at school and with life skills." I am there to dry the tears, hide the expression, and bring solace.

Medical Evaluation 1:
I dig blindly through my purse for a tissue. Dr. Burgess has just given her final assessment. Moderate Autism Spectrum Disorder. "How will I tell my husband?" I say, as my son lays his head on my lap. But what I mean is, "How am I going to do this?" My husband knew, had suggested the evaluation. Even my special education degree had not prepared me for this.

Home:
The kids are finally asleep after two hours of rocking my oldest and letting my youngest cry himself to sleep. The exhaustion is bone deep. "What if it is autism?" I ask my husband. "Then we'll deal with it. You're the teacher. You'll know what to do, or you'll figure it out." "But if he has autism, then so do I."

I . . . I . . . me . . . me . . . we . . . *have* AUTISM.

After MET 1:
We have been here for almost an hour. Since we were out of Spanish copies of the developmental history form, I am orally translating. Mom seems so happy to have someone who takes her seriously. She tells me about the family's experiences at the last school. They were told that their child behaved badly because of their lack of parenting skills. Mom tells how they would pry their screaming child from the car to get him into the school building. Dad feared the truancy officer but was worn out with the daily struggle. I cannot count the number of times they thank me and our school staff for finally listening.

THANK YOU for *hearing* us, *believing* us, being there for us.

Kindergarten day 2:
The coolness of the smooth wood beneath my fingers is calming. I place five blocks down in a line, then stack four on top, centering them. Everything else in the room is blurred as I focus. There is a low hum and a sense of colors, shapes and movement, but the blocks have my attention. Together we create. "Oh!" I have forgotten to check the chair where my mom has been sitting. It's empty! My stomach twists and I cannot breathe. Out the door I run. She is not there. I keep running.

Keep running.
Keep running.

At the park:
My son runs to the playground. He wiggles his little body in the sand, smiling as thousands of grains find their way down his shirt and into his shorts. A sand mosaic designs his sweaty face. He stands up and jogs off. I sigh and call him back, but he keeps going. I follow him, repeating my command. He giggles and runs. I reach him just before he steps into the busy street. Grasping at the solidness of his body, I feel only fluid movement as he sifts into sand through the deceptive security of my arms. I stand alone in a barren desert. The deep anguish of failure rising to a shattering scream.

Support group:
"At least I know now and can start to figure out how to help my son." Smiling and nodding, I think to myself, "Yes, it's a start, but it's a long journey. Be prepared to learn as much about yourself as your child."

After adult autism evaluation:
Back in my car, I pop some gum in my mouth, chew, chew. "You do not qualify as an individual with autism. Most likely you have had enough life experiences to overcome any of its limitations." I think back to the evaluation tasks. Tasks I might have used with very young children. I wonder . . . if they had placed me in a noisy, bright room full of strangers for a sudden meet-and-greet . . .

Related quote:

> Despite the fact that legislative loopholes, budget problems, and lack of public awareness still prevent many eligible students from receiving the services they deserve, one must stand back and marvel at the progress that has been made in special education since the 1950s, when only a handful of children with particularly severe needs were served in the schools, if they were served at all . . . it is far better for a child to have her special learning needs identified and addressed in school rather than to languish unrecognized in a regular classroom or be excluded from school entirely . . . concerned . . . negativity . . . *disability, disorder, deficit . . . dysfunction* . . . what they *can't* do rather than on what they *can* do. (Rapp & Arndt, 2012, p. 3) [emphasis added]

Parent conference:
"It's nice to meet you. I'm enjoying getting to know Roberto. I love his humor and he is a great helper." His mother replies, "Es burro, I know. He doesn't listen. He's just lazy." I hope that I can convince her that her child really is a pleasure to have in class. And help her understand learning disabilities.

Burro: Spanish word for donkey, also derogatory term for someone who is perceived as dumb, stubborn and/or lazy.

Biblioburro: A hardworking animal that, with his person, brings books to rural areas.

Burro, or burrito: Sustenance, consisting of a non-descript pouch with a surprising filling of (multiplicities and potentialities of) ingredients, to be savored. In how many ways has this mother come across the stereotype of the *lazy Mexican*? At *work*, on *TELEVISION*, in movies? And why might she relate it to her own child, a child who is struggling to perform "normal?" (See, Bebout, 2018).

Gifted parent meeting:

A trickle of sweat weaves down the middle of my back as I stand up to greet everyone. Not expecting a full house, I had not requested a translator. I take a deep breath and go through the agenda in English and Spanish, explaining the gifted programming for the new school year as quickly as possible. When I open for questions, a very concerned father stands. In Spanish, he asks, "Entonces, *¿qué le pasa* a mi hijo? ¿Y cómo lo ayudamos? So what is *wrong* with my son? And how do we help him?" I am taken off guard. I have never had a parent of a newly identified gifted student ask that question.

Resource room (also, see discussion in interlude):

"I'm stupid. I can't read."

"You're a great problem solver, scientist, and you have deep thoughts about literature. We can work together on the reading decoding. Everyone learns differently and at different paces."

"Then why am I the only one in 5th grade who can't read? Everyone is supposed to learn the same way and at the same time. Go visit my class. You'll see."

New book:

"I'm stupid. I can't be read."

"Now honey, just give it time. Your illustrations are wonderful and they clearly support your written text."

"None of the people in this family have read me yet. I'm tossed from the shelf to the floor to the couch. I'm hardly ever opened at all! I was better off scraps of paper and drops of ink. Maybe I could've been folded into an airplane instead. Then, at least Bobby would have enjoyed me."

"Bobby will enjoy you someday. You must be patient."

"Bobby's mom loves YOU. She reads you almost every day."

"And look at me! Dog-eared, stained, ripped and written on. The life of a book is not easy."

"It's easier when you are loved. NOBODY likes me."

Related quote:

"The infinite variety of human attributes suggests that what is undesired or stigmatized is heavily dependent on the social context and to some extent arbitrarily defined" (Brown, 2013, p. 147).

Meeting neurodiversity:

"What are you?"
"A celebration."
"Not a disorder?"
"Human diversity."
https://www.youtube.com/watch?v=aWxmEv7fOFY

Related quote:
". . . change the conversation about students with special needs from a *disability* discourse to a *diversity* discourse" (Armstrong, 2012, p. 5)

CHANGE the conversation about students
from a *deficit* discourse to a *DIVERSITY* discourse.

Beginning of the school year:
Curriculum map: The third-grade team is expected to stick to me as closely as possible so that we can ensure that all content has been covered by the end of the year. 80% of your class should master each skill following my timeline. For those who do not, you will be designing Response to Intervention (RTI).
Me: I have students on IEPs in this class. Some of them learn better using methods other than the direct instruction that is outlined in the teacher's manual you have listed.
Curriculum map: Not my concern. You can supplement them with other methods, but the special ed teacher will worry about that in the resource room.
Base-ten blocks: (Sighs)
Related quote:
"So we are left with our current educational system: serving all students, with variable success, and facing struggles in funding, achievement, and assessment" (Rapp & Arndt, 2012, p. 28).
Research interviews:
As I prepare for my third interview, I think back to the other teens I have spoken with. Each, very open about injustice and the bullying occurring in their schools. A deep rooted unacceptance of difference. What started as a study on school climate for twice exceptional students has become much more. Race and giftedness. Gender, dyslexia, and anxiety. Just words? Identities? I would not wish their school experiences on anyone.

Spacing students.
Spacing students.
S   p   a   c   I   n   g   students

Related quote:
". . . real and imagined borders between general education and segregated special education spaces represent physical artifacts of social stigma around difference from a dominant norm . . ." (Siuty, 2019, p. 1033).

Kindergarten recess:
Screeech-scrat, screech-scrat. Forward, back, forward, back. I pat my spring horse on the head and gaze out onto the rest of the huge playground. The chaotic movement, the grouping and regrouping of children and equipment, the grass and sand flying; it seems senseless to my horse-friend and I. Screech-scrat, screech-scrat. Forward, back, forward. I slowly raise my hands and form a camera with my fingers. Then, I shift my fingers to make a tv screen. I pan, zoom in, focus, watch. Hmmm. I pan again, zoom in, watch. Children in their natural habitat, a curious animal. The "tv screen," like so much else, separates them from me.

Related quote:

. . .by creating a special category of teachers and paraprofessionals- helps reinforce the idea that students with disabilities are so different from their typical peers that a completely new branch of education needed to be developed . . . A very different way to structure special education would be in place if the social model of disability had been the theory that anchored decisions about how to provide a free appropriate public education for children with disabilities. (Rapp & Arndt, 2012, pp. 28–29)

A very different way to structure education would be in place if . . .

Differentiation and "enrichment" were available to all . . .
    Accommodations and modifications were available to all . . .
Individual students were taught by their jagged learning profiles . . .
    Supported   encouraged
        motivated
        confidence   care
  Creativity   uniqueness
    Each person and each gift indispensable.

Related quotes:
"In the 1800s, schools were often one room with a single teacher for all grades, and the teacher taught any child able to attend" (Rapp & Arndt, 2012, p. 33).

The social construction of special education includes thinking about labels, and that has sometimes led to treating individual children who have the same disability label as if they are all the same. The result has been programs that are designed to serve groups of children who may in actuality have very different needs. (Rapp & Arndt, 2012, p. 30).

The AUTISM Class

The GIFTED Program
The SPEECH Program
The School for the BLIND.

Student *with autism* or *autistic student*?
Student *with deafness* or *deaf student*?
Student *with giftedness* or *gifted student*?
Student *with tallness* or *tall student*?
Student *with nearsightedness* or *nearsighted student*?

Teacher's lounge:
Two IEPs walk into a teacher's lounge. They introduce themselves over lunch and, as always in the teacher's lounge, talk turns to students. IEPa is a veteran. He has been revised, reworked, and rewritten over the last few years, with the help of MET1 and MET2, to better design educational programming for student N. (IEPa is attempting to keep the student's name confidential, of course.)

IEPb: I'm so new to all this. How did your team design the best educational programming in the least restrictive environment (LRE) for N?
IEPa: Well, N has learning disabilities in reading decoding, math computation, and written expression. N needs a lot of repetition and small group tutoring. N gets frustrated and needs frequent breaks or else N has a meltdown and needs to be removed from the regular classroom. N has a behavior plan, with rewards and consequences. Plus, N's an English learner and doesn't have much support at home. It's definitely an uphill battle.
IEPb: Wow, it seems like N has many needs. So . . . frequent breaks, repetition, behavior plan . . .
IEPa: Yes, and N spends a lot of time in the resource room. N's about three years behind in math and four years behind in reading. We are working hard to get him caught up.
IEPb: It seems as if you and your team have your work cut out for you. My student will probably be receiving all services in the regular classroom. He has amazing artistic and mechanical skills. He holds deep discussions in literature, history and science and leads his class in mathematical problem solving. When I did a home visit, I found out that he speaks three languages, English, Spanish and Yaqui, which turns out to be a Native American language used across the

Arizona-Sonora border (Trujillo, 1997). I've been observing him this first week at school and I'm completely impressed.

IEPa: It doesn't sound like your student needs services at all. Why is he in special ed?

IEPb: Oh, he qualifies under various categories. In fact, he's just received a medical diagnosis of ADHD on top of his learning disability diagnoses. But his classroom environment has been designed to allow him flexibility in how he learns and does his work. He is able to use his strengths throughout the day, and those strengths are used to help him improve in his areas of challenge.

IEPa: He must not need repetition or have behavior problems if he is spending so much time in the regular classroom.

IEPb: Actually, memory is one of his challenges according to his latest eval, but it turns out that using hands-on, authentic tasks has really enhanced his learning retention. I guess having a real-life, whole body experience to hang an idea or fact onto makes all the difference for him.

(Lunch bell rings.)

IEPa: I've gotta scoot. I have a meeting afterschool to prepare for.

IEPb: Yeah, me too. It was nice talking to you!

(Later, the school dismissal bell rings.)

IEPa: Good afternoon, all.

IEPb: (Walks in behind IEPa) Good afternoon, good to see you again IEPa. Are you helping with the meeting today?

IEPa: Oh, it's N's IEP meeting. New school, but I'm sure we will just need to tweak a few things.

IEPb: Oh . . . um, I didn't realize your N was the same as my student, N. They sounded like completely different students.

Special Education Teacher: Good morning team. We have been working toward this day for the last few weeks with meetings, home visits, and classroom observations. N, you have shared some about your future aspirations. So today we will review all that we have compiled and design a new IEP. We are so happy to have N at our school this year. He has so many strengths that will be invaluable to his classmates.

IEPa: (bewildered) . . .

· · · _ _ _ · · ·

SOS

Movie theater:

My husband and I leave theater number 7 hand in hand heading toward the lobby exit. A couple walks toward us, hand in hand. One carries a drink and the other carries a bag of popcorn in their free hands. My heart and mind do a double take and I ask myself, "Why?" Why should it surprise me to see a couple with Down Syndrome doing the same thing I am doing? Conscious?

AWARE?
Woke?

Related quote:
". . . critical ability identity exploration, discussions on ability privilege, and ability bias assessments . . ." (Siuty, 2019, p. 1045)

Interlude

The first section of dreaming/s emerged as memories, imaginings, and stories. Many tensions between perceptions, emotions, feelings, affects, and orientations were felt, from stigma to acceptance, identification to identity, deficit to diversity, and standardization to individuality. Conflict arose through the play between the cold, sterile conference room and the comfort of a tissue or a listening ear, or the solid, little body and a grasping at loose sand. New perspectives also came to light in sharing the dreaming/s with others. One colleague mentioned, referring to the resource room memory above, that the words we use when talking with a student might unintentionally communicate to them that their feelings are wrong. In attempting to show a student that they are not stupid, we might overlook the need they have for us to *validate their feelings*. There is good reason for feeling stupid when we think about their lived realities. This needs to be considered before reciting a litany of their strengths to disprove their assertion of "being stupid," which only verifies that they are wrong again.

This emerging awareness of the tensions between orientations, conflicts between practices, and the possibility of unintentionally hurtful communications produces discomfort. At times, the disparities between values and practice become so evident as to create emotional and physical distress, much like the churning stomach I have felt when teaching in school environments that were not in line with my philosophy of teaching and learning. I have been grateful to have administrators that I could talk with openly about my concerns. But, even with open communication, the final verdict is "this is just the way it is" and "we do the best we can within the constraints we are given." For me, working in an educational system with a constantly churning gut was unbearable. Since teachers no longer had license to design environments for *mutual respect*, that demonstrated the belief that each student was able to think and contribute productively to the learning environment, I decided to leave elementary teaching for a doctoral program. And now, I face the same incongruencies from a new angle, as a becoming educational researcher and teacher educator.

The systematic injustices discussed in the prelude are present in all facets of education, and, whether a kindergarten teacher, a principal, or an educational researcher, one must become aware of their foundation on white supremacy and their far-reaching impact. The siloed "educations," standardization of curriculum, and gatekeeping are all part of the ableist educational culture new teachers are assimilated into at their first job, or even before, in teacher education programs and internships. With awareness, or knowledge, we can begin to move toward change with radical love (Fromm, 2000). Taking responsibility, with mutual respect and care, we might first begin by dreaming the possible, or even dreaming of that which seems impossible.

What if the educational system was based on the main tenets of DSE? How would roles, labels, services change? How would the IEP process change? How might the focus of education shift to one where all students are perceived as learners with potential, who need guidance in developing lifelong thinking, creative learning, and problem-solving practices? Might the general education system be restructured to support each student's strengths as much as areas of challenge? Where each teacher uses their individual strengths in collaboration with other teachers to get the job done? Where interdependence is appreciated over independence? What if educators just stopped thinking about: normal, average, deviant, control, manage, atypical, falling behind, behavior problem, special needs, advanced . . .? What if . . .?

Related quote:

"[R]ethinking human potential means generating a conception of human potential conducive to creating a system of education that provides opportunities for all yet promotes and accommodates to a variety of talent development trajectories and pathways conducive to realizing individuals' potential" (Dai, 2020, p. 6).

Dreaming/s

Juana greeted Roy as she set her coffee on a corner work table. She scooped up the white board markers and her planner. It would be a typical day for their homeroom class. Juana wrote the agenda on the white board:

Wednesday, September 10, 2040
8:00–8:20 Class meeting
8:20–9:50 Literacy Development
9:50–10:10 Health break
10:10–11:40 Math Development
11:40–12:10 Lunch and health break

12:10–1:40 Collaborative Projects, Apprenticeships, Electives or Seminars
1:40–1:50 Health break
1:50–3:20 Collaborative Projects, Apprenticeships, Electives or Seminars
3:20–3:30 Class check-in and dismissal

Meanwhile, Roy reviewed student schedules. During literacy development, Juana would hold individual reading conferences with Shawn, Maya and Pedro then would lead a small group of four students in a discussion on metaphors. They were also planning a metaphor skit to perform for the class next week. Roy had already updated the reading journal prompts and set up the laptops. He would begin with half the class, reviewing speech-to-text, text-to-speech, and online book access on the laptops. Then he would be holding reading conferences with Jake, Susana, and Mikey. During writer's workshop, an author would be skyping in. The students had already prepared questions for him. After, they would have about a half hour to work on their writing pieces. They were all at various points in the writing process. He and Juana would make sure everyone had updated their progress charts. Some students would be participating in peer writing conferences today as well. Roy checked his email for the guest author's confirmation.

Juana knew that Roy would have everything prepared for literacy development, so she prepared for math development. Wanda would be joining remotely for math, being that she is a five-year-old student in one of the early childhood homerooms across campus and her schedule did not allow for her to walk to their room. Juana made sure the projector and camera were ready to go. With this technology, Wanda would be able to work collaboratively alongside the multi-aged primary elementary students from this class. Today's whole group task was to design an aquarium that could hold 2 gallons of water. The students had already determined that 2 gallons would be needed to hold the number of goldfish they planned to purchase. Juana reviewed the teaching team's list of possible questions, concerns, and directions that the students might take during the task. This list included references to math content standards across early, primary, upper elementary and middle school bands, with a focus on process. The goal was to guide students in becoming mathematicians, critical and creative thinkers, and problem solvers. After the task, there would be about a half hour for practice work. Juana straightened up the shelf with manipulatives and games to ensure that the practice materials were easily accessible to every student. She would be playing multiplication games with a group of three and Roy would be playing time bingo with a few others.

Roy read the confirmation email from the author and heaved a sigh of relief. "Perfect! We are all set for this morning," he said to Juana. Afternoons had been a bit rough, but the students had finally adjusted to the transition to projects, electives, apprenticeships, and seminars. Most of the class would spread out across the school to work on various collaborative projects, take electives to learn more about specific domains, such as drama, basketball, geology, or woodwork, or participate in seminars delving into social issues. Zuleima, though, was apprenticing with a seamstress that came to work with her three times a week in the mentoring center. The other days of the week Zuleima practiced what she learned and worked on her own design project.

The phone rang. Juana answered and said, with wide eyes, "Ok, great, we will be ready!" before turning to Roy. "A new student! And class starts in 15 minutes." Roy smiled, "Just starting the transition process or did someone forget to keep us in the loop?" Juana laughed, "No, thank goodness. He is just starting the transition process. He'll be with us for the class meeting, then will be working on his learning profile in the welcome center and might check in to the class remotely at various times throughout the day to see what we are up to." He might be ready to fully transition to their homeroom class by Friday.

Between 7:50 and 8:00 AM, students trickled into the classroom, hanging their backpacks on wall hooks and finding a comfortable spot in the open area. Some sat on the floor, others pulled up a bean bag. Melody came in dragging her feet and said, "I can't seem to wake up today." Roy asked her to consider what activities might help her "wake up." She decided on one and headed to the back of the room to do some wall push-ups, then a few chin-ups on the installed bar. Joey overheard the conversation and shuffled over to the sink to splash water on his face. Juana and Roy joined the students on the floor. Melody walked toward the group, stopping only to pick up the talking stick. "Good morning everyone," she said, "Please remember to respect the person with the stick by waiting your turn to speak. Today, we will start with Jake. How are you? And what are you looking forward to today?" Jake responded and was about to pass the talking stick to the next person when the door opened. Nancy walked in with the new student and introduced him as Jerry. All eyes were suddenly on Jerry. Melody walked up to him and greeted him, then explained that they were having a class meeting and asked him if he would like to choose a spot to sit. He hesitated by the door watching everyone. Juana said, "Some students like to sit on the floor, others on the bean bags. Sometimes one of us will sit on a chair nearby or even stand up. It depends on how we feel that day." Jerry slowly sank into a chair at a table near the open space. Jake passed the talking stick to the next person. Once Roy was done with his turn, he passed it to Jerry and asked him, "How are you today, Jerry?" Jerry shrugged his shoulders and held out the talking stick, which was taken by Zuleima.

As the class moved to prepare for literacy development, Nancy called Jerry. Juana and Roy smiled at Jerry and told him that they were glad that he was going to be with this class and that they were looking forward to getting to know him better. Roy explained that everyone would be working on reading and writing projects next and that he could peek in on them from the welcome center's laptop. Jerry's eyes widened as he slowly walked out of the room, watching the students pull out boxes with books and folders or head over to the laptops. Students moved to different spaces in the room and settled in to work. One student was reading on a swing and another was walking in circles listening to something on headphones. Two students were reading together by the door.

Later that day, after bus duty Juana asked Roy, "Well, how do you think today went?" Roy considered his answer. Not everything had gone according to plan. There was that little accident during math that took a while to clean up. Susana hurt herself during a health break and was upset for half the morning. Wanda kept covering her camera, making the remote collaborative learning difficult. Amanda, the Somali language mentor, had been out sick. And they would need to brainstorm with Jake's elective teacher and the occupational therapist (OT) about how to leverage his strengths during painting tasks. But Roy said, "We have a wonderful class of neurodiverse students who respect each other, learn collaboratively and independently, and are learning to be reflective and self-directed learners and thinkers. They understand that learning is lifelong and that whatever they choose to do affects those around them. This is how I dreamed teaching would be as a student at the university."

Juana smiled and said, "I've heard stories about how things were done in the early 2000's. How could educators place students in programs according to test scores or disability labels? There were special teachers that taught groups of students based on those scores and labels instead of their individual learning profiles. And every ten-year-old had to learn from the same book and be evaluated on the same summative assessments as every other ten-year-old. As if they were clones! I'm happy to be teaching in 2040."

Juana and Roy stepped into the teacher's collaboration room to meet with Ananí, their professional development co-facilitator from the nearby university, and Don, the school co-facilitator. Everyone opened their eJournals for reflection. During the discussion, Pam, the school compliance officer, stopped in to mention some dates for IEP and therapist consultation meetings. Most of the real IEP preparation work happened beforehand through the learning profile process in place for all students. The therapist consultations were helpful for instructional planning for the whole class, as well as in the development of educational plans for students without the federally mandated IEPs. Nancy also stopped in with a preliminary learning profile for Jerry which outlined his strengths, challenges, and interests. Finally, the team turned to intern applications, reviewing philosophy, pedagogy, and diversity statements (in text, picture, and/or video essay formats), and began to consider which university students might fit well with their homeroom class.

Coda

In the last section, I endeavored to imagine consilience, through dreaming/s, by blurring the siloed "educations," disability studies with(in) the "educations," teachers with students, and typical with atypical, therefore transforming "the real world" of education into one possible future reality. Both sections of dreaming/s presented actual and virtual realities across educational spaces and times as a practice of autoethnographic self-study (Arndt & Tesar, 2019). Each of these, dreaming/s, self-study, and autoethnography provided different affordances for an emergent methodology. Dreaming/s provided a methodology for acknowledging emerging events and questions that are usually kept "silent in 'the real world'" (Arndt & Tesar, 2019, p. 136). As self-study, I initiated, through writing, an interactive and improvement-oriented space for acknowledging prevalent, but harmful, discourses in education; discourses for which I have personally partaken in as teacher, parent, and student, but am working toward exposing as a researcher. Also, because systemic change requires a cultural shift and the support of many, I called upon the use of autoethnographic practices when using "multiple layers of consciousness" and "shifting aspects of self" to write about experiences of broad social import (Hamilton, et al., 2008, p. 22). Public education is a social context that affects almost every person in today's world. The educational systems we have today are both products of our sociopolitical histories and progenitors of our possible sociopolitical futures.

The "educations" and disability studies each have distinct sets of values, theories, practices, and histories but converge at individual, human points within the public-school system. Systemic structures have been designed in ways that continually propagate disparities within and across these systems and most educators, having become acclimated to the current culture of education, are unaware of the part they play in upholding ableist and unjust systems (Siuty, 2019). The ongoing underrepresentation of students from minoritized groups in gifted education and their overrepresentation in the special education being only one example (Waitoller, 2020; Yaluma & Tyner, 2020). Because the tenets of DS are not often discussed in teacher education or during professional development, teachers often do not engage with social-political views of disability, interact with individuals with disabilities, envision fully inclusive schools, or even presume competence of all students (Hunter, n.d.; Rapp & Arndt, 2012). Self-study through dreaming/s is one strategy for questioning one's own perceptions and orientations of disability, ability, and education at the intersections of power and identities. In this chapter, I engaged in interactive critical self-reflection through writing, including memories, dialogues, pictures, narratives, and scholarly quotes to question my own assumptions. Autoethnographic self-study extends this thinking-writing to reflect on educational culture and possibilities for envisioning systemic change. In the last section, I imagined a possible future classroom by using a disability studies lens to sift through and merge effective teaching methods found across general, gifted, and special education. Consilience for the "educations" and disability studies, then, emerges through collaborative envisioning of possible multiple realities.

My journey through the "educations" and disability studies as a neurodivergent-teacher-parent-student-researcher and future teacher-educator continues. As we move forward interdependently, in collaborative self-study, in speculative dreaming/s and through radical love, let us continue to imagine and create future realities in education where school structures engender strength-based learning experiences for all students, promote lifelong learning, and practice thinking skills that lead to attainment of student aspirations, regardless of labels.

REFERENCES

Annamma, S. A., Boelé, A. L., Moore, B. A., & Klingner, J. (2013). Challenging the ideology of normal in schools. *International Journal of Inclusive Education, 17*(12), 1278–1294.

Armstrong, T. (2012). *Neurodiversity in the classroom: Strength-based strategies to help students with special needs succeed in school and life.* ASCD.

Arndt, S., & Tesar, M. (2019). Reconfiguring narrative methodologies: Thresholds of realities in post-qualitative methodologies. In S. Farquhar & E. Fitzpatrick (Eds.), *Innovation in narrative and metaphor* (pp. 133–145) Springer.

Baum, S. M., & Novak, C. (2010). Why isn't talent development on the IEP? SEM and the twice exceptional learner. *Gifted Education International, 26*(2–3), 249–260.

Bebout, L. (2018). US Latina/os and the white imagination. In L. G. Mendoza (Ed.), *The Oxford encyclopedia of Latina and Latino literature.* Oxford University Press. https://oxfordre.com/literature/view/10.1093/acrefore/9780190201098.001.0001/acrefore-9780190201098-e-647

Berne, P., Morales, A. L., Langstaff, D., & Invalid, S. (2018). Ten principles of disability justice. *WSQ: Women's Studies Quarterly, 46*(1), 227–230.

Blanchett, W. J. (2006). Disproportionate representation of African American students in special education: Acknowledging the role of white privilege and racism. *Educational Researcher, 35*(6), 24–28.

Blanton, L. P., Pugach, M. C., & Boveda, M. (2014, September). Teacher education reform initiatives and special education: Convergence, divergence, and missed opportunities. *CEEDAR Center.* https://ceedar.education.ufl.edu/wp-content/uploads/2014/09/LS-3_FINAL_09-20-14.pdf

Brown, L. C. (2013). Stigma: An enigma demystified. In L. J. Davis (Ed.), *The Disability Studies Reader* (pp. 147–160). Routledge.

Carlson, D. L. (2020). The (un)certainty of post-qualitative research: Textures of life-of-in-motion as articulation. *Qualitative Inquiry, 27*(2), 1–5.

Crabtree, L. M., Richardson, S. C., & Lewis, C. W. (2019). The gifted gap, STEM education, and economic mobility. *Journal of Advanced Academics, 30*(2), 203–231.

Crenshaw, K. (1991). Mapping the margins: Intersectionality, identity politics, and violence against women of color. *Stanford Law Review, 43*(6), 1241–1299.

Dai, D. Y. (2020). Introduction to the special issue on rethinking human potential: A tribute to Howard Gardner. *Journal for the Education of the Gifted, 43*(1), 3–11.

Davis, L. J. (2013). Introduction: Disability, normality, and power. In L. J. Davis (Ed.), *The Disability Studies Reader* (pp. 1–14). Routledge.

Dudley-Marling, C., & Gurn, A. (Eds.). (2010). *The myth of the normal curve* (Vol. 11). Peter Lang.

Fish, R. E. (2017). The racialized construction of exceptionality: Experimental evidence of race/ethnicity effects on teachers' interventions. *Social Science Research, 62*(2017), 317–334.

Fish, R. E. (2019). Teacher race and racial disparities in special education. *Remedial and Special Education, 40*(4), 213–224.

Fromm, E. (2000). *The art of loving: The centennial edition.* A&C Black.

Hamilton, M. L., Smith, L., & Worthington K. (2008). Fitting the methodology with the research: An exploration of narrative, self-study and auto-ethnography. *Studying Teacher Education, 4*(1), 17–28.

Hunter. (n.d.). Mission/statement of purpose of Disability Studies in Education. http://www.hunter.cuny.edu/conferences/dse-2012/mission-and-tenets-of-dse

Jung, L. A., Frey, N., Fisher, D., & Kroener, J. (2019). *Your students, my students, our students: Rethinking equitable and inclusive classrooms.* ASCD.

Kaufman, S. B. (2013). *Ungifted intelligence redefined: The truth about talent, practice, creativity, and the many paths to greatness.* Basic Books.

Kaufman, S. B. (2018). *Twice exceptional: Supporting and educating bright and creative students with learning difficulties.* Oxford University Press.

Lemann, N. (2000). *The big test: The secret history of the American meritocracy.* Farrar, Straus and Giroux.

Longmore, P. (2013). Heaven's special child: The making of poster children. In L. J. Davis (Ed.), *The Disability Studies Reader* (pp. 34–41). Routledge.

Mena, J., & Russell, T. (2017). Collaboration, multiple methods, trustworthiness: Issues arising from the 2014 International Conference on Self-study of Teacher Education Practices. *Studying Teacher Education, 13*(1), 105–122.

Ottwein, J. K. (2019). Working toward equitable gifted programming: The school psychologist's role. *Psychology in the Schools, 57*(6), 937–945. https://doi.org/10.1002/pits.22353

Padia, L. B., & Traxler, R. E. (2020). (Special) education is political; (Special) education is social justice. *Journal of Critical Thought and Praxis, 10*(1), Article 3.
Rapp, W. H., & Arndt, K. L. (2012). *Teaching everyone: An introduction to inclusive education.* Paul H. Brookes Publishing.
Richardson L., & St. Pierre, E. A. (2018). Writing: A method of inquiry. In N. K. Denzin & Y. S. Lincoln (Eds.), *The SAGE handbook of qualitative research* (5th ed.) (pp. 959–978). SAGE.
Rose, T. (2016). *The end of average: Unlocking our potential by embracing what makes us different.* HarperCollins.
Sabatino, C. A., & Wiebe, C. R. (2018). Bridges Academy: A strengths-based model for 2e. In S. B. Kaufman (Ed.), *Twice exceptional: Supporting and educating bright and creative students with learning difficulties* (pp. 301–321). Oxford University Press.
Sawyer, K. (2019). *The creative classroom: Innovative teaching for 21st-century learners.* Teachers College Press.
Siuty, M. B. (2019). Inclusion gatekeepers: The social production of spatial identities in special education. *International Journal of Qualitative Studies in Education, 32*(8), 1032–1047.
Trujillo, O. V. (1997). Tribal approach to language and literacy development in a trilingual setting. In J. Reyhner (Ed.), *Teaching indigenous languages* (pp. 10–21). Northern Arizona University.
Wall, S. S. (2016). Toward a moderate autoethnography. *International Journal of Qualitative Methods, 15*(1), 1–9.
Worrell, F. C., Subotnik, R. F., Olszewski-Kubilius, P., & Dixson, D. D. (2019). Gifted students. *Annual Review of Psychology, 70* (2019), 551–576.
Yaluma, C. B., & Tyner, A. (2020). Are U.S. schools closing the "gifted gap"? Analyzing elementary and middle schools' gifted participation and representation trends (2012–2016). *Journal of Advanced Academics, 32*(1), 1–26.

Chapter 15

I Still Have Joy

Disability Justice as Praxis, Theory, and Research in a Special Education Teacher Preparation Program

Gloshanda Lawyer

Black joy . . . most people imagine joy as feelings of happiness, lack of suffering or pain, all things positive. But Black joy goes much deeper than that. We know there was a time before all of this when we could exist freely as our whole selves and at some point I would like to get back to that. But in modern times, in these times, Black joy is inseparable from the struggle for freedom. In discussing the meaning of Black joy to them, one Black artist posed the question: What does it mean to take off into flight toward something you've always known to be true? We have always known that we are worth full humanity. We are worth full access to humanity no matter what and how our bodies and/or minds look like or how they function. As a person who has gone through the U.S. education system categorized as "gifted" (read: having a mind that functions in ways that are divergent but uplifted in many educational spaces) but who also had unaccommodated needs because giftedness does not fit with dependency; as someone who has been trained as a Special Education educator and researcher and now works within academia, I have come to the conclusion that you can't have authentic, fully actualized Black joy without Disability Justice and radical love. Because Black joy is resisting any system, any ideology, any group or individual that seeks to remove our worth or mold us into something that is "more acceptable" by a system that was never created to accept us. And that is what I have always known to be true.

As I reflect back on my past and present experiences, and now realizing that my experiences were not isolated to me (see Hernandez-Saca et al., 2020), I sense a collective resistance in this moment, which has been a recurring theme on this journey. My doctoral experience was a journey full of "resisting" both for myself and for others who did not look like me, but their struggles looked like mine. Yet, I was unprepared for the responses from classmates, potential future colleagues, professors and administrators within the Special Education department at my university, and even my students. We were in the South. I was one of two Black doctoral students in my department, a single mother, a multilingual, and an outsider (new to the state), with no support system. They were all White, all bought in to and were fully committed to the medical model of disability, and were all women. Did the visibility of my Blackness prevent them from recognizing my actions were rooted in radical love? Was it my refusal to accept my socially constructed position of inferiority that caused them to target my humanity? These were questions I often asked myself when I would openly discuss the intersections of disability and LGBTQIA identities and why we need to incorporate diverse reading materials in our pedagogical approaches. Or when I would discuss how Deaf, DeafBlind, DeafDisabled, and Hard of Hearing students of Color make up 50 percent or more of our K-12 student population in a teaching and interpreting field that is 90 percent White, cis-heterosexual, hearing, women, and Christian (my students were 100 percent White and hearing and 99 percent Christian and women) they need to be prepared to provide representation of Deaf, DeafBlind, DeafDisabled, and Hard of Hearing adults of Color. I would often get head nods in the classroom from students but then have formal letters of complaint filed against me with the head of the department (who was a former special education teacher and school psychologist and whose background and ideologies aligned more closely to my students and classmates than mine). Or in class when I would remind a classmate that it is important to not silence the comments of our Deaf classmate who has experienced personally and vicariously the traumas of the systems that have benefited you as a hearing White woman who only teaches Deaf students but gets to go home to unhindered communication access. And the result is a complaint to the department head that I am intimidating and silencing her professional expertise. As more and more of these experiences became my daily reality, as students tried to get me fired from my teaching assistant position (which they did not know was unpaid); as the department administrator told me I would never succeed in Special Education research and attempted to hinder my dissertation studies, tried to censor my dissertation chairs, and effectively prevented me from participating in my graduation ceremony; as my fellowship stipend and primary means of income were constantly "late" or "having an issue processing"; it was here that it became clear that the same system that criminalizes and vilifies People of Color is the same system that pathologizes Disabled bodies (Annamma, 2018). With this recognition of how the system was at play, I pressed forward to continue to operate in Disability Justice and radical love.

This critical autoethnography (Boylorn & Orbe, 2014) explores how I used Disability Justice at first unknowingly and then intentionally to center multiple points of difference within Special Education programs. Despite the many and persistent ways that my efforts toward radical love and justice were rejected and outright targeted, I pressed forward to expose my students and classmates to critical theories and concepts from Cultural Studies and Multicultural Education. Additionally, my Deaf White nonbinary classmate and I co-facilitated the transition of the Deaf and Interpreter Education department from a medical model of teacher training to a Bilingual, Bicultural model (more aligned with the social/cultural model of disability) infused with social justice throughout the program (Lawyer et al., 2020). I pressed forward by using American Sign Language (ASL) in classes so that my Deaf classmate could have direct communication access and not always receive second-hand information, even when White interpreters refused to voice for me. This meant I then had to re-state my own comments in English for our hearing classmates. I did all these things despite the reactions launched at me because radical love is not just about me. It's about humanizing us all so that we can all be accepted and free. It's about taking advantage of every moment possible to impact change and to be the change with the hope that these seeds will make a better society for future generations. And in that, I find joy.[1]

THE NECESSITY FOR CRITICAL AUTOETHNOGRAPHY

Critical autoethnography is an essential tool for sharing my experience as a practitioner, doctoral student, and now professor within Deaf Education, a field considered within the Special Education umbrella in the United States. Drawing roots from critical ethnography, critical autoethnography addresses lived experience of unfairness and injustice within a specific domain or context (Boylorn & Orbe, 2014). Critical autoethnography centers what Madison (2012) calls "politics of positionality" (p. 7) and how our positions of privileges oftentimes are in play with our experiences of marginalization (Boylorn & Orbe, 2014). The politics of positionality are often ignored within Special Education and professionals and researchers are essentialized as a collective group of helpers who are "benevolent, beneficial, and socially just" (Connor, 2013, p. 496). This benevolence is rooted in colonization and writhe with contradiction, seeking for students to be "taught to or helped to assimilate to prescribed norms . . ." (Coomer, 2019, p. 2) as a way to advance equality while simultaneously pathologizing their students at the intersections of dis/

ability and other marked identities (Thorius, 2019). Within Deaf Education all professionals wear the benevolent mask of what I call the "hearing helper" (Lawyer, 2022), entering the field to help "fix deafness" and research how "deafness" negatively impacts the life of an individual so that new interventions can be developed to improve the quality of life for those who are Deaf, DeafBlind, DeafDisabled, and Hard of Hearing. When the field automatically assumes this positionality for the professionals who enter it, there is no space created for self-reflection or to engage in questions about how our experiences impact those we purport to help.

Critical autoethnography is a method that allows me to make sense of who I am within the context of my profession, my advocacy, and my activism and the spaces these three aspects intersect in my life. In this space of intersection, critical autoethnography allows me to "write as an Other, and for an Other" (Boylorn & Orbe, 2014, p. 19). Though this story is about me and my actions, it is also about the ways I (un)successfully negotiated the interactions of various identities within the space of Special Education. Though I cannot detail all of my experiences here, I use my personal narrative to describe some ways I engaged in Disability Justice with the hopes that my experiences can serve as an example of ways to move forward and as a site of critique about who I am and how I approached this work. I do this by first situating Special Education in order to challenge ahistoricism about the field, describing where Disability Studies in Education fits in my experience because it can provide an ideological bridge leaving Special Education and moving toward Disability Justice, and then I explore Disability Justice and provide specific examples of how it saved by giving me a lens to analyze my lived experiences and how it challenged me to remove the boundaries between how I addressed Disability in my professional spaces and my personal spaces.

SITUATING SPECIAL EDUCATION

Special Education is a field that has historically been rooted in the medical model and deficit model regarding difference (Connor, 2013). It is important to know that *difference* from a medical model has not only been limited to how student bodies and minds function; difference has also applied to racialized groups, those who use one more multiple languages other than English, and those of lower social classes as these groups have often been disproportionately overrepresented in Special Education in the United States (Connor, 2013; Losen & Orfield, 2002). Ironically, from my observations, the professionals who enter the field of Special Education tend to be unaware of the overrepresentation and the pathologization of students from marginalized backgrounds (Artiles, 1998; Patton, 1998). Most Special Education programs do not call for critical self-reflection as one goes through coursework and student teaching. So it is important to name the stance of Special Education to understand why special educators' training, coursework, and pedagogical stances tend to perpetuate harm against marginalized and disabled populations of students.

The goal of Special Education is to (re)habilitate and minimize the effects of disability for better functioning in society. Analyzing the social, political, emotional, economic, and institutional contexts of schooling practices within U.S. capitalist society, "success is measured in a child's ability to participate and contribute to the social order and to contribute to society through gainful employment. As a result, schooling supports the existing social structure in a class-based society" (Lawyer, 2018, p. 91). Disability is perceived as disrupting the development of "socially moral" and "productive citizens" and creating dependence, therefore, in need of intervention to promote access to independence and future employment opportunities. This is why I focused my doctoral studies on expanding on how disability, race, class, heteronormativity, and other axes of identities are mutually constructed and maintained through colonization and capitalism.

Disability Studies in Education (DSE) provides a stance that is ideologically opposed to traditional Special Education approaches to teaching and research. There are several points of contrast worth highlighting here that are embodied in the tenets of DSE. First, while Special Education positions disability as an attribute within a person through a clinical and rehabilitative lens and ignores how systems are disabling and that *normalcy* is an unobtainable, intangible concept that changes so that certain people are excluded; DSE examines disability in how it is socially constructed within specific historical, social, and cultural contexts (Taylor, 2006) and this construction shifts based on said contexts and how it benefits those who are superordinated within oppressive systems (Connor, 2013). Second, I like to think of Special Education as akin to the banking model of education (Freire, 1970) wherein disabled children are likened to empty vessels, who by nature of their disability cannot contribute to their learning or society and are waiting to be filled by a competent/skilled and most often abled professional. Contrastingly, DSE assumes competence of disabled individuals (Connor et al., 2008); they have inherent value and much to offer society in their unique ways. The other two tenets of DSE (a) "privilege the interests, agendas, and voices of people labelled with disability/disabled people" and (b) "promote social justice, equitable and inclusive educational opportunities, and full and meaningful access to all aspects of society for people labelled with disability/disabled people" (Connor et al., 2008, p. 448). The ultimate goal of DSE is to effectively advocate for more meaningful educational inclusion (Connor et al., 2008).

GIVEN LANGUAGE AND A FRAMEWORK TO GROW WITH

The tenets of DSE draw parallels to those of Disability Justice. However, it is important to note that I came to DSE as a doctoral student because of and through my educational access/privilege, and I believe that if I had not entered a doctoral program, I would not have been exposed to DSE as a Special Education teacher or a Teacher for the Deaf. I came to Disability Justice more authentically through lived experience and interactions with those engaged in and living the work of Disability Justice. This is important to note because though DSE does important boundary work related to teaching pedagogy and research, I believe that Disability Justice engages across contexts and focuses particularly on our individual and collective actions. Talila Lewis (2016) described disability as:

> The tie that binds—it is represented across race, socio-economic class, gender, sexual orientation and faith. Black people, people of color, our indigenous and native nations, low and no income community members, and women, are all disproportionately represented in the class of disability [and therefore, needs a framework that] cuts across identities and movements. (para. 9)

That framework is Disability Justice. Disability Justice is a developing advocacy framework that was developed by disabled queers and activists of color Patty Berne, Mia Mingus, Leroy Moore, Stacey Milbern, Eli Clare, and Sebastian Margaret beginning in roughly 2005 (Sins Invalid, 2019). Disability Justice holds that in order to understand ableism, you must also address how it interrelates with white supremacy, capitalism, heteropatriarchy, and colonialism because these systems all construct an ideal body/mind (Berne, 2015). This framework understands that:

a) all bodies are unique and essential;
b) all bodies have strengths and needs that must be met;
c) we are powerful, not despite the complexities of our bodies, but because of them; and
d) all bodies are confined by ability, race, gender, sexuality, class, nation state, religion, and more, and we cannot separate them. (Sins Invalid, 2020)

Before coming to learn and witness Disability Justice in action, I had no idea that I was engaging in the work. My practice of justice spanned all areas of my life: my pedagogy as a teacher (as I journeyed to unpack my Applied Behavioral Analysis training, my Special Education training, and my Deaf

Education training and discern what was humanizing in my pedagogy and what was not); my life as a member of multiple marginalized communities; fight for food justice (Simpson, 2017) and access to social systems as a person who spent my early years living in poverty; my studies as a first generation college-turned doctoral student; my language justice as a multilingual person working with families of various countries and backgrounds; my budding educational research; and my approaches to training future teachers and interpreters for the Deaf. Yet I did not know I was doing Disability Justice work. From Disabled siblings engaging in Disability Justice work, I was gifted with the language to name my living praxis/practice. I learned about the ten principles of Disability Justice (Berne, 2015); Sins Invalid, and I share them with you here in the ways that I enacted them in Special Education contexts both past and present.

DISABILITY JUSTICE: MY IMPERFECT PRACTICE

We know that each person has multiple community identifications, and that each identity can be a site of privilege or oppression . . . the very understanding of disability experience itself being shaped by race, gender, class, gender expression, historical moment, relationship to colonization and more.—Berne, 2015

INTERSECTIONALITY

Having grown up in a predominantly Black U.S. and Latino community most of my life, I was used to knowing "Black and ____" or "Latino and ___" identity folk. They were "grannies" who were "forgetting things," cousins with seizure disorder, alcoholic "aunties," speed thinking/talking uncles, elders with cancer, grandmas with diabetes and high blood pressure needing help medicating themselves and the list goes on. This was my "normal." I didn't step out of that normal until I was 17 and went away to a predominantly white institution leaving the Deep South for Minnesota. In the nine years I lived there, I became accustomed to being the only one. I was often the only Black person in a 100 lecture auditorium or one of a handful in a 600 lecture course. I became hyper-visible in those years. In my master's degree in Special Education (focus on Deaf Education and Early Childhood Special Education), I was the only Black student for those two years. After completing my degree and entering the Deaf school, I was the first Black teacher in the school's twenty-five-year history; though there were a handful of Black and Brown (hearing and Deaf) paraprofessionals. Since my leaving in 2014, they have yet to hire another Black teacher however, they have increased the representation of Deaf Black and Brown U.S.-born and immigrant paraprofessionals. When I went into my doctoral program in Tennessee, the experience was the same. It's important to know that this is representative of the field of Deaf Education. Only about 10 percent of our field are People of Color; a huge underrepresentation of teachers and administrators when compared to the 50 percent plus student population of color. So it's not hard to believe that when I became a doctoral teachers assistant for the undergrad and master's level courses, I was the first Black, woman-identified, and the youngest teacher they had ever had.

I often discussed in my courses "Black and Brown and Indigenous" Disabled and Deaf children and the need to consider culturally appropriate ways of engaging with them and their families. After getting a few class sessions of getting blank looks, and after receiving a complaint that I was always discussing race and making my White women students feel oppressed, I asked them to explain the student populations they envisioned they would be working with. None of the fifteen students that first year, and only two of the nineteen the second year ever envisioned teaching Deaf or Disabled students of color. It never even crossed their minds. Yet in all my years of teaching, I could count on two hands the number of White Deaf students or White Disabled students I had worked with. I felt like I was constantly, unintentionally challenging every belief or idea my students held. For class assignments they would create lessons that required parents to purchase or provide materials. I would pose questions such as: why not use materials already available in the school, or design projects that are accessible to all students regardless of income level? I would give examples of how the lessons could be adapted or changed for something else that could accomplish the same language goals. Regarding language, students would often discuss the "word gap" and how that could be applicable to Deaf students. I would discuss that the word gap is actually classist, racist, and ableist in how the language "differences" are framed as a deficit. I provided historical evidence of how immigrant and Black U.S.-born children were often overrepresented in speech therapy. I would discuss how I previously worked with Deaf children who were physically disabled and labeled as nonverbal and how professionals assumed they were not intelligent. However, it was important to recognize how intersectionalities related to race, ability, class, and immigration status often played into these misconceptions. What I did not imagine was how difficult it would be for my students to internalize the information and experiences I had shared with them. After further unpacking, many of them had never interacted with a Deaf individual outside of the ASL teachers they had at the university. They had no idea that Deaf people could also be Disabled, could also be LGBTQIA+. It never crossed their minds that the experiences of low-income and no-income Deaf people would be different from those who came from wealthy backgrounds. They never conceptualized a multilingual Deaf person. All they imagined was Deaf, White, and users of ASL. I think as a professional, the naivety of my students who would become future teachers and interpreters, brought me to two realizations: (1) this was one of the first moments I became extremely fearful for Deaf, DeafBlind, DeafDisabled, and Hard of Hearing children from diverse language, class, gender, sexuality, SES, race, and ability and (2) now I understand why the state of Deaf Education is where it is. I knew then that my dissertation work would explore the experiences of multiply marginalized Deaf, DeafBlind, DeafDisabled, and Hard of Hearing within the U.S. schooling system.

Reflects our understanding of ableism in the context of other historical systemic oppressions, thus we are led by those who most know these systems.—Berne, 2015

LEADERSHIP OF THOSE MOST IMPACTED

I recall sitting in my doctoral seminar as my classmates and I discussed interventions for children with autism/autistic children. One classmate who also engages in Disability Justice work asked "what have the Autistic adults told you?" The ASL interpreters in the room stopped signing. The Typewell transcription cursor blinked with no words on the screen. The room fell silent for what felt like several minutes. Then the classmate responded: I have never met an adult with autism. I must have been unable to control the signs of shock displayed on my face. In his twenty years of experience in Special Education, he had never interacted with an adult who identified as having autism. And I could not understand how. I remember the first time an Autistic adult told me how applied behavioral analysis (ABA) traumatized them (see Broderick & Roscigno, 2021; Broderick, 2011; Roscigno, 2019). I remember going to Twitter and reading threads of other Autistic adults who felt the same way. And I cried that day. I cried because it took me back to when I worked as a bilingual behavior therapist for toddlers with autism. I went into their homes every day for 3-hour sessions and trained them and their parents using ABA. I remember the day my non-autistic supervisor applauded my ability to adhere to the "techniques," how I presented at my university for a class assignment in the Special Education department for my masters and the non-autistic professors wanted to recruit me into the Autism program track because of my "potential." I wondered how many little autistic spirits I had snuffed out and what kinds of trauma I caused. I wondered how long it would take those three-year-olds, then turned nine-year-olds to heal from the traumas I inflicted on them. From then on I decided to let the voices of Autistic adults guide me in my interactions with Autistic children and how to care for them and instruct them in humanizing ways. I thought about my classmate, and I wondered when he would (if ever) have that moment. I made it my goal to teach my students the importance of listening to Disabled adults because they have already lived the life we are trying to co-create with our students. They are the best knowers of what it takes to succeed as their authentic selves and therefore the ones who can best help us and our students imagine and obtain the future they want.

We value our people as they are, for who they are, and that people have inherent worth outside of commodity relations and capitalist notions of productivity.—Berne, 2015

RECOGNIZING WHOLENESS

We value the teachings of our lives and understand that our embodied experience as a critical guide and reference pointing us toward justice and liberation—Berne, 2015

SUSTAINABILITY

Keeping in mind the lessons I learned through my doctoral program with classmates and my future interpreter and teacher candidates in Special Education, I now as a professor make it a priority to uplift the voices of Deaf and Disabled students (of Color) in my courses. I realize that this is very delicate work and requires so much relationship building for it to be successful. In my experiences, I feel that I have had more successes building these relationships with my students who are most marginalized. I like to believe that is one of the ways I can recognize their wholeness. I try to also help others in the classroom recognize wholeness. Oftentimes in my courses I serve as moderator/facilitator for discussions because there is always a tension between the heterosexual, cisgender, White, hearing, often women-identified students who share from their professional perspectives/experiences and the Deaf, DeafDisabled, DeafBlind, and Students of Color who share from their lived experiences but may not yet have professional experience. When I notice these conversations have the potential to become unhealthy, I often remind the group of the importance of silent reflection. A person's lived experience holds so much value and it's worth holding space for that value to be shared and transmitted. Denying that is to convey that their lived experience is invalid, and no one has the right to invalidate someone's lived experience. Instead, you can silently reflect on what feelings are evoked in you and why those feelings are evoked. Unfortunately, I have been told by colleagues that this approach has been critiqued by some dominant group students as "silencing," as being "anti-hearing," and "anti-White." So it appears that while marginalized students feel they are able to find their voices in my courses, dominant group students feel that wholeness and sustainability are finite resources and that for one group to gain, means theirs must be taken away.

We bring flexibility and creative nuance to engage with each other, that we value exploring and creating new ways of doing things that go beyond able-bodied/minded normativity.... We can share responsibility for our access needs without shame—Berne, 2015

COLLECTIVE ACCESS

Bringing collective access into my coursework has been by far one of the most noticeably impactful practices for me and my students. It is one of the ways I feel radical love is most undeniable and quickly rewarding. For a field like Deaf Education which also includes DeafBlind students, it is surprising how many professionals have never had meaningful interactions with DeafBlind individuals. So when it comes to navigating a classroom space that is often labeled "visual space" because of the use of American Sign Language, there is often the question of how to accommodate a DeafBlind student. Many DeafBlind students now have their own intervener, tactile interpreter, support service provider (SSP), or Pro-Tactile interpreter. Therefore, many teachers rarely have direct (tactile) communication with their DeafBlind student. When I was a preschool teacher with DeafBlind students, I made it a goal to have direct instruction time or social time with my students. I learned their communication styles, I played directly with them, chatted directly with them, and encouraged their classmates to do the same. Now as a professor, that continued. Every DeafBlind student has different needs and preferences. Some may include large print, high contrast colors, slower pace of discussion, frequent breaks, etc. Now with our doctoral classes online via Zoom video conference, additional adaptations had to be made. Everyone in my courses is responsible for accessibility. Additionally, access and accommodations benefit everyone. This summer some of the ways we made accessibility work in a course taught in ASL: (a) prerecorded all lectures in ASL using a shirt that contrasted with my dark brown skin tone that was approved by the DeafBlind student, (b) include image descriptions for all images shared, (c) put my English notes/transcripts in the "presenter notes" section of the presentation slides, (d) upload the video prior to class to allow download time, (e) allow students to review videos in class and ask questions, (f) spotlight each signer which forces everyone to sign one person at a time and to pause and wait for the spotlight to be placed on them, (g) sign everything that is posted in the chat box, (h) have 10–15 minute breaks every hour (for 4 hour long courses), and (i) restating comments that students might have missed. Students are always keeping everyone accountable with comments like "wait for the spotlight," "in the chat (person) said . . .," "it might be time for a break," etc. By far, the level of community that has been developed through this practice of intentional access has been uplifting to witness.*

The very nature of our mind/bodies resists conforming to a capitalist "normative" productive standard, with the actual construction of "disability" derived from the exploitation of the body in an economy that sees land and human as components of profit.—Berne, 2015

ANTI-CAPITALIST POLITIC

We can attempt to meet each others' needs as we build toward liberation, without always reaching for state solutions . . .—Berne, 2015

INTERDEPENDENCE

Universities are major capitalist microsystems. I have witnessed how Deaf Students of Color because of their tuition waivers in our state are often denied educational grants. This means that while students who may have full-time jobs are receiving grants to pay for their flights to our hybrid program and cover their lodging and rental car expenses six times per semester, Deaf Students of Color are expected to pay those expenses out of pocket. I watched as this financial barrier became a breaking point for potentially exiting the program before completing the degree. I refused to allow that to happen. Six times a semester, I would open up my home for any student who could not afford or did not feel safe to sleep in a hotel. This decision resulted in weekends with a packed house, beautiful connections, healthy home-cooked meals for everyone, and students who deserved to be given the opportunity to gift the field with their full Deaf selves! This also showed how much we need one another. Capitalism tells us that our worth is based on what we can do/achieve independently. However, we continue to find creative solutions by allowing and trusting one another to meet our needs.

Shifts how social justice movements understand disability and contextualize ableism, lending itself toward a united front politic.—Berne, 2015

COMMITMENT TO CROSS MOVEMENT ORGANIZING

Valuing and honoring the insights and participation of all of our community members and therefore are committed to breaking down ableist / patriarchal / racist / classed isolation between people with physical impairments, people who identify as "sick" or are chronically ill, "psych" survivors and those who identify as "crazy," neurodiverse people, people with cognitive impairments, people who are a sensory minority, as we understand that isolation ultimately undermines collective liberation.—Berne, 2015

COMMITMENT TO CROSS DISABILITY SOLIDARITY

As I continue to grow through Disability Justice and constant learning and unlearning, I find that I am more and more intentional about building across movements and contexts. I engage in Disability Justice both in academia, in my birth-12 work, and in social contexts. This is my way of bridging the "theory" and the "practice." I leave no aspect of my life untouched because disability touches all aspects of my life. That is why I argued for bringing culturally sustaining pedagogy (Paris, 2012; Paris & Alim, 2014) and an intersectionality framework for research (Garcia & Ortiz, 2013) in Deaf Education as a doctoral student and that is why I created a theory of colonization that stepped outside of academic conceptualizations of the U.S. Deaf populations and accounted for multiple axes of oppressions and privileges.

How do we move together—as people with mixed abilities, multiracial, multi-gendered, mixed class, across the orientation spectrum—where no body/mind is left behind.—Berne, 2015

COLLECTIVE LIBERATION

As a person who was raised under the practices of several collective cultures, I always tell my current Deaf Studies and Deaf Education students whether undergraduate, master's, or doctoral level that my motto for my classes is "we move together." The first day of my courses I explain that we are a unit. If one person does not understand, as a group we can work together to make the information clear. If one person needs many breaks, then the entire class takes a break so that no one feels left behind. There have been times when a diabetic student was ill and needed to eat before our 4-hour long master's level class. I would inform that class that we would be officially starting 30 minutes later and that everyone can take advantage to get a meal if needed. I would still make myself available at the scheduled start time for questions, elaborations, or just for students to debrief about particular experiences. However, one of the challenges with this approach for me was that I value respecting student's privacy and the students who were unaffected (not diabetic) would complain that I was not respecting their time and it's my job to start class on time. Most of the time these were dominant students in the class and their complaints (both to other students in the class and to my superiors) would result in Disabled students problematizing their disability and needs and feeling more discouraged about disclosing those needs to the class and other professors. These situations were a reminder that I needed to find more effective ways to get nondisabled students and students from individualistic backgrounds to buy in and commit to collective liberation. This continues to be an area of struggle for me. Yet I remain committed to continuing to implement this in my teaching because the impact might not be today, I may continue to get backlash, but hopefully one day these future practitioners see the value in leaving no one behind.

POINTS FOR MOVING FORWARD

Here I leave you with some points of reflection for moving forward in your work as practitioners in whatever field you may be in as I firmly believe that the principles of Disability Justice can and do apply to all contexts. Your positionality is political, whether you choose to engage with it or not, others do. As professionals in Special Education, self-study is essential because we have potential to impact change on all levels of society if we are willing and able to acknowledge and act against all forms of injustice (Lawyer et al., 2020). This acknowledgment and action against injustices applies to our pedagogical practices and research alike. First, if you do not know where to start, make examining reflexivity and positionality a common practice in your courses and research processes and writings (Garcia & Ortiz, 2013). Second, interdisciplinary approaches to learning and research are vital to advancing equity within the demographics of professionals who have access to entering the field as well as for the improved lives of our students. A field that results in the overrepresentation of Disabled children in detention centers (Mader & Butrymowicz, 2014) and higher incarceration rates (Children's Defense Fund, 2007) is proof that silos in education create spaces that cause and perpetuate harm even beyond their physical spaces/places. Interdisciplinary approaches would bring greater awareness and accountability and force an expansion of the ways of knowing and being that are accepted within Special Education. Third, and similar to point two, we must analyze all systems (i.e., educational, medical, carceral, etc.) because they are all interconnected and mutually sustaining therefore if any form of oppression and injustice is allowed to exist in one of these systems, it is sustaining the existence of oppression in all of these systems. Dismantling them all is the only way to reach full humanity for us all. The following questions are points that I often reflect on in my work and with my students, I hope that they may provide you with some points for consideration to continue the dialogue within yourself and with others: (a) does my pedagogy, advocacy, and research approaches benefit the most marginalized of the marginalized in the ways *they* want to be benefited; (b) why are these pedagogies and methods uplifted in this context; (c) how did I come to inherit and implement these pedagogies and methods; (d) if I rejected these pedagogies and methods who would be harmed; and (e) what would or could be reimagined in their place? (Lawyer, 2022).

NOTE

1. Italicized font used in this chapter represents my critical autoethnographic texts and experiences.

REFERENCES

Annamma, S. A. (2018). *The pedagogy of pathologization: Dis/abled girls of color in the school-prison nexus*. Routledge.
Artiles, A. J. (1998). The dilemma of difference: Enriching the disproportionality discourse with theory and context. *The Journal of Special Education, 32*(1), 32–36.
Berne, P. (2015, June 9). *Disability Justice - a working draft*. https://www.sinsinvalid.org/blog/disability-justice-a-working-draft-by-patty-berne
Boylorn, R. M., & Orbe, M. P. (2014). *Critical autoethnography: Intersecting cultural identities in everyday life*. Taylor and Francis.
Broderick, A. A. (2011). Autism as rhetoric: Exploring watershed rhetorical moments in applied behavior analysis discourse. *Disability Studies Quarterly, 31*(3). https://dsq-sds.org/index.php/dsq/article/view/1674/1597
Broderick, A. A., & Roscigno, R. (2021). Autism, inc.: The autism industrial complex. *Journal of Disability Studies in Education, 2021*, 1–25.
Children's Defense Fund (CDF). (2007). *America's cradle to prison pipeline*. Children's Defense Fund.
Connor, D. J. (2013). Who "owns" dis/ability? The cultural work of critical special educators as insider-outsiders. *Theory and Research in Social Education, 41*(4), 494–513.

Connor, D. J., Gabel, S. L., Gallagher, D. J., & Morton, M. (2008). Disability studies and inclusive education-- implications for theory, research, and practice. *International Journal of Inclusive Education, 12*(5–6), 441–457.

Coomer, M. N. (2019). Deconstructing difference and inclusion in educational research: reflections on the international journal of qualitative studies in education special edition on difference. *International Journal of Qualitative Studies in Education, 32*(3), 1–5.

Freire, P. (1970). *Pedagogy of the oppressed.* Herder & Herder.

Garcia, S. B., & Ortiz, A. A. (2013). Intersectionality as a framework for transformative research in special education. *Multiple Voices for Ethnically Diverse Exceptional Learners, 13*(2), 32–47.

Hernández-Saca, D. I., Martin, J. L., & Meacham, S. (2020). The hidden elephant is oppression: Violence within the academy, and finding strength in self-study. *Studying Teacher Education: A Journal of Self-Study of Teacher Education Practices, 16*(1), 26–47.

Lawyer. G. (2022). Theorizing the curriculum of colonization in the U.S. Deaf context: Situating DisCrit within a framework of decolonization. In S. A. Annamma, B. Ferri, and D. Connor (Eds.), *DisCrit Expanded: Inquiries, Reverberations & Ruptures* (pp.179–198). New York, NY: Teachers College Press.

Lawyer, G., Shahan, C., Holcomb, L. K., & Smith, D. H. (2020). First comes a look at the self: Integrating the principles of social justice into a teacher preparation program. *Odyssey: New Directions in Deaf Education, 21*(2020), 66–70.

Lewis, T. L. (2016). Keynote. *2016 Minnesota Governor's Council Martin Luther King, Jr. Statewide Celebration.* https://www.talilalewis.com/blog/archives/01-2016

Losen, D., & Orfield, G. (2002). *Racial inequity in special education.* Harvard University Press.

Mader, J., & Butrymowicz, S. (2014). Special education too often leads to jail. *The Hechinger Report.* https://www.clarionledger.com/story/news/2014/10/25/pipeline-to-prison-system-fails-special-ed-students/17917859/

Madison, D. S. (2012). *Critical ethnography: Method, ethics, and performance.* Sage Publications.

Paris, D. (2012). Culturally sustaining pedagogy: A needed change in stance, terminology, and practice. *Educational Researcher, 41*(3), 93–97.

Paris, D., & Alim, H. S. (2014). What are we seeking to sustain through culturally sustaining pedagogy? A loving critique forward. *Harvard Educational Review, 84*(1), 85–100.

Patton, J. M. (1998). The disproportionate representation of African Americans in special education: Looking behind the curtain for understanding and solutions. *The Journal of Special Education, 32*(1), 25–31.

Roscigno, R. (2019). Neuroqueerness as fugitive practice: Reading against the grain of applied behavioral analysis scholarship. *Educational Studies, 55*(4), 405–419.

Simpson, N. (2017). Disabling justice? The exclusion of people with disabilities from the food justice movement. In S. J. Ray & J. Sibara (Eds.), *Disability Studies and the environmental humanities: Toward and eco-crip theory* (pp. 403–421). University of Nebraska Press.

Sins Invalid. (2019). *Skin, Tooth, and Bone: The Basis of Movement Is Our People, a Disability Justice Primer* (2nd ed.). Primedia eLaunch LLC.
Sins Invalid. (2020, June 16). *What is disability justice?* https://www.sinsinvalid.org/news-1/2020/6/16/what-is-disability-justice
Taylor, S. J. (2006). Before it had a name: Exploring the historical roots of disability studies in education. In S. Danforth & S. L. Gabel (Eds.), *Vital questions facing disability studies in education* (pp. xiii–xxiii). Peter Lang.
Thorius, K. A. (2019). Facilitating en/counters with special education's cloak of benevolence in professional learning to eliminate racial disproportionality in special education. *International Journal of Qualitative Studies in Education, 32*(3), 323–340.

Conclusion

Holly Pearson, Catherine K. Voulgarides, and David I. Hernández-Saca

Dear readers,

While this chapter is located at the back of the book, this is not the end. If you think you will find a list of goodies for the next steps, you are sorely mistaken and have not fully understood the purpose of the book! Please return to the beginning of the book and start over. Just kidding. But, yes, there are no "IKEA" instructions on how to assemble together *a disability justice radical love meta-critical emotionality consiliencatory boundary* work praxis. As seen with each of the amazing contributors, they all found, forged, and interwove their paths in different ways. While there is an array of reasons—the desire/desperation to make a difference, to process, to find a voice/identity, to cease the intergenerational cycle of trauma and pain, and/or to survive—the one thing all of these reasons have in common is intuition—listening/feeling/trusting from within.

Too often when we sense something is off, we freeze or ignore the inner voice—whether it is because of hesitation, fear, confusion, shame, guilt, denial, and/or anger, which are both sociologically and psychologically engendered and in turn materially, culturally, socially, economically, and emotionally and affectively experienced and (de)constructed (Ahmed, 2004; Zembylas, 2021). This is not a moment of criticism but *instead* a moment of recognition and awareness. Within this space of recognition and awareness is where *disability justice radical love meta-critical emotionality consiliencatory boundary* work praxis stems and is deeply rooted within. (Re)learning to listen/feel/trust our intuition is vital in engaging with individual and collective boundary engagement. To not be able to listen/feel/trust our intuition is like being a tree with no roots. A tree with no roots will easily sway to influences and eventually collapse in exhaustion. To do boundary work is to build and grow your roots—starting and returning within—in alignment with your values. This is not easy nor not as common as it should be. Why? Because we all have been socialized to prioritize external validation over listening/ feeling/trusting within. It is not as strange as it sounds considering the different forms of external validation (e.g., grades, compliments, applause, weight, income) we were exposed to from a young age. These forms of external validation have the greatest built-in accountability.

This is not the case with inner work. Consider when was the last time you were held accountable or "rewarded" (e.g., praise, monetary value, a sticker, a grade) for checking in with yourself? To sit down and ask yourself—how am I doing? What am I feeling right now? *Oh* (somber tone or realization) is correct. We exist in a society that does not encourage us to value ourselves but instead encourages a toxic culture of competitive comparison meritocratic and oppression Olympics. Yet, as we have encountered across all the narratives—breathing life into *disability justice radical love meta-critical emotionality consiliencatory boundary* work praxis ironically stems from within all of us—our insecurities, dreams, values, beliefs, heritage, and legacies. In other words, valuing each other's humanity is where we must begin and keep returning to. It is here, within these spaces of humanizing that tension, differences, healing, connections, breathing, and love weave together in the creation of this praxis. Therefore, this work cannot be scripted—like a prescription pad or a recipe. There are no damn shortcuts. This work fundamentally comes down to embracing ourselves as who we are—as complex messy imperfect beings and listening/feeling/trusting our instincts as this provides us clarity and the ability to engage in boundary work that aligns with our values and beliefs. Boundary work cannot be done in isolation. It also cannot be done parroting someone else's values and beliefs. Boundary work must begin from within. From here is where we can begin to not only grow our roots deep but also extend out different directions like branches as we build upon each other's wisdom, lived experiences, values, beliefs, and knowledge.

As noted at the beginning, in a firm and gentle nudge—this conversation is far from done and is very much dependent on each other to sustain this conversation. The intent of this book is to facilitate critical awareness and a deeper understanding of the fault lines at the boundaries between traditional special education and Disability Studies in Education (DSE). Specifically, the authors' grappling with their boundary work and artifacts, we hope, informs your *disability justice radical love meta-critical emotionality consiliencatory boundary* work praxis for internal and external justice and individual and collective agency among the parallel systems of support of special and general education. We also hope that an interdisciplinary and intersectional DSE paradigm can further provide guidance in your personal, professional, and programmatic future transformational actions and change as advocates, allies, and/or co-conspirators inside and outside the educational system, especially in the context of disruption and freedom from the hegemony of traditional special education and white and Ability supremacy. We encourage you to revisit the questions that each of the authors posed at the end of their chapters as you continue to reimagine the boundary work for global intersectional dis/Ability liberation and struggle. As you continue to engage in this work, do not forget to ask yourself:

"How am I doing?"
"What brought me here?"
"What are my values?"

REFERENCES

Ahmed, S. (2004). Affective economies. *Social Text, 22*(2), 117–139.
Zembylas, M. (2021). The affective turn in educational theory. In *Oxford Research Encyclopedia of Education.* https://oxfordre.com/education/view/10.1093/acrefore/9780190264093.001.0001/acrefore-9780190264093-e-1272.

Index

ability supremacy, 32, 41, 217, 262–63, 265, 268–73, 275
ableism, 56–57, 182, 183, 215, 229, 304, 306, 316; disbelief that sign language is a natural language, 183
ableist ideology, 47
academic underachievement, 186
academy, 218
access, 151–52, 155, 160; access is love, 158, 162, 164
accommodations, 313
activist, 155, 164
activity systems, 79, 83, 84, 88, 91, 93
Adams, Glenn A., 228
Adichie, Chimamanda Ngozi, 40
adjuncts, 217–18
advocacy, 97, 105, 111, 113, 115, 225, 229
African: culture, 172; languages, 172; tradition, 171
agency, 225, 263
Akkerman, Sanne, 31, 219
Allen, Daniel, 38
Allman, Paula, 31
Almond, David, 196
Altruistic Shield, 269
Americans with Disabilities Act (ADA), 194, 203
Anastasiou, Dimitris, 20

Anderson, Leon, 220, 222, 228
Annamma, Subini, 39
anti-ableism, 54, 61, 64, 66
anti-immigrant, 221
anti-Islamic rhetorics subjectify people medical scrutiny through the pathologizing lens of race, dis/ Ability, nationality and immigration, 220
anti-racism/anti-racist, 194, 200, 203, 261–62, 272
Anyon, Jean, 14
Artiles, Alfredo J., 31, 215
arts-based research, 62, 63
Ashton-Warner, Sylvia, 12
assessment, 134–37, 142
assistive technology, 32, 217, 219
attention deficit hyperactivity disorder (ADHD), 100
audism, 183
auditory learning disability, 31, 34–35, 42–44, 226
augmentative and alternative communication (AAC), 136, 142
aural-oral, 177
autism spectrum disorder (ASD), 105, 113
autoethnographic texts, 32, 42; autoethnography, 32, 173–75, 303–5, 321–22

Badar, Jeanmarie, 20
Baglieri, Susan, 19, 219
Bakker, Arthur, 31, 219
bargaining, 184
Beck, Clive, 12
behavior, 309–10, 314–15
Bell, Christopher, 228
benevolent, 186
Berne, Patricia, 16, 18, 20, 34, 215
Big D Discourse, 226
bilingual in Spanish and English, 224
binary boundaries, 304
Black, Indigenous, and People of Color (BIPOC), 34, 219–20, 227
Bochner, Arthur, 31, 42
Boskovich, Lisa, 42
boundary work, 5–6, 216–17, 224–25, 228, 236–39, 343–44; boundaries of special education and disability studies in education, 215–17; boundary crossing, 239; boundary workers, 195, 198, 199, 207; preservice teacher preparation at the boundaries, 219
Brandenburg, Robyn, 31, 44
Brantlinger, Ellen, 15, 20, 38
Brienes, Wini, 18
Brown vs. Board of Education of Topeka. *See* Civil Rights Movement
Buber, Martin, 126, 130–32, 133, 138, 141
Bullough, Robert V., 44
Burns, Victoria F., 218
Butler, Brandon, 12

Calderón-Almendros, Ignacio, 31
Cannon, Mercedes, 41, 46
capabilities for, 205; caring community, 207; complexities of, 196; compliance as, 196; ethic of, 196, 197, 199–203, 207; feminist, 197; fucked up, 198; geographies of, 200
capacity/capacity orientation, 287, 289–90, 296–97

capital/capitalism/capitalist, 16, 194, 197, 200, 205, 215
capitalist notions of productivity, 215
care: aesthetic, 201; broken, 198, 199, 206
Castelló, Montserrat, 216
Chandler-Olcott, Kelly, 218
change. *See* inclusion, inclusive reform
Chanmugam, Amy, 218
charity, 172, 186
check-in questionnaire, 223
checklists, 261–62, 265, 269–76
child find, 136, 142
Chirema, 179
Cioè-Peña, Maria, 218
civil rights: educational, 23
Civil Rights Movement, 12, 18
class meeting, 319
coalition, 148, 151, 154, 162–63
collaborative autoethnography, 239–42; data analysis, 241; data collection, 240–41
collage, 63
Collier, Lorna, 34
colonial, 178; languages, 178; precolonial, 179
coloniality of power, 227
communality, 173
community, 298
conceptual framework, 217
conferences, 261, 273
connor, david, 12, 13, 15, 16, 19, 21, 25, 34, 37–39, 215, 219
consilience, 16, 21, 24, 27, 31, 33, 41–42, 44, 78–80, 87, 91, 92, 215, 237–39, 241, 245, 253–54, 263, 273, 303, 305, 308, 321–22; consiliencatory approach, 215; contextualized, 237, 239, 241, 248, 251–52. *See also* Critical Consilience Emotion Praxis at the Boundaries
Context Principle, 307
Cosier, Megan, 215
Costa, Arthur L., 44

co-teaching, 217–18, 220, 223, 317–21; co-teaching as co-mentoring, 222, 228; co-teaching experiences of graduate assistants of color and faculty of color, 218; mentor-mentee relationship, 228
Council for Exceptional Children, 19
Counter-hegemonic, 297
COVID-19 crisis, 223
creativity, 313
Crenshaw, Kimberlé Williams., 41, 46, 216, 230
critical analytic autoethnography, 221–22; analytic reflexivity, 221–22; commitment to theoretical analysis, 221; complete member researcher status, 221; dialogue with informants beyond the self, 221; narrative visibility of the researcher's self, 221
critical and courageous dialogues, 216
critical awareness, 316
critical consilience emotion praxis, 48; critical emotion revolutionary praxis for liberation, 31
critical consilience emotion praxis at the boundaries, 32, 48
Critical Disability Studies (CDS), 215, 220; CDS paradigm, 215; counter-narrating, 220; Critical Disability Studies in Education (CDSE), 219; disability studies, 231; White Disability Studies, 228
Critical Emotion Praxis, 215, 217, 224–25, 229–30; critical consiliencatory critical emotion praxis counter-narrating generativity, 215–17, 224–25, 230; critical emotional revolutionary praxis, 3; generativity, 216–17, 224–25, 230
critical friendship, 222
critical pedagogy, 183, 237, 238, 244–46; objects of education, 183; subjects of own autonomy and emancipation, 183

Critical Race Theory (CRT), 151, 155, 202
critical self-reflection, 303, 305, 316, 322
critical self-study in teacher education, 34
critical special education, 41, 194, 197
critical special education scholarship, 235
critical theory, 222, 230
Crow, Jayne, 218
Cultural Historical Activity Theory (CHAT), 76, 78–79, 216, 237–39, 253–54; activity system, 238–39, 242, 245, 248, 252–54; agency as collective, 216; agents of collaborative and transformational change, 216; transformative ethico-ontoepistemology, 216, 219
culturally relevant and sustaining pedagogy, 219
cultural reciprocity, 104
culture of compliance, 220
curriculum, 57–59, 64; fragments, 149, 157–58; maps, 312
curriculum and instruction, 205
Cycle of Legislation, 127

Danforth, Scot, 15, 23, 31
data sources, 240–41
Davis, Lennard, 36
deaf: cycle of low expectations, 184; education, 180, 184, 186; non-deaf, 172, 173
debilitation, 148
decision-making, 197
decolonization, 262, 272–73
deficient, 283; aspirants of hearing society, 187; focused special education, 185
deficit assumptions, 218
deficit-focus, 307, 310, 312, 314–15
deficit narratives, 229
deficit thinking, 186, 215, 227; deficits, 180, 183

democracy/democratic, 194, 195, 197, 198, 200
Derrick Bell, 217
de Saint-Exupéry, Antoine, 126, 131, 132, 134–36
Deviance, 281–82, 291–92
Devor, Aaron, 18
diagnoses. *See* labels
differentiation, 312–13, 319–20
dilemma of difference, 96
Dirth, Thomas P., 229
dis/ability, 49, 230, 263–64, 267, 273; capitalization of a, in dis/ability, 231; dis/abled, 216, 219; disabled people of color, female immigrants-specifically from the global south, 221
dis/ability critical race studies, 194, 197, 198
disability, 75–78, 84–88, 92, 147–51, 194, 197, 203, 205; conceptual understandings of, 17–20; critical disability studies, 149–50, 155–57, 162, 166; deficit-based perceptions of, 13, 26; disability and whiteness, 148; feminist disability studies, 156–57, 162, 165; as love, 198, 199; rights, 21; self-disclosure, 21; as a social construct, 305, 308, 313; social model of, 18, 20; social-political views of, 321
disability identification and disabled identity, 235–36, 255
disability identity, 54, 58–60
disability justice, 2, 16, 20, 41, 76, 80–81, 83, 88–89, 91, 125, 126, 128, 130, 140, 178, 182, 186, 201, 215, 217, 220; CDS paradigm and Disability Justice Consiliencatory approach, 215; disability justice principles, 236–37
disability justice consilience. *See* Disability Justice
disability language, 303, 314
disability representation, 57–58, 62, 68

disability studies, 22, 31, 35, 36, 39–40, 125, 140, 141, 194, 196, 199, 207, 263, 267, 274, 303–5, 308, 321; Department of Special Education (DSpED), 32; Disabilities Studies Reader, 36; Disability Studies in Education (DSE), 11, 12, 31, 37, 235–39 (DSE scholars in teacher preparation programs, 236; educator's disposition toward, 20–23; inception, 15; purpose, 15; subfield of disability studies, 19; tenets of, 20, 235–36; traditional special education, 236–38); disability studies in education and intersectionality, 39; disability studies quarterly, 36; a history of disability studies, 35, 37; interdisciplinarity, 22
Disability Studies in Education (DSE), 97, 999, 100, 108, 114, 115, 117, 118
disabled community scholars and activists of color, 237
discipline, 282, 291–92
DisCrit, 110, 116. *See also* Dis/ability Critical Race Studies
disproportionality, 117, 219, 223, 307. *See also* underrepresentation; overrepresentation
diversity, 219
division of labor, 187
doctoral candidates of Color, 217
Dolmage, Jay Timothy., 220
Down syndrome, 103–4, 109–10, 113
dreaming/s, 303–4, 308, 316–17, 321. *See also* emergent methodology
DSE-SIG-AERA: American Educational Research Association (AERA), 39
Dugan, Kimberly, 218
Dunhamn, Jane, 40
Dysconscious racism, 219

educational systems, 312, 316–17, 321
Education for All Handicapped Children Act, P.L., 12, 18, 94–142
The "Educations", 303, 305, 308, 321

Eisner, Elliot, 18
Electives, 318–20
Ellis, Carolyn, 31, 42
El Salvador, 43, 224
emergent/emergence, 197, 207
emergent methodology, 321. See also dreaming/s
emotional and behavioral disturbance (EBD), 97–98, 112
emotionality, 220
emotional labor, 199, 206
Endo, Rachel, 220
English language, 217; English Language Learner (ELL), 45, 223–24, 226; English Language Teaching, 264, 273
epistemologies of the South, 227
Erevelles, Nirmala, 220
ethical/ethics/ethos, 195, 197–201, 204; ethical practice, 220; love ethic, 207
Eurocentrism, 227
Evans, Daryl, 36
exclusionary, 283, 291, 297
exonerating construct, 182
expansive notions of, 197; racial, 205; Social, 207. See also care; givers, as justice

Faber, Adele, 13
faculty of Color, 217, 219, 222; emerging scholars of Color, 218; female educators of Color, 218; female faculty of Color, 218; male faculty of Color, 218
failure, 281–82, 291
feminism/feminist/feminine, 196, 197, 201, 208. See also care; ethical/ethics/ethos; disability justice
Ferguson, Diane, 15
Ferguson, Phil, 15, 37
Ferri, Beth, 13, 19, 20, 37
Fletcher, Jack M, 227
flexible grouping, 318, 320
flexible seating, 319–20
Foucault, Michel, 34, 216

Found poetry, 64
Freese, Anne, 12
Freire, Paolo, 41, 47, 126, 129–31, 133, 136–38, 140, 141, 228, 262, 265–66, 269
Fromm, Erich, 31
full citizenship, 305, 308, 316
funding, 305, 307, 310

Gabel, Susan, 15, 16, 23
Gabel, Susan Lynn, 31
Gallagher, Deborah, 13, 15, 16, 19, 20, 227
Garbett, Dawn, 12
Garnett, Kate, 12, 25
Gartner, Allan, 20
Gatekeepers, 306
Gee, James, 35, 226
gender bias, 226
general education, 84–85, 88, 92; general education and special education binary, 235, 237–38; general educators, 76, 82–85, 90–92
geography/geographies, 200
Gerlach, Beth, 218
giftedness, 307, 311
Gitlin, Andrew David, 44
givers, 204; consilience, 195, 208; impetus to, 195; as justice, 194, 197, 201; patronizing, 193; as a practice, 200; as a praxis, 200, 203; providers, 205; racialized nature of, 200; relational, 201, 207; savior/care complex, 198, 206, 207; for self/other, 195, 205, 207; for students with disabilities, 196; trauma-informed, 200; womanist, 202; work, 198–200
Glaser, B. G., 44
Global Imperialism, 219
global north, 227
Global South, 218, 227, 229
Goffman, Erving, 126, 131, 139, 141
Grant, Melva, 12
grit, 262, 269–71, 273

Groce, Nora, 36
growth mindset, 262, 271
Gutiérrez, Kris, 216, 226
Gutstein, Eric, 219

Hall, Melinda, C., 216, 220
Hallahan, Daniel, 17, 18
Hang, Qi, 218
Harris, Angela, 217
Harry, Beth, 23, 97, 105–6, 113, 117–18
hearing impaired, 173, 178
hegemony, 32; challenging the hegemony of positivism, 37, 46. *See also* Positivism; counter-narrate the hegemony of whiteness and ableism in educational institutions, 218; hegemonic epistemologies of dis/ability at the intersections of power and identity, 219; hegemony, traditional hegemonic structures of special education, 215, 226, 228, 230; hegemony of traditional psychological science, 228; traditional special education, 215–16, 219; white, patriarchal, and Ableist hegemonic power structures, 217, 229
hermeneutic cycle of critical reflection, 225
Hernández-Saca, David, 32–34, 41, 43–46, 218–19, 224
Heshusius, Lous, 38
Heumann, Judith, 17
Hey, Steve, 36
higher education, 215, 220, 228
historically multiply marginalized individuals, families, and communities, 237
historicity, 237–39, 242, 252–53
Hooks, Bell, 119–20
hope, 195
humanization, 31, 49
human potential, 306, 317

ideals, 16
identification processes, 307–10

identity, 303–4, 306–10, 314, 321
identity language, 139, 142
ideological becoming, 227
immigrant and refugee students of Color, 217, 223, 225–26; immigration, 224–25
inclusion, 195, 196, 205, 207, 306, 308, 317–21; inclusive education, 16, 19, 21, 75, 79–81, 88, 90, 217, 219, 235–36, 240, 242, 250–51, 253; inclusive reform, 76, 78–83, 89, 91
Individual Education Program (IEP), 12, 23, 100, 106–7, 128, 136–39, 142, 314–15, 320
individualism, 16
Individuals with Disabilities Education Act (IDEA) of 2004, 98, 101, 111, 116, 137, 139, 194, 215, 220
institutional critique, 305, 316
instructional planning, 312, 318–20
intellectual disability, 98, 103, 112, 116
interactive introspection, 175
interdisciplinary, 219; interdisciplinary relationships, 235, 236, 243, 250, 251
intersectional/intersectionality, 11, 12, 18, 25, 39, 54, 56–57, 69, 105, 112, 148, 156–57, 165, 217, 219–20, 222–23, 284, 297–98, 303–5, 307–8, 312; intersectional disablism, 227
inventorying, 174, 175
Iqtadar, Shehreen, 222, 227

Jaggedness Principle, 307, 313
Journal of Learning Disabilities, 19
joy, 248–53

Kallick, Bena, 44
Kauffman, James, 17, 20
Kelchtermans, Geert, 220
Kendi, Ibram X., 261–62
Kliewer, Chris, 38
Kohl, Herbert, 12
Kosnik, Claire, 12, 42, 215, 222
Kozleski, Elizabeth B., 31, 215

labeling, 100, 103, 112–13, 115, 120
labels, 306, 308–11, 314–15, 320. *See also* self-labeling
Ladson-Billings, Gloria, 219
Laissez faire, 186
Langstaff, David, 16, 18, 20
language, 186; inaccessible, 186; of instruction, 186; language and culture, 307, 309, 311, 314–15, 317; language-handicapped, 181, 183; language mentor, 320; signed, 183; spoken, 183
LatCrit, 202
Latina/o Critical Theory. *See* LatCrit
Latino ethnicity, 224; Latinx, 226
learning disabilities/disabled, 19, 31, 184; and trauma, 34
learning disability quarterly, 19
Letterman, Margaret, 218
LGBTQIA, 43, 222
linguicism, 227, 229
Linton, Simi, 18, 27
Lipsky, Dorothy, 20
The Little Prince, 131, 133, 134
Living as an international student and a recent immigrant woman of Color from the Global South, 225–26
Lorde, Audre, 275
love/loving, 195, 197, 200, 206–8, 282, 287, 291, 294, 296–98. *See also* ethical/ethics/ethos
low expectations, 182, 184

maintenance, 236
Marshmallow Test, 271
master narratives: of intersectional dis/abilities, 219, 224; of learning disabilities, 227; of policy, 219
Matsi, 179
Matte, Nicholas, 18
Mazlish, Elaine, 13
Mccourt, Frank, 12
medical evaluation, 305, 309
medical model of disability, 84–86, 172, 215; medical-psychological model of disability, 219

Meekosha, Helen, 220
merit badges, 261–62, 265, 271–76
Meritocracy, 87, 267–68, 270
meta-cognition, 225; meta-cognitive process and awareness, 225, 226
meta-feeling processes, 227
Michail, Domna, 20
Microaggression, 13
Middle-class norms, 13
midwest, 217
Miller, Richard, 215
Million, Dian, 225
Minority Versus Majority, 224
Mintzberg, Susan, C., 218
Mitchell, David, 38
modifications, 313
Monroe, Lorraine, 12
Moore, Mignon R., 218
Morales, Aurora, 16, 18, 20
Morelock, John R., 218
more-than-human ontology, 304
Morton, Missy, 15, 16
mother, 294–95
multi-age instruction, 318
multidisciplinary evaluation team (MET), 308, 314
multilingual female, 227
multiple pathways, 312, 319
munching, 3
Museus, Samuel D., 45, 227
Muslim, 227
mute, 178

Naidich, Thomas P., 47
Narian, Srikala, 23, 26
narrative/narrative inquiry, 281, 285
narrative analysis, 241
needs, 203, 205–7
Nelson, Nancy, 216
neoliberal/neoliberalism, 148, 195, 198, 200, 204, 206
Nepantla, 149, 158, 162–63
neurodivergence/neurodiversity, 263–65, 268, 274, 311–12
No Child Left Behind (NCLB), 129

normal, 97–98, 101, 104, 109, 115, 119, 120, 122–23, 182; ideology of, 182; normalcy, 96–97, 103, 109–11, 113, 116, 121; normalize, 182

Ocasio-Stoutenberg, Lydia, 23
occupational therapy, 320
Office of Education Ombuds, 58
One Out of Five: Disability History and Pride Project, 53, 57–59
onto-epistemological turn, 219
organizations: The Association for Severely Handicapped (TASH), 38; The Coalition of Open Inquiry in Special Education, 38; Early Cross-pollination between Critical Special, 37; International Western Social Science Association (WSSA), 35; Modern Language Association, 36; The National Black Disability Studies Coalition (NBDC), 39–40 (Black Disability Studies, 39–40); National Council for Learning Disabilities, 19; National Social Science Association of the United States (NSSA), 35; Society of Disability Studies (SDS), 35; Study of Chronic Illness, Impairment, and Disability within the NSSA, 35
Ovens, Allan, 12
overrepresentation, 97, 306, 321. *See also* disproportionality

Pakistan, 224
Palestine, 43, 224; Palestinian, 224
pandemic, 193, 196
parents, 127, 128, 131, 137, 138, 140, 308–11
Paris, Django, 219
pathways principle, 307
patriarchy, 20, 194; paternalism, 197, 200, 204
Patton, James W., 219
Patton, Lori Davis, 45, 227
Pearson, Holly, 31, 215

pedagogy, 22, 25, 75, 91
people of Color, 216, 224; historically and systematically minoritized individuals of color with and without dis/abilities, 216; students of color, 223
personal, professional and programmatic selves, 32, 34–35, 42, 44, 46, 215, 218, 225, 230
person first language, 136, 139, 142, 178
personhood, 179
Peters, Susan, 37
poetry, 241–53. *See also* three-voice poems
positionality, 239–40
positivism, 37–38, 45, 47, 194
postsecondary educators of Color, 217
post-traumatic growth (PTG), 34
post-traumatic stress disorder, 224
power, 79–81, 83, 88, 91, 92
power dynamics, 218
practice, 88, 90
Praxis, 236, 240, 242–43, 245, 247–48, 253–54
Predominantly White Institution (PWI), 31, 217
pre-professional teaching, 184
Price, Jeremy N., 218
Professional development co-facilitators, 320
programs, 314
proverbs, 172
psychic disequilibrium, 2
psycho-emotional disablism, 40
Pullen, Paige, 17, 18

Rabren, Karen, 218
race, 148, 151–55, 165; racial reckoning, 230; racism, 215, 227
race-evasiveness, 25
radical love, 16, 41, 48, 85, 91, 149, 157, 158, 161–66, 172, 184, 217, 229, 261–62, 265–70, 272–76, 287, 317, 322; false sense of, 184
Redmond, Sonjia Parker, 228

Reid, D. Kim, 19
relationships/relatedness, 126, 128–35, 138–42
research interviews, 312
resilience, 262, 271
resistance, 293–94, 297
resource room, 311
respect, 290–91, 294
restorative practices, 287
Rice, Nancy, 37
Rich, Adrienne, 2
rights, 196, 197; civil, 194; rooted in Rights, 58. *See also* Americans with Disabilities Act (ADA); Individuals with Disabilities Education Act (IDEA) of 2004
Ripley, Amanda, 271
of risk, 202
Rogoff, Barabra, 32
Ruiz-Román, Cristobal, 31
Russell, Tom, 222

Samaras, Anastasia P., 12, 44, 216, 222
Scheer, Jessica, 36
Schlessinger, Sarah, 23, 26
School climate, 312, 316, 320
school compliance officer, 320
schooling, 75–77, 85–88, 91; purpose, 87
Schuck, Sandy, 222
Schultle, Ann K, 42
scientism, 45, 47
segregated classrooms, 12, 19, 23
Seidel, John, 36
self-labeling, 311
self-study, 16, 175, 186, 303–5, 321–22
self-study in teacher education, 215–17, 221, 223, 225–26, 228; critical incidents, 221, 226; public good, 221; self-reflection, 221, 223; self-study as counter-narrative, 223, 225; tacit knowledge from their practices cognizant, 221
sensory tools and strategies, 309–10, 313, 319

separation, 312–13
serve/service, 193, 206, 207
Shona, 178–80
Shuttleworth, Russell, 220
sign language, 185; native-like competency, 185; use of, 186
simultaneous communication, 183
Sins Invalid, 16, 18, 20, 220
Skrtic, Thomas, 20
smartness, 268, 271, 278
Smith, Lesley, 218
Smith, Phil, 12, 15
Snyder, Sharon, 38
socially constructed, 85–87, 92
social model, 85–86
sociocultural model, 172, 179
South Asian Female Student and Instructor of Color, 224; South Asian, 227
special education (SPED), 31, 32, 34, 79–86, 88–92, 147–51, 155–56, 164–66, 186, 224, 261–62, 265, 267–68, 274–75; concerns of, 11; for deaf learners, 185; discipline, 18; further actively disabling, 184; as an institution, 15; limitations, 15–16; special education law, 32, 33, 217, 219; special education services, 310–15, 320; special education students, 89; special education teachers, 84, 92; techniques, 186; traditional special education, 32, 42
speech and language impairment, 224; communication, 224; speech and language pathology, 224
Spoon Theory, 1
standardization, 306, 312, 316, 320
standards, 177, 182, 187
Stetsenko, Anna, 216, 219
stigma, 126, 130–32, 136, 139, 307, 310–11, 314, 316
Strauss, A. L., 44
strengths-based schooling, 306, 314–15, 317–21
student voice, 58, 61

success, 270–71, 274
systematic injustices, 303, 317
systems of thought, 216

talent development, 306–7, 317
teacher education preparation, 216, 235–36, 239–40, 253–54; prepare ALL preservice and in-service teachers for diverse classrooms and society, 218; preservice Teacher Preparation, 216–17, 219; teacher education, 61–62, 68; teacher education programs, 20–24
teacher interns, 317, 320
teachers, 172, 184; held to account, 184
technology integration, 318
tension, 4–5
testing, 135, 136, 138
theoretical Framework, 217
theory, 236, 247, 254
third space, 216, 226; third and brave spaces, 225–26, 230
Thomas, Carol, 41
Thomas, Lynn, 12
Thorius, Kathleen King, 215
Three-Voice Poems, 242–52
Tidwell, Deborah, 31, 42
Tough, Paul, 270
traditional and subjective special education disability Labels, 217
transition process, 314–15, 319
transition programming and planning, 217, 219
trauma, 193. *See also* care
twice exceptional students, 312

U.S. Education System, 217, 224; U.S. Public Education, 217
Ubuntu, 178, 179

unconditional: acceptance, 187; love, 182
underrepresentation, 306, 321. *See also* disproportionality
Universal Design for Learning (UDL), 195, 200

Valle, Jan, 19, 23
Valle, Jan W., 220
Vanassche, Eline, 220
Van den Berg, Femke Marij, 219
Vasconselos, Erica, 12
voice, 216, 218
voicing, 177
Voulgarides, Catherine M., 215, 220
Vygotskian Zone of Proximal Development, 225

Ward, Devery, 19
Ware, Linda, 15, 31, 37–38
white fragility, 271
whiteness, 20, 148, 151–54, 217; white femininity, 148
white property, 217
white supremacy, 32, 45, 217, 305–6, 317; racist ideology, 48; structures based on, 307; whiteness, 45
Wilson, Edward O., 31, 34, 42, 217
Wolfensberger, Wolf, 18
Womanist, 202
work, 237–39, 250, 253. *See also* consilience

xenophobia, 227

Yoon, Irene H., 43

Zembylas, Michalinos, 215
Zola, Irving Kenneth, 36
Zubal-Ruggieri, Rachael, 36

About the Contributors

Brittany Aronson is an associate professor in teacher education at Penn State University. She teaches classes in sociocultural foundations, sociology of education, and multicultural education. In her scholarship, she focuses on preparing educators to work against oppressive systems as well as critical policy analyses of both popular and political discourse. Her research interests include critical teacher preparation, social justice education, critical race theory, critical whiteness studies, and educational policy. Dr. Aronson earned a PhD in learning environments and educational studies from the University of Tennessee in 2014.

Christina A. Bosch is an educator, scholar, and assistant professor in the department of literacy, early, bilingual and special education at the California State University Fresno. Bosch holds a PhD in Special Education from the University of Massachusetts Amherst, an MEd in Mind, Brain and Education from Harvard University, an MA in Special Education: Learning Disabilities from American University, and a BA in English from the University of Vermont. She has taught in (and learned from) a wide range of grade levels and instructional contexts and is a former RAND Faculty Leader, Fulbright Scholar, HASTAC Scholar, and NSF CADRE fellow.

David J. Connor, EdD, is a professor emeritus of Hunter College (Learning Disabilities and Instructional Leadership Programs) and the Graduate Center (Urban Education Program), City University of New York. He taught in New York City for thirty-five years, from high schoolers to doctoral students. Throughout his career, he has always been interested in issues of equality, particularly in regard to dis/ability and race. He is the author/editor of many articles, book chapters, and books, including: *DisCrit: Disability Studies and Critical Race Theory* (2016) co-edited with Subini Annamma and Beth Ferri; *Contemplating Dis/Ability in Schools and Society: A Life in Education* (2018); *Rethinking Disability: A Disability Studies Approach to Inclusive Practices* (2019) (second edition) co-authored with Jan Valle; *How Teaching Shapes Our Thinking About Dis/abilities: Stories from the Field* (2021), co-edited with Beth Ferri; and *DisCrit Expanded: Inquiries, Reverberations & Ruptures* (2022), co-edited with Subini Annamma and Beth Ferri. He is currently working on a book with two teachers, Sarah Bickens and Fran Bittman, called Embracing Diversity: *Teachers' Everyday Practices in Secondary English Language Arts Classrooms*. He also writes fiction.

M. Nickie Coomer is an assistant professor of education at Colorado College. She teaches classes on urban education, special education, and disability activism in schooling contexts. Her research includes an interdisciplinary approach to study contexts of emotional and behavioral disability in schools, the intersection of race and disability in schools, teacher identity and agency, and narrative methodologies. Dr. Coomer earned a PhD in urban education studies from the Indiana University School of Education-Indianapolis (IUPUI) in 2021.

Danielle M. Cowley is an associate professor of education at Alfred University. Her primary teaching responsibilities include graduate courses in the areas of inclusive and comprehensive literacy instruction, best practices for inclusion, and humanistic behavior supports. Dr. Cowley's research interests include inclusive education, disability studies in education, urban school reform, gender in schooling, and comprehensive literacy instruction for students with significant disability labels. She has published several book chapters and in journals such as *PowerPlay: A Journal of Educational Justice, the Journal of Literary and Cultural Disability Studies*, and *Race Ethnicity and Education* and has presented her research at numerous national and regional conferences. Dr. Cowley was the recipient of the 2014 AERA-sponsored Disability Studies in Education Outstanding Dissertation Award for her research with adolescent girls with disabilities. In 2019 she was the recipient of the College of Education Faculty Excellence in Teaching Award from the University of Northern Iowa.

Ashley Cartell Johnson is a senior clinical lecturer in and coordinator of inclusive special education and disability studies at Miami University. In 2019, she was awarded the Excellence in Education: Inventive Educators Award for securing funding to promote a college access program that was collaboratively designed with Disabled students on Miami's campus. Her research examines issues of social justice and disability in schools through the method of currere.

Deborah J. Gallagher is a professor in the Department of Special Education at the University of Northern Iowa. Her research interests center on the philosophy of science as it pertains to research on disability, pedagogy, and inclusive education. In addition to authoring and co-authoring numerous publications, she has presented invited papers both internationally and nationally and is a founding member of the Disability Studies in Education Special Interest Group at the American Educational Research Association.

JPB Gerald is an adult educator and recent graduate of the EdD program at CUNY–Hunter College in Instructional Leadership. He identifies as Black and neurodivergent, though he spent most of his life unaware of the latter. His scholarship focuses on language education, ability, racism, and whiteness. He hosts a podcast called Unstandardized English and has had his writing published in academic journals (NYS TESOL, BC TEAL), practitioner magazines (*Language Magazine*), and national newspapers (*The Washington Post*). His first book, on the harm caused by the centering of whiteness in language education was published by Multilingual Matters in September 2022. He lives with his wife, young son, and dog in New York, on stolen Munsee Lenape and Canarsie territory.

David I. Hernández-Saca, PhD, is an associate professor of disability studies in education in the Department of Special Education at the University of Northern Iowa (UNI). Dr. Hernández-Saca is a former 8–12 multi-subject teacher and his teaching responsibilities at UNI include undergraduate teacher preparation courses in the areas of post-school transition programming and special education law, assistive technology, and advocacy and activism from a DSE interdisciplinary and intersectionality approach. Dr. Hernández-Saca's research nucleus of his research agenda is problematizing the common-sense assumptions of learning disabilities (LD). Dr. Hernández-Saca's three lines of inquiry include (1) the emotional impact of LD labeling on conceptions of self; (2) the role of emotion and affect in teacher learning about social justice issues; and (3) examining violence within the academy against historically multiply marginalized and non-hegemonic scholars at their intersections of power and identities for their well-being and healing. What ties all three of his lines of inquiry together is his commitment to educational equity through an interdisciplinary and intersectional research design and methodology. Overall, Dr. Hernández-Saca investigates these as they relate to historical equity issues in general education and special education and current movements for inclusive education at the boundaries of traditional special education and DSE.

Shehreen Iqtadar, EdD, is an Assistant Professor of Bachelor's in Inclusive Education Program at Rowan University. Her primary teaching responsibilities at Rowan include teaching courses in the undergraduate teacher preparation programs from Critical Disability Studies in Education (C-DSE). As a female researcher of color, and recent immigrant to the United States, she is specifically sensitive to the issues of power, justice, and students' intersectional identities within the edu-cation system. Her two lines of inquiry include: (a) student voice and identity work in urban education systems at the intersections of race, immigration, class, gender, and dis/ ability, and (b) transnational educational equity for theory, praxis, and policy. She has published handbook chapter in *SAGE Handbook of Inclusion and Diversity in Education* and peer-reviewed articles in journals such as *Race, Ethnicity and Education* (REE), *Disability Studies Quarterly* (DSQ), *Education Policy Analysis Archives, and Educational Policy*. In her recent publication, she has engaged in policy analysis of the United Nations Convention on the Rights of Persons with Disabilities (UNCRPD) to examine the complexity of the global education policy and the expansion of Global-South informed Disability Critical Race Studies (DisCrit).

Gloshanda Lawyer, PhD (she/ella or they/elle), is founder of COCOA Language Advocacy and Consulting LLC, a BIPOC/Disabled supporting organization that promotes Language Justice and Disability Justice through interpretation services, advocacy, and consulting. Through COCOA, Gloshanda also engages in research at the community, national, and international levels on: critical theory; colonization of Deaf, DeafBlind, DeafDisabled, and Hard of Hearing body/minds and Deaf Education; and multilingualism for DDBDDHH populations. She provides workshops, trainings, and consultations on multilingualism and DDBDDHH populations. She is a practitioner of Reproductive Justice, Language Justice, and Disability Justice for Black and Disabled birthers in the United States and the Global South. She has been an educator and multilingual interpreter for more than ten years. She is one part of Myers & Lawyer, a Black multilingual researcher/interpreter duo that engages in research, consultation, training, and resource development for BIPOC interpreters.

Amanda L. Miller (she/her) is an assistant professor and critical educator in the Division of Teacher Education at Wayne State University in Detroit, Michigan. Her research is framed by humanizing approaches to inquiry, critical theories (e.g., disability critical race theory, critical spatial theory), and qualitative and visual methods, including photovoice and cartography. Her research focuses on how school systems, policies, and practices impact girls of color, including girls who identify with or have been labeled with disabilities, as well as how they create joy and care in schools. Amanda is particularly interested in learning from and with girls of color because their experiences and perspectives are vital to truly transform schools. She also works with educators to create classroom and school communities that are culturally responsive, culturally sustaining, and inclusive and families to generate equitable and just family-school-community partnerships. Amanda collaborates on multiple projects, including a grant-funded youth participatory action research project led by two Black girls in high school focused on dismantling the school-to-prison nexus grounded in the experiences and perspectives of Black girls in middle school and high school. She has recently authored/co-authored publications in *Disability & Society*, *International Journal of Inclusive Education*, *International Journal of Qualitative Studies in Education*, and *Teachers College Record*. In 2020, she was awarded the Outstanding Dissertation Award from the AERA Disability Studies in Education SIG and the Dissertation of the Year Award from the University of Kansas School of Education.

Martin Musengi, PhD (Wits), MEd, BEd, CE (UZ), is associate professor of deaf and special needs education at Great Zimbabwe University (GZU) where he was Chairperson (Head of Department) of the Jairos Jiri Centre for Special Needs Education from 2015 to 2018. He is currently director of quality assurance and academic planning at GZU. He is a Fulbright scholar (Gallaudet University—Washington, DC), who has published forty-five articles and book chapters as well as two books. He serves on the editorial board of *GZU's School of Education* official journal and the *Journal of New Vision in Educational Research (JoNVER)* and is also a board member of the *Journal Deafness and Education International*. A teacher of the deaf since 1986, his abiding research interests are in deaf education from school to higher education levels. From 2021 to 2025 he has the honor and privilege to serve as a member of the international committee of the International Congress on the Education of the Deaf (ICED). The ICED may well be the oldest continuously held conference in any branch of education in the world (since 1878).

Lydia Ocasio-Stoutenburg, PhD, is an assistant professor in special education at Penn State University. As a mother-scholar-advocate, her focus has been on promoting equity through advocacy among families across educational, clinical, and community settings. Driven by the desire to challenge deficit-based attitudes and limited opportunities for her son, her research interests have been on disability intersectionality and systemic inequities experienced by families with multiple historically marginalized identities. She is also a fierce advocate for other parents of children with Down syndrome, from the prenatal period across the lifespan. Through counternarratives, her goal has been to share hope and highlight strengths, particularly among Black, Brown, and Indigenous families, as well as individuals with intellectual and developmental disabilities. Lydia is the co-author of two books on parent and caregiver advocacy for children with disabilities, *Meeting Families Where They Are: Building Equity Through Advocacy with Diverse Schools and Communities* and, its companion volume, *Case Studies in Building Equity Through Advocacy in Special Education.*

Holly Pearson (no preferred pronouns) is a contingent assistant professor in the Department of Sociology and Criminology at Framingham State University. Their research interest draws upon interdisciplinary lens exploring institutional diversity and equity in higher education from a spatial, geographical, and architectural lens. She has published research on the impact of disability studies curriculum, tension between disability and diversity, spatiality of intersectionality in higher education, and experiences of multiply marginalized faculty in universities and colleges. Outside of academia, they are a yoga instructor and an aspiring baker.

Amy J. Petersen is a professor in the Department of Special Education at the University of Northern Iowa. Dr. Petersen's research interests include inclusive education, qualitative methodology, and disability studies in education. She has published several book chapters and in journals such as *Harvard Educational Review*, *International Journal of Qualitative Studies in Education*, *Disability Studies Quarterly*, and *Equity & Excellence in Education*. Dr. Petersen was the recipient of the Regents Award for Faculty Excellence in 2020.

Ganiva Reyes is an associate professor in the Department of Teaching, Curriculum and Educational Inquiry at Miami University. Her research revolves around issues of justice in education. She draws from feminist of color theories and pedagogies of care to study social inequities in teaching and schools. Her other research interests include gender and sexuality.

Sarah Schlessinger, EdD, is a professor of education at the Relay Graduate School of Education in the Department of Teaching Exceptional Learners. Her research and teaching focus on social justice as it is enacted through inclusive classroom practices, specifically referring to notions of normalcy, marginalization, and exclusion and the intersections of race, class, and ability. This research interest lies predominantly in the field of teacher education and professional development. Dr. Schlessinger was the recipient of the 2015 AERA-sponsored Disability Studies in Education Outstanding Dissertation Award. She is co-author of the book *Narratives of Inclusive Teaching: Stories of Becoming in the Field* (2021).

Chelsea Stinson (She/her) is an assistant professor of education in the School of Health Professions and Education at Utica College in Utica, New York. Her research focuses on the experiences of emergent bilingual youth labeled as disabled and their families across migration and education contexts, as well as the knowledge, emotions, and policy contexts of teachers who support multiply marginalized students. To this end, she aims to contribute to a critical, generative understanding of equity and justice through inclusive education. As a former K-12 English language teacher, Stinson specialized in supporting students dually identified as English language learners (ELLs) and students with disabilities. In her current position, she aims to uphold her commitment to students and families through school-based consultation, offering local and global professional learning opportunities, and supporting early-career and established educators in cultivating praxical knowledge (i.e., deeply connected and mutually informing theoretical and practical knowledge) through rich, contextual, experiential learning. She has recently authored and co-authored publications in *International Journal of Inclusive Education*, *TESOL Quarterly*, *International Journal of Qualitative Studies in Education*, and *TESOL Journal*, as well as several forthcoming book chapters and encyclopedia entries. Most importantly, Stinson is the proud mother of energetic, inquisitive twin daughters and caregiver of two *very* good dogs.

Jane Strauss holds BA-Biology, BS-Education, JD, and MAPA degrees from a variety of Universities, but that is far from the whole story. She stumbled through K-12 education, generally on the margins, without any explanation for her peculiar social and learning challenges. Whenever possible, Jane found interdisciplinary studies or created them herself—up to and including her first undergraduate degree, essentially a study of Urban Social and Biological Ecology. Her twice-exceptional nature was discovered only in her late 20s and defined accurately in midlife—gifted and autistic. Since that time, Jane has lectured, researched, advocated, written, and challenged sacred cows within medical, educational, and social service systems, often perpetrating change in spite of inertia. Jane is a parent to five neurodiverse young adults and became a home educator before it was fashionable after seeing how poorly the public education system dealt with their gifts and challenges. Jane was recently appointed to the Board of Directors of Israel Elwyn, an organization which works with all ethnic groups in Israel providing independent living services, mainstream employment services, and other programs with the goal of full inclusion of all disabled people in that country. Jane had a younger brother who passed away in 2021. He was a musician, writer, and teacher and also diagnosed on the spectrum in midlife. Ironically, when going through his bookshelves after his death, Jane found *I and Thou*, several books by Friere, *The Little Prince*, and a copy of *Consilience*. On the spot, she decided to dedicate the work contained in this book in his honor—this one's for you, Mike Strauss, wherever your essence may be.

Maria T. Timberlake (she/her), PhD, is an associate professor in the Foundations and Social Advocacy Department at the State University of New York, Cortland. She is a former general and special educator who now prepares preservice teachers for inclusive dual certification. Her research focuses on the interpretation of ambiguous policy language (i.e., "access" and "achievement"), how teachers understand the meaning of disability, select pedagogical approaches, and the implications of those decisions for students whose communication, sensory needs, perceived intellect, and troubling behavior make them vulnerable to being misunderstood and underestimated. Her work has appeared in academic journals across a spectrum of areas including *Teaching and Teacher Education, Research and Practice in Severe Disabilities, International Journal of Inclusive Education*, and the *Journal of Autism and Developmental Disorders*. Maria is also the director of the undergraduate research program at SUNY Cortland where she works with faculty across the disciplines to facilitate student engagement in intellectual inquiry and investigation. She is leading campus efforts to increase access to research and mentoring opportunities for underrepresented and first-generation college students. She is the club advisor for an organization of students who identify as disabled and is currently conducting research with student partners on the experiences of disability disclosure.

Sarah Arvey Tov is a PhD candidate and instructor at the University of Washington College of Education committed to anti-racist, anti-ableist, and anti-oppression education. Her research, teaching, and learning prioritizes collaborative, intersectional, and intergenerational projects for and by the disability community. As part of a team of disabled filmmakers, educators, and activists, Sarah co-designed the One Out of Five: Disability History and Pride Project (http://bit.ly/One_Out_of_Five), which has been used across general and special education K-12 classrooms and teacher education programs. Her current work attends to culturally sustaining pedagogies and disability justice in the development of curriculum that uplifts disability identity, community, and culture. She utilizes arts-based methods in her teaching and research as expressions of hope, joy, and resistance.

About the Contributors   365

Ananí M. Vasquez is a doctoral candidate in the Learning, Literacies, and Technologies program at Arizona State University. She is a former elementary teacher and teacher coach who combines her experiences in general, bilingual, gifted and special education(s) to envision an inclusive education. As a teacher educator, she has been an instructor for elementary mathematics, math methods, and early childhood special education courses through which she has advocated for developing inclusive environments where multiple modes of thinking, learning, communicating, and interacting are accepted and encouraged. Ananí draws on creativity theory, disability studies in education, the neurodiversity paradigm, process philosophy, and arts-based inquiry while working with others toward post-oppositional educational transformation. Her area of research is *Neurodiversity and Creativity in Education and Research Methods*. Ananí is part of a beautifully neurodiverse family that includes her husband and two teens.

Catherine Kramarczuk Voulgarides is assistant professor at the City University of New York (CUNY)—Hunter College in the Department of Special Education. She received her PhD from New York University in Sociology of Education. Her scholarship is interdisciplinary. She focuses on understanding how schools are both sites of educational opportunity and marginalization for nondominant students, specifically examining how notions of equity, access, and opportunity are constructed in policy and law; how educational policies and laws impact educational inequity; and how the social, historical, and cultural contexts of schools relate to educational inequity. She published her first book with Teachers College Press in 2018, entitled *Does Compliance Matter in Special Education: IDEA and the Hidden Inequities of Practice*, which won the Outstanding Publication Award in 2020 by the Disability and Society Section of the American Sociological Association (ASA). Her work has appeared in journals such as *Sociology of Education, Review of Research in Education, Theory into Practice,* and *Multiple Voices,* among others. She has also received funding for her work from the William T. Grant Foundation, the American Educational Research Association, and the Spencer Foundation.